# Cholesterol Cures

From Almonds and Antioxidants to Garlic,
Golf, Wine and Yogurt—325 Quick and Easy
Ways to Lower Cholesterol and Live Longer

Richard Trubo, Mary Carroll and the Editors of
**PREVENTION** Magazine

Medical Adviser: William P. Castelli, M.D.
Medical Director, Framingham Cardiovascular Institute

Rodale Press, Inc.
Emmaus, Pennsylvania

*Cholesterol Cures* was first published in 1996 by Rodale Press, Inc. The recipes in this revised edition have been adapted from *The No-Cholesterol (No Kidding!) Cookbook*, copyright © 1991 by Mary Carroll and Hal Straus.

Copyright © 1997 by Rodale Press, Inc.
Cover design copyright © 1995 by Andrew Newman Graphic Design

**Library of Congress Cataloging–in–Publication Data**

Trubo, Richard.
   Cholesterol cures : from almonds and antioxidants to garlic, golf, wine and yogurt—325 quick and easy ways to lower cholesterol and live longer / Richard Trubo, Mary Carroll and the editors of Prevention Magazine.—Rev. ed.
       p.     cm.
   "The recipes in this revised edition have been adapted from The no-cholesterol (no kidding!) cookbook, © 1991 by Mary Carroll and Hal Straus"—t.p. verso.
   ISBN 0–87596–453–2 hardcover
   1. Low-cholesterol diet.   2. Hypercholesteremia—Diet therapy.
I. Carroll, Mary Harrison.   II. Prevention Magazine.   III. Title.
RM237.75.T78   1997
613.2'84—dc21                         96–47691

**Distributed in the book trade by St. Martin's Press**

2  4  6  8  10  9  7  5  3  1  hardcover

### *Cholesterol Cures* Editorial Staff

**Senior Managing Editor:** Edward Claflin
**Managing Editor:** Sharon Faelten
**Editors:** Julia VanTine, Susan G. Berg
**Contributing Writers:** Lisa Delaney, Jack Forem
**Assistant Research Manager:** Anita Small
**Researchers:** Hilton Caston, Valerie Edwards-Paulik, Theresa Fogarty, Sandra Salera-Lloyd
**Copy Editors:** Kathy D. Everleth, Amy K. Kovalski
**Art Director:** Jane Colby Knutila
**Associate Art Director:** Faith Hague
**Cover Designer:** Andrew Newman
**Book Designers:** Acey Lee, Joe Golden/Melonhead Studio
**Studio Manager:** Stefano Carbini
**Layout Artists:** Joe Golden/Melonhead Studio
**Nutrition Consultants:** Sonja L. Conner, R.D.; Anita Hirsch, R.D.
**Manufacturing Coordinator:** Patrick T. Smith
**Office Staff:** Roberta Mulliner, Julie Kehs, Bernadette Sauerwine, Mary Lou Stephen

**Rodale Health and Fitness Books**
**Vice-President and Editorial Director:** Debora T. Yost
**Design and Production Director:** Michael Ward
**Research Manager:** Ann Gossy Yermish
**Copy Manager:** Lisa D. Andruscavage
**Book Manufacturing Director:** Helen Clogston

# CONTENTS

## Part III: The 30/30 Menu Plan to Cut Cholesterol *Fast*

## Part IV: What's Cooking in the No-Cholesterol Kitchen

## Part V: The Fat and Cholesterol Finder

# FOREWORD

In 1948, the town of Framingham, Massachusetts, gave the world a great gift. Half of its residents allowed doctors to study them—and, in the decades that followed, their children, grandchildren and great-grandchildren—to help the medical community unravel the mysteries of heart attack and stroke. For over 45 years, this study—known as the Framingham Heart Study—has been used to reveal the three biggest risk factors of heart disease: high levels of LDL cholesterol (the bad stuff; more about LDL in the following pages), high blood pressure and smoking. The Big Three are followed closely by overweight, lack of exercise, diabetes and stress.

Some of you might be wondering, "Aren't some people genetically predisposed to high cholesterol?" The answer is yes. But as the risk factors above show, we have to take some responsibility for having high cholesterol. After all, about 4 billion of the 5.7 billion people on the planet don't have high cholesterol. The average cholesterol level in central China, for example, is 125 milligrams/deciliter. The Masai people of Africa have cholesterol levels averaging 135 milligrams/deciliter. And in the less urban sections of Latin America, cholesterol levels hover under 150 milligrams/deciliter.

Fortunately, we can undo the harm caused by high-fat diets, inactivity and other harmful factors. That's where this book comes in. It focuses on cholesterol cures—that is, simple things virtually anyone can do to lower his or her blood cholesterol. Most of these cures focus on the foods we eat (or don't eat) and the lifestyle choices we make. This book also provides scores of no-cholesterol and low-fat menus and recipes that can help you start *now* to lower your cholesterol—to help you reap the health benefits right away.

But be advised: There's no such thing as a magic bullet. Choosing to take antioxidant supplements, for example, or to eat more garlic while continuing to eat a high-fat diet is unlikely to affect your cholesterol for the better. And use your common sense: Consider these cures as an adjunct to a doctor's care, particularly if your cholesterol is over 200 milligrams/deciliter.

For years, the American Heart Association, the National Cholesterol Education Program of the National Heart, Lung and Blood Institute (part of the National Institutes of Health in Bethesda, Maryland) and other health organizations have run huge public-service campaigns to alert the public to the risk factors that can lead to heart disease. So many of us know what we have to do to take care of our hearts. But knowledge is useless if it's not paired with action.

I encourage you to mount your own personal campaign. To do so is to validate one of the foremost conclusions of the Framingham Heart Study: that the promise—and the privilege—of good health lies in our own hands.

—William P. Castelli, M.D.

~❦~

# INTRODUCTION

## *Your Personal Anti-Cholesterol Action Plan*

The fact that you've picked up this book says something very good about you: You understand that keeping your cholesterol in check is crucial to your good health. Maybe you've been told by your doctor that your cholesterol reading is on the high side and you need to bring it down a few points. Or maybe yours is right where it should be, and you want to make sure it stays that way. Whatever your reason, you're taking a very important first step by finding out what you can do to maintain your cholesterol at a healthy level.

Even more important is actually following through and doing something. And that's when even the best intentions can get stymied.

It's understandable, really. Many cholesterol-reduction plans tell you only about the "shouldn'ts"—especially all of those favorite foods that you shouldn't be eating. But what kind of an incentive is deprivation? Some folks decide that they just can't give up the foods they love, so instead they forgo any attempts to lower their cholesterol. Others "behave" themselves for a while, then feel so wracked with guilt for indulging even once that they jump off the cholesterol-control bandwagon for good.

If you're thinking, "There has to be a better way to cut cholesterol". . . you just may find it right here.

*Cholesterol Cures* defies the notion that getting to and maintaining a healthy cholesterol level requires a certain amount of sacrifice and suffering. The book's premise is simple: If you have a cholesterol-reduction plan that you can live with, you'll stick with it and succeed.

Now since everyone has different needs and different lifestyles, a one-size-fits-all plan obviously won't work. So *Cholesterol Cures* gives you options. By all means consider all of them—but then you can choose the ones you're most comfortable with.

Here's a brief overview of what you'll find in the pages ahead—and a few suggestions for using this book most effectively.

• If you're going into battle, as they say, it pays to know a little bit about the enemy. So think of part 1 as a dossier on cholesterol: what it is, what it does and how much of it your body needs. We recommend reading this section first to better understand why managing your cholesterol is so important.

• Then in part 2 you can choose your weapons for your anti-cholesterol action plan. This section profiles 60 individual remedies, along with hundreds of proven strategies for incorporating them into your day-to-day living. Any one of these tips can nibble points off your cholesterol reading. Select those that fit in with your lifestyle.

• Looking for fast results? You might want to give the eating plan in part 3 a try. Developed and reviewed by nutritionists—and tested by one of the editors of *Prevention* Magazine Health Books—it gives you a full month's worth of menus, with three complete meals plus snacks every day. As our editor discovered, by following this plan you can cut your total cholesterol by as many as 30 points in just 30 days.

• The recipes in part 4 work equally well as a follow-up to the 30-day menu plan and in conjunction with part 2's cholesterol-cutting strategies. Each of the 200 culinary creations is 100 percent cholesterol-free and low in fat.

• The Fat and Cholesterol Finder in part 5 can help you keep tabs on your intake of dietary bad guys. It features nutrient analyses for more than 500 foods, which are categorized as "low," "acceptable" or "high" according to their saturated fat content. Aim low for the most heart-smart selections.

Just imagine: You have in your hands all of the information you need to achieve and maintain a healthy cholesterol level safely, sensibly and effectively. And you can do it without giving up your favorite foods, without going hungry, without taking powerful prescription drugs. Controlling your cholesterol just got a whole lot easier.

# PART I

# The Lowdown on High Cholesterol

# THE HEART OF THE MATTER

## Cutting Cholesterol Has Big Health Benefits

Not so long ago, when red meat, whole milk and creamery butter topped the country's culinary Hit Parade, high blood cholesterol was considered the medical equivalent of a mosquito bite.

Not anymore. Doctors now know that high blood cholesterol sets the stage for a host of debilitating health conditions, including atherosclerosis, heart attack and stroke.

To add insult to injury, high cholesterol has a nasty way of sneaking up on you (which may be why you're reading this book). If you've been ambushed by high cholesterol's sneak attack, you're not alone. The blood cholesterol levels of 60 percent of us exceed 200 milligrams/deciliter, even though the National Cholesterol Education Program has designated blood cholesterol levels of less than 200 milligrams/deciliter as desirable. And almost 30 percent of us have high cholesterol—technically, 240 milligrams/deciliter or above.

But take heart. While elevated cholesterol is a significant risk factor for heart disease, it's a risk that you can control. "There are solid studies showing that watching your diet, exercising regularly and reducing your stress level can slow or perhaps even reverse atherosclerosis," says Marianne Legato, M.D., associate professor of clinical medicine at Columbia University College of Physicians and Surgeons in New York City and author of *The Female Heart.*

3

## HOW HIGH IS HIGH?

Some people can rattle off their cholesterol levels as quickly as their Social Security numbers. But if you require some translation, consult these guidelines, designated by the National Cholesterol Education Program. (All readings are in milligrams/deciliter.)

**TOTAL CHOLESTEROL**

| | |
|---|---|
| Desirable | Less than 200 |
| Borderline high | 200 to 239 |
| High | 240 or above |

**LDL CHOLESTEROL**

| | |
|---|---|
| Desirable | Less than 130 |
| Borderline high | 130 to 159 |
| High | 160 or above |

**HDL CHOLESTEROL**

| | |
|---|---|
| Desirable | Above 35 |

If you've already been diagnosed with heart disease, there's every reason for hope. Studies show that even people with severe heart disease can turn their health around. One benchmark study—the Lifestyle Heart Trial, led by Dean Ornish, M.D., president and director of the Preventive Medicine Research Institute in Sausalito, California, and author of *Dr. Dean Ornish's Program for Reversing Heart Disease*—concluded that people with heart disease can often stop or even reverse their conditions with lifestyle changes alone.

Most likely, you can do it, too.

## Why You Should Wage a Plaque Attack

To fire up your resolve, we've listed the most significant benefits of reducing your cholesterol.

***You can slow or even reverse the progression of atherosclerosis.*** In atherosclerosis, fatty deposits called plaques clog the walls of the coronary arteries, the vessels that supply oxygen-rich blood to the heart. Atherosclerosis can lead to coronary heart disease, or blockages in the coronary arteries. If left untreated, these blockages can choke off the heart's supply of blood and lead to a heart attack.

Lowering your cholesterol can reduce your chances of atherosclerosis and coronary heart disease. One landmark study, the Lipid Research Clinics Coronary Primary Prevention Trial, found that for each 1 percent you lower your total cholesterol, the probability of developing coronary heart disease or having a heart attack falls 2 percent. The same study found that as cholesterol levels dip, so does the incidence of chest pain (angina) and coronary bypass surgery.

***You can reduce or eliminate your reliance on cholesterol-lowering medication.*** While people with extremely high cholesterol may need cholesterol-lowering drugs, "drugs are the second line of defense," says John McDougall, M.D., creator and head of the McDougall Program at St. Helena Hospital in Santa Rosa, California,and author of *McDougall's Heart Medicine*. "Diet and lifestyle changes are the foundation for recovering from coronary heart disease."

***You can reduce your risk of stroke.*** One study has found that elevated cholesterol can produce abnormal amounts of a chemical that can cause spasms in the carotid artery in the neck, which supplies blood to the brain. If these spasms interrupt blood flow, they could trigger a mini-stroke, or a transient ischemic attack.

***If you have diabetes, you can troubleshoot potential problems.*** Some research suggests that women with diabetes have twice the risk of coronary heart disease of women without diabetes; both women and men with diabetes have about twice the risk of the general population. People with diabetes also tend to have high levels of triglycerides, another blood fat implicated in coronary heart disease. If you have diabetes, lowering your cholesterol and controlling other risk factors such as high blood pressure and overweight can cut down the chances of developing diabetes-related heart and blood vessel problems.

***You can extend your quantity of life.*** The renowned Framingham Heart Study, which has tracked the health of the residents of Framingham, Massachusetts, for more than four decades, has shown that the lower cholesterol levels fall, the lower the chance of heart attacks and sudden death.

***You can enhance your quality of life.*** Taking charge of elevated cholesterol now could mean the difference in the future between shuttling to and from the doctor's office (or to and from the hospital) and enjoying a full, happy, healthy life.

ᴎ᷎ᴇᴎ

# A CHOLESTEROL PRIMER

## *The ABCs of LDL and HDL*

You've decided that it's high time to give cholesterol its walking papers. After all, you think, anything that has proven ties to two of the nation's top killers—heart disease and stroke—must be up to no good. And the less of it that's floating around your bloodstream, the better off you'll be.

Unfortunately, it's not quite as simple as that. To begin with, your body needs a certain amount of cholesterol to carry out some of its most essential functions. What's more, there's a particular kind of cholesterol that is actually heart-friendly, and depleting its supply could have serious effects on your cardiovascular health.

So before you launch your anti-cholesterol offensive, it might not be a bad idea to get a little better acquainted with the "enemy." For starters: What exactly is this stuff, anyway?

### The Good, the Bad and the Murky

Cholesterol is a soft, waxy substance found in every human cell, in blood and in food. The kind found in food is called dietary cholesterol. Only animal-based foods such as meat and dairy products contain dietary cholesterol; it's not found in plant-based foods such as fruits, vegetables, beans and grains.

As mentioned earlier, cholesterol isn't as evil as you might think. Your body actually needs the stuff, and your cells make what they need. Your liver, for example, uses cholesterol to make bile acids, which help you digest food.

But too much cholesterol circulating in your blood can lead to trouble. One study, the Multiple Risk Factor Intervention Trial, evaluated nearly 360,000 American men, none of whom had yet experienced a heart attack. After seven years, the investigators found that men with total cholesterol above 220 milligrams/deciliter had twice the risk of dying of coronary heart disease as men with total cholesterol of 180 milligrams/deciliter or less. Men with readings of 245 milligrams/deciliter had triple the risk.

Studies of women show that before menopause, women's levels of blood cholesterol tend to average about ten points lower than men's. At menopause, however, the gap closes, and women seem to run the same risk as men.

## A Tale of Two Proteins

Cholesterol doesn't dissolve in blood, so it can't get to where the body needs it on its own. It has to hitch a ride on special carriers called lipoproteins. There are two major types of lipoproteins: low-density lipoprotein (LDL) and high-density lipoprotein (HDL). LDL, the "bad" cholesterol, is packed with cholesterol, while HDL, the "good" cholesterol, is mostly protein.

If there's too much LDL in your blood, it gets deposited on the walls of your arteries as fatty clumps. If these clumps break free, they

---

### MEN: LOWER YOUR CHOLESTEROL, IMPROVE YOUR LOVE LIFE?

Men with high total cholesterol and low levels of "good" HDL cholesterol may be prime candidates for impotence, several studies show.

In one study, researchers gave a group of 3,371 men physical exams, including cholesterol tests. Each man visited the clinic twice, with an average of 22 months between visits.

In that time, 71 men developed impotence. But men with total cholesterol above 240 milligrams/deciliter were 83 percent more likely to suffer from impotence, compared with men whose total cholesterol was below 180 milligrams/deciliter. Also, men whose HDL exceeded 60 milligrams/deciliter were 70 percent less likely to be impotent, compared with men whose HDL was below 30 milligrams/deciliter. Atherosclerosis may cause impotence by reducing blood flow to the penis, the researchers speculated.

Another study, which examined the various causes of impotence in Massachusetts men, found that the men's risk of impotence rose as their HDL levels dipped.

can cause the blood to clot. A clot that cuts off the flow of blood to the heart can cause a heart attack; a clot that blocks blood flow to the brain can trigger a stroke.

HDL, on the other hand, is a cardiovascular hero. It patrols your arteries, hauling cholesterol away from the arteries and back to the liver for dumping. Experts agree that the higher your HDL, the better your cardiovascular health is likely to be. One study has concluded that for each one milligram/deciliter rise in HDL, the risk of coronary heart disease declines 2 to 3 percent.

## What's Your Ratio?

You're most likely familiar with your total cholesterol, or the sum of your HDL and LDL values and other blood fats. To determine whether your blood fats fall within a desirable range, your doctor will evaluate your cholesterol ratio—that is, your total cholesterol divided by your HDL cholesterol. Experts agree that the ideal ratio is 4 to 1 or lower.

---

### WOMEN: HEED YOUR HDL

Before they reach menopause, women have significantly lower rates of coronary heart disease than men their ages. Why? In a word: estrogen. This female sex hormone appears to raise women's stores of heart-healthy HDL cholesterol. "Women tend to have higher HDL than men, which may be one reason why they have less heart disease than men—at least in their premenopausal years," says Peter Wood, D.Sc., Ph.D., professor emeritus of medicine at Stanford University School of Medicine.

After the onset of menopause, a woman's total and "bad" LDL cholesterol rise and her HDL wanes, most likely because of a dwindling supply of estrogen. "Postmenopausal women's heart attack rates eventually catch up with those of men their ages," says William P. Castelli, M.D., medical director of the Framingham Cardiovascular Institute, a wellness program at Metro West Medical Center in Framingham, Massachusetts. But take heart: "Women can raise their HDL by quitting smoking, losing weight and getting regular exercise," says Dr. Castelli.

Let's say you discover that your total cholesterol is 250 milligrams/deciliter and your HDL is 50 milligrams/deciliter. Dividing your total cholesterol (250) by your HDL (50) gives you a ratio of 5 to 1. But cutting your total cholesterol to 200 milligrams/deciliter while holding your HDL at 50 milligrams/deciliter will shrink your cholesterol ratio to a more desirable 4 to 1. In fact, doctors participating in the Physicians' Health Study—an ongoing study of over 22,000 American doctors conducted at Harvard Medical School and Brigham and Women's Hospital in Boston—found that cutting just one unit from their ratios of total to HDL cholesterol slashed their heart attack risk by 53 percent!

## Five Can't-Miss Tips for Controlling Cholesterol

So now you know what it takes to shape up your total cholesterol reading: You want to pare down your LDL cholesterol while making sure that your HDL level holds steady or even goes up a few points. And really, it's not as hard—or as painful—as you may think.

Experts say that you can get the upper hand on cholesterol simply by adapting the following five strategies. In fact, these make sense for anyone who wants to lead a healthy lifestyle, whether or not high cholesterol is a concern.

**Eat less fat.** We now get about 37 percent of total calories from fat, down from 42 percent in the 1960s. This is great news, since consuming too much fat, particularly saturated fat, has been linked to an increased risk of coronary heart disease. But we still have a ways to go: The American Heart Association recommends getting no more than 30 percent of calories from fat. Other experts suggest 25 percent or even lower. The menu plan in part III (page 217) and the recipes in part IV (page 251) will help you begin a no-cholesterol, low-fat eating program.

**Lose weight.** Folks who follow low-fat, low-cholesterol diets and lose excess weight tend to have easier times reducing their total and "bad" LDL cholesterol than people who don't drop the extra pounds, says Margo Denke, M.D., associate professor of medicine in the Center for Human Nutrition at the University of Texas Southwestern Medical Center at Dallas.

One study of 150 people who were overweight concluded that

folks who lose just 10 to 15 percent of excess body weight—and keep it off—may help afford themselves long-term protection from coronary heart disease.

Dropping extra pounds may also boost "good" HDL cholesterol. In a study of 2,400 people, women experienced a 2 percent increase in LDL and a 2 percent drop in HDL for every five pounds they gained.

"Being overweight is the most common cause of low HDL in women," says Dr. Denke. "It's important to get down to an ideal body weight to bring HDL back up."

**Exercise.** The Framingham Heart Study found that people who were physically active for more than an hour a week had significantly higher HDL levels than those people who exercised less than an hour a week.

**Stop smoking.** Smoking can lead to atherosclerosis and can deflate HDL by as much as 15 percent. So quitting can significantly improve your cholesterol profile.

"Quitting smoking can reverse the negative effect on HDL in just 60 days," explains Robert Rosenson, M.D., director of the Preventive Cardiology Center at Rush-Presbyterian-St. Luke's Medical Center in Chicago.

**Reduce your stress level.** Several studies suggest that emotional stress can elevate cholesterol levels, so keeping cool may help keep the lid on your cholesterol.

# PART II

# 60 Surefire Cholesterol-Clobbering Remedies

# ALCOHOL

## *Making an Informed Decision*

Drinking protects your heart. Right?

Wrong. Or at least not quite right.

But that's the message some Americans came away with some years ago, when a few studies indicated that moderate drinking is associated with reduced risk of coronary heart disease. The truth is, deciding whether to imbibe to protect your heart isn't as simple as pledging to eat less saturated fat and more soluble fiber.

On the one hand, there's evidence that moderate consumption of alcohol can help reduce the risk of coronary heart disease as well as help raise levels of "good" HDL cholesterol. On the other hand, many experts question the wisdom of encouraging people to drink for their health. In fact, some health professionals suggest that the decision to drink moderately to benefit heart health be made with the guidance of a physician. Experts are equally clear on another point: If you don't drink, don't start. This chapter can help you make an informed decision about the benefits—and risks—of moderate drinking to raise HDL and lower heart disease risk.

Why does moderate alcohol consumption seem to raise HDL cholesterol? Experts aren't sure. "We don't entirely understand the effect of alcohol on HDL," says Peter O. Kwiterovich, Jr., M.D., professor of medicine and director of the Lipid Research and Atherosclerosis Unit at Johns Hopkins University School of Medicine in Baltimore and author of *The Johns Hopkins Complete Guide for Preventing and Re-*

*versing Heart Disease.* "But it's pretty clear from epidemiological studies that people who drink moderately do better than people who don't drink at all."

"The data are clear that a drink or two a day lowers your heart attack risk," agrees William P. Castelli, M.D., medical director of the Framingham Cardiovascular Institute, a wellness program at Metro West Medical Center in Framingham, Massachusetts.

According to data from the second National Health and Nutrition Examination Survey, average levels of HDL cholesterol were higher among drinkers than among abstainers, no matter what their age, sex or race. Also, as alcohol consumption increased, so did HDL levels—an average increase of 5.1 milligrams/deciliter for daily or weekly use. (This study suggests reducing your risk of coronary heart disease by means other than alcohol consumption, however.)

For seven years, the Multiple Risk Factor Intervention Trial followed a subgroup consisting of 11,688 middle-age men who were at high risk for heart disease. During that time, those who consumed about two drinks per day (with each drink equal to 4 ounces of wine, 12 ounces of beer or 1.5 ounces of 80-proof spirits) had higher HDL levels than nondrinkers. This alcohol intake seemed largely responsible for a 22 percent reduced chance of death from heart disease, researchers said.

Researchers at Kaiser Permanente Medical Center in Oakland, California, studied the alcohol consumption patterns of nearly 129,000 people. Those who had one to two drinks a day were 30 percent less likely to die from coronary heart disease than those who did not drink. But people who had six or more drinks a day had a 60 percent greater risk of death from noncardiovascular causes than nondrinkers.

Dr. Kwiterovich and his colleagues had 56 men with low levels of HDL either drink one beer a day or abstain from alcohol. After two months, there were no differences in HDL levels between the two groups. But the beer drinkers experienced a 10 percent increase in apoprotein A-I, the major protein component of HDL. This protein is believed to help extract cholesterol from the cells and move it to the liver for excretion. Alcohol also makes blood platelets less sticky, which cuts the risk of clot formation and reduces the risk of heart attack, and raises blood levels of an enzyme called tissue-type plasminogen activator, or tPA, which helps keep blood clots from forming.

Researchers at Harvard Medical School and Brigham and Women's Hospital in Boston measured blood levels of tPA in 631 male doctors. These doctors—participants in the Physicians' Health Study, a study of 22,000 American doctors—gave blood samples and reported on their drinking habits. Researchers found that tPA levels rose with drinking frequency. The doctors who consumed two or more drinks a day had 35 percent higher levels of tPA than doctors who rarely or never drank. What's more, the doctors who drank more had significantly higher levels of HDL cholesterol than the doctors who didn't.

## Booze: No Magic Bullet

If you think that simply hoisting a beer stein or sipping your favorite Bordeaux will have a beneficial effect on your cholesterol level, think again. "Two glasses of wine a day will have a modest effect upon your HDL, and even that modest effect is beneficial," says Dr. Castelli. "But if you're looking for a magic bullet, this isn't it."

Further, overimbibing to benefit your cholesterol level is risky, say experts. "Alcohol is like coffee—it has some theoretical benefits and some potential risks," says Neal Barnard, M.D., president of the Physicians Committee for Responsible Medicine in Washington, D.C. Risks include developing certain cancers and provoking cardiac arrhythmias, cirrhosis of the liver and high blood pressure, says Dr. Castelli.

"It appears that women have an increased risk of breast cancer from increased alcohol consumption, even at the moderate levels recommended as potentially beneficial for heart disease," says Marla Mendelson, M.D., assistant professor of medicine at Northwestern University Medical School in Chicago. "So women who have a significant risk of developing breast cancer have to think twice about drinking."

There are other issues to consider. "If you have high blood pressure, alcohol can raise it more," says Frederic J. Pashkow, M.D., cardiologist at the Cleveland Clinic Foundation in Cleveland and author of *50 Essential Things to Do When the Doctor Says It's Heart Disease.*

What's more, alcohol can actually raise triglycerides by lowering the concentration of an enzyme used to break them down. "Even having a glass of wine with dinner every night can substantially raise triglycerides in people who are overweight or who have hereditary triglyceride problems," says Thomas Bersot, M.D., associate professor of medicine at the University of California, San Francisco.

The bottom line? If you choose to imbibe, do so in moderation—and if you don't drink, don't start, says Margo Denke, M.D., associate professor of medicine in the Center for Human Nutrition at the University of Texas Southwestern Medical Center at Dallas.

Dr. Barnard agrees. "I suggest that people follow a low-fat diet. I'm not sure that adding alcohol to that would be helpful."

*See also* Grape Juice, Wine

ᴖ᯾ᴗ

# ALMONDS

## *Food of the Gods*

In ancient Greece, the almond was so popular that it was nicknamed the Greek nut. And centuries later, we still crave this sweet, crunchy nut, whether as a snack or as an ingredient in many main dishes and desserts.

But almonds are more than just delicious. These nuts are loaded with calcium, which keeps bones and teeth strong; vitamin E, an antioxidant vitamin thought to reduce the risk of heart disease and certain types of cancer; and magnesium, which helps regulate blood pressure.

Almonds, and nuts in general, are also high in monounsaturated fat, which has been shown to lower total and "bad" LDL cholesterol without detrimentally affecting the "good" HDL cholesterol. Nearly two-thirds (65 percent) of the total fat of almonds is monounsaturated.

### The Heart-Healthy Fat

Researchers at Loma Linda University in Loma Linda, California, examined the link between eating nuts—including almonds, walnuts and peanuts—and a reduced risk of heart disease in more than 31,000 Seventh-Day Adventists. The researchers found that those who ate nuts more than four times a week had about half of the risk of suffering a heart attack (fatal or nonfatal) of those who ate nuts less than once a week. Twenty-nine percent of the nuts consumed were almonds.

"There are several possible reasons why almonds and other nuts seem to be capable of lowering blood cholesterol levels," says Gary E. Fraser, M.D., Ph.D., professor of medicine at Loma Linda University School of Public Health and head of the study. "Almost certainly, nuts' high level of monounsaturated fat is a major factor. But nuts are also a very good source of an amino acid called arginine, which is a dietary precursor of a chemical called nitric oxide, a major EDRF (endothelium-derived relaxing factor)." This chemical, which is released in the lining of the artery wall, seems to help prevent atherosclerosis, explains Dr. Fraser.

One of the most comprehensive studies of the almond/cholesterol link was conducted by Gene A. Spiller, D.Sc., Ph.D., director of the Health Research and Studies Center in Los Altos, California, and author of *The Superpyramid Eating Program*. In Dr. Spiller's study, 26 men and women ate a low-fat, low-cholesterol diet brimming with vegetables, fruits, grains, beans and low-fat dairy products for nine weeks. They avoided foods such as butter, margarine, fatty fish, most meats and ice cream. After following this low-fat baseline diet for two weeks, these individuals also began eating about three ounces of raw almonds a day and using almond oil instead of other vegetable oils.

When these individuals added almonds to their diet, their total daily fat intake rose from 67 to 90 grams a day; about 37 percent of their daily calories came from fat. But after three weeks of following the almond-rich diet, these folks' average total cholesterol plummeted from 235 to 215 milligrams/deciliter. What's more, their average LDL cholesterol fell 21 points—from 154 to 133 milligrams/deciliter. Their HDL cholesterol levels remained steady.

Why did the total and LDL cholesterol levels of these men and women decline, despite their eating more fat? Perhaps because the extra fat derived from the almonds is monounsaturated, speculate Dr. Spiller and his colleagues. "But if these men and women had been getting 40 percent of their calories from mostly saturated fat—if they had had bacon for breakfast, steak for dinner and butter on their bread—you wouldn't want to add many almonds on top of that," says Dr. Spiller. Dr. Spiller's study further concluded that following a diet higher in total fat than usually recommended can still help lower cholesterol if the diet is high in plant foods.

## Nutty Ways to Enjoy Almonds

Grabbing a fistful of raw, unsalted almonds is one way to take advantage of these nuts' power to lower cholesterol. Here are some others.

• To enjoy the flavor of almonds without the added fat or salt of the canned kind, toast the nuts yourself. Here's how: Spread whole raw almonds in a single layer across a shallow pan. Place the pan in a cold oven, then heat to 350°. Stir the nuts occasionally. When they're lightly toasted (8 to 12 minutes), remove from the pan and cool.

You can microwave almonds, too. Place ½ cup of raw almonds on a microwave-safe plate or bowl. Then zap the almonds for two to six minutes on high power, stirring once a minute. Let cool.

• Sprinkle your cereal, waffles or pancakes with slivered almonds. Or stir ground-up almonds into nonfat or low-fat yogurt.

• "Sprinkle almonds in your salads," says Dr. Spiller. To prepare almonds for salads, toss raw almonds into a pot of boiling water for about a minute (a cooking method called blanching). Drain the almonds and remove the skin, suggests Dr. Spiller. Then toast the nuts as above, chop and add to the greens.

• Add almonds to a variety of soups, including vegetable soup, suggests Dr. Spiller. "Grind or chop the almonds before adding to the soup," he advises.

• Stir chopped or ground-up almonds into cooked vegetables and pasta dishes.

• Replace small amounts of meat, fish or chicken in main dish casseroles with ground almonds. You'll boost your consumption of healthier monounsaturated fat while you reduce your intake of saturated fat.

## Go Nuts without Gaining Weight

One ounce of almonds (about 20 to 25 nuts) contains about 170 calories. So these nuts aren't exactly a low-calorie snack. But you don't have to deprive yourself of almonds' cholesterol-busting potential, says Dr. Spiller. Just indulge wisely.

"Some people are afraid they'll gain weight if they add almonds to their diets," says Dr. Spiller. "But their weight often stays the same, probably because as they eat more almonds, they tend to cut down on other foods and replace animal protein with plant protein. You should do the same."

If you're over your desirable weight, however, don't go nuts over almonds, advises Dr. Spiller. "Don't follow your big meal of the day with three ounces of almonds," he says. "Add almonds to your diet in place of something else."

# ANTIOXIDANTS

## *The Plaque-Attacking Cardio-nutrients*

Low in fat, high in fiber and cholesterol-free, fruits and veggies are crucial components of a heart-healthy diet. But there may be another reason to load up on produce. There's evidence that the antioxidant nutrients—vitamins C and E and beta-carotene, which converts to vitamin A in the body—may protect against high blood cholesterol levels. These "supernutrients," which are abundant in fresh fruits and vegetables, may even help prevent heart disease.

Many studies that associate a high intake of antioxidant vitamins with a lower risk of coronary heart disease and improvement in cholesterol have found these benefits in dosages that are more than the

Daily Values (DVs) for these nutrients. The DV for vitamin C is 60 milligrams. The DV for vitamin E is 30 international units. There is no DV for beta-carotene, but most experts recommend consuming 5 to 6 milligrams of this nutrient per day. Some authorities recommend taking antioxidant supplements to bridge the gap between the DVs and these theoretically therapeutic doses of antioxidants. Other experts consider supplements a "promising but unproven" means of lowering the risk of cardiovascular disease.

But gulping down antioxidant supplements won't compensate for a high-fat, artery-clogging diet, say experts. The best way to lower your cholesterol—and protect your heart—is to follow a low-fat, low-cholesterol diet, they say. Here's what's known about the antioxidant/cholesterol link.

## Antioxidants to the Rescue

Experts believe that antioxidants help thwart a number of chronic illnesses, including heart disease, by foiling the activity of free radicals. These cell-damaging chemical compounds are produced both inside and outside the body. Free radical damage can eventually lead to disease, including heart disease. Antioxidant vitamins may help stem this cellular damage.

Further, antioxidants may help boost "good" HDL cholesterol and help artery-clogging LDL cholesterol resist oxidation. This chemical process, researchers believe, increases the likelihood of LDL collecting in the arteries.

"LDL is the major cholesterol-carrying molecule in the bloodstream," says Thomas Bersot, M.D., associate professor of medicine at the University of California, San Francisco. Oxidized LDL is more likely to be "trapped" by macrophages, certain cells in the walls of the arteries. When LDL starts to collect inside the macrophages, it sets up a chemical chain reaction that can accelerate oxidation and other artery-clogging processes.

"The accumulation of LDL in the macrophages initiates the entire cascade of events in atherosclerosis," says Dr. Bersot. "If you can prevent LDL from oxidizing, you may reduce the risk of developing hardening of the arteries."

## E-liminating Heart Disease

A number of studies have demonstrated an association between a higher intake of antioxidant supplements—particularly vitamins C and E—and a lower risk of heart disease.

Researchers in the Health Professionals Study, conducted at Harvard Medical School and Harvard School of Public Health, followed 40,000 healthy male health care workers for four years, tracking how many developed heart disease during that time. They found that the men who consumed the most vitamin E had a lower risk of heart disease. Men who took 100 or more international units of vitamin E for at least two years cut their risk of heart disease by 37 percent, relative to the men who did not take any supplements.

A parallel Harvard study evaluated more than 87,000 healthy female nurses for eight years. Women who consumed the most vitamin E were found to have a 34 percent reduced risk of developing heart disease compared with women who consumed the least vitamin E. Women who had taken vitamin E supplements for at least two years had a 41 percent lower chance of developing coronary disease than those who didn't. And women who consumed the most beta-carotene had a 22 percent reduced risk of heart ailments compared with women who consumed the least amount of this nutrient.

Researchers at the University of California, Los Angeles, found that men who consumed the most vitamin C had a 45 percent reduced risk of dying of heart disease; women, a 25 percent reduction in risk. The researchers used data from the first National Health and Nutrition Examination Survey, which included information about the vitamin intakes of more than 11,000 people.

## Pumping Up HDL

The studies above did not specifically explore the relationship between blood cholesterol levels and antioxidants. But other research has examined the possibility that antioxidants may help raise HDL cholesterol and interfere with the oxidation of LDL.

"Several studies have shown that if you progress from consuming a relatively low amount of vitamin C—below 60 milligrams a day—up to about 200 to 300 milligrams a day, you'll experience a dose-related increase in HDL cholesterol," says Jeffrey Blumberg, Ph.D., chief of the Antioxidants Research Laboratory at the Jean Mayer USDA Human Nutrition Research Center on Aging at Tufts University in Boston. "This might account for some of the benefits of vitamin C in heart disease."

A study published by the New York Academy of Sciences in New York City, which compared the heart disease risks of 696 men and women ages 60 and over, found that consuming more than 180 milligrams of vitamin C a day—over three times the DV—was associated with higher HDL cholesterol and lower blood pressure than consuming less than the DV of vitamin C a day. And at the Human Nutrition Research Center on Aging at Tufts, researchers found that higher blood vitamin C (ascorbic acid) levels were associated with elevated HDL cholesterol and lower LDL cholesterol in over 1,200 people.

Researchers at the University of California, San Diego, conducted two studies to determine the effects of vitamin E and beta-carotene—used individually, in combination and together with vitamin C—on the oxidation of LDL. In the first phase of the study, eight people consumed 60 milligrams of beta-carotene per day for three months. Then for another three months, these folks added 1,600 international units of vitamin E a day to the beta-carotene. And for yet another three months, these individuals added 2,000 milligrams of vitamin C to the vitamin E and beta-carotene. In the second phase of the study, these individuals consumed only vitamin E supplements (1,600 international units a day) for five months. Researchers concluded that long-term use of vitamin E in high doses hindered the oxidation of LDL by 30 to 50 percent. Beta-carotene did not seem to affect LDL's resistance to oxidation.

## The Great Debate: Food or Supplements?

Some researchers, including Dr. Blumberg, believe that the DVs—set at levels designed to prevent nutritional deficiencies—are too low to help fight disease. "Going by only the nutritional deficiency criteria, the DVs are absolutely correct," says Dr. Blumberg. "But if you ask 'How much vitamin C do I need to reduce my risk of heart disease, cancer or cataracts?' you'd get a much different answer than the DVs."

What's more, some people may find it difficult to even reach the

## GOOD FOOD SOURCES OF ANTIOXIDANTS

What do clams, kale and cantaloupe have in common? They're all brimming with antioxidant vitamins. Here's a short list of other antioxidant-rich fare.

**VITAMIN C**

| | |
|---|---|
| Broccoli | Mangoes |
| Brussels sprouts | Oranges |
| Cantaloupe | Papaya |
| Cauliflower | Peppers |
| Clams | Potatoes |
| Grapefruit | Watermelon |
| Green peppers | |

**VITAMIN E**

| | |
|---|---|
| Asparagus | Sunflower seeds |
| Cereal (fortified) | Sweet potatoes |
| Kale | Vegetable oil |
| Liver | Wheat germ |
| Nuts | Whole-grain products |
| Pumpkin seeds | |

**BETA-CAROTENE**

| | |
|---|---|
| Apricots | Peaches |
| Cantaloupe | Spinach |
| Carrots | Sweet potatoes |
| Mangoes | Tomatoes |
| Papaya | Yellow squash |

DVs. In fact, a government survey found that just 9 percent of Americans eat the recommended minimum of five servings of fruits and vegetables a day. And it's difficult to consume potentially therapeutic amounts of some antioxidants through diet alone, say experts.

An important part of the answer, according to Dr. Blumberg, is antioxidant supplements. He recommends consuming between 250 and 1,000 milligrams of vitamin C, between 100 and 400 international units of vitamin E and between 6 and 30 milligrams of beta-carotene a day in supplement form. These doses are safe, says Dr. Blumberg. Consuming large amounts of beta-carotene may give the skin a yellow or orange tint in some people, however. Also, taking large amounts of vitamin C has been reported to cause diarrhea, while extremely high doses of vitamin E may cause headaches and diarrhea. So be sure to check with your doctor before taking antioxidant supplements.

Because supplements can't compensate for bad dietary habits, it's crucial to follow a healthy diet rich in fruits, vegetables, whole grains, low-fat or nonfat dairy products and small amounts of meat, poultry and fish. "Rather than rely on supplements, eat foods rich in antioxidants," says Dr. Bersot. "They'll provide antioxidant vitamins as well as other nutritional substances that may be beneficial."

*See also* Beta-Carotene

꙳

# APPLES

## *Put the Crunch on Cholesterol*

The next time you bite into a sweet, juicy McIntosh, consider this: Apples may very well help keep the doctor away—by lowering your blood cholesterol and protecting your heart.

The ingredient in apples that wallops blood cholesterol? Pectin, a sticky substance found in fruits and vegetables that works as a natural cholesterol cutter. "Pectin is a soluble fiber that helps draw cholesterol out of the system," says Audrey Cross, Ph.D., associate clinical professor at Columbia University's Institute of Human Nutrition in New York City. The average apple contains 1.08 grams of pectin.

Apples also contain flavonoids, certain chemicals that seem to short-circuit the process that leads "bad" LDL cholesterol to accumulate in the bloodstream. Dutch researchers who conducted a five-year study of 805 men ages 65 to 84 found that the men who ate the most flavonoids (also found in onions, tea and wine) were 50 percent less likely to have a first heart attack and die of heart disease than those who consumed the least.

You need to munch more than an apple a day to reap the full benefits of this fruit's power to clobber high cholesterol. But adding more apples and other high-fiber fruits and vegetables to your diet is a step in the right direction.

## Scrubbing Clogged Arteries Clean

There's a wealth of evidence that points to apples' ability to help cut blood cholesterol. In a study conducted by David L. Gee, Ph.D., professor of food science and nutrition at Central Washington University in Ellensburg, Washington, 26 men with elevated cholesterol (ranging from 200 to 255 milligrams/deciliter) were divided into two groups. The first group ate three cookies with added apple fiber per day. These cookies contained a total of 14.5 grams of fiber, an amount equal to that found in four to five apples. The second group ate regular cookies. Otherwise, the men ate what they always ate.

After six weeks, the cookie-eating group's total cholesterol dropped an average of 15 points, or 7 percent. No improvements were seen in the placebo group.

In a follow-up study conducted by Dr. Gee and graduate student Karen Spencer, 25 men with cholesterol levels ranging from 200 to 270 milligrams/deciliter drank 20 ounces a day of FiberRich, a commercial apple juice brimming with pectin. After six weeks, the men's total cholesterol levels dipped an average of 10 percent, and their LDL cholesterol fell an average of 14 percent.

Other studies have pointed to apples' ability to lower blood cholesterol levels. In a French study, 30 healthy men and women added two to three apples to their diets each day for a month. Total cholesterol fell in 80 percent of these individuals, by an average of 14 percent. One person's cholesterol plummeted 29 percent! HDL cholesterol, the "good" kind, rose slightly as well.

# The Not-So-Forbidden Fruit

Perhaps the simplest way to take advantage of apples' power to pare blood cholesterol is to eat the raw fruit itself, say experts. "A fresh apple is a great snack food," says Evelyn Tribole, R.D., a dietitian in Beverly Hills, California, and author of *Healthy Homestyle Cooking*. But there are other ways to enjoy the delicious taste of apples. Try these suggestions.

• Mix sliced apples with a low-fat cheese, sprinkle with fresh chives and serve on romaine lettuce. You might also toss sliced apples with raisins, almonds and cooked chicken and splash the salad with tarragon vinegar.

• Add apples to baked goods. "You can grate apples into almost anything that you bake, including low-fat muffins and cakes," says Tribole. Try grating one large apple into a recipe that yields six large muffins.

• Sauté a side dish. Sautéed apples are a delicious accompaniment to meat (preferably leaner cuts). After sautéing turkey cutlets, for example, remove the meat from the pan and add sliced peeled apples to the meat juices. Sauté the apples for five minutes, then stir in ½ cup of apple juice and cook until the apples are soft (about three minutes). Serve with the cutlets.

• Bake a guilt-free pastry. Chop up some apples, add cinnamon and a little sugar, wrap the apples in phyllo dough and bake, suggests Tribole. "You'll end up with something like apple strudel that's very low in fat," she says.

As healthful as apples are, you can sabotage their goodness. "Consuming apples in a pie with a thick crust loaded with butter isn't the best way of eating them," says Sheah Rarback, R.D., director of nutrition at the University of Miami School of Medicine's Mailman Center. You can indulge your sweet tooth occasionally, says Rarback. But if you want to help lower your blood cholesterol, it's best to munch fresh apples or to prepare them in some other healthy way, she says.

To keep apples crisp, wrap them in a plastic bag and store them in the refrigerator. Apples kept at room temperature soften ten times faster than refrigerated fruit.

# AVOCADOS

## *This "Fat" Fruit Fights Cholesterol*

Fattening. Oil-soaked. Hell on the waistline.

If you're like many people, you might use epithets like these to describe the otherwise tasty avocado. But hold the name-calling for a second. If you're trying to lower your blood cholesterol, you may want to indulge in this green fruit once in a while: Avocados are high in monounsaturated fat, which is known to reduce LDL, or "bad," cholesterol. Avocados are especially rich in oleic acid, the same cholesterol-busting monounsaturate found in olive and canola oils.

The only catch: Avocados are extremely high in fat. And consuming too much of any fat, even monounsaturated fat, isn't a good idea, say experts. Eaten sparingly, however, avocados just might help you chip a few points off your cholesterol count—deliciously.

## Going Down, Down, Down

The connection between avocados and lower blood cholesterol began with a hunch: A team of Australian researchers suspected the link and decided to test their theory. In this study, 15 women alternated between a low-fat, high-carbohydrate diet (21 percent fat calories) and an avocado-enriched diet (36 percent fat calories) in which they ate from ½ to 1½ avocados per day.

After three weeks on the avocado-rich diet, the women's total cholesterol fell from an average of 236 to 217 milligrams/deciliter, or 8.2 percent, compared with 4.9 percent after three weeks on the low-fat plan. More significantly, however, "good" HDL cholesterol plummeted an average of 14 percent on the low-fat plan and not at all on the avocado diet. As a result, the ratio of total cholesterol to HDL increased 10.4 percent in the women on the low-fat plan but decreased 14.9 percent in the avocado-eaters.

Avocados may also be a dietary asset for people with non-insulin-dependent (or Type II) diabetes, for whom consuming too many carbohydrates can cause triglyceride and blood sugar problems. A Mexican study found that partially replacing carbohydrates with monounsaturated fat lowered triglycerides in 16 women with Type II diabetes. In this study, the women ate a baseline diet for one month. They then alternated between two diets. The first diet was high in monounsaturated fat (40 percent total fat calories), derived primarily from avocados. The second food plan was high in complex carbohydrates (20 percent total fat calories).

Both diets lowered the women's total cholesterol slightly. But their triglycerides fell 20 percent on the avocado-enriched diet, compared with 7 percent on the high-carbohydrate plan. The women's blood sugar levels were not affected by either diet.

## Get Monos in Moderation

Avocados contain zero dietary cholesterol, which is found only in animal-derived foods such as eggs, milk and meats. But don't gobble avocados with abandon: From 71 to 88 percent of this fruit's calories come from fat. "Using one-eighth of an average avocado in a salad adds about five grams of fat," says Janet Lepke, R.D., a dietitian in Santa Monica, California, and a spokesperson for the American Dietetic Association.

Most people don't eat more than half of an avocado at a time, however. "You shouldn't consume too much of any fat, saturated or unsaturated," says Wahida Karmally, R.D., director of nutrition at the Irving Center for Clinical Research at Columbia-Presbyterian Medical Center in New York City and a member of the American Heart Association's nutrition committee. So substitute avocados for foods high in saturated fat rather than add avocados to an already high-fat diet, recommends Karmally.

## A Little Goes a Long Way

Many people stud their salads with chunks of avocado or add a few slices of the fruit to a sandwich. But you might try these serving suggestions, too.

- Try topping your baked potato with mashed avocado, suggests the California Avocado Commission. A tablespoon of butter contains 100 calories, mostly from saturated fat. A tablespoon of mashed avocado, on the other hand, contains 20 calories, mostly from monounsaturated fat.
- To perk up baked chicken, "top it with slices of avocado before serving," suggests Tammy Baker, R.D., a nutritionist in Cave Creek, Arizona, and a spokesperson for the American Dietetic Association.
- The next time you make potato salad, use less mayonnaise and add some mashed avocado instead. You'll consume less saturated fat and dietary cholesterol and more heart-healthy monounsaturated fat.
- Slice an avocado in half, remove the seed and stuff the fruit with chicken, seafood or pasta salad prepared with low-fat or cholesterol-free mayo. To keep the avocado from turning brown, rub the flesh with a little lemon juice.

*Note:* If you buy avocados that aren't yet ripe enough to eat, you can speed up the ripening process by putting them in a paper bag and setting them aside for a few days.

# BARLEY

## *Full of Fiber—And Flavor*

**M**an has been growing and eating barley since the dawn of civilization. Yet here in the United States, barley, which has been called the world's oldest grain, is virtually unknown—overshadowed by rice and wheat and grown mostly to feed livestock and brew beer.

But you don't have to be a chicken farmer or a home brewer to appreciate barley, especially if you're watching your cholesterol: A number of studies have found that this tasty grain can help push down elevated cholesterol levels.

The reason? Fiber. Barley is especially rich in soluble fiber—the gluey, sticky stuff that hinders the body's ability to absorb fat and cholesterol—particularly beta-glucans, the same type of fiber found in oats that has been shown to lower blood cholesterol. The oils in barley may help poke holes in high cholesterol levels as well.

## A Fiber Gold Mine

Here's what researchers have discovered about the cholesterol-battling properties of barley.

Investigators at Texas A & M University in College Station had 79 people with blood cholesterol readings of 230 milligrams/deciliter or higher follow a low-fat, low-cholesterol diet for a month. These individuals also consumed either 30 grams of barley bran flour or 3 grams of barley oil extract each day. After 30 days, total cholesterol dipped about 7 percent in both groups. What's more, "bad" LDL cholesterol fell by 6.5 percent in the barley flour group and by 9.2 percent in the barley oil group.

Interestingly, "good" HDL cholesterol dropped in the barley flour group by 7.8 percent but not in the group taking the barley oil. "That's probably because the barley oil group had a fall in triglycerides (another blood fat implicated in heart disease), which may have increased in the barley flour group," says William P. Castelli, M.D., medical director of the Framingham Cardiovascular Institute, a wellness program at Metro West Medical Center in Framingham, Massachusetts.

In a study led by Rosemary K. Newman, Ph.D., professor of foods and nutrition at Montana State University in Bozeman and a leading researcher of barley, 22 men and women with elevated blood cholesterol consumed either oat or barley flour, both of which were added to bran muffins, breakfast cereals and flatbreads. After six weeks, both groups' total cholesterol fell 12 points. But the barley-eaters' LDL cholesterol slid 24 points, from 173 to 149 milligrams/deciliter. By contrast, the oat-eaters' LDL cholesterol declined 11 points, from 157 to 146 milligrams/deciliter.

---

### KNOW YOUR BARLEY

Here's a barley glossary to help you distinguish between the most common forms of this versatile grain.

*Pearl barley.* The most readily available form of barley, added to soups, salads, pilafs and casseroles. In processing, the grain's double outer husk and its bran layer (along with some nutrients) are removed, and the kernels are steamed and polished.

*Hulled barley.* Only the outer husk of the grain is removed, which preserves more of its nutrients. Most people use hulled barley in soups and stews.

*Pot barley.* Part of the grain's bran layer is left intact. And as its name implies, pot barley is usually added to soups and stews.

*Barley flakes.* These flattened barley grains are usually prepared as a form of hot cereal but can also be mixed into baked goods.

---

In an Australian study, 21 men with elevated cholesterol alternated between eating barley bran and eating wheat bran for four weeks each. Both types of bran were added to foods such as breads, spaghetti, biscuits and muesli (a type of cereal). Researchers found that the men's average total cholesterol was 6 percent lower, and their LDL cholesterol 7 percent lower, when they consumed the barley diet than when they followed the wheat plan.

## Roughage Up Your Diet

Barley boosters insist that the taste of their favorite grain is second to none. "Barley has a nutty flavor that some people really enjoy," says Dr. Newman.

You'll find the most common form of barley, called pearl barley, in the pasta and rice aisle of many supermarkets. You can find other types of barley, such as pot barley and barley flakes, in health food stores.

And if you think the only way to use barley is to add it to soups, think again. You can add this versatile grain to salads, casseroles and side dishes. "You can use barley like any other grain," says Janet Lepke, R.D., a dietitian in Santa Monica, California, and a spokesperson for the American Dietetic Association. Here are a few ideas to get you started.

• Not ready to buy—or cook—barley on your own? Conduct a taste test first. Barley is found in a variety of prepared foods, including soups, cookies, crackers and rice pilaf mix. (Read labels to make sure that the product doesn't contain lots of fat, sodium or sugar.) Or try breakfast cereals that contain barley, such as Multi Grain Cheerios or Quaker Multi Grain Oatmeal.

• You can substitute barley in almost any recipe that calls for rice, says Linda Van Horn, R.D., Ph.D., associate professor of preventive medicine at Northwestern University Medical School in Chicago. That means using it in recipes for stuffed peppers and rice pilaf, for example. Suggests Lepke, "Instead of serving a vegetarian stew over long-grain rice, try using a mixture of barley and couscous."

• Add pearl barley to rice and to macaroni salad, says Lepke. "Try adding cold barley to a tomato salad flavored with dill," she suggests.

• For a tasty side dish, the National Barley Foods Council suggests combining 3 cups of hot cooked barley with 1 cup of plain yogurt, ⅓ cup of sliced green onions and two to three teaspoons of curry powder. Or mix in ½ cup of crumbled feta cheese, two tablespoons of minced sweet onions, three tablespoons of fresh mint and one tablespoon of fresh lemon juice.

• Add a small amount of cooked barley to meat loaf, suggests Mary Donkersloot, R.D., a dietitian in Beverly Hills, California, a spokesperson for the California Dietetic Association and author of *The Fast Food Diet*. You'll boost your consumption of fiber while you slash your intake of artery-clogging animal protein.

• If you enjoy baking bread, add barley flour to your favorite bread recipe, says Dr. Newman. But take note: Barley contains very little gluten, the substance that helps give bread its volume. "So the barley flour shouldn't be more than ¼ to ⅓ percent of the total amount of flour," advises Dr. Newman.

• Similarly, if you make your own fresh pasta, try using barley flour, suggests Dr. Newman, by substituting barley flour for part of the wheat flour.

# BEANS

## *Mean Heart-Smart Cuisine*

Think the bean is peasant food? Think again. The formerly humble legume has become hot stuff, especially among folks who want a high-protein, low-fat and inexpensive alternative to red meat.

What's more, beans can help deal a knockout blow to elevated cholesterol: Many varieties are loaded with soluble fiber, which has been proven to help lower cholesterol. "Beans also contain omega-3 fatty acids and loads of calcium," says Neal Barnard, M.D., president of the Physicians Committee for Responsible Medicine in Washington, D.C. Omega-3 fatty acids, also found in certain fatty fish, are a type of polyunsaturated fat, which helps prevent cardiovascular disease.

Beans' nutritional pedigree and culinary versatility mean they're perfect in virtually any dish, from fiery chili to savory soups. Best of all, whipping up quick, healthy bean dishes can be as simple as opening a can. Want more good reasons to pile your plate with beans? Read on.

At the University of Kentucky in Lexington, James W. Anderson, M.D., professor of medicine and clinical nutrition in the university's College of Medicine and author of *Dr. Anderson's High-Fiber Fitness Plan,* and his colleagues instructed 20 men with cholesterol levels exceeding 260 milligrams/deciliter to eat about 1½ cups total of pinto and navy beans a day. After three weeks, the men's total cholesterol fell an average of 56 points, while their "bad" LDL cholesterol plunged 51 points.

And in another study led by Dr. Anderson, 28 men with high cholesterol ate one eight-ounce can of beans in tomato sauce every day for three weeks. The men's total cholesterol dropped 10.4 percent, and their triglyceride levels declined 10.8 percent.

Researchers in New Zealand put 40 people with high cholesterol on a low-fat diet to which either cooked beans or oat bran was added. These folks' total cholesterol declined slightly on both diets.

But their "good" HDL cholesterol rose significantly when they ate the beans rather than the oat bran.

## The Basics of Bean Cookery

Don't know beans about beans? Don't fret: These tips can get you started.

• If you want to use dried whole beans, you'll need to soak them. Soak the beans in cold water overnight, so they'll be ready to cook the next day. Or try the quick soak method: Boil the beans for two minutes, then set them aside to soak for an hour or so.

• To bypass soaking or quick soaking altogether, opt for lentils and split peas, suggests Dr. Anderson. These legumes don't require soaking and cook up in a fraction of the time of dried beans. "While split peas and lentils are a little lower in fiber than the beans we used in our studies, they should still help lower cholesterol," says Dr. Anderson.

---

### CAN'T BEAT THESE BEANS

Want to add fiber power to your cholesterol-lowering diet? Load up on these legumes.

| LEGUME (½ CUP COOKED) | SOLUBLE FIBER (G.) |
| --- | --- |
| Kidney beans | 2.8 |
| Cranberry beans | 2.7 |
| Lima beans | 2.7 |
| Black beans | 2.4 |
| Navy beans | 2.2 |
| Lentils | 2.0 |
| Pinto beans | 1.9 |
| Great Northern beans | 1.4 |
| Chick-peas | 1.3 |
| Split peas | 1.1 |

• Add canned beans to soups, salads and casseroles, suggests Dr. Anderson. Rinse the beans to remove excess sodium.

• To give stews a fiber boost, add a can of chick-peas, kidney beans, lima beans or black beans.

• Enjoy burritos made with beans instead of beef, suggests Dr. Barnard. "There's nothing better than a homemade bean burrito with jalapeño peppers," he says. Try topping your burrito with low-fat or nonfat cheese and a dab of nonfat sour cream.

• Mix any type of mashed canned beans with chopped onions, fresh garlic and low-sodium tamari (a kind of soy sauce), suggests Michael Klaper, M.D., health director of the Royal Atlantic Health Spa in Pompano Beach, Florida, and author of *Vegan Nutrition: Pure and Simple*. Spread the mixture on crackers or spoon into taco shells.

• Add a trickle of olive oil and some fresh garlic to mashed canned garbanzo beans and spread on your favorite bread, suggests Dr. Klaper.

• Explore the ways different cultures use beans. You might try making a spicy Cuban black bean soup; Middle Eastern hummus (a savory spread of chick-peas, lemon juice, garlic and fresh mint, served with pita bread); Italian *pasta e fagioli* (pasta with beans); or Southern-style hoppin' John (black-eyed peas and rice—hold the ham).

• If you're dining in a Mexican restaurant, avoid refried beans, says Martin Yadrick, R.D., a dietitian in Manhattan Beach, California, and a spokesperson for the American Dietetic Association. "Traditional re-fried beans are prepared with lard," he says. "Ask for pinto beans or black beans, which contain a minimal amount of fat."

## Degassing Legumes

Beans can cause gastrointestinal distress in some people. The gas-producing culprits: stachyose and raffinose, sugars that are the by-products of beans, says Linda Van Horn, R.D., Ph.D., associate professor of preventive medicine at Northwestern University Medical School in Chicago. To help prevent gas, "soak beans before you cook them and discard the water they've been soaking in," advises Dr. Van Horn. "Soaking beans breaks down some of these sugars."

You might also consider trying a product called Beano. This over-the-counter product really does help reduce gas in some people, according to a study conducted at the University of California, San Diego. Folks who consumed eight drops of Beano after the first bite of a meal of meatless chili seemed to experience fewer gas eruptions than those who had taken a placebo, according to these individuals' self-reported symptoms.

⚜

# BETA-CAROTENE
## *Crunch a Carrot, Collar Heart Disease*

Beta-carotene was once thought to be like the straight man in a vaudeville act, always playing second banana to vitamin A, the nutritional star of the team. Beta-carotene's only role, nutrition experts assumed, was as a so-called precursor to vitamin A, because the body converts beta-carotene to vitamin A on an as-needed basis and excretes what it can't use.

Many medical experts believe that beta-carotene plays a vital role in fighting heart disease, but the evidence doesn't all point one way. In a 12-year study of nonsmoking physicians with an average age of 49, no benefit could be found from taking the supplements, according to William P. Castelli, M.D., medical director of the Framingham Cardiovascular Institute, a wellness program at Metro West Medical Center in Framingham, Massachusetts. He contrasts that study with one of the largest cholesterol-lowering trials in the United States, which showed that people had a 72 percent lower risk of heart attack if they had a high concentration of carotenoids in their blood. He concludes that getting beta-carotene (and other carotenoids) from foods like leafy green vegetables offers some protection against the oxidation of LDL.

## Banking on Beta

Beta-carotene is a carotenoid, one of a group of compounds that give certain plants their red, orange and yellow pigments. There's compelling evidence that people whose diets are high in beta-carotene—found in green leafy vegetables such as kale, broccoli and spinach and in yellow-orange fruits and vegetables such as cantaloupe, mangoes, carrots and sweet potatoes—are somehow protected from heart disease.

In the benchmark Nurses' Health Study conducted at Harvard Medical School, researchers analyzed eight years of dietary records kept by 87,245 healthy female nurses. From that information, the researchers were able to estimate the nurses' intakes of several nutrients, including beta-carotene. The researchers found that the nurses whose diets were highest in beta-carotene had a 22 percent lower risk of heart attack and a 40 percent lower risk of stroke than those who consumed the lowest amounts of this nutrient. Another study, which analyzed the beta-carotene intakes of 1,299 older men and women in Massachusetts, showed that the individuals who consumed the most beta-carotene were 45 percent less likely to die from heart-related problems than those who consumed the lowest amounts.

The study that really attracted the attention of the medical community, however, was a clinical trial (the type of experiment considered to yield the most reliable scientific evidence) known as the Physicians' Health Study. This study, also conducted at Harvard Medical School and at Brigham and Women's Hospital in Boston, was designed to test whether aspirin and beta-carotene would help prevent heart disease and cancer in 22,071 male doctors.

In a subset of this study involving 333 doctors who had already had heart attacks, the researchers found the first evidence of the potential benefit of taking 50 milligrams of beta-carotene—the amount found in two cups of cooked carrots—every other day. This group of doctors was divided into four subgroups: The first group received placebos; the second group received only aspirin; the third group received only beta-carotene; and the fourth group received both beta-carotene and aspirin. After five years, researchers found that the doctors who took only beta-carotene experienced no change in heart attack risk. The aspirin-only doctors lowered their risk of heart attack by 40 percent. But the doctors who took both beta-carotene and aspirin had zero heart attacks in five years.

## Karate Chops to Artery Plaque

So exactly how might beta-carotene help thwart heart disease? Experts aren't sure. But one widely accepted theory postulates that beta-carotene keeps LDL cholesterol from oxidizing.

Oxidation is the chemical reaction that turns a banana brown and mushy. To some degree, this process occurs in your body, too. In the oxidation process, free radicals—highly reactive, unstable oxygen molecules that wreak havoc in the body—damage, or oxidize, LDL. Free radicals are formed naturally in the body as well as by toxic substances such as cigarette smoke and pollution. Experts theorize that oxidized LDL becomes stickier, clings to artery walls and forms the fatty streaks of plaque that signal the first signs of heart disease.

Fortunately, we're afforded some protection from these marauding molecules—and that's where beta-carotene and the other antioxidants come in. In test-tube studies, antioxidants display a kind of "over my dead body" behavior, shielding LDL from free radicals and sacrificing themselves to the oxidation process instead.

So the higher your intake of antioxidants, the slower the rate of oxidation, and the longer oxidation is delayed, theorizes Paul LaChance, Ph.D., professor of nutrition at Rutgers University in New Brunswick, New Jersey. That would explain why people whose diets are high in beta-carotene and other antioxidants are less likely to have heart disease and heart attacks, says Dr. LaChance.

## How Much Is Enough?

At this writing, there is no established Daily Value for beta-carotene and no medical consensus on how much of this nutrient the body needs to stiff-arm heart disease, says Dr. LaChance. Some studies suggest that anywhere from 15 to 30 milligrams a day of beta-carotene is protective. How much is that, food-wise? A medium carrot contains 12 milligrams of beta-carotene, and a sweet potato, 15 milligrams.

But you might need even less beta-carotene than that, says Dr. LaChance. He analyzed the nutritional content of two weeks' worth of menus from the American Heart Association's anti–heart disease diet and the cancer prevention diet of the National Cancer Institute in Rockville, Maryland, and found that both diets supply an average of six milligrams of beta-carotene a day. Yet for many, intake falls woefully short of the six milligrams. "The typical American consumes only about a third of (the American Heart Association and National Cancer Institute average)—from 1.5 to 2 milligrams," says Dr. LaChance. "So there's a gap. My argument is, why not fill that gap and see what happens?"

You can meet the six-milligram quota by consuming just one serving of a yellow-orange fruit or a dark green leafy vegetable a day, says Dr. LaChance. Getting even more beta-carotene through food is safe and may do your heart good, he says (although if consumed in very high doses, this nutrient can tint the skin orange).

By the way, that six milligrams of beta-carotene translates to 10,000 international units of vitamin A, which is double the Daily Value for vitamin A (5,000 international units). But preformed vitamin A doesn't help you meet your beta-carotene needs, Dr. LaChance notes.

## Best-Bet Ways to Boost Your Beta

The bad news: Certain ways of preparing and cooking fruits and vegetables can rob you of beta-carotene, says Dr. LaChance. The good news: You can prevent this theft. Dr. LaChance offers the following nutrient conservation strategies.

• If you can't get fresh fruits and vegetables, opt for frozen products. They tend to contain more beta-carotene than the canned kinds.

• Opt for broccoli spears rather than chopped broccoli, and cut carrots into hefty chunks instead of dicing them. The smaller the area, the more surface area that is exposed, allowing more nutrients to escape.

• Steam vegetables or zap them in the microwave (in a microwave-safe container without added liquid) to minimize cooking time and beta-carotene loss. Should you opt to steam your veggies, use very little water. The more water you use, the more beta you lose.

• Make a one-pot meal, such as a stew or soup. Because the juice from the carrots or broccoli becomes part of the broth, you don't lose as much beta-carotene.

• Add liquid from cooked vegetables to soups, stews, gravies and sauces.

• Snack on vegetables, not chips. To work an extra serving or two into your day, munch raw carrots or broccoli spears with a couple of tablespoons of low-fat dip or a wedge of low-fat cheese. Like all fat-soluble nutrients, beta-carotene is best absorbed when consumed with a bit of fat.

## Supplements Are Fine, Food Is Better

It shouldn't be hard to get a full day's supply of beta-carotene through food. But if you are always on the go and can't be sure you'll have the time to lunch on a spinach salad or even to snack on a carrot or two, you might consider taking beta-carotene in supplement form, says Dr. LaChance. Beta-carotene is sold over the counter (often in 15-milligram doses) and is included in some multivitamin/mineral supplements.

Many experts, including Dr. LaChance, say it's preferable to eat more beta-carotene-rich foods (and more fruits and vegetables in general) than to rely on supplements, however. "There are more advantages to eating whole foods" than to taking supplements, says Dr. LaChance. "Antioxidants don't work in isolation," he notes. "When you take in more beta-carotene, you also get more of the other antioxidants and more folate (a B vitamin), fiber and minerals."

You'll also consume more of the 400 or so other carotenoids, which may further boost beta-carotene's heart-healthy benefits. In fact, some studies suggest that total carotenoid intake is strongly associated with a reduction in heart disease or heart attack risk—perhaps even more strongly than beta-carotene alone. That's another good reason for you to tuck in to a fluffy sweet potato.

*See also* Antioxidants

cﾟﾉﾟﾉ

# CALCIUM

## *The Multi-talented Mineral*

Drink your milk! It's good for growing bones."
As a kid, you probably heard this maternal refrain hundreds of times. And Mom was right: Milk—or rather the calcium in milk—does help build strong bones. Calcium is also the first line of defense against osteoporosis, the crippling bone-thinning disease that afflicts about 24 million people, mostly women, over age 65.

But along with fracture-proofing your bones, calcium might also help protect your ticker: Some studies indicate that calcium may play a role in lowering blood cholesterol. While the jury is still out on this theory, the evidence is intriguing. Read on.

## How Calcium Licks LDL

Heart disease experts have suspected since the 1950s that calcium might lower cholesterol. But most of their studies, while promising, have yielded less than sensational results. That's because most of the early research focused on the effects of calcium on total cholesterol. More recent studies have analyzed calcium's effects on the separate components of total cholesterol, LDL (the "bad" kind) and HDL (the "good" kind), which experts consider more sensitive measures of heart disease risk. And the news is encouraging.

Researchers at the University of Texas Southwestern Medical Center at Dallas, headed by Margo Denke, M.D., associate professor of medicine in the Center for Human Nutrition, put 13 men with moderately high cholesterol on either a high-calcium diet (2,200 milligrams of calcium per day) or a low-calcium diet (410 milligrams of calcium per day) for ten weeks. For the next ten weeks, the men resumed their regular diets. During the study's final ten weeks, the men who first consumed the high-calcium diet followed the low-calcium plan, and vice versa.

The researchers found that the men's total cholesterol fell an average of 6 percent on the high-calcium diet. Even more significantly, their LDL cholesterol dropped an average of 11 percent. Since experts generally agree that every 1 percent decrease in LDL cholesterol results in a 2 percent decrease in heart disease risk, these individuals' risk dropped over 20 percent.

In another study, researchers at the Hennepin County Medical Center in Minneapolis had 56 men and women with mildly to moderately high blood cholesterol follow a low-fat diet and consume 1,200 milligrams of calcium a day. These folks' LDL cholesterol dropped 4.4 percent, which theoretically decreased their heart disease risk by nearly 10 percent. What's more, their HDL cholesterol increased 4.1 percent.

How might calcium reduce cholesterol? According to the University of Texas study, calcium may both block the absorption of saturated

---

## CALCULATE YOUR CALCIUM QUOTA

Chances are you won't find a single-dose multivitamin/mineral supplement that contains 100 percent of the optimal amount of 1,000 milligrams of calcium. And if you're a woman over age 50 or a man over age 65, you need even more calcium: 1,500 milligrams per day (150 percent of the Daily Value). So you may want to consider taking a calcium supplement. Here's how to find out if you're giving your heart and bones a steady supply of this essential nutrient.

1. Determine your calcium goal.
2. Subtract 300 milligrams for each serving of milk, yogurt, cheese or calcium-fortified orange juice that you typically consume each day.
3. Subtract any calcium that you may get from a multivitamin/mineral supplement. Most supplements contain 200 milligrams or less.

If, after your calculations, you're coming up short of your calcium goal, you need to take a calcium supplement, says William P. Castelli, M.D., medical director of the Framingham Cardiovascular Institute, a wellness program at Metro West Medical Center in Framingham, Massachusetts.

fat and bind with cholesterol-containing bile acids in the digestive system. The body then excretes these acids, giving excess cholesterol the boot, too. In fact, the men in the University of Texas study excreted 13 percent saturated fat while following the high-calcium diet, compared with only 6 percent while on the low-calcium plan.

## Nonfat Ways to Bone Up Your Diet

Whether the link between increased calcium consumption and lower blood cholesterol will be borne out by further study remains to be seen. Still, "there are many good reasons to increase your calcium intake," says Robert Heaney, M.D., professor of medicine at Creighton University School of Medicine in Omaha, Nebraska, and an expert on calcium.

The most crucial reason? Many people simply don't get enough of this vital mineral. The optimum intake is 1,000 milligrams a day for women ages 25 to 50, menopausal women (ages 51 to 65) who take estrogen and men ages 25 to 65. That amount jumps to 1,500 milligrams a day for menopausal women who don't take estrogen and for all men and women over age 65. Yet it's estimated that 50 percent of women over age 35 consume less than 500 milligrams of calcium a day—far less than they need.

Fortunately, it's easy to fortify your heart and bones with calcium. Simply eat more low-fat or nonfat milk, yogurt and cheese, which contain all of the calcium of whole-milk dairy products with much less of the artery-plugging saturated fat. Other good sources of calcium include sardines and canned salmon, calcium-fortified orange juice and green vegetables, particularly bok choy and kale.

## Choosing a Supplement

If you suspect that you're not getting enough calcium through your diet, you might consider taking calcium supplements, available in drugstores and health food stores, says Dr. Heaney. The most common supplements contain calcium carbonate.

The following guidelines can help you choose calcium supplements properly, says Dr. Heaney.

• Take calcium supplements in small doses—500 milligrams or less at a time.

• Take calcium carbonate supplements with meals to ensure good absorption, says Dr. Heaney. He recommends chewable supplements: "They disintegrate best," he says. Avoid "natural source" calcium carbonate supplements made from bonemeal, dolomite or oyster shell, however. Some studies indicate that these products may contain unhealthy amounts of lead.

• Limit your intake of fatty foods, caffeine, alcohol and tobacco products. All can hinder calcium absorption.

• Make sure to get the Daily Value of vitamin D (400 international units): It's essential for calcium absorption. Eat foods fortified with vitamin D, including skim milk and some breads and cereals. Or consider taking a daily multivitamin/mineral supplement that meets 100 percent of your daily vitamin D requirement.

• Try to avoid calcium supplements that contain aluminum. This chemical can deplete the body's supply of phosphate, which it needs to absorb calcium, says Dr. Heaney. "But if you have a peptic ulcer and need to take supplements that contain aluminum, make sure you get extra calcium," he advises.

• Don't take calcium supplements with high-fiber wheat bran cereals: These cereals can reduce calcium absorption by 25 percent.

• Drink lots of water to help avoid constipation, a possible side effect of calcium supplements.

Supplements are not a substitute for a low-fat diet or cholesterol-lowering drugs (if your doctor has prescribed them), says Dr. Denke. But "if you're eating a low-fat, low–saturated fat, low-cholesterol diet, some additional calcium may be helpful," she says. "Women might want an extra 1,000 milligrams a day of calcium—it can also help protect against osteoporosis." For men, taking an additional 800 milligrams of calcium over the optimal amounts may be sufficient, she says.

While research indicates that calcium does not heighten the risk of kidney stone formation, if you have kidney stones, it's still a good idea to check with your doctor before taking calcium supplements. In fact, says Dr. Heaney, "a high-calcium diet may protect against the absorption of oxalic acid, the principal risk factor in the formation of kidney stones."

~ঙ্কুঌ

# Canola Oil

## *The Lightest of All*

Safflower and corn oils, which are high in polyunsaturated fat, can lower "bad" LDL cholesterol. But there's a trade-off: Polyunsaturated fat can cause "good" HDL cholesterol to slide, too. And coconut and palm kernel oils (the so-called tropical oils) are brimming with saturated fat, which can launch your blood cholesterol into an upward trajectory and stop up your coronary arteries.

Enter canola oil. This super oil can lower LDL cholesterol while it maintains or even raises HDL cholesterol. That's because canola oil is high in monounsaturated fat, the kind associated with reducing blood cholesterol.

## Promising Results

A number of studies have shown that canola oil can be effective in reducing elevated cholesterol. For example, at the Kenneth L. Jordan Heart Foundation and Research Center in Montclair, New Jersey, and Elmhurst General Hospital in Queens, New York, 36 people with either high blood cholesterol or high blood pressure added one ounce (about two tablespoons) of canola oil to their diets per day, using it in place of other oils and spreads. After four months, these individuals' average total cholesterol fell from 254 to 248 milligrams/deciliter, and their LDL cholesterol dipped from 173 to 160 milligrams/deciliter. What's more, these folks' HDL cholesterol rose slightly, from 47 to 51 milligrams/deciliter.

Researchers at the University of Helsinki in Finland compared the effect on blood cholesterol of a diet high in monounsaturated fat and a diet high in polyunsaturated fat. For two weeks, the researchers fed 59 people a baseline diet that was high in saturated fat. Then these individuals alternated between two diets—the first enriched with canola oil, and the second, with sunflower oil. Both diets supplied 38 percent of calories from fat. But the sunflower oil diet was higher in polyunsaturated fat and lower in monounsaturated fat.

After 25 days on each diet, total cholesterol among men and women on the canola-enriched diet dropped 15 percent, and LDL cholesterol levels dipped 23 percent below the baseline level. By comparision, the total cholesterol of the sunflower oil group decreased 12 percent, and the LDL cholesterol fell 17 percent from the baseline. Neither diet affected these individuals' levels of HDL cholesterol.

## What about Olive Oil?

How does canola oil fare against olive oil, also touted for its ability to slash LDL while it maintains or even raises HDL cholesterol?

Canola oil and olive oil have virtually the same effect on blood cholesterol, says Alice H. Lichtenstein, D.Sc., assistant professor of nutrition at Tufts University in Medford, Massachusetts, and a scientist at the Jean Mayer USDA Human Nutrition Research Center on Aging in Boston. "The effects on LDL cholesterol are comparable," says Dr. Lichtenstein. "No one is saying that there's an advantage to using olive oil over canola oil, or vice versa."

And while canola oil is lower in monounsaturated fat than olive oil, it is also lower in saturated fat. "Of the five vegetable oils lowest in saturated fat—canola, olive, corn, safflower and sunflower—none is lower than canola," says Evelyn Tribole, R.D., a dietitian in Beverly Hills, California, and author of *Healthy Homestyle Cooking.* "Canola oil contains 6 percent saturated fat, and olive oil 15 percent saturated fat."

The bottom line? You can use both canola oil and olive oil as part of a heart-healthy diet. The best course of action, advises Tribole, is to replace the saturated fat in your diet, such as butter, with unsaturated fat, such as canola oil.

## Salads, No—Popcorn, Yes

Unlike olive oil, canola oil doesn't have a pronounced flavor. But that's not necessarily a disadvantage, especially if you don't enjoy the robust flavor of olive oil.

In fact, canola oil's subtle flavor can be a plus—it's a natural choice for some dishes. "You can use canola oil in place of safflower or corn oil," says Tammy Baker, R.D., a nutritionist in Cave Creek, Arizona, and a spokesperson for the American Dietetic Association. Try substituting canola oil for butter when you're sautéing vegetables or in baked goods and sauces, suggests Baker, or when you're making popcorn. When not to use canola oil, says Baker: in salad dressings. It's way too bland to add flavor to your fixin's.

However you decide to use canola oil, keep it fresh. Oils high in monounsaturated fat tend to go bad faster than other oils. So if you haven't used up a bottle of canola oil about a month after opening it, store it in the refrigerator.

# CARROTS

## *Fight Cholesterol with Fiber Power*

Crisp and crunchy, carrots may well qualify as the ultimate healthy snack. They're brimming with beta-carotene and vitamin C— antioxidant nutrients believed to help protect against a variety of ailments, including cancer—as well as with vitamin A. What's more, these sweet, crunchy veggies are packed with soluble fiber, the kind proven to help deflate blood cholesterol.

More specifically, carrots are rich in calcium pectate, a certain type of soluble fiber that may bestow special cholesterol-lowering power, according to Peter D. Hoagland, Ph.D., a research chemist for the U.S. Department of Agriculture. Dr. Hoagland's research indicates that calcium pectate helps to bind bile acids, the substances that assist in the digestion of fats and in the transportation of cholesterol out of the body.

A study conducted outside the United States seems to back Dr. Hoagland's research. Scientists at Western General Hospital in Edinburgh, Scotland, had five people eat 200 grams of raw carrots (about two carrots) each morning. After three weeks of this morning ritual, the people's cholesterol levels fell 11 percent. And their cholesterol remained lowered for another three weeks after they stopped eating the daily carrots.

Cooked carrots appear to help lower cholesterol just as well as raw carrots, says Dr. Hoagland. "The fiber in cooked carrots seems to have the same ability to bind bile acids as the fiber in raw carrots," he says. "Calcium pectate still ends up in the gut, where it can interact with bile acids."

Here's how to add more carrots to your diet.

• Make sure carrots are fresh. If you're buying them by the bunch, choose the ones with the freshest-looking tops: The fresher the greens, the fresher the carrots, says Mindy Hermann, R.D., a nutrition consultant in Mount Kisco, New York. "If you buy bagged carrots, feel the vegetables through the bag and avoid those that feel flabby or rubbery," says Hermann.

• Many experts suggest steaming carrots to preserve their nutrients. Boiling carrots drains 50 percent of their beta-carotene and 90 percent of their vitamin C.

• Try snacking on prewashed, prepeeled baby carrots. "Try them with a nonfat dip—nonfat sour cream or yogurt mixed with a dry dip mix," says Evelyn Tribole, R.D., a dietitian in Beverly Hills, California, and author of *Healthy Homestyle Cooking*.

• Want to make a dish bursting with fiber and antioxidant vitamins? "Make a sweet-potato-and-carrot casserole, and season it with a little ginger or nutmeg," suggests Mona Sutnick, R.D., Ed.D., a dietitian in Philadelphia and a spokesperson for the American Dietetic Association.

• Make roasted carrots, suggests Barbie Casselman, a nutrition consultant in Toronto. Here's how: Spray sliced carrots with no-stick cooking spray, arrange them on a no-stick baking sheet and bake at 425° for 20 to 25 minutes. "When you make carrots this way, no one misses the cream sauce," says Casselman.

<br>

❦

# CHICKEN

## *A Decent Choice Made Better*

For years, the ultimate in fine dining was a nice, thick, juicy steak. But when doctors started telling us what consuming too much fatty red meat could do to our coronary arteries—and to our hearts—many of us modified our carnivorous ways and started eating more chicken.

"Generally speaking, chicken contains less saturated fat and more polyunsaturated fat than beef," says Gene A. Spiller, D.Sc., Ph.D., director of the Health Research and Studies Center in Los Altos, California, and author of *The Superpyramid Eating Program*. Three ounces of lean, broiled filet mignon contains 8.5 grams of fat, 3.2 grams of it saturated. The same amount of skinless chicken breast contains 3.1 grams of fat and less than 1 gram of saturated fat.

But hold on. While eating plates of red meat the size of Idaho isn't a good idea, all red meat isn't necessarily bad for you, say experts. Nor is all chicken necessarily good for you: If you're trying to lower your blood cholesterol, eating three or four pieces of fried chicken is definitely not what the doctor ordered.

To make poultry a part of a heart-healthy diet, say experts, you need to choose the right cuts of chicken and prepare them with little or no fat. "Think lean when you put chicken on your table," says Dr. Spiller.

## Poultry Pointers

These suggestions can help you trim the fat—and a significant number of calories—from chicken.

• Buy the leanest birds. Broilers and fryers are lower in fat than roasters.

• Bake, broil or roast chicken. These cooking methods allow the fat to drip off the bird. Frying chicken, on the other hand, adds fat and calories.

• Eat "light." The white meat portions of a chicken contain less fat than the dark meat, and the breast is the leanest part of the bird: Three ounces of skinless chicken breast gets 19 percent of its calories from fat, while a whole skinless chicken leg—thigh and drumstick—gets a whopping 40 percent of its calories from fat.

• If you can't resist dark meat, eat smaller amounts of it less often, suggests Susan Kleiner, R.D., Ph.D., a nutritionist in Seattle and author of *The High-Performance Cookbook*. While a thigh or drumstick contains more fat than a breast, "dark meat still contains less fat than most beef, relatively speaking," says Dr. Kleiner.

• Coat a pan or wok with nonfat cooking spray and stir-fry chicken with fresh or frozen vegetables, herbs and spices. Or make chicken fajitas, suggests Janet Lepke, R.D., a dietitian in Santa Monica, California, and a spokesperson for the American Dietetic Association. "Sauté strips of chicken breast with red and green peppers, onions and tomatoes in a teaspoon of oil with some chicken broth, or sauté the strips in white wine and garlic with fajita seasoning," suggests Lepke. Then stuff the mixture into a soft corn or flour tortilla.

• Microwave skinless chicken breasts and top them with salsa, low-fat spaghetti sauce or lemon-pepper seasoning. (Make sure the chicken is cooked thoroughly.)

• Pass up fast-food fried chicken, which is loaded with sodium, fat and cholesterol. But if you must indulge, stem the damage: Eat one or two pieces of chicken and fill up on vegetables, rice, a baked potato or a salad with low-fat or nonfat dressing, advises Mary Donkersloot, R.D., a dietitian in Beverly Hills, California, a spokesperson for the California Dietetic Association and author of *The Fast Food Diet*.

• Better yet, make your own "fried" chicken in the oven, suggests Evelyn Tribole, R.D., a dietitian in Beverly Hills, California, in her book *Healthy Homestyle Cooking*: Coat skinless chicken breasts with egg whites (not the yolks), a small amount of flour and cornflake crumbs and bake at 375°.

## To Skin or Not to Skin

If you consider the crispy, crunchy skin the best part of the chicken, being told not to indulge may leave you feeling deprived. So if you know you're not going to give up the skin, at least practice damage control.

"If you insist on leaving the skin on, you definitely shouldn't fry the chicken, which will add more fat," says Bettye Nowlin, R.D., a dietitian in Los Angeles and a spokesperson for the American Dietetic Association. "Instead, you should roast or broil your chicken, keep your portion size small and avoid high-fat foods for the rest of the day."

If you're serious about reducing your intake of dietary fat, however, it's best to avoid the skin altogether, says William P. Castelli, M.D., medical director of the Framingham Cardiovascular Institute, a wellness program at Metro West Medical Center in Framingham, Massachusetts. "Take off the skin and toss it out!" he says. Think of it this way: By stripping off the skin, you'll slash your intake of saturated fat in half and save yourself some calories in the bargain.

There is some good news about chicken skin, however: Despite what you may think, you don't have to remove the skin before you cook chicken. Researchers at the University of Minnesota found that removing the skin after cooking rather than beforehand doesn't affect the fat content of the meat. "The fat that's in the skin stays there—it doesn't migrate into the meat," says dietitian Linda Dieleman, R.D., of the University of Minnesota Inter-College Nutrition Consortium in St. Paul.

As a bonus, "leaving the skin on during baking will help keep the chicken moist," says Lisa Lauri, R.D., nutrition consultant at North Shore University Hospital in Manhasset, New York.

～❈～

# CHILI PEPPERS

## *Fire Up Your Blood Fats*

For some thrill-seeking folks, eating chili peppers is as exhilarating as skydiving or rock climbing. Eyes streaming, noses leaking, these self-proclaimed fire-eaters—who call riding the wave of chili pepper heat mouth surfing—enjoy setting their tongues ablaze. And they never seem to run out of ways to send their mouths into meltdown: Chili aficionados add their favorite pepper to soups, stews, salsas and sauces, roast them and stuff them with cheese, even add them to ice cream.

But those with flame-resistant gullets may actually reap some health benefits from chili peppers. These pungent peppers are high in vitamin A, which is thought to boost immunity and protect against cancer, and vitamin C, which may help deflate blood pressure. Even more significantly, capsaicin—the substance that gives chili peppers their bite—may also help lower triglycerides, a type of blood fat implicated in heart disease. Chili peppers may even reduce the risk of heart attack and stroke by increasing the blood's ability to break up dangerous clots.

It appears that capsaicin (also used to relieve psoriasis and arthritis pain) may impact more on triglycerides than on cholesterol. But the few studies that have explored the connection between capsaicin and blood fats have yielded intriguing results. When researchers in India fed capsaicin to laboratory rats along with their normal diet, for example, the rodents' triglyceride levels fell, although their cholesterol levels weren't affected. Researchers at the Ohio State University College of Medicine in Columbus also administered capsaicin to rats; these rodents' triglycerides fell as well.

The best news of all? Despite chili peppers' fearsome reputation, it's entirely possible to enjoy their three-alarm flavor without losing taste buds in the process. You just have to know how to handle the heat—and proceed with caution. Here's how.

## Small Peppers Pack Big Heat

There are over 100 kinds of chili pepper, and they're available in a variety of forms, including fresh, dried and powdered. But when it comes to generating heat, not all chilies are created equal.

You can't always judge a chili pepper's heat by its size or color. Generally speaking, the smaller the pepper, the hotter it is: Small, narrow chili peppers, including the cayenne and serrano, pack more capsaicin than larger, milder peppers, such as the poblano and Anaheim.

The jalapeño pepper is one of the most popular chilies in the United States. But while most people consider this plump, bright red or dark green pepper a real stinger, its heat pales in comparison with that of the habañero, the most blistering chili of all.

"It's the hottest pepper on record," says Dave DeWitt, author of *The Whole Chile Pepper Book*. A measurement called the Scoville unit is used to determine the heat of chili peppers, he explains. While the jalapeño pepper averages about 5,000 Scoville units, "a habañero can measure 500,000 Scoville units—100 times hotter than a jalapeño!" says DeWitt.

Chili connoisseurs say the habañero's fire is short-lived. But when your mouth is on fire, a minute or two can seem like an eternity, so try this pepper at your own risk.

## Red-Hot Chili Tips

When it comes to using chili peppers, you're limited only by your imagination (and your courage). Here are a few common—and un-common—uses for these fiery delicacies.

• Spice up a salad with a small amount of chili peppers, suggests DeWitt. If you're using dried chilies, be aware that they tend to be hotter than fresh peppers.

• Mix a tiny bit of chopped chili peppers into mayonnaise or salad dressing, suggests dietitian Nancy Gerlach, R.D., food editor of *Chili Pepper Magazine*. Or add cayenne or any type of ground chili pepper to barbecue sauce. "But bear in mind that capsaicin is soluble in oil," she notes. Translation: The longer chili peppers sit in mayonnaise or salad dressing, says Gerlach, the hotter these condiments will get. So skimp on the amount of chili you use, at least at first.

• Add chili peppers to your homemade chili. "Both the type and amount of chili peppers you use are matters of personal preference," says DeWitt. "Some people use a base of green chili peppers; others prefer red." Let your taste buds be your guide, he adds.

• Add fresh or powdered chili peppers to your favorite bread recipe, suggests Gerlach, who uses both chopped green chilies and red chili powder in her homemade loaves. "Chilies give bread a real bite," she says.

• As odd as it may sound, try adding a small amount of pureed chili peppers to ice cream, suggests DeWitt. "Jalapeño ice cream is one of the more unusual chili pepper dishes," he says. "It's quite a sensation—cold and hot at the same time." (Opt for low-fat or nonfat ice cream, of course.)

## Mouth Surfing 101

Just as you wouldn't jump into a pool without knowing how to swim, you shouldn't handle—or eat—chili peppers before you know the finer points of going for the burn. These hints can help.

• Chili peppers can burn more than your mouth—they can scorch your skin, too. So after you handle chilies, wash your hands with soap and water before you touch your eyes or face. Better yet, wear gloves while chopping chili peppers, especially if you have a cut on your hand or finger. Also, avoid inhaling the peppers' fiery fumes: "The capsaicin can burn your eyes and lips," says Gerlach.

• It's simpler to add chili heat to a dish than to subtract it, says De-Witt. "So add the chili peppers carefully and taste as you go," he cautions. "It's easy to make the food literally too hot to eat."

• If you're unfamiliar with chili peppers, use some commonsense caution. "See how hot the food is before you start wolfing it down," says DeWitt.

If, despite your best efforts, eating a fiery chili pepper dish leaves you screaming for relief, don't gulp water—that will spread the capsaicin throughout your mouth, says DeWitt. Rather, drink a glass of milk or eat a few spoonfuls of yogurt. Milk contains a protein called casein that can help smother capsaicin's flames. Rice, bananas and bread may douse the flames, too.

# CHROMIUM

## *Big Benefits from a Mighty Mineral*

Some of the most intriguing research in the nutritional fight against high cholesterol has to do with a trace mineral whose name reminds most people of the shiny stuff on the bumpers of cars: chromium.

## A STRIKE AGAINST DIABETES

People with diabetes run an increased risk of developing heart disease. For them, chromium may improve glucose tolerance, which is a measure of how well glucose, or sugar, is absorbed into the blood and transported into the cells, according to Richard A. Anderson, Ph.D., lead scientist at the U.S. Department of Agriculture Human Nutrition Research Center in Beltsville, Maryland.

Most people with diabetes have glucose intolerance, a condition in which blood sugar levels are out of control. That's because insulin, a hormone that helps control blood sugar levels, doesn't work properly. Chromium particularly benefits people who already have diabetes by making insulin work more effectively.

In one study, Dr. Anderson, a leading expert on chromium, had 17 people—8 of whom had mild glucose intolerance—eat a chromium-poor diet. After a month, Dr. Anderson divided these people into two groups. While both groups continued on the low-chromium diet, the first group took 200 micrograms of chromium per day. The second group received placebo pills. Five weeks later, the groups were switched, with the first group receiving the placebo pills and vice versa.

The chromium supplements didn't affect blood sugar levels in the glucose-tolerant folks. But the blood sugar levels of the glucose-intolerant people rose nearly 50 percent less when they were taking chromium supplements than when they didn't take these supplements. The upshot? Chromium may reverse glucose intolerance, says Dr. Anderson.

Some studies indicate that chromium, which helps control the way your body uses sugar and fat, may boost the body's stores of "good" HDL cholesterol. "When people who follow a normal diet—which tends to be marginally chromium-deficient—consume more chromium, their cholesterol and triglyceride levels benefit," says Richard A. Anderson, Ph.D., lead scientist at the U.S. Department of Agriculture Human Nutrition Research Center in Beltsville, Maryland, and a leading expert on chromium.

What's more, chromium may help people with glucose intolerance avoid developing non-insulin-dependent (Type II) diabetes. Having diabetes increases the risk of developing heart disease. (See "A Strike against Diabetes.")

## The Cholesterol Connection

Researchers at Oklahoma State University in Stillwater had 21 people ages 60 and over take 150 micrograms of chromium every day for three months. Another 21 people took a placebo.

Chromium takers with normal cholesterol exhibited no change in their cholesterol levels. But chromium takers with high cholesterol saw their total cholesterol go down 12 percent and their "bad" LDL cholesterol plummet 14 percent. Just as important, their levels of HDL cholesterol didn't change.

In a second study conducted at Oklahoma State University, researchers had 24 people ages 55 and over take one of three supplements: chromium (210 micrograms), copper or zinc. After two months, the total cholesterol of the folks taking the chromium fell 12 points, from 217 to 205 milligrams/deciliter. When these individuals stopped taking the chromium, their total cholesterol crept up again. Copper and zinc had no effect on cholesterol levels.

In Jerusalem, 76 heart disease patients—about one-third of whom also had Type II diabetes—consumed either a 250-microgram chromium supplement or a placebo every day for 7 to 16 months. The total cholesterol of the men in the chromium group didn't change. But their HDL cholesterol increased by 21 to 25 percent.

Investigators at the Medical Hospital and Research Centre in Moradabad, India, had 104 patients with Type II diabetes follow either a chromium-rich diet (129 micrograms of chromium a day) or their usual diets, which contained 69 micrograms a day. After two months, the high-chromium group saw their total cholesterol fall 10 percent, their LDL cholesterol decline 12 percent and their HDL cholesterol jump 7 percent. The cholesterol of the low-chromium group didn't change.

## Getting Enough Chromium

The Daily Value for chromium is 120 micrograms. The average American man consumes 33 micrograms of the mineral a day, and the average woman, 25 micrograms. "We collected data on 32 people over seven consecutive days, and not one of them averaged even 50 micrograms of chromium over that one-week period," says Dr. Anderson.

Good sources of chromium include turkey ham, grape juice, broccoli, unpeeled apples, green beans and whole-wheat products. So, apparently, are some breakfast cereals. "Total breakfast cereal is very high in chromium," says Dr. Anderson. "One serving contains nearly 27 micrograms of chromium, which is probably as much as you'll get from everything else you eat all day."

But you need to watch the rest of your diet, too, says Dr. Anderson—especially if you have a sweet tooth. Consuming too many highly processed, sugary foods can rob the body of chromium (which is excreted through the urine). According to Dr. Anderson, "Eating lots of simple sugars may also increase your need for chromium supplements because you're consuming fewer chromium-rich foods. So you need to pay attention to your overall diet as well as to the amount of chromium you're getting."

Dr. Anderson recommends taking a multivitamin/mineral supplement containing 50 to 200 micrograms of chromium. "One leading brand contains 100 micrograms of chromium," he says. "That extra 100 micrograms a day can serve as an insurance policy should there be a deficiency in your diet."

If you have diabetes, you may need even more chromium, says Dr. Anderson—about 400 to 600 micrograms a day. Is consuming this amount of chromium safe? Yes, says Dr. Anderson. "We've been studying chromium for decades, and we've never documented a single case of a negative effect," he says. Still, check with your doctor before taking more than a 200-microgram supplement per day.

❧

# COFFEE

## *Enjoy Your Java in Moderation*

Whether you linger over designer lattes at trendy coffee bars or savor fresh, strong joe from your trusty old percolator, one thing's for sure: When it comes to the relationship between coffee consumption and elevated blood cholesterol, there's controversy brewing.

Some studies suggest that coffee can raise cholesterol levels; others conclude just the opposite. Most of the studies conducted in the United States have found that people who don't drink coffee have higher rates of coronary heart disease than coffee drinkers! In fact, the prestigious Framingham Heart Study concluded that drinking up to five cups of coffee a day may actually have lowered the risk of coronary heart disease, says William P. Castelli, M.D., medical director of the Framingham Cardiovascular Institute, a wellness program at Metro West Medical Center in Framingham, Massachusetts.

The good news is, consuming moderate amounts of coffee does not appear to raise the risk of heart disease. What's more, some experts say that a cup or two of coffee a day shouldn't significantly affect your cholesterol level. (No large studies have been conducted on the effect of other caffeinated foods or drinks—such as chocolate or cola—on blood cholesterol levels.)

But caffeine can affect the body in other ways. Consumed in large amounts, it can sap bone strength and accelerate the heart rate. Further complicating the coffee/cholesterol issue: the role of nicotine. Some studies note that avid coffee drinkers tend to smoke more than people who drink coffee in moderate amounts, and smoking has definitely been implicated in the development of coronary heart disease.

## The Caffeine/Cholesterol Connection

Investigators have conducted numerous studies on the relationship between coffee, elevated cholesterol and heart disease. Results have been inconclusive, however. Some of these studies show that when it comes to coffee and cholesterol, much depends on how the coffee is prepared, according to Dr. Castelli. "Boiled coffee, like the kind drunk in Scandinavia and Turkey, tends to raise cholesterol and the risk of heart disease," says Dr. Castelli. "But filtered coffee does not raise cholesterol or increase the risk of heart disease."

Researchers at Boston University polled 858 women hospitalized with a first heart attack and an equal number of healthy women on their health habits, including coffee consumption. Researchers found that compared with non–coffee drinkers, women who said they drank five to six cups of coffee a day had a 40 percent greater risk of having a heart attack; women who drank seven to nine cups, a 70 percent greater risk. But women who drank less than five cups of coffee a day had no higher risk than women who didn't drink coffee at all.

Investigators at Kaiser Permanente Medical Center in Oakland, California, evaluated the relationship between coffee and tea intake and mortality rate—including deaths from coronary heart disease—in nearly 129,000 people. After an eight-year follow-up period, neither coffee nor tea was found to have increased the overall death rate in these individuals. Drinking four or more cups of coffee a day was tied to a slightly higher risk of death from heart attack, however.

Researchers at Johns Hopkins Medical Institutions in Baltimore had 100 healthy men drink varying amounts of filtered coffee: 24 ounces of regular coffee, 12 ounces of regular coffee, 24 ounces of decaffeinated coffee or no coffee at all. After eight weeks, the men who drank the 24 ounces of regular coffee a day experienced small increases in their total cholesterol, due to slight rises in their "bad" LDL and "good" HDL cholesterol. The researchers concluded that these small increases in LDL and HDL together "should not affect coronary heart disease risk." That's because small changes in HDL can protect against much larger changes in LDL, explains Dr. Castelli.

In Israel, researchers analyzed coffee and tea consumption and cholesterol levels in 5,369 people. The investigators' conclusion: The individuals who drank five or more cups of coffee a day had higher levels of total cholesterol—as much as 18 milligrams/deciliter higher—than the individuals who abstained from coffee. The researchers also noted that the people who drank the most coffee in their study were also the most likely to have negative health habits, especially smoking. "It is conceivable that the increased cholesterol levels in smokers may be confounded by coffee drinking," wrote the researchers.

Some coffee drinkers may make other lifestyle choices that may be responsible for elevating their cholesterol levels, suggests Connie Diekman, R.D., a dietitian in St. Louis and a spokesperson for the American Dietetic Association. For example, "caffeine tends to stimulate hunger in certain people," says Diekman. "Some people may respond by eating foods that increase their cholesterol levels. But it's difficult to isolate the effect of caffeine on cholesterol and to determine whether the increases in cholesterol are caused by caffeine or by something else."

## WHAT ABOUT DECAF?

You drink decaffeinated coffee, so it can't possibly affect your cholesterol. Right? Not so fast. In one study, decaffeinated coffee raised levels of "bad" LDL cholesterol, while regular, caffeinated coffee did not.

Scientists at the Lipid Research Clinic at Stanford University had 181 healthy middle-age men drink several cups of regular, drip-filtered coffee a day. After two months, some of the men switched to decaf; others continued to drink regular coffee. After another two months, the decaf drinkers saw their LDL cholesterol increase significantly. The regular-coffee drinkers experienced no such changes in LDL. Further, the LDL cholesterol levels of the decaf drinkers were 6 percent higher than that of the regular-coffee drinkers.

The researchers' conclusion: It is not the caffeine in coffee but some other factor in the decaf that's responsible for the increase in LDL cholesterol.

But William P. Castelli, M.D., medical director of the Framingham Cardiovascular Institute, a wellness program at Metro West Medical Center in Framingham, Massachusetts, remains skeptical. "This is just one study," he says.

## Watch the Lattes

Most people don't have to be overly anxious about their caffeine intakes, says Robert J. Nicolosi, Ph.D., director of the Cardiovascular Research Center at the University of Lowell in Massachusetts. "In my view, avoiding caffeine is not one of the lifestyle interventions you need to be most concerned about," says Dr. Nicolosi. While it's possible that caffeine may contribute to elevated cholesterol, he says, "the evidence is very weak at this point."

Diekman concurs. "If you enjoy coffee in moderation and it's not affecting your body—such as accelerating your heart rate—continue to drink it," she says. "But keep in mind that coffee provides no nutritional value. So make sure it's not crowding nourishing beverages (such as juice or skim milk) out of your diet."

Also, pay attention to flavored and specialty coffees, including those served at the local coffee bar, says Barbie Casselman, a nutrition consultant in Toronto. Some coffee beverages contain large amounts of high-fat milk and syrup, so you may be sipping more fat and calories than you realize.

"Most people think that a cappuccino is 6 ounces of coffee and 2 ounces of whipped milk," says Casselman. "But a regular-size cappuccino is actually 2 ounces of espresso plus a cup of milk; in a large cappuccino, there are 12 ounces of milk. If whole milk is used, you might be consuming about 200 calories and eight grams of fat in that 12 ounces of milk. You could eat a dessert for that!"

## Coffee Caveats

The jury is out on whether there's an association between coffee consumption and elevated blood cholesterol. But there's less doubt, say experts, that caffeine can affect your nerves—and your bones.

"I consider caffeine to be a mind-altering drug, in the same category as nicotine and alcohol," says Dr. Nicolosi. "Some people are super-sensitive to caffeine and become hyperactive when drinking coffee." These individuals should consider limiting their consumption of caffeine, he says.

Caffeine may also encourage the development of osteoporosis, the bone-thinning disease that affects many women (and men) later in life, says Isadore Rosenfeld, M.D., author of *Doctor, What Should I Eat?* "Caffeine steals calcium from the body by causing more of it to be excreted in the urine," says Dr. Rosenfeld. He notes, though, that "there's some research to show that drinking a glass of skim milk a day can offset the losses caused by coffee. So make sure you're getting plenty of calcium from milk and other sources."

Two health conditions in which some experts advise reducing or completely eliminating caffeine are heart disease and pregnancy. They recommend that people at high risk for heart attack consider drinking less coffee—under four cups a day, according to some research. And while it's not certain whether caffeine can harm a developing fetus, cautious mothers-to-be may choose to avoid caffeine during their entire pregnancies, recommends Evelyn Tribole, R.D., a dietitian in Beverly Hills, California, and author of *Healthy Homestyle Cooking.*

*See also* Smoking Cessation, Tea

෴

# COMPLEX CARBOHYDRATES

## *Eat Your Fill without Filling Your Arteries*

It used to be that when you wanted to shed a few pounds, you gave up bread, potatoes and pasta. Doctors thought they were fattening. But times have changed, and so has the scientific understanding of carbohydrates: Researchers now know that carbohydrates, the body's primary source of fuel, can help fill us up without necessarily filling us out. What's more, some studies have found that replacing saturated fat with a particular kind of carbohydrate—complex carbohydrates, found primarily in grains and starchy vegetables—can help lower blood cholesterol.

So feel free to enjoy that plate of pasta or that slice of fresh-baked bread. Prepared correctly and eaten in moderation, foods high in complex carbohydrates can make low-fat, low-cholesterol eating a breeze. Here's how to power up your diet while helping to trim down your cholesterol.

## Complex Carbohydrates: Simply Delicious

There are two types of carbohydrates: sugars (simple carbohydrates) and starches (complex carbohydrates). Simple carbohydrates are abundant in fruits, vegetables, honey, corn syrup, milk and sugarcane. Complex carbohydrates are found primarily in breads, pastas, rice and other grains, beans and potatoes.

There's a lot to recommend complex carbohydrates. Starches release their energy more slowly than sugars, making you feel fuller longer. Further, foods high in complex carbohydrates tend to be low in fat and high in fiber—both soluble fiber, which has been proven to lower blood cholesterol, and insoluble fiber, which helps keep you regular and protect against colon cancer.

The government recommends that we eat 6 to 11 servings of breads, cereals, rice and pastas per day. While that may seem like a lot, filling up on complex carbs isn't as hard as you might think, says Mindy Hermann, R.D., a nutrition consultant in Mount Kisco, New York.

"A couple of slices of toast for breakfast equals two servings," says Hermann. "If you have a turkey burger for lunch, the bun counts as another two servings. The bag of pretzels you have as an afternoon snack may count as two servings, depending on the size of the bag. And a big plate of pasta for dinner might add up to four servings. That's ten servings right there."

## So Long, LDL

Several studies have linked the decreased intake of saturated fat and increased consumption of complex carbohydrates with lower levels of blood cholesterol. In one study, R. James Barnard, M.D., of the University of California, Los Angeles, analyzed information on almost 4,600 people who took part in the Pritikin Longevity Center's lifestyle modification program. Forty percent of these individuals had been diagnosed with coronary heart disease, while 43 percent had high blood pressure. These men and women all followed a high-complex-carbohydrate, high-fiber, low-fat, low-cholesterol diet and exercised each day, mainly walking. After three weeks of this diet and exercise regimen, the men's total and "bad" LDL cholesterol had fallen 24 and 25 percent, respectively, while the women saw their total and LDL cholesterol decline 21 and 19 percent, respectively.

Researchers at the National Institutes of Health branch in Phoenix and the Medlantic Research Foundation in Washington, D.C., put 11 people on one of two diets. The first group followed a diet composed of 65 percent carbohydrates (mostly complex carbohydrates) and 21 percent fat. The second group ate a diet that contained 43 percent carbohydrates and 42 percent fat (mostly saturated fat). Then the groups switched diets. Researchers found that these folks' total cholesterol was 184 milligrams/deciliter on the high-fat diet, compared with 164 milligrams/deciliter on the carbohydrate-rich diet. Their LDL cholesterol was 125 milligrams/deciliter on the high-fat plan, compared with 108 milligrams/deciliter on the high-carbohydrate program. The probable reason for the decline? "Substituting complex carbs for saturated fat improves the body's metabolism of LDL, so it's removed from the blood more rapidly," theorizes William P. Castelli, M.D., medical director of the Framingham Cardiovascular Institute, a wellness program at Metro West Medical Center in Framingham, Massachusetts.

## Pass the Spuds, Pass Up the Butter

Want to tank up on cholesterol-busting complex carbs? Follow these simple tips.

• Try to avoid processed foods, which tend to contain added fat, salt and sugar, advises dietitian Marilyn Guthrie, R.D., manager of health promotion for Virginia Mason Medical Center in Seattle. So eat baked potatoes instead of potato chips and whole-grain cereals instead of the highly refined, sugary kinds, says Guthrie. (You might also opt for plain white or brown rice instead of preseasoned rice mixes, which can be high in fat and sodium.)

---

### GOOD NEWS FOR PASTA LOVERS

Still think carbohydrates pack on the pounds? Here's some food for thought.

Researchers at the University of Michigan in Ann Arbor asked almost 500 obese men and women for a top ten list of their favorite foods. After analyzing these individuals' responses, the researchers noted that these folks often confused foods high in fat—doughnuts, ice cream, salty snacks and the like—with carbohydrate-rich foods, such as bread, rolls, cereals and rice. Moreover, more men and women reported craving fatty foods than carbohydrate-rich foods.

The upshot? The researchers found no evidence that craving carbohydrate-rich foods causes obesity. But yearning for fat as opposed to carbohydrates may well be associated with weight gain. In fact, added the researchers, people trying to lose weight might do well to indulge their cravings for carbohydrates rather than to suppress them. Just make sure you splurge on a whole-wheat bagel with jelly—not a jelly doughnut.

- Make room for fruits and vegetables. Apples, bananas, blackberries, prunes, pears, parsnips, acorn squash, corn and yams are rich sources of complex carbs and fiber. If fresh vegetables aren't available, opt for frozen—they're just as high in fiber and nutrients.

- Learn to eat bread (preferably the whole-grain kind) without butter. You might top your morning toast with sugar-free jam or apple butter or even learn to enjoy the delicious simplicity of plain whole-grain bread.

- Jazz up vegetables with herbs instead of butter or cream sauces, says Sue Chapman, executive chef at Skylonda Fitness Retreat in Woodside, California. "Flavor broccoli with rosemary, and bok choy with chopped cilantro, chives or scallions," she suggests.

- Sprinkle baked potatoes with Parmesan cheese, suggests Guthrie. You might also try nonfat sour cream or a dab of spicy brown mustard or low-fat salad dressing.

- Don't drown carbo-packed pastas in fatty meat sauces and cheeses. Instead, flavor spaghetti with low-fat tomato sauce or a drizzle of olive oil, fresh garlic and parsley.

## Can Pasta Make You Fat? The Facts

A while back, you couldn't turn on the television or pick up a newspaper without being confronted by this ugly little phrase: "Pasta makes you fat." Well, does it or doesn't it? Here's what you need to know.

According to some experts, people who produce too much insulin—the hormone that helps metabolize starches and sugars—may gain weight on a high-carbohydrate, low-fat diet. These experts theorize that such "insulin-resistant" people may comprise up to 25 percent of the population.

But other health professionals say that for the remaining 75 percent of us who are not insulin-resistant, whether pasta leads to weight gain depends on how much of it we eat and what we ladle on top of it.

There's some evidence that a high-carbohydrate diet can raise triglycerides (a type of blood fat implicated in heart disease) and lower levels of HDL cholesterol (the "good" kind) in insulin-resistant people, says Wahida Karmally, R.D., director of nutrition at the Irving Center for Clinical Research at Columbia-Presbyterian Medical Center in New York City, a member of the American Heart Association's nutrition subcommittee and part of a research study examining this issue. But you can't blame pasta for your excess pounds "unless you eat loads and loads of it," says Karmally. "It's the overall carbohydrate intake that counts, not just pasta, or just rice, or just potatoes."

"You have to distinguish between complex carbohydrates and simple carbohydrates," says Dean Ornish, M.D., president and director of the Preventive Medicine Research Institute in Sausalito, California, and author of *Dr. Dean Ornish's Program for Reversing Heart Disease.* "Complex carbohydrates—fruits, vegetables and grains—do not raise your insulin level and blood sugar." Dr. Ornish recommends that pasta-lovers avoid sauces and toppings containing fatty ingredients such as butter, oil, cream and sausage.

*See also* Beans, Fiber, Fruit, Vegetables

# COOKING

## *From the Frying Pan into the Steamer*

**I**s there life after fettuccine Alfredo and fried chicken? The answer is a resounding yes. But as more and more health-conscious folks have learned, eating for (rather than to) your heart's content means changing not only what you eat but how you prepare it.

Some of the following culinary tricks help trim the fat from old favorites; other tips update traditional cooking methods with healthier ones. You'll also discover how to sneak low-fat ingredients into your favorite dishes, with your taste buds none the wiser.

As you try new ways of preparing old favorites, you might think of yourself as a culinary explorer, navigating the dangers of the high-fat, high-cholesterol jungle to discover the brave new world of heart-smart cuisine. "The challenge is to cut the fat from our diets while still

---

## LOW-CHOLESTEROL COOKING 101

Here are the basics of low-cholesterol cookery.

- Trim all visible fat from meat before cooking, advises Nancy Baggett, author of *100% Pleasure: The Low-Fat Cookbook for People Who Love to Eat.* Also, before you eat poultry, you should remove the skin.
- Bake, broil, braise, grill, boil or steam foods, advises dietitian Marilyn Guthrie, R.D., manager of health promotion at Virginia Mason Medical Center in Seattle.
- In baked goods use skim milk rather than whole milk, advises Baggett. "Your taste buds will never notice the difference," she says.
- When stir-frying or sautéing foods, use a no-stick cooking spray. Or you can replace each tablespoon of oil in a recipe with a teaspoon of oil plus a few tablespoons of chicken or beef broth, says Baggett.

---

enjoying our foods," says dietitian Marilyn Guthrie, R.D., manager of health promotion at Virginia Mason Medical Center in Seattle. Once you've met that challenge, you'll get a free bonus: the satisfaction of knowing that you're helping to protect your heart and the hearts of those you care about. So get cooking!

## Slimmed-Down Homestyle Favorites

We asked several well-known dietitians and cookbook authors for their advice in creating healthy versions of some high-fat, high-calorie "forbidden" foods. Here are their tasty tips.

### Chilies and Chowders

***Chili con carne.*** If you choose to add ground beef or turkey to your chili, "stir-fry the meat and drain off the fat before adding it to the pot," says Wahida Karmally, R.D., director of nutrition at the Irving Center for Clinical Research at Columbia-Presbyterian Medical Center in New York City and a member of the American Heart Association's nutrition committee. A better idea: Replace some or all of the

---

## LOW-FAT ALTERNATIVES TO HIGH-FAT INGREDIENTS

Want to make your next meal a cholesterol-busting bonanza? Cut the fat—and the cholesterol—with these heart-smart substitutes.

| WHEN YOU NEED ... | USE ... |
| --- | --- |
| Butter, lard or shortening | No-stick cooking spray; olive or canola oil |
| Cream | Evaporated skim milk; skim milk; 1% low-fat milk |
| Oil or margarine | Applesauce (for muffins and quick breads) |
| Sour cream | Nonfat or low-fat plain yogurt; pureed 1% low-fat cottage cheese with a little lemon juice |
| Whipped cream | Whipped evaporated skim milk |
| Whole eggs | Egg substitute; egg whites |
| Whole milk | Evaporated skim milk; skim milk; 1% low-fat milk; reconstituted nonfat dry milk |

---

beef with beans, which contain virtually no fat and lots of cholesterol-busting soluble fiber, says Karmally.

**Clam chowder.** Substitute 1 percent low-fat milk for whole milk and evaporated skim milk for cream, suggests Evelyn Tribole, R.D., a dietitian in Beverly Hills, California, and author of *Healthy Homestyle Cooking.* And if you usually add bacon to your chowder recipe, "use a dash of liquid smoke instead," she says.

## Casseroles and Pasta Dishes

**Beef Stroganoff.** Instead of using canned cream of mushroom soup, the traditional ingredient in this family favorite, "mix an envelope of onion-mushroom soup mix with a cup of evaporated skim milk and some cornstarch," says Tribole. Bring the sauce to a boil, add the beef and serve over noodles with a dollop of nonfat yogurt, if desired.

**Lasagna.** "Layer the noodles with vegetables instead of with fatty meats such as sausage," suggests Julia Della Croce, author of *The Veg-*

*etarian Table.* She suggests roasting or grilling (not frying) zucchini or eggplant, then layering the vegetables with the noodles. To further defat lasagna, opt for reduced-fat ricotta cheese and light spaghetti sauce.

**Spaghetti and meatballs.** Substitute a tangy blend of chopped fresh tomatoes, basil, garlic and balsamic vinegar for the traditional meat- or sausage-filled sauce, suggests Dean Ornish, M.D., president and director of the Preventive Medicine Research Institute in Sausalito, California, and author of *Dr. Dean Ornish's Program for Reversing Heart Disease.* For meatballs, "try adding crumbled soy burgers—they taste just like meat," says Dr. Ornish. Or use one of the many vegetable burgers on the market.

**Tuna noodle casserole.** Old-style tuna casserole is often prepared with oil-packed tuna, whole milk, fatty cheeses and cream of mushroom soup. As an alternative, JoAnna Lund, author of *The Original Healthy Exchanges*, recommends using water-packed tuna, a cup of reduced-fat Cheddar cheese and a can of Campbell's Healthy Request cream of mushroom soup.

## More Main Dishes

**Meat loaf.** Use egg whites instead of whole eggs, along with very lean ground beef, says Lynn Fischer, author of *Healthy Indulgences.* In fact, consider replacing half of the ground beef with a packaged soy mixture (available in most health food stores), she suggests. To keep the meat loaf moist, add chopped onions, celery, carrots, mushrooms, green peppers or the whites of hard-boiled eggs. Fischer also suggests baking the meat loaf in a perforated pan; suspend the pan over a rack so that the fat can drain off.

**Pizza.** Lund uses reduced-fat mozzarella, reduced-calorie tomato sauce and "skinny" toppings such as lean ground turkey and fresh vegetables. "I use ¾ cup of cheese and about eight ounces of ground meat for a pizza that serves six," she says. "You'll never miss all of that high-fat sausage and cheese."

**Quiche.** Try making Lund's crustless Cheddar cheese–carrot quiche. She replaces whole milk with nonfat dry milk, eggs with egg substitute and whole-fat Cheddar cheese with three ounces of the reduced-fat variety.

**Sloppy joes.** Use 90 percent lean ground beef or ground turkey instead of regular ground beef, suggests Lund. To pump up the flavor of this very lean meat, "mix ½ cup of chunky salsa with a can of tomato sauce," says Lund. "I also add a tablespoon of brown sugar substitute, which gives the meat just a hint of Southwest barbecue."

## Sauces and Stuffings

***Fettuccine sauce.*** Blend nonfat cream cheese, skim milk and nonfat cottage cheese in a food processor for about four minutes, then heat, suggests Fischer. Add ¼ cup of very lean diced ham and 1 cup of peas, if desired, she says.

***Quick and healthy gravy.*** To prepare a tasty make-ahead sauce for chicken, freeze chicken stock in ice cube trays, suggests Sue Chapman, executive chef at the Skylonda Fitness Retreat in Woodside, California. "When you're ready to make the sauce, melt a few cubes, then add a bit of red wine and some fresh herbs such as rosemary," she says. "This sauce delivers the flavor of a traditional gravy without the fat."

***Stuffing.*** Here is Tribole's reduced-fat version of a holiday favorite: Preheat the oven to 350°. Sauté chopped onions, celery and mushrooms in a no-stick skillet coated with a no-stick cooking spray. Place unseasoned cornbread stuffing in a two-quart casserole, add the sautéed vegetables and some defatted chicken broth, then bake for 30 to 40 minutes.

## Miscellaneous Goodies

***French toast.*** Dunk your bread in egg substitute instead of whole eggs, suggests Fischer, and "fry" it in a no-stick skillet coated with a no-stick cooking spray rather than butter. You can enjoy French toast with a small amount of maple syrup, says Fischer; "just don't top it with a big hunk of butter," she advises.

***Potato salad.*** Replace whole hard-boiled eggs with just the egg whites and whole-fat mayonnaise with the reduced-fat or nonfat variety, suggests Fischer. "The nonfat mayonnaise products available today are wonderful," she says. To boost the flavor of this salad, "try adding chopped Spanish onions, celery, dill pickles and scallions," she says.

*See also* Chicken, Eggs, Fish, Lean Meat, Low-Fat Diet, Margarine, Mediterranean Diet, Skim Milk, Vegetables, part 4.

꙳

# DESSERTS

## *Sweet Satisfaction—Guaranteed*

If you are watching your cholesterol but can't seem to tame your sweet tooth, don't despair: You can have your cake and eat it, too, while keeping your cholesterol at a heart-healthy level. Low-fat, low-calorie dessert classics such as fresh fruit and sugar-free gelatin can go a long way toward satisfying an urge for something sweet. And if you're hit with an out-and-out craving for chocolate, you can either trim the fat from your favorite home-baked desserts or head to any supermarket: Most now carry a wide array of reduced-fat cookies, cholesterol-free baked goods and nonfat yogurt.

But beware: Some fat- and cholesterol-free sweets can be loaded with calories. Moreover, indulging in these treats can too often help pile on the pounds—definitely not a heart-smart move. So you'll need to look beyond the "no cholesterol" hype that often adorns these products' labels. On the other hand, treating yourself to an occasional hot fudge sundae most likely won't jeopardize an otherwise low-fat diet, say experts.

### Living *La Dolce Vita*

What's for dessert? Try one of these delicious suggestions.

• You can't pick a healthier dessert than fresh fruit. For an extra-special treat, create an elegant fruit salad using exotic fruits such as fresh pineapple, kiwifruit, mangoes and blueberries.

• Put a peeled banana in a plastic bag and pop it in the freezer, suggests Michael Klaper, M.D., health director of the Royal Atlantic Health Spa in Pompano Beach, Florida, and author of *Vegan Nutrition: Pure and Simple.* "When the banana is frozen, slice it and sprinkle it with chopped nuts," says Dr. Klaper. Try freezing seedless grapes, too.

• Jazz up sugar-free gelatin with sliced fresh fruit or a dollop of low-fat whipped topping. Or prepare sugar-free chocolate or vanilla pudding with 1 percent low-fat milk.

• If it's cookies you crave, try one of the many reduced-fat or nonfat varieties on the market. But beware: Low-fat cookies aren't necessarily low in calories—or fat, for that matter. Case in point: Reduced-fat Oreos get 33 percent of their calories from fat, while regular Oreos get 39 percent of their calories from fat. Beware, too, of "cholesterol-free" cookies, cakes and pastries: Many of these products are made with palm or coconut oil—both of which are full of artery-clogging saturated fat—or partially hydrogenated vegetable oil, which contains cholesterol-raising trans-fatty acids.

• Screaming for ice cream? Opt for a cup of sherbet, which contains just 4 grams of fat (compared with 24 grams of fat for premium ice cream), or nonfat sorbet. "Ice milk and low-fat or nonfat frozen yogurt are other good alternatives," recommends Lisa Lauri, R.D., nutrition consultant at North Shore University Hospital in Manhasset, New York. Many people enjoy sugar-free fudge bars and fruit pops, too.

• Angel food cake, made with cholesterol-free egg whites, is a luscious low-fat dessert. "Top your piece of cake with sliced strawberries," suggests James W. Anderson, M.D., professor of medicine and clinical nutrition at the University of Kentucky School of Medicine in Lexington and author of *Dr. Anderson's High-Fiber Fitness Plan*. Or treat yourself to a few tablespoons of whipped topping—it'll cost you just two grams of fat, says Dr. Anderson.

• To lighten up strawberry shortcake, "make the biscuits with canola oil instead of butter and use half of a biscuit per serving rather than a whole one," suggests Susan Purdy, author of *Have Your Cake and Eat It, Too: 200 Luscious, Low-Fat Cakes, Pies, Cookies, Puddings and Other Desserts You Thought You Could Never Eat Again*. Also, try replacing whipped cream with nonfat vanilla frozen yogurt.

• Yearning for a slice of pie? Whip up a treat that is equally tasty but has a fraction of the fat. "Make a low-fat piecrust out of phyllo dough," suggests Marilyn Cerino, R.D., nutrition consultant at the Benjamin Franklin Center for Health of Pennsylvania Hospital in Philadelphia. "Then fill the shell with mounds of strawberries just before you're ready to serve it. It tastes wonderful."

• Substitute low-fat cream cheese for the regular variety in your favorite cheesecake recipe, says Purdy. Or use nonfat cottage cheese: "It's a wonderful addition to cheesecake because it provides a creamy mouthfeel." Put the cottage cheese through a strainer, then puree it in a food processor or blender until it has the consistency of sour cream.

Purdy also suggests reducing the number of eggs you use. If your recipe calls for three whole eggs, "try using one whole egg plus two whites," she says.

• The next time you bake brownies, replace the standard semisweet chocolate with unsweetened cocoa and the butter with a cup of pureed prunes, suggests Purdy. "The prunes keep the brownies moist, and the overall fat content is about one-fifth of the fat in a traditional brownie recipe," she says. Also, "butter" the brownie pan with a no-stick cooking spray.

• You can slim down chocolate cake by replacing a significant portion of unsweetened or semisweet chocolate with cocoa, using fewer egg yolks and reducing the amount of fat, says Purdy. "If the recipe calls for a cup of butter or shortening, for example, use ⅔ cup," she says. To further reduce the amount of fat, substitute nonfat or low-fat yogurt for a small portion of the butter or shortening, says Purdy.

• Defat other home-baked treats. "When you bake a cake, for example, substitute two egg whites for every whole egg," suggests Lauri. "And if your recipe calls for ⅓ cup of oil, use ⅓ cup of applesauce instead." These substitutions work for boxed mixes, too, notes Lauri.

• To trim the fat from a boxed brownie mix that calls for eggs and oil, "use egg substitute instead of whole eggs and nonfat yogurt in place of the oil," says Janet Lepke, R.D., a dietitian in Santa Monica, California, and a spokesperson for the American Dietetic Association. "The brownies will be chewy and gooey—just as they should be."

## When Temptation Strikes

You may never feel cheated by opting for a spicy baked apple over apple pie or nonfat frozen yogurt over premium ice cream. On the other hand, never say never, says Cerino. "If you adore hot fudge sundaes, indulge once in a while," she says. "It's no big deal, as long as you don't have one on a regular basis."

"If you're dreaming of apple pie, have some," adds Sheah Rarback,

R.D., director of nutrition at the Mailman Center at the University of Miami School of Medicine. Eat a smaller piece of pie than you would have in the past, suggests Rarback, or spend your fat calories on the pie and curb your fat intake for the rest of the day. "But avoid feelings of deprivation," advises Rarback. "Any food can fit into a low-fat diet. What counts is how often you eat it, how much of it you eat and what else you're eating."

~ ❧ ~

# EGGS

## *You Don't Have to Give Them Up*

Can't remember the last time you ate a three-egg omelet? You're not alone. Many people have cut down on eggs—or have even given them up entirely—as part of their efforts to lower their blood cholesterol.

Unfortunately, however, you may be eating more eggs than you know. Besides the occasional omelet you savor at Sunday brunch or the odd fast-food breakfast sandwich you wolf down on the drive to work, you most likely are also consuming eggs in many packaged and cooked foods, including cakes and pastries, pasta dishes and meat loaf and bottled sauces and dressings.

But don't despair: It's entirely possible to cook delicious dishes using egg whites or commercial egg substitute (which many people say is a lot tastier than it used to be). Or you might choose to eat whole eggs in moderation. Any way you crack it, though, you can still savor the flavor of eggs and be kind to your coronary arteries.

### Attack of the Killer Cholesterol

Eggs aren't all bad. One large egg is brimming with vitamins E and B$_{12}$, folate, riboflavin, phosphorus and iron and contains less than two grams of saturated fat. Eggs pack plenty of protein, too. "Eggs are the best-quality, least expensive protein we can eat," says Wanda Howell, R.D., Ph.D., assistant professor of nutritional sciences at the University of Arizona in Tucson.

So why can't we enjoy eggs as often as we wish? Because "most of the protein in the egg is in the white; all of the cholesterol is in the yolk," explains Dean Ornish, M.D., president and director of the Preventive Medicine Research Institute in Sausalito, California, and author of *Dr. Dean Ornish's Program for Reversing Heart Disease*. The yolk of one average egg contains 213 milligrams of dietary cholesterol—more than two-thirds of the daily limit of 300 milligrams recommended by the American Heart Association (AHA).

The AHA says that healthy adults can eat up to four whole eggs per week but advises people with elevated cholesterol to limit themselves to one whole egg per week. "Because eggs—or, more specifically, egg yolks—are a concentrated source of dietary cholesterol, you shouldn't overdo them," says Chicago dietitian Alicia Moag-Stahlberg, R.D., a spokesperson for the American Dietetic Association.

Don't get hung up on eggs while disregarding the rest of your diet, though. While cutting back on dietary cholesterol can help lower your blood cholesterol, "reducing your intake of total and saturated fat will help even more," says Dr. Howell.

## Breaking Free of the Yolk

As mentioned previously, only egg yolks contain dietary cholesterol, which means you can eat as many egg whites as you wish. Doesn't sound like much of a treat, you say? Get creative! Here are some ideas to get you started.

• It's possible for you to create an appetizing breakfast without using whole eggs. "You don't have to sacrifice flavor," says Evelyn Tribole, R.D., a dietitian in Beverly Hills, California, and author of *Healthy Homestyle Cooking*. "Try making French toast with egg whites and skim milk. Or make egg-white omelets stuffed with bell peppers, mushrooms and onions. Chopped green chilies work well, too." But don't sauté all of those vegetables in butter. Use a no-stick cooking spray instead.

---

## LOVE TO BAKE? LOSE THE YOLKS!

You don't have to forgo baking—or eating—your favorite cakes, cookies and muffins because you're cutting back on eggs. Here's how to bake yolk-free treats.

**Baking with egg whites.** Not using egg yolks won't significantly affect the texture of baked goods, says Evelyn Tribole, R.D., a dietitian in Beverly Hills, California, and author of *Healthy Homestyle Cooking.* "Most likely, you won't notice the difference," says Tribole. She recommends substituting two beaten egg whites for each whole egg.

If you're baking a product that calls for three or four whole eggs, however, substituting that many egg whites may create too much liquid. In that case, you may want to use an egg substitute.

**Baking with egg substitute.** Some experts suggest replacing each whole egg with ¼ cup of egg substitute. But you can use more or less of this product to suit your taste.

---

- Make cholesterol-free *huevos rancheros*, suggests Marvin Moser, M.D., clinical professor of medicine at Yale University School of Medicine and author of *Week by Week to a Strong Heart.* Simply fold scrambled egg whites into a taco or tortilla, then top the eggs with spicy salsa.
- Add chopped egg whites from hard-boiled eggs to tuna salad. Making the salad with reduced-fat or nonfat mayonnaise will slash your intake of dietary cholesterol even more.

## Try This Tasty Impostor

Yearning for a plate of steaming scrambled eggs? You can indulge your craving with egg substitutes. These products consist primarily of egg whites, with other ingredients—including nonfat milk, food coloring, vegetable oil and vitamins—added to mimic the taste and texture of real eggs and to boost nutritional value. Most egg substitutes contain zero cholesterol and one to four grams of fat per serving.

Use an egg substitute as you would egg whites or even whole eggs. You can make a tasty omelet by adding chopped onions, mushrooms, peppers and reduced-fat or nonfat cheese to egg substitute, for example. Or you might mix this product with flavored bread crumbs to batter-coat baked chicken (without the skin).

If you have tried egg substitute in the past but didn't care for it, you might want to give it another try, says Tribole. "Some of the newer egg substitutes taste much more like real eggs," she says. And the more brands you try, the more likely it is that you'll find a brand you like.

There's one advantage to using egg substitute over egg whites, says Tribole: It's yellow, so it looks like the real thing. "If you like scrambled eggs and you're really into eye appeal, use egg substitute," she says. And with more and more restaurants offering omelets and scrambled eggs made with egg substitute, it's not difficult to follow your program away from home.

## Three Ways to Have Your Eggs and Eat Them, Too

Sometimes only real eggs will do. If you have elevated cholesterol levels, most doctors agree that it's smart to stick to the AHA's guidelines and limit yourself to one whole egg per week. So if egg whites or egg substitute just isn't for you, it's possible to occasionally eat whole eggs as part of an overall low-fat, low-cholesterol diet. Try these suggestions.

• "Buy small or medium-size eggs, which contain a little less cholesterol than larger eggs," suggests James W. Anderson, M.D., professor of medicine and clinical nutrition at the University of Kentucky College of Medicine in Lexington and author of *Dr. Anderson's High-Fiber Fitness Plan.*

• Don't scramble or fry eggs in bacon grease or butter—both are full of saturated fat. Instead, prepare eggs in a no-stick skillet coated with a no-stick cooking spray. Or try eating eggs hard-boiled or poached, suggests Dr. Howell.

• As mentioned, one egg uses up most of the AHA's recommended daily intake of dietary cholesterol. "So if you eat an egg on Sunday, make Monday an egg-free or low-cholesterol day," says Sheah Rarback, R.D., director of nutrition at the University of Miami School of Medicine's Mailman Center. "Concern yourself not with every meal, or even with every mouthful, but with your diet as a whole."

∿❧∾

# EXERCISE

## *Work Your Body, Boost Good Cholesterol*

You've just dragged yourself home from a frantic day at work, and the idea of climbing aboard your stationary bike or popping *Buns of Steel* into the VCR is just too exhausting to contemplate. Frankly, all you want to work is your remote.

If you'd rather channel-surf than feel the burn, you're not alone. Only about one in ten of us is physically active for a half-hour or more a day. That's unfortunate, because exercise is one of the most powerful weapons we have to keep our hearts healthy and our cholesterol under control.

The good news is, getting into the exercise habit can be easier than you think, even if you haven't worked up a sweat in years. What's more, say many experts, a half-hour of exercise a day is all that it takes to improve your cholesterol profile and lower your risk of developing heart disease, high blood pressure and diabetes.

Want to exchange a half-hour a day for a lifetime of good health? You can. Read on to find out how.

### The Dream Team

According to scientific evidence, exercise helps boost levels of "good" HDL cholesterol, which helps whisk "bad" LDL cholesterol out of the body. "It is thought that exercise's ability to reduce the risk of heart disease comes mostly from its ability to increase HDL cholesterol," says James Rippe, M.D., director of the Center for Clinical and Lifestyle Research at Tufts University School of Medicine in Boston and co-author of *Dr. James Rippe's Complete Book of Fitness Walking.*

A high HDL level is associated with a decreased risk of heart disease. For every one-point increase in HDL, risk of heart disease sinks by 2 percent for men and 3 percent for women. So if you're a woman who raises your HDL reading from 45 to 55 milligrams/deciliter, you'll slash your risk of heart disease by about 30 percent!

Exercise appears to trigger a chain of physiological events that increase the efficiency of an enzyme called lipoprotein lipase, says Michael Miller, M.D., director of preventive cardiology at the University of Maryland School of Medicine in Baltimore. This enzyme attacks triglycerides, another type of blood fat implicated in heart disease. "As lipoprotein lipase breaks down triglyceride-rich particles, it also produces substances that help make HDL," says Dr. Miller. So people who exercise tend to make more HDL and have lower triglyceride levels, he says.

Researchers at the University of Hawaii at Manoa in Honolulu studied the effect of exercise on HDL levels in ten separate studies involving about 700 people. The researchers found that for each 6.2 miles per week that a person jogged, HDL climbed three milligrams/deciliter in both men and women.

Regular exercise can also help you lose weight, which can further improve your cholesterol profile, says William P. Castelli, M.D., medical director of the Framingham Cardiovascular Institute, a wellness program at Metro West Medical Center in Framingham, Massachusetts. One well-known study has determined that for every eight pounds a person sheds, HDL rises about three points. And for every eight pounds gained, HDL declines about two points.

## Walk, Cycle, Golf . . . Or Just Scrub the Tub

Think you have to become a marathon runner to raise your HDL and slash your risk of heart disease? Think again. Thirty minutes of moderate-intensity exercise a day can do it, say experts convened by the Centers for Disease Control and Prevention in Atlanta and the American College of Sports Medicine. According to these experts, "The scientific evidence clearly demonstrates that regular, moderate-intensity physical activity provides substantial health benefits."

These experts define moderate exercise as the equivalent of walking two miles at a brisk pace. Other moderate-intensity exercises include cycling for pleasure, playing golf (pulling the cart or carrying clubs), cleaning the house and mowing the lawn with a power mower.

Even better, you can accumulate this 30-minute minimum in short bursts of activity rather than all at once, say experts. So walking instead of driving short distances, or pedaling a stationary bicycle while you watch your favorite sitcom, can confer substantial health benefits. Best of all, the couch potatoes among us stand to gain the most from increasing their physical activity.

Consult your doctor before you start any exercise program, particularly if you are a woman over age 50 or a man over age 40, are overweight, have diabetes or heart disease or have ever fainted or experienced chest pains while exercising. And remember to start slowly and to listen to your body. "Intense physical activity in people not used to it is very dangerous," says Dr. Castelli.

## The One-Two Punch That Can KO Cholesterol

While exercise has been proven to lower the risk of coronary heart disease, exercise combined with a low-fat diet can pack an even stronger punch.

Researchers in Germany had one group of men with chest pain exercise at home for a half-hour a day as well as participate in two one-hour group exercise sessions per week. The men also followed a low-fat, low-cholesterol diet. Another group of men were encouraged—but not required—to exercise regularly and consume a low-fat diet.

After a year, the LDL cholesterol of the men who both dieted and exercised dropped an average of 8 percent, and their HDL climbed 3 percent. What's more, only 23 percent of the men experienced progression in the blockages of their coronary arteries. And in another 32 percent, the disease process actually regressed. By contrast, the LDL and HDL cholesterol of the men in the control group didn't change, and 48 percent experienced progression of these arterial blockages.

Researchers at Stanford University School of Medicine, led by Peter Wood, D.Sc., Ph.D., professor emeritus of medicine, had one group of moderately overweight people follow a low-fat, low-cholesterol diet. A second group followed the same diet but also exercised three times a week. After a year, the exercisers raised their HDL levels by an average of 13 percent. By contrast, the diet-only group raised their HDL 2 percent.

---

## HOW TO FIND YOUR TARGET HEART RATE

While you work out, periodically check your pulse to make sure you're in your target heart range, suggests James Rippe, M.D., director of the Center for Clinical and Lifestyle Research at Tufts University School of Medicine in Boston and co-author of *Dr. James Rippe's Complete Book of Fitness Walking.*

To get the low number for your range, subtract your age from 220, then multiply that figure by 0.6. To get the high number for your range, subtract your age from 220, then multiply by 0.85.

If you're 52 years old, for example, you'd subtract 52 from 220, which equals 168. Multiply 168 by 0.6, which equals 100.8 (low number for your range). Multiply 168 by 0.85, which equals 142.8 (high number for your range). So your heart rate should remain between 101 and 142 as you exercise.

Some experts suggest that there's a simpler way to gauge whether you're overextending yourself. "If you can't carry on a conversation during exercise, you're overdoing it," says John McDougall, M.D., creator and head of the McDougall Program at St. Helena Hospital in Santa Rosa, California, and author of *McDougall's Heart Medicine.*

---

## Nine Heart-Healthy Fitness Tips

No doubt about it: Starting an exercise program can be tough. But it's equally difficult to deny the proven benefits of regular exercise, from a healthier heart to a better shape. So drop the excuses, don your sweats and get moving! These tips can help make it easier.

• Put your goals in writing. You're more likely to stick to an exercise program if you know what you want to accomplish and write it down, says exercise physiologist Peter Snell, Ph.D., assistant professor of internal medicine at the University of Texas Southwestern Medical Center at Dallas. "Start keeping a workout log," he suggests. "The log will be a record of what you've accomplished and will help keep you on track."

• Find a workout you enjoy. From fencing to in-line skating to yoga, there's a wealth of fitness options that you may not have considered. So explore the alternatives. "When you're having fun being

---

## CAN PUMPING IRON HELP PUMP UP HDL?

Most health professionals recommend aerobic exercise to help raise "good" HDL cholesterol and protect against heart disease. But there's some preliminary evidence that a nonaerobic activity—weight training—may help lower cholesterol as well.

Researchers at the Department of Veteran Affairs Medical Center and the University of Arizona, both in Tucson, enrolled 46 women in a weight-training program. These women pumped iron for an hour three times a week. Another group of women acted as a control group, sticking to their normal exercise habits.

After five months, the women involved in weight training saw their total cholesterol drop from 184 to 171 milligrams/deciliter. More significantly, however, their "bad" LDL cholesterol plummeted 12 percent, from 116 to 102 milligrams/deciliter, without significantly affecting their HDL levels.

---

physically active, you're much more likely to keep going, week after week, month after month," says Darlene A. Sedlock, Ph.D., associate professor of kinesiology at Purdue University in West Lafayette, Indiana.

• Go at your own pace. "Don't adhere to the adage 'No pain, no gain,'" says Dr. Sedlock. "Do what you're capable of doing. You'll find that exercise becomes easier and easier."

• Schedule a "happy hour" for exercise. "If you commit to working out at a particular time and place, you'll have a greater chance of meeting your goals," says Dr. Rippe. Try taking an aerobics class that meets during your lunch hour, for example. Or enjoy a brisk walk after dinner.

• Work out with a friend who's at a similar fitness level, suggests Dr. Snell.

• Vary your activities—walking on Monday, cycling on Wednesday, a round of golf on Sunday and so forth. If you walk regularly, "give yourself a change of scenery by varying your walking route," advises Dr. Rippe. Should you grow weary of your regular Tuesday-night step class, drop in on that Friday-night funk aerobics class you've been meaning to try.

- Adapt to the weather. "In cold weather, dress in layers that you can remove as your body heats up," says Dr. Rippe. In warm weather, he says, wear loose clothing and drink lots of water before and during your workout. In stormy weather, try walking on an indoor track at the health club or at the mall.
- Add more activity to your day. At work, you might forgo your midmorning coffee break and go on a short walk instead. Or resolve to take the stairs instead of the elevator at least once a day.
- Reward yourself for meeting your exercise goals. Buy a new shade of lipstick or a new tie. Splurge on some new workout gear. "Even a hot bath can be a reward," says Dr. Rippe.

*See also* Golf, Walking

∽✿∾

# FIBER

## *Give Your Arteries the All Clear*

Say "fiber," and many of us think "laxative"—not exactly anyone's favorite noun. But fiber's power to unclog your backed-up plumbing is only part of the story. Numerous studies suggest that fiber can help unplug your arteries, too, by scuttling elevated cholesterol.

Fiber, the part of plant foods that the body can't digest, passes through your system pretty much intact. There are two basic types of fiber: soluble and insoluble. Soluble fibers such as pectin, psyllium and guar gum, found in foods such as oat bran, barley, dried beans, peas and apples, seem to help control the way your body produces and eliminates cholesterol. "Soluble fiber helps lower serum cholesterol," says Alicia Moag-Stahlberg, R.D., a dietitian in Chicago and a spokesperson for the American Dietetic Association. Insoluble fiber, abundant in whole-grain products, fruits, vegetables and cereals, is the stuff that helps keep you regular, speeding food through the system and bulking up your stool.

While soluble fiber is the cholesterol buster, filling up on grains, beans, fruits and veggies can benefit more than your blood fats. Scientists believe that eating a fiber-rich diet may help reduce the risk of developing colon cancer, diabetes and other ailments as well as heart disease. All in all, good reasons to munch something that crunches—and that doesn't mean chips.

## The Incredible Bulk

Scientists have conducted numerous studies of fiber's power to stomp cholesterol. In one study, James W. Anderson, M.D., professor of medicine and clinical nutrition at the University of Kentucky College of Medicine in Lexington and author of *Dr. Anderson's High-Fiber Fitness Plan,* and his colleagues divided 146 people with moderately elevated cholesterol into three groups. The first group ate their usual diets. The second group followed a low-fat diet that contained 15 grams (about a half-ounce) of fiber. The third group consumed a low-fat diet packed with 25 grams of fiber.

After a year, the low-fat, high-fiber group's total cholesterol had fallen 13 percent, compared with a 9 percent drop in cholesterol for the low-fat group and a 7 percent decrease in the folks who ate their usual diets. Researchers noted that the fiber boost came from common foods easily added to an ordinary diet—one bowl of cooked oat bran cereal, two small bowls of cooked oatmeal or about five ounces of canned beans a day.

Researchers at Stanford University School of Medicine had 16 people consume 15 grams of soluble fiber (including pectin and psyllium) a day. These folks' total cholesterol fell 8.3 percent, and their "bad" LDL cholesterol dropped 12.4 percent, in just one month. Another Stanford study found that cholesterol declined as soluble fiber consumption increased. Individuals who consumed 5 grams of soluble fiber per day for a month lowered their LDL cholesterol 5.6 percent, while those who consumed 15 grams of soluble fiber saw their LDL cholesterol plunge 14.9 percent.

There's also evidence that adding soluble fiber to a diet already low in fat can further slam cholesterol. Researchers from the United

# SOURCES OF SOLUBLE FIBER

Want to clamp down on high cholesterol? Chomp into these foods—they're high in soluble fiber, the kind that helps lower blood cholesterol.

| FOOD | TOTAL FIBER (G.) | SOLUBLE FIBER (G.) |
| --- | --- | --- |
| All-Bran cereal (⅓ cup) | 8.6 | 1.4 |
| Apple, with skin (1 small) | 2.8 | 1 |
| Barley, raw (2 Tbsp.) | 3 | 0.9 |
| Blackberries (¾ cup) | 3.7 | 1.1 |
| Blueberries (¾ cup) | 1.4 | 0.3 |
| Brussels sprouts (1 cup) | 5 | 2.6 |
| Carrot, raw (1) | 2.3 | 1.1 |
| Chick-peas (½ cup) | 4.3 | 1.3 |
| Corn bran, raw (2 Tbsp.) | 7.7 | 0.1 |
| Figs, dried (3) | 4.6 | 2.2 |
| Grapefruit, pink (1) | 1.4 | 0.3 |
| Honeydew, cubed (1 cup) | 0.9 | 0.3 |
| Kidney beans, cooked (½ cup) | 6.9 | 2.8 |
| Lentils, boiled (½ cup) | 5.2 | 0.6 |
| Lima beans, canned (½ cup) | 4.3 | 1.1 |
| Oat bran, dry (⅓ cup) | 4 | 2 |
| Okra (1 cup) | 7.3 | 2.9 |
| Orange (1 small) | 2.9 | 1.8 |
| Pear (1 small) | 2.9 | 1.1 |
| Peas, frozen, cooked (½ cup) | 4.3 | 1.3 |
| Pinto beans, cooked (½ cup) | 5.9 | 1.9 |
| Plums, red, with skin (2 medium) | 2.4 | 1.1 |
| Potato, baked (1) | 5 | 1.2 |
| Pumpernickel bread (1 slice) | 2.7 | 1.2 |
| Raisins, seedless (½ cup) | 1.6 | 0.8 |
| Spaghetti, whole-wheat, cooked (1 cup) | 5.4 | 1.2 |
| Spinach, boiled (½ cup) | 1.6 | 0.5 |
| Sweet potato, baked (1) | 2.7 | 1.2 |
| Turnips, cooked (½ cup) | 4.8 | 1.7 |
| Wheat germ, toasted (¼ cup) | 5.2 | 0.8 |
| White/navy beans, cooked (½ cup) | 6.5 | 2.2 |

States, Canada and Switzerland had 43 people with high cholesterol follow either a low-fat, high-soluble-fiber diet or a low-fat, high-insoluble-fiber diet for four months. Then the group that followed the soluble-fiber plan consumed the diet high in insoluble fiber, and vice versa, for another four months. These folks' total and LDL cholesterol were 5 percent lower when they consumed the diet rich in soluble fiber than when they followed the high-insoluble-fiber plan, researchers found.

## If It Crunches, Eat It

Many of us consume less fiber than we should, notes Moag-Stahlberg. "Americans consume about 12 grams of fiber (less than a half-ounce) a day," she says. "We should be eating about 25 to 30 grams (about an ounce) per day." Fortunately, it's easy to fiber up your diet. The following tips can help.

• Be sure to eat the skins of fruits and vegetables (such as apples and potatoes) as well as fruits with edible seeds, such as figs and blueberries.

• Try to get your fiber from foods rather than fiber supplements, recommends Moag-Stahlberg. These products lack other nutrients found in fiber-rich foods, she says. "Fruits and vegetables contain antioxidant vitamins, for example, which may help prevent heart disease and cancer," she says.

• Don't consume a day's worth of fiber in one sitting, advises Susan Kleiner, R.D., Ph.D., a nutritionist in Seattle and author of *The High-Performance Cookbook.* "Eat high-fiber foods throughout the day," she advises. "Don't depend on a high-fiber cereal whose manufacturer claims that 'you can get all of your fiber in one bowl.'"

• Drink eight to ten glasses of water a day, advises William P. Castelli, M.D., medical director of the Framingham Cardiovascular Institute, a wellness program at Metro West Medical Center in Framingham, Massachusetts. Fiber absorbs fluid as it passes through the body; not drinking enough water can lead to constipation.

• To minimize gas and bloating—common side effects of consuming more fiber—add fiber-rich foods to your diet slowly, says Dr. Anderson.

• Don't gobble fiber to compensate for eating high-fat foods, says Dr. Castelli. As Dean Ornish, M.D., president and director of the Preventive Medicine Research Institute in Sausalito, California, says in *Dr. Dean Ornish's Program for Reversing Heart Disease*, "A bowl of (oatmeal) is an ideal breakfast, but it won't undo the effects of a ham and cheese omelet on the side."

*See also* Barley, Beans, Fruit, Grapefruit, High-Fiber Cereals, Oats, Vegetables, Vegetarian Diet

‿❊﹏

# FISH

## *The Brain Food That's Good for Your Heart*

If you sometimes feel like you're swimming upstream in the fight to lower your blood cholesterol, fish can help you turn the tide. Not only is fish low in saturated fat, but it also contains oils called omega-3 fatty acids, highly polyunsaturated fats that can work small miracles in your body. In most studies, the anchorlike omega-3's have dragged down high cholesterol concentrations to healthier levels.

"Omega-3's appear to decrease blood levels of VLDL (very low density lipoprotein), which is manufactured by the liver," says Peter O. Kwiterovich, Jr., M.D., professor of medicine and director of the Lipid Research and Atherosclerosis Unit at Johns Hopkins University School of Medicine in Baltimore and author of *The Johns Hopkins Complete Guide for Preventing and Reversing Heart Disease*. As VLDL measurements plummet, so may blood cholesterol levels and triglycerides, another blood fat implicated in heart disease. The two most common omega-3 fatty acids are eicosapentaenoic acid and docosahexaenoic acid.

Omega-3 fatty acids also appear to help lower blood pressure, a significant risk factor for heart attack and stroke. Moreover, omega-

3's help keep blood platelets from clinging to one another, which can defend against blood clots that may trigger a heart attack or stroke.

Generally speaking, the fattier the fish, the more omega-3 fatty acids it contains, says Margo Denke, M.D., associate professor of medicine in the Center for Human Nutrition at the University of Texas Southwestern Medical Center at Dallas. Interestingly, fish don't manufacture omega-3's. They derive these fats from ocean foods such as saltwater algae and other cold-water vegetation. "So cold-water trout, salmon and mackerel are good sources of omega-3's, while farm-raised catfish isn't," says Dr. Denke. Other fish rich in omega-3 fatty acids include herring and bluefin tuna.

---

## BEST CHOICES FOR OMEGA-3'S

Here's the omega-3 fatty acid content of common varieties of fish. The higher the better, when you're trolling for unwanted cholesterol.

### HIGH LEVELS OF OMEGA-3'S

| | |
|---|---|
| Albacore tuna | Lake trout |
| Atlantic herring | Pacific herring |
| Atlantic mackerel | Pacific mackerel |
| Atlantic salmon | Pink salmon |
| Bluefin tuna | Rainbow trout |

### MEDIUM LEVELS OF OMEGA-3'S

| | |
|---|---|
| Bluefish | Striped bass |
| Channel catfish | Swordfish |
| Halibut | Turbot |
| Red snapper | Yellowfin tuna |

### LOW LEVELS OF OMEGA-3'S

| | |
|---|---|
| Atlantic cod | Rockfish |
| Brook trout | Sole |
| Carp | Sturgeon |
| Flounder | Yellow perch |
| Haddock | Yellowtail |
| Pacific cod | |

But fish has even more going for it than the cholesterol-clobbering omega-3's. Depending on the way it's prepared, fish is also lower in dietary fat than red meat or even poultry. Three ounces of broiled or baked cod, for example, contains 89 calories, 47 grams of cholesterol and less than 1 gram of fat.

## Why This School of Fish Gets High Marks

Some of the earliest research into the heart-healthy benefits of fish dates back to studies of the Greenland Eskimos. Researchers found that despite the Eskimos' high-fat diet, they had a low incidence of heart disease, which was linked to their heavy consumption of fish.

Subsequent studies have borne out the connection between omega-3's and heart health. Researchers in Denmark gave 11 men with high levels of blood cholesterol and triglycerides daily supplements of omega-3's in one of three different doses (two, four or nine grams). No matter what the dose, the men's total cholesterol, triglycerides and ratio of total cholesterol to "good" HDL cholesterol declined. Also, the higher the dose of omega-3's, the lower the numbers dropped: Total cholesterol fell 11 percent in the men taking the two-gram dose of omega-3's but dove 22 percent in those taking the nine-gram dose. The men's levels of HDL increased as well, with larger improvements as doses rose.

At the Oregon Health Sciences University in Portland, six healthy men alternated between one of two diets that contained varying amounts of total and saturated fat. The men consumed each diet for three weeks, both with and without omega-3 fatty acids.

Researchers found that adding omega-3's to the men's diets significantly reduced their total cholesterol, regardless of how much saturated fat they consumed. Their triglycerides declined even more dramatically—by 41 percent if they were on a high-fat diet with fish oils and 31 percent if they were following a low-fat diet with fish oils.

In South Africa, researchers alternated 28 men and women between a red-meat diet and a fish-only diet that included sardines and salmon. After six weeks on the fish diet, these individuals' total cholesterol declined significantly. What's more, their "bad" LDL cholesterol was 9 percent lower on the fish diet than on the red-meat regimen.

# Falling for Fish—Hook, Line and Sinker

To reap the maximum benefits from omega-3's, most doctors suggest that we eat fish two or three times a week. But they're less certain of how much fish we should eat. "There's no clear evidence that we need a specific amount of fish oil in our diets," says Dr. Denke. "Fish is a good alternative to chicken and red meat." (But it's best to follow an overall cholesterol-lowering diet that includes plenty of fresh fruits and vegetables, grains and low-fat dairy products as well as fish, meat and poultry.)

The following tips can help you choose and prepare fish that pleases both your taste buds and your ticker.

• Stock up on canned tuna or salmon—it's an easy, inexpensive way to consume omega-3's. To save on calories, buy fish that's packed in water rather than oil.

• If you're buying whole fresh fish, look for clean, tight scales, bright, clear eyes (rather than cloudy or sunken) and red or pink gills. The flesh should also spring back into place when touched.

Further, "fish should have a clean smell, not a strong odor, and the surface of the fish should be moist but not slimy," says A. Garth Rand, Ph.D., professor of food science at the University of Rhode Island in Kingston. Or opt for cleaned, gutted fish—it is more convenient and keeps longer, he adds.

• Unlike red meat, fish has little in the way of visible fat, so in that respect, it doesn't need trimming. But if you're preparing a fatty fish such as mackerel, tuna or swordfish, cut away the darker flesh, says Dr. Rand; it's usually higher in fat.

• The healthiest ways to prepare fish include broiling, baking, grilling and steaming. Don't overcook fish, however. "If the fish's moisture runs out during lengthy cooking, so will some of its nutrients," says Dr. Rand.

You might also stir-fry fish with vegetables, herbs, spices and a small amount of low-sodium soy sauce. "Some kinds of fish make for better stir-fries than others," says Evelyn Tribole, R.D., a dietitian in Beverly Hills, California, and author of *Healthy Homestyle Cooking*. "Stir-fried shrimp, lobster and scallops are wonderful choices."

• If you love fried fish, try this healthy alternative from the American Heart Association: Dip fish fillets in flour and sauté them in a small amount of a polyunsaturated oil. Then place the fish on a heated platter, add some crushed raw garlic and lemon juice to the oil and drizzle the seasoned oil over the fish before serving.

Or "oven-fry" fish, suggests Tribole. "Coat the fish in egg whites—no yolks—and bread crumbs, then bake until crispy," she says. "Squeeze some lemon or orange juice over the fish and sprinkle on some dill."

You might also top the fish with fresh or dried parsley, basil, tarragon or thyme, says Tribole.

• Skewer chunks of fish, onions, tomatoes and peppers and grill fish kabobs. "Preparing kabobs is easy, and most people enjoy them," says Tribole.

• For a quick and healthy meal, microwave fish fillets in a microwave-safe dish along with onions, mushrooms and peppers, suggests James W. Anderson, M.D., professor of medicine and clinical nutrition at the University of Kentucky College of Medicine in Lexington and author of *Dr. Anderson's High-Fiber Fitness Plan.* Or create a quick and tasty entrée by combining fish with your favorite vegetables and grains, says Dr. Anderson.

• If you're dining out, order a seafood appetizer. It will stoke you with omega-3's while it dampens your craving for higher-fat courses. Try boiled shrimp spritzed with lemon juice, smoked salmon served with a platter of raw vegetables or pickled herring. (For more tips on how to order a heart-smart seafood dinner, see "Best Bets on Seafood Menus" on page 92.)

## Fish Oil Capsules: A Worthy Alternative?

Can you attack high cholesterol by simply swallowing fish oil supplements?

Maybe, maybe not. A few studies suggest that fish oil supplements, which contain omega-3's extracted from fatty fish, may have some health benefits. One study that examined data on 2,030 men under age 70 who had had heart attacks found that whether the men ate fatty fish (salmon, trout, mackerel or sardines) at least twice a week or took three 500-milligram fish oil capsules a day, their chances of dying during the two-year study period fell 29 percent.

But some doctors say that more studies are needed to prove a rela-

## BEST BETS ON SEAFOOD MENUS

Craving steamed lobster, broiled scallops or grilled scrod? Go ahead, indulge: According to a national survey, most seafood dishes at mid-priced seafood restaurants are low in fat. It's simply a matter of angling for the right entrées.

The Center for Science in the Public Interest bought take-out portions of a variety of appetizers, side dishes and entrées from 32 seafood restaurants across the country. The center then made a "composite" of each dish (equal portions of nine restaurants' fried fish, for example) and sent it to independent laboratories for nutritional analysis. Among the study's best-bet dishes:

- Clam chowder (1½ cups, 7 grams of fat)
- Broiled or grilled scallops (six ounces, 3 grams of fat)
- Broiled low-fat fish such as haddock, cod, scrod, sole and flounder (six ounces, 5 grams of fat)
- Blackened catfish (six ounces, 15 grams of fat)

The worst fish dishes: fried anything. That includes fish sandwiches at fast-food restaurants, say experts. "Some people believe that if they order fish sandwiches, they're taking good care of themselves," says Wahida Karmally, R.D., director of nutrition at the Irving Center for Clinical Research at Columbia-Presbyterian Medical Center in New York City and a member of the American Heart Association's nutrition committee. "But eating a fish sandwich may be even worse than eating a plain burger because of all of the fat in the batter."

tionship between fish oil and lower rates of cardiovascular disease. "There may be instances in which people with very high triglyceride levels can benefit from fish oil capsules," says Wahida Karmally, R.D., director of nutrition at the Irving Center for Clinical Research at Columbia-Presbyterian Medical Center in New York City and a member of the American Heart Association's nutrition committee. "But these capsules have not been shown to lower LDL cholesterol."

Moreover, researchers at Tufts University in Medford, Massachusetts, analyzed popular brands of fish oil supplements and found that they didn't contain sufficient amounts of vitamin E, which is added to help keep the omega-3's in the capsules from breaking down.

So what's the bottom line? "The best way to consume any nutrient is to consume it in food," says Susan Kleiner, R.D., Ph.D., a nutritionist in Seattle and author of *The High-Performance Cookbook.* "Our bodies absorb nutrients most efficiently through food."

If you do choose to take omega-3 supplements, however, consult your doctor first, says Dr. Kleiner. Some research shows that large doses of fish oil may thin the blood and may raise the risk of excessive bleeding or stroke. For these reasons, the American Heart Association advises people to take fish oil supplements only under a doctor's supervision.

~❊~

# FLAXSEED

## *Small but Mighty*

You never know where the next cholesterol fighter is going to come from. Case in point: flaxseed. The fiber and fatty acid in this underutilized grain team up to wield awesome cholesterol-controlling powers.

Flaxseed is brimming with soluble fiber, a substance also found in fresh fruits and vegetables that is known to wallop "bad" LDL cholesterol. What's more, this seed is packed with linolenic acid, a polyunsaturated fat also found in canola oil that's similar to the cholesterol-lowering omega-3 fatty acids in fish. Together, the fiber–linolenic acid offensive may clip double-digit points off your LDL cholesterol.

Much of the credit for discovering flaxseed's ability to lower blood cholesterol belongs to Tom Watkins, Ph.D., laboratory director of the Kenneth L. Jordan Heart Foundation and Research Center in Montclair, New Jersey. Dr. Watkins and his research team have gathered data on flax for years, and his facility has baked enough flaxseed bread to clean out the coronary arteries of a small army.

Dr. Watkins believed that flaxseed's high concentration of linolenic acid might help lower blood cholesterol. To test his theory, he began to bake flaxseed bread, first at home and then in his lab. "The easiest way to consume flaxseed is to bake it into bread," says Dr. Watkins, who experimented with different recipes and formulas. "I ate the bread myself for more than a year, and some of the people in our clinic tried it, too."

In Dr. Watkins's first study, 15 men and women with blood cholesterol above 240 milligrams/deciliter ate three slices of bread made with flaxseed (10 percent of each loaf by weight) per day. These individuals also consumed an additional 15 grams of ground flaxseed a day. After three months, these folks' total cholesterol took a tumble from an average of 266 to 248 milligrams/deciliter. And their LDL cholesterol fell from an average of 190 to 171 milligrams/deciliter, a 10 percent decline.

In a second study conducted by Dr. Watkins, 13 people with moderately elevated blood cholesterol ate six slices of either wheat bread or flaxseed bread per day. In this study, flaxseed made up 30 percent of the weight of each loaf. After six weeks of eating the flaxseed bread, the average total cholesterol fell about 10 percent, from 223 to 201 milligrams/deciliter. What's more, LDL cholesterol fell 18 percent, from 162 to 133 milligrams/deciliter—which translates into a probable reduction in heart attack risk of 30 to 40 percent. By contrast, when eating the wheat bread, the participants' total and LDL cholesterol decreased about 6 percent.

Researchers in Canada have studied the effects of flaxseed on blood cholesterol, too. In one experiment at the University of Toronto and St. Michael's Hospital, also in Toronto, nine healthy young women consumed flaxseed flour either in breakfast cereal, soup, juice or yogurt or in bread or muffins. After one month, the flaxseed had reduced the women's total cholesterol by 9 percent and their LDL cholesterol by 18 percent—without lowering their "good" HDL cholesterol.

## Bake a Heart-Healthy Loaf

Want to consume flaxseed as part of a low-fat, low-cholesterol diet? Bake a loaf of flaxseed bread, using the recipe below.

You can buy flaxseed in many health food stores that sell grains.

Grind the seeds to the consistency of cornmeal using a blender or coffee mill. As a general rule, ⅔ cup of flaxseed yields 1 cup of meal.

Flaxseed bread has a mild, nutlike taste, says Dr. Watkins. While it might go without saying, don't slather flaxseed bread with butter: It's too high in saturated fat. "Some people spread the bread with a little jelly or simply toast the bread and eat it plain," says Dr. Watkins.

Adding flaxseed to your diet may make you feel bloated and gassy, especially at first. To minimize these side effects, eat one slice of flaxseed bread a day and build up to three to six slices a day.

---

## FLAXSEED BREAD

1½  teaspoons active dry yeast
2  tablespoons + 1¼ cups warm water
3  tablespoons honey
1  tablespoon canola oil
½  teaspoon salt
1  cup flaxseed meal
1¼  cups whole-wheat flour
1¾  cups bread flour

In a large bowl, dissolve the yeast in 2 tablespoons of the water. Set aside for about 5 minutes, or until bubbly.

Mix in the honey, oil, salt and remaining 1¼ cups water. Add the flaxseed meal, whole-wheat flour and 1 cup of the bread flour. Mix well.

Stir in enough of the remaining ¾ cup bread flour to make a soft, kneadable dough. Turn out the dough onto a lightly floured surface. Knead for 10 minutes, or until smooth and elastic.

Coat a 9″× 5″loaf pan with a no-stick cooking spray. Shape the dough into a loaf and place in the pan. Cover; let rise in a warm place until doubled in bulk, about 1 hour.

Bake at 350° for 40 to 45 minutes, or until the loaf is browned on top and sounds hollow when tapped. Cool.

*MAKES 1 LOAF; 12 SLICES.*

---

PER SLICE: 179 CALORIES, 4.2 G. TOTAL FAT, 0.4 G. SATURATED FAT, 0 MG. CHOLESTEROL, 3.0 G. DIETARY FIBER, 95 MG. SODIUM.

⁂

# FRUIT

## *Bananas, Berries and Other Fiber-Full Favorites*

When you top your breakfast cereal with strawberries or plunge your fork into a slice of watermelon, it's good news for your taste buds—and your cholesterol level. With few exceptions, fruit is virtually nonfat, so it can help keep your arteries clean as a whistle. Further, fruit is packed with fiber—both the insoluble kind, which helps keep you regular and is associated with a reduced risk of colon cancer, and the soluble kind, proven to whittle down elevated cholesterol levels.

"Grapefruit, apples and strawberries are just some of the good sources of soluble fiber," says Wahida Karmally, R.D., director of nutrition at the Irving Center for Clinical Research at Columbia-Presbyterian Medical Center in New York City and a member of the American Heart Association's nutrition committee. So are pears, prunes and bananas. Most fruits contain a soluble fiber called pectin, a gummy substance that acts as a natural cholesterol cutter.

### Prune Your Blood Fats

There's considerable evidence that the soluble fiber in fruits and vegetables helps suck up artery-clogging cholesterol and escort it out of the body.

Researchers at the University of Minnesota in Minneapolis and the University of California, Davis, had 41 men with mildly to moderately high cholesterol add 12 prunes a day to their regular diets. After a month, the men's total cholesterol dropped significantly, from about 230 to 225 milligrams/deciliter, and their "bad" LDL cholesterol fell from 158 to 151 milligrams/deciliter.

In a study conducted in India, researchers had 61 men with high blood pressure—a significant risk factor for heart disease—add between one and two pounds of guava, a tropical fruit, to their regular daily diets. Another group of 59 men consumed their normal diets minus the guava. After 12 weeks, the guava-eaters' total cholesterol had plunged nearly 10 percent, their blood pressure and triglyceride levels had dipped, and their "good" HDL cholesterol had increased 8 percent.

Apparently, the guava-eaters consumed less dietary fat and more potassium—which may help lower blood pressure and protect against stroke—than the guava-free group. But there's nothing special about guava, say experts. The main point is that eating fruit—nearly any kind of fruit—instead of dietary fat can have dramatic results on cholesterol levels.

This conclusion seems to be borne out by another study, also conducted in India. In this study, 621 people at risk for coronary heart disease followed a low-fat, low-cholesterol diet for a month. Next, 310 of those individuals were told to increase their intakes of fruits and vegetables to 400 grams (about 14 ounces) or more a day. The folks who maxed out on fruits and veggies saw their cholesterol drop by 6.5 percent, their LDL cholesterol plunge by 7.3 percent and their HDL cholesterol rise by 5.6 percent. Those who didn't eat the extra fruits and vegetables saw no significant improvements.

There's yet another heart-healthy reason to fill up on fruit. Many varieties of fruit—particularly berries, cantaloupe and citrus—are brimming with vitamin C, an antioxidant nutrient that some studies have linked to lower rates of heart disease. Researchers at the University of California, Los Angeles, studied more than 11,000 adults for ten years and found that individuals who consumed the most vitamin C had a lower risk of dying of heart disease and a lower death rate overall than individuals with the lowest intakes of vitamin C.

## Seven Scrumptious Ways to Feast on Fruit

Sure, you can munch more apples. But there are other ways to meet your fruit quota, too. Try these juicy suggestions.

• Sample the more exotic fruits that you see at the corner fruit stand or in the produce section of your supermarket. Discovering the delights of kiwifruit, passion fruit, mangoes, papayas and fresh pineapple can make eating more fruit an adventure rather than a chore.

• If you're more the classic type, treat yourself to a classic dish: fruit salad. "Slice up some melon, apples, bananas and peaches, and top the fruits with a bit of shredded coconut," suggests Michael Klaper, M.D., health director of the Royal Atlantic Health Spa in Pompano Beach, Florida, and author of *Vegan Nutrition: Pure and Simple*. (Don't overdo the coconut, though—it's very high in saturated fat.) Splash fruit juice over the salad to further boost the flavor, says Dr. Klaper.

• Stir sliced fresh strawberries or bananas into a cup of low-fat or nonfat vanilla yogurt.

• Top pancakes or waffles (prepared with a low-fat mix) with fresh fruit, suggests James W. Anderson, M.D., professor of medicine and clinical nutrition at the University of Kentucky College of Medicine in Lexington and author of *Dr. Anderson's High-Fiber Fitness Plan*. Try bananas, strawberries, fresh or frozen peaches, blueberries or even apples sautéed with a pinch of cinnamon and nutmeg. "You can add fruit to pancake and muffin recipes, too," says Dr. Anderson.

• Make a fruit salsa to accompany grilled chicken, fish or turkey. Here's a simple recipe: Peel and dice half of a ripe pineapple, three

## AN APPLE A DAY—AND THEN SOME

The government recommends that we eat five servings of fruits and vegetables a day. While that may sound like a lot, it's really not that hard to do, notes Bettye Nowlin, R.D., a dietitian in Los Angeles and a spokesperson for the American Dietetic Association.

The cup of orange juice and half of a grapefruit that you have at breakfast each count as one serving, says Nowlin. "So does the piece of fruit you have as an afternoon snack," she says. "And when you count the baked potato and cup of salad you might have at dinner—which each count as one serving—five servings isn't that hard to reach."

kiwifruit and half of a melon. Combine with generous amounts of chopped mint and cilantro. Let stand for at least 30 minutes before serving.

• Substitute pureed prunes for butter or margarine in homemade brownies and other chocolate baked goods, suggests Evelyn Tribole, R.D., a Beverly Hills, California, dietitian, in her cookbook *Healthy Homestyle Cooking*. "They add a naturally sweet flavor and chewy texture," she writes. "Best yet, a half-cup of prune puree will save you nearly 800 calories and over 100 grams of fat."

• Whip up a frothy fruit drink. "I call them smoothies," says Dr. Klaper. "Just blend your favorite fruit—say, bananas or strawberries—with some very cold water." These frosty blender drinks are especially refreshing on a summer day, says Klaper.

## Fiber Up without Fattening Up

While fruit is a delicious part of a low-fat, low-cholesterol diet, you should keep the following points in mind.

First, whole fruits pack significantly more cholesterol-lowering pectin than fruit juices, says Martin Yadrick, R.D., a dietitian in Manhattan Beach, California, and a spokesperson for the American Dietetic Association.

Even a pulp-filled juice can't deliver the fiber of the fruit itself, notes Yadrick. That doesn't mean you shouldn't enjoy your favorite juice; it just means that you should consume whole fruits as well.

Also, don't gorge on avocados. While this fruit is rich in monounsaturated fat, the kind that can help lower LDL cholesterol, you don't want to consume too much of any type of fat.

Happily, you can splurge on an occasional avocado, says Marilyn Cerino, R.D., nutrition consultant at the Benjamin Franklin Center for Health of Pennsylvania Hospital in Philadelphia. "Many people feel that there's no substitute for really good guacamole," says Cerino. So if a rich, nutty-tasting avocado or spicy guacamole is your weakness, she says, "don't feel like you're cheating—eat it slowly and enjoy it every once in a while."

*See also* Antioxidants, Apples, Avocados, Grapefruit, Pectin

~✲~

---

# GARLIC

## *A Pungent Plaque Attacker*

If you're fond of garlic-laden pasta (or other dishes prepared with this aromatic member of the onion family), you're automatically paving the way toward good heart health. Numerous studies indicate that garlic may help overpower high cholesterol levels.

Garlic contains allicin, a compound that is activated when the bulb is cut, crushed or cooked. When allicin, which contains sulfur, reacts with oxygen, it breaks down into other compounds that give garlic its distinctive odor and, medical experts speculate, provide its apparent cholesterol-busting abilities.

Garlic also appears to keep blood platelets from clumping together, preventing clots that could trigger a heart attack or stroke. Garlic may also stimulate the blood's natural clot-dissolving processes, which helps get rid of clots that do form.

But this aromatic herb isn't revered for its health benefits alone. Countries from Italy to India have an enduring love affair with the "stinking rose," and Americans consume about 250 million pounds of fresh garlic a year. Should you prefer to help clear your arteries without clearing the room, however, you might opt for garlic supplements, which are odorless pills and powders created to offer the health benefits of garlic without offending the noses of those around you.

## Praise the Bulb and Pass the Breath Mints

Garlic hasn't been conclusively proven to reduce cholesterol. But the evidence associating garlic with reductions in total and "bad" LDL cholesterol continues to accumulate.

Researchers at Tulane University School of Medicine in New Orleans gave 42 men and women with elevated cholesterol either 900 milligrams of garlic extract (divided among three capsules) or a placebo every day. After 12 weeks, the total cholesterol of the folks taking the garlic extract fell 6 percent, from 262 to 247 milligrams/deciliter, and their LDL cholesterol plunged 11 percent, from 188 to 168 milligrams/deciliter. (The National Cholesterol Education Program recommends that LDL cholesterol should not exceed 130 milligrams/deciliter.) By contrast, the total and LDL cholesterol of those consuming the placebo fell only 1 and 3 percent, respectively.

In one European study, 40 patients with high cholesterol consumed either 900 milligrams of garlic powder or a placebo every day for 16 weeks. The total cholesterol of the garlic powder group fell an average of 21 percent, and their triglycerides—another blood fat implicated in heart disease—fell 24 percent. The total cholesterol of those taking the placebo declined only 3 percent, while their triglycerides fell 5 percent.

At Tagore Medical College in India, 222 people who had had one heart attack consumed six to ten grams of garlic (about two to three cloves) every day for three or more years. Another group of 210 people took a placebo. Not only did the garlic-eaters' cholesterol levels fall an average of 9 percent, their risk of dying or of having a second heart attack declined as well. The cholesterol of the individuals taking the placebo didn't change.

Experts aren't certain how much garlic might put the kibosh on cholesterol levels. One study that was conducted in the Netherlands concluded that it would take 7 to 28 cloves of garlic a day to help curb cholesterol. Fortunately, a more recent study conducted in the United States indicates that significantly smaller doses of garlic may do some good.

At New York Medical College in Vahalla, Stephen Warshafsky, M.D., and his colleagues in the Section of General Internal Medicine pooled data from five top studies, involving more than 400 people, of garlic's effects on cholesterol levels. According to Dr. Warshafsky's analysis of the groups studied, one-half to one clove of garlic a day appears to lower blood cholesterol an average of 9 percent.

## Tips for Garlic Lovers

Whether you're a card-carrying garlic fan or looking for convenient ways to work this healthful seasoning into your diet, you're sure to benefit from one or more of these tips.

• "One of the easiest ways to use garlic is to chop it up, crush it and sauté it in a little olive or canola oil," says Herbert Pierson, Ph.D., vice-president of Preventive Nutrition Consultants in Woodinville, Wisconsin, and former project director of the Cancer Preventive Designer Food Project at the National Cancer Institute in Rockville, Maryland. "Then you can add it to soups, stews and many other dishes that would benefit from the flavor of garlic."

• Add ground fresh garlic to salad dressings and marinades, suggests Mary Donkersloot, R.D., a dietitian in Beverly Hills, California, a spokesperson for the California Dietetic Association and author of *The Fast Food Diet.*

• If you'd rather not handle fresh garlic, opt for commercially prepared garlic paste or minced garlic in oil. You might also try garlic powder (made from dehydrated and pulverized cloves), garlic oil (distilled from cloves) or aged garlic extract (a water-based garlic product). One large garlic clove is equal to ½ teaspoon of garlic powder and 1 teaspoon of minced garlic.

• Store commercially prepared minced garlic in oil in the refrigerator and garlic powder in a cool, dark cabinet.

• Add garlic to your orange juice. Yes, you read right. "Add an odor-modified substance such as aged garlic extract to orange juice," says Dr. Pierson. "The juice tends to cover up even the slightest garlicky odor." His recipe: Blend three eight-ounce glasses of orange juice, a whole orange and a tablespoon of aged garlic extract liquid.

• If you don't enjoy the taste of garlic, consider trying garlic supplements (available in health food stores and most drugstores). The supplement used in some of the studies Dr. Warshafsky analyzed, Kwai powder tablets, contains the equivalent of 2.7 grams of fresh garlic in each 900-milligram dose. One clove of garlic equals about 3 grams of fresh garlic.

• Don't use garlic salt. This product can be loaded with sodium, which is associated with a rise in blood pressure. What's more, garlic salt doesn't possess the health benefits of fresh garlic.

Consumed in large amounts, garlic can cause a variety of side effects, including heartburn, gas, skin irritation and, rarely, allergic reactions in sensitive individuals. If you experience garlic-induced discomfort, reduce the amount of garlic you're consuming, advises Dr. Pierson. Or try cooking fresh garlic instead of eating it raw.

---

### GETTING GARLIC INTO YOUR DIET—GRACEFULLY

Try these handy strategies the next time you eat or cook with garlic.

#### TO BANISH GARLIC BREATH

Love fresh garlic but hate garlic breath? Try roasting the bulbs, says Audrey Cross, Ph.D., associate clinical professor at Columbia University's Institute of Human Nutrition in New York City. "Roasting garlic helps reduce its odor and some of its sharpness," she says. "Brush the garlic with olive oil to keep it from drying out, then oven-roast the whole clove."

#### TO AVOID GARLIC-SCENTED HANDS

If you want to use fresh garlic rather than the commercially prepared kind but don't want the smell clinging to your hands, consider investing in an electric chopper, suggests Janet Lepke, R.D., a dietitian in Santa Monica, California, and a spokesperson for the American Dietetic Association. "The garlic is chopped and ready to use in seconds," she says.

---

Cooking garlic tends to weaken its irritating properties, he says.

Also, since garlic has been shown to delay blood-clotting time, consult your doctor before consuming garlic or garlic supplements if you're taking blood-thinning drugs, advises Dr. Pierson.

# GOLF

## *Another Heart-Healthy "Green"*

Sure, lots of doctors golf. But few would think of recommending this popular pastime as a way to strengthen the heart, shed pounds or lower blood cholesterol.

So here's news that should bring joy to golfers everywhere: Some experts say that golfing regularly can help you achieve all of these health goals—if you leave the cart at the clubhouse and walk the fairway instead.

No one would compare the health benefits of a weekly round of golf with keeping up a regular fitness program, of course. But this sport's potential health perks shouldn't be ignored, says Edward A. Palank, M.D., a cardiologist and director of the New Hampshire Heart Institute in Manchester. While it isn't an aerobic activity like running, tennis or swimming, "golfing does provide some positive cardiovascular benefits," says Dr. Palank, who has studied the effect of golfing on blood cholesterol. "If you golf three times a week and walk the course each time, you may be walking 12 to 15 miles." Combined with following a low-fat diet, getting regular exercise—including walking—has been shown to lower total and "bad" LDL cholesterol levels.

## Driving Down Bad Cholesterol

Can lining up putts really help deflate blood cholesterol? Maybe, maybe not. In Dr. Palank's study, 28 sedentary men golfed an average of three times a week, walking about 14 miles a week in the process. Dr. Palank tested these golfers' blood cholesterol at the beginning and end of the golf season (May to September). Dr. Palank also tested the blood cholesterol of 16 nongolfing men.

After four months, the total cholesterol of both the golfers and the nongolfers had fallen—an average of 17 points for the golfers and 15 points for the nongolfers. But more important, LDL cholesterol plummeted much more in the golfers—13 points, compared with 3.4 points in the men who didn't golf.

The golfers' levels of HDL cholesterol increased only slightly, suggesting that exercise more vigorous than golf is necessary to significantly boost the body's level of this "good" cholesterol. But the golfers' overall ratio of HDL to total cholesterol improved significantly, while HDL cholesterol fell in the nongolfers.

Golfing regularly might also help you control your weight, says Darlene A. Sedlock, Ph.D., associate professor of kinesiology at Purdue University in West Lafayette, Indiana. And the lower your percentage of body fat, the lower your risk of high levels of total and LDL cholesterol. The golfers in Dr. Palank's study lost an average of 1.4 pounds, which may have helped reduce their cholesterol, says Dr. Palank.

What's more, a round of golf can burn over 600 calories in the average 150-pound man, according to Dr. Sedlock. That figure is based on walking an 18-hole course, taking four hours to play one round of golf and carrying your own clubs, she says.

## Tips for Iron Johns and Janes

Supplement playing golf with another form of aerobic exercise such as swimming or cycling, recommends Dr. Palank. "Your goal should be to find an activity you like and pursue it," he says. "If you enjoy playing golf, play it—but you have to get out of the cart."

Besides walking the fairway, carry your clubs in a lightweight bag instead of letting a caddy carry them, suggests Dr. Palank. He also suggests using a variety of club sizes to vary your physical motion a bit. You might also arrive early for your game, so you can walk the perimeter of the course before your golfing partners arrive, says Dr. Palank.

One additional tip: Watch yourself at the 19th hole—the clubhouse watering hole, that is—so you don't munch high-fat snacks after your game. There's no quicker way to undo the health benefits of golf than to overindulge before you leave the country club grounds!

*See also* Exercise

# GRAPEFRUIT

## *The Secret Is in the Pectin*

Some people see grapefruit as the ultimate diet food, right up there with cottage cheese, melba toast and celery sticks. Others view it as a tasty way to begin a low-fat breakfast or as a delicious, sun-ripened snack. But whatever your opinion of grapefruit, one thing is clear: This tart, pink- or white-fleshed fruit can help put the squeeze on high cholesterol.

"It's really a wonderful fruit," says James J. Cerda, M.D., professor of medicine at the University of Florida College of Medicine in Gainesville, who finds no need for understatement when discussing the fruit he has studied for decades.

Grapefruit's pulpy membrane—the stuff that separates one section of the fruit from another—is loaded with pectin, a type of soluble fiber that Dr. Cerda says may actually reverse the buildup of fatty deposits in the coronary arteries. And while most of grapefruit's pectin is concentrated in the membrane, the fruit itself contains 3.9 percent pectin, enough to help take a bite out of high blood cholesterol. As a bonus, grapefruit is packed with vitamin C and beta-carotene, a derivative of vitamin A that may help reduce the risk of certain types of cancer and heart disease.

If you're a bona fide grapefruit fan, so much the better. But even if you're not, you can still get more of this citrus's cholesterol-clobbering pectin into your diet—without having to eat the fruit itself. Read on to find out how.

## Putting Grapefruit to the Test

How does grapefruit help send cholesterol levels south? Ask Dr. Cerda and his colleagues, who studied the effects of grapefruit pectin on the cholesterol levels of 27 people. But not just any people: These folks were deemed to be at moderate to high risk for coronary heart disease because of their elevated cholesterol levels. "We recruited men and women who were unable or unwilling to alter their lifestyles—who weren't going to start exercising or eating a low-fat diet or stop smoking or drinking," says Dr. Cerda. "They were real couch potatoes. Our objective was to see if despite this adverse set of circumstances, these individuals' cholesterol levels would improve simply by adding grapefruit pectin to their diets."

In this study, the men and women consumed either 15 grams (about three teaspoons) of pectin in capsule form or a placebo every day for four weeks. Then for another four weeks, the people consuming the pectin took the placebo, and vice versa.

The results? These folks' total cholesterol dropped an average of 7.6 percent, from 275 to 254 milligrams/deciliter, when they consumed the pectin supplement as opposed to the placebo. What's more, their "bad" LDL cholesterol plummeted an average of 11 percent, from 195 to 174 milligrams/deciliter.

"These figures are extraordinary because these people didn't make any other lifestyle adjustments," says Dr. Cerda. "We didn't ask them to start walking three miles a day or to curb their fat intakes—we asked them just to take grapefruit pectin."

In another study conducted by Dr. Cerda and his colleagues, 14 miniature pigs (called microswine) were fed a high-fat diet for more than a year—long enough for the pigs to develop severely plaque-clogged coronary arteries. Then for another nine months, half of the pigs continued on this same fatty diet plus 3 percent grapefruit pectin. The remaining seven pigs were fed the same diet but with no added pectin.

After nine months, the pigs' arteries were examined. While the pectin had not significantly lowered the pigs' cholesterol levels, this soluble fiber had stopped the progression, or reduced the extent, of the plaque buildup in the animals' coronary arteries and aortas. In fact, the coronary arteries of the pigs who hadn't consumed pectin had narrowed an average of 45 percent, while the arteries of the pectin-fed pigs had narrowed only 24 percent.

Okay, the study was conducted on pigs, not humans. But pigs' cardiovascular systems are similar to ours, notes Dr. Cerda, and further study may conclude that what's good for swine is good for humans, too.

## The Juicy Details

Want to get more grapefruit into your diet? The following tips can get you started.

• To begin with, select brightly colored grapefruit with thin, fine-textured skin, advises Sharon Tyler Herbst, author of *The Food Lover's Tiptionary.* "The heavier grapefruit are, the juicier they'll be," she says. "And generally speaking, the thinner the skin, the juicier the grapefruit."

• Sprinkle half of a grapefruit with brown sugar and bake it, suggests Evelyn Tribole, R.D., a dietitian in Beverly Hills, California, and author of *Healthy Homestyle Cooking.* "Baked grapefruit is a tasty dessert," says Tribole. Baking grapefruit also tames its natural tartness—good news if you're craving an especially sweet treat.

• Serve grapefruit sections as an accompaniment to spicy foods such as chili.

• Drizzle a tablespoon of honey or maple syrup over slices of kiwifruit and peeled sections of orange and grapefruit. Sprinkle the fruits with cinnamon and nutmeg, then serve over raw fresh spinach dressed lightly with olive oil.

## A Grapefruit "Supplement"

To make a dent in elevated cholesterol, says Dr. Cerda, you'd need to eat two or three grapefruit a day—too much for the average person to swallow. So Dr. Cerda and his colleagues created ProFibe. This product, a tasteless powder that contains grapefruit pectin and other water-soluble fibers, can be blended into beverages, sprinkled onto salads or cereals or mixed into baked goods.

Dr. Cerda recommends that people with moderately elevated blood cholesterol consume about 15 grams of ProFibe a day. "It's one more tool people can use to lower their cholesterol," says Dr. Cerda. (For more information about ProFibe, which is available through mail order, write to Cer-Burg Enterprises, P.O. Box 245, Hawthorne, FL 32640, or call 1-800-756-3999.)

Another way to get more pectin is to step up your intake of soluble fiber–rich fruits, vegetables and grains, advise experts.

# GRAPE JUICE

## *The Teetotalers' Toast of Choice*

**A**s mentioned elsewhere in this book, drinking wine or other alcoholic beverages in moderation has been shown to boost "good" HDL cholesterol and reduce the risk of coronary heart disease. But if you choose not to imbibe, here's good news: According to one study, grape juice may have the same benefits as wine—including the ability to keep red blood cells from clumping together to form the clots that can lead to a heart attack. While more study is needed, grape juice could be the heart-smart teetotaler's beverage of choice.

## The Power of Flavonoids

There's evidence to suggest that antioxidant compounds called flavonoids reduce the "stickiness" of blood-clotting cells called platelets, which in turn lowers the risk of coronary heart disease and heart attack, says John D. Folts, Ph.D., director of the University of Wisconsin Coronary Artery Thrombosis Research and Prevention Lab at the University of Wisconsin Hospital and Clinics in Madison. Flavonoids are found in the skin, stems and seeds of grapes, says Dr. Folts.

In research conducted at the University of Wisconsin, study participants—that is, Dr. Folts and several colleagues—drank varying amounts of grape juice. They then tested one another's blood to monitor its clotting activity. Dogs were also tested, using a different method. The researchers' conclusions: Purple grape juice has the same anticlotting properties of red wine. (Dr. Folts and his colleagues used purple grape juice rather than the red or white variety because darker juice contains more flavonoids, according to Dr. Folts.)

Since there are 800 to 900 different kinds of flavonoids, "it's going to be a massive task to determine which of the flavonoids are the most significant," says Dr. Folts. His research has shown, however, that one of these flavonoids, quercetin, inhibits platelet stickiness—and more. "Quercetin is a better antioxidant than even vitamin E," says Dr. Folts. "So it may also reduce heart disease risk by preventing the oxidation of 'bad' LDL cholesterol." Oxidation is a chemical process that makes LDL cholesterol stickier and thus more likely to cling to arterial walls.

Other research has speculated that resveratrol, a fungus-fighting chemical produced in the skin of grapes, may help lower cholesterol. One study, for example, has shown that purified resveratrol appears to lower cholesterol in rats, and grape juice contains more resveratrol than many wines. But Dr. Folts credits the anticlotting properties of quercetin or other flavonoids with the fruit's potential heart-healthy benefits. "Resveratrol didn't show platelet-inhibiting properties," he says.

## How Much Juice?

It appears to take three times as much grape juice by volume to reap red wine's preventive effects, according to Dr. Folts. "Our studies have determined that there's a measurable antiplatelet inhibition from two glasses of red wine," he says. "It would probably take six glasses of grape juice to achieve the same effect."

Besides drinking grape juice, you can boost your intake of flavonoids by eating more fresh fruits and vegetables, suggests Dr. Folts. "There's a fair amount of quercetin in apples," he says. "Broccoli and kale are other good sources."

*See also* Alcohol, Wine

~✿~

# HIGH-FIBER CEREALS

## *Winning the Grain Game*

Who says cereal is just for breakfast? Certainly not the typical American. In fact, over 90 percent of the folks who responded to one survey said they eat cold cereal at least once a week; 4.5 times per week was the average. Forty percent said they eat cold cereal as a snack. And almost 25 percent said they occasionally break out the cornflakes for dinner!

That's good news—if they're spooning up high-fiber, whole-grain products (rather than brands that tend to come with secret decoder rings). Many cereals deliver a day's worth of energy-giving complex carbohydrates, vitamins and minerals in one power-packed bowl and contain little or no fat, says James W. Anderson, M.D., professor of medicine and clinical nutrition at the University of Kentucky College of Medicine in Lexington and author of *Dr. Anderson's High-Fiber Fitness Plan*. Most important, some brands are good sources of cholesterol-clobbering soluble fibers such as oat gum and psyllium, he says.

So whether you spoon up a low-fat, high-fiber cereal as an A.M. eye-opener or a P.M. snack, rest assured: You're giving your heart a gift.

Of course, the high-sugar cereals that come in Day-Glo colors and in flavors not found in nature aren't likely to contain much soluble fiber, says Dr. Anderson. Worse, however, are the so-called all-natural cereals that are loaded with nuts, honey, dried fruits and other ingredients that drive their fat and calorie counts sky-high, he says. So to separate the wheat from the . . . er, chaff, prepare to do some sleuthing when you navigate the cereal aisle.

## Cholesterol-Slicing Action in Every Spoonful

Several studies have analyzed the effect of high-fiber cereal on blood cholesterol. In one study, researchers at the University of Minnesota in Minneapolis had 58 men with high cholesterol follow a low-fat, low-cholesterol diet for six weeks. For the next six weeks, the men ate the same diet, with one adjustment: They also consumed a pectin-enriched cereal, a psyllium-enriched product or cornflakes, which contained no soluble fiber.

The men's total cholesterol declined about 4 percent on the low-fat diet alone. But the total cholesterol of the men who ate the low-fat diet and the pectin-enriched cereal dropped 6.4 percent, and their "bad" LDL cholesterol fell 8.4 percent. The men who consumed the psyllium-enriched cereal saw their blood fats drop even more: Their total cholesterol dropped 9.2 percent, and their LDL cholesterol plummeted 9.7 percent. The total and LDL cholesterol of the cornflake-eaters didn't change.

In another study, researchers at the University of Toronto had 18 people with high cholesterol eat either a psyllium-enriched cereal or a wheat bran cereal. After two weeks, the total cholesterol of the folks who consumed the psyllium-added cereal dropped 8.4 percent, and their LDL cholesterol plummeted 11.1 percent. The researchers concluded that psyllium-enriched cereal may help cut the risk of coronary heart disease.

## Read between the Lies . . . Um, Lines

Stroll down the cereal aisle of almost any supermarket, and you'll see healthful, high-fiber cereals competing for space with box after box of the sugar-coated stuff. Don't be fooled by cereals that look nutritious but aren't. These tips can help you spoon up cereal's maximum cholesterol-busting benefits.

• Choose a cereal that contains at least three grams of fiber and one gram or less of fat per serving, advises Dr. Anderson.

• Consider trying a product enriched with psyllium, which contains a significant amount of soluble fiber, suggests William P. Castelli, M.D., medical director of the Framingham Cardiovascular Institute, a wellness program at Metro West Medical Center in Framingham, Massachusetts. "Replacing a daily high-fat breakfast, such as eggs and bacon, with a breakfast of cereal high in soluble fiber and skim milk can lower cholesterol from 8 to 16 percent within a month," says Dr. Castelli. You'll find several brands on the market, including Bran Buds and FiberWise.

• "Look for as whole a grain of cereal as you can find," advises Michael Klaper, M.D., health director of the Royal Atlantic Health Spa in Pompano Beach, Florida, and author of *Vegan Nutrition: Pure and Simple.* "The box should say 'whole oats,' 'whole barley' or 'whole millet.' One brand to try is Kashi, a blend of oats, long-grain brown rice, rye, barley and other whole grains, suggests Kay Stanfill, R.D., adjunct assistant professor in the Department of Nutritional Sciences at the University of Oklahoma Health Sciences Center in Oklahoma City. "It's a wonderful mix of whole grains, and you can eat it cold or hot," she says.

• Avoid granola-type cereals—they're generally loaded with fat. If you opt for a low-fat granola, however, make sure it's also low in sugar, sodium and calories, says Dr. Anderson.

• To slash fat even more, splash cereal with skim milk rather than 2 percent or even 1 percent low-fat milk.

• Top high-fiber cereal with fruit. Peaches, strawberries, bananas and raisins will help spike a cereal's fiber content even higher.

• If you enjoy hot cereal but need a break from oatmeal, try barley, roasted buckwheat kernels (also known as kasha) or millet, available in supermarkets and health food stores, suggests Dr. Anderson. These grains are prepared the same way you cook any hot cereal, and they're microwaveable, too. The only catch: Adding cream or butter will negate these cereals' cholesterol-lowering benefits. So stir in your favorite nonfat fruit-flavored yogurt instead, says Dr. Anderson.

- Mix cold cereal with nonfat yogurt for a tasty, low-fat snack.

*See also* Barley, Fiber, Oats, Psyllium

# LEAN MEAT

## *The Red Scare Is Over*

If you have elevated cholesterol, you should avoid red meat. Right?

Not necessarily. Despite what you may have heard, experts say that you don't have to forgo steak and burgers entirely to keep tabs on your cholesterol. The key to making red meat part of a low-fat, low-cholesterol diet is to eat smaller portions of leaner cuts, says Susan Kleiner, R.D., Ph.D., a nutritionist in Seattle and author of *The High-Performance Cookbook*.

What's more, red meat is a great source of protein, iron, zinc and B vitamins. But a little bit of red meat goes a long way, and experts still advise against broiling up a steak too often. "Red meat is high in saturated fat, so you shouldn't overdo it," says Janet Lepke, R.D., a dietitian in Santa Monica, California, and a spokesperson for the American Dietetic Association.

### Trimming Down the Fat of the Land

For many Americans, eating king-size portions of ribs and roast beef is a thing of the past. According to the U.S. Department of Agriculture (USDA), our consumption of beef plummeted from 88.8 pounds per person in 1976 to 62.8 pounds in 1992.

But just when it seemed that Americans would abandon red meat in a mad stampede, the nation's beef producers grew innovative, crossbreeding traditional beef cattle with leaner animals, giving cattle lower-fat feed (which makes their meat less fatty) and sending animals to market at a younger age, when their meat is leaner. Meat packers and butchers are also trimming more visible fat from beef right in the supermarket or butcher shop.

These changes in the raising and packaging of beef mean that in some cases, red meat is lower in fat, cholesterol and calories than it used to be. In fact, the fat content of retail beef declined 27 percent during 1990 and 1991, according to the National Cattleman's Association. Moreover, "some of the leaner cuts of red meat contain less fat than skinless chicken thighs," says Tammy Baker, R.D., a nutritionist in Cave Creek, Arizona, and a spokesperson for the American Dietetic Association.

## Here's the Beef

A few studies have beefed up the argument that red meat can be part of a cholesterol-lowering diet.

In a study at Baylor College of Medicine in Houston, two groups of men with high blood cholesterol levels were placed on a five-week stabilization diet in which 40 percent of their calories came from fat. These men then switched to one of two low-fat test diets in which they ate either chicken breast or lean beef (choice strip loin steak) for five more weeks. The beef contained 8 percent fat, and the chicken, 7 percent fat.

After five weeks, both groups' total cholesterol decreased significantly—7.6 percent for the meat-eaters and 10.2 percent for the poultry-eaters. The men's "bad" LDL cholesterol also dropped significantly on both diets, although not to desirable levels. The researchers concluded that lean beef and chicken are interchangeable in a low-fat, low-cholesterol diet.

In an Australian study, researchers placed ten people on a very low fat diet that contained lean beef with the fat trimmed off. These individuals' total cholesterol fell significantly within a week. But when beef fat (in the form of drippings) was added to these folks' diet, their total cholesterol rose. The researchers concluded that it was the beef fat, not the beef itself, that raised these individuals' blood cholesterol.

Further, they wrote, the low-fat diet with lean beef (but without the fat drippings) was just as effective at lowering cholesterol as other low-fat diets that were tested.

## A Carnivore's Guide to Cholesterol Busting

To make red meat part of your low-fat, low-cholesterol diet, keep these shopping guidelines and serving suggestions in mind.

• Choose the leanest cuts of meat. If you're shopping for pork, select the tenderloin, leg and shoulder. If you're buying lamb, choose the arm and loin.

• The leanest cuts of beef usually carry the label "USDA select." On average, select beef contains 20 percent less fat than "choice" beef and 40 percent less fat than "prime." Extra-lean ground beef contains just 10 percent fat based on weight.

• You can estimate the fat content of a cut of meat just by looking at it, according to Mary Donkersloot, R.D., a dietitian in Beverly Hills, California, a spokesperson for the California Dietetic Association and

### THE KINDEST CUTS

The following cuts of beef are among the leanest. Figures are for three ounces cooked. By comparison, the same amount of rib eye steak contains 10 grams of fat and 191 calories. And three ounces of short ribs packs 15.4 grams of fat and 251 calories.

| MEAT | FAT (G.) | CALORIES |
|---|---|---|
| Eye of round | 4.2 | 143 |
| Top roast | 4.2 | 153 |
| Tip round | 5.9 | 157 |
| Top sirloin | 6.1 | 165 |
| Chuck roast | 7.6 | 189 |
| Top loin | 8 | 176 |
| Flank | 8.6 | 176 |
| Tenderloin | 8.6 | 177 |

author of *The Fast Food Diet.* "Check to see how much white marbling the meat has," she suggests. The more marbling, she says, the more fat.

• Eat red meat only a couple times a week and keep the servings small, advises Baker. "The suggested serving size is about three ounces," she says. "That's a little smaller than the palm of your hand or about the size of a deck of cards." Agrees Dr. Kleiner, "Sixteen-ounce steaks are no longer the way to go."

• Cut away all visible fat from red meat before you cook it. While trimming the fat won't affect its taste much, it will dramatically reduce your intake of fat and calories.

• "If you eat meat, broil it," suggests Gene A. Spiller, D.Sc., Ph.D., director of the Health Research and Studies Center in Los Altos, California, and author of *The Superpyramid Eating Program.* "Let the fat drip off the meat, but don't let it drain on hot charcoal or a hot burner, which will create undesirable fumes."

• If you're wondering how to make do with a three-ounce serving of meat, get creative: Start thinking of meat as an ingredient of the main course rather than as the main course itself, says Evelyn Tribole, R.D., a dietitian in Beverly Hills, California, and author of *Healthy Homestyle Cooking.* "Three ounces of lean ground beef combined with spaghetti is satisfying," says Tribole. "Or stir-fry ground beef and make a low-fat beef stroganoff" using nonfat plain yogurt instead of sour cream.

Lepke agrees that an entrée should most often feature grains and vegetables, with beef playing a supporting role. "Let's say you want to make a stew," she says. "You'd be better off using more garbanzo beans or vegetables" and less beef.

• Substitute whole or ground turkey or chicken in recipes that call for beef. Make turkey burgers instead of hamburgers, or meat loaf with ground turkey instead of ground beef. "But the less fatty the meat, the drier it can get," says Tribole. She suggests adding a medium-size grated apple to a pound of ground turkey. "The apple will give the turkey a nice texture without adding extra fat," she says.

• "Marinate meat in something flavorful," suggests Marilyn Cerino, R.D., nutrition consultant at the Benjamin Franklin Center for Health of Pennsylvania Hospital in Philadelphia. A savory marinade: a blend of fresh orange juice, light soy sauce, olive oil, garlic and ginger. "You can use this mixture to marinate strips of meat or chicken that you plan to stir-fry," says Cerino. "And if the meat is tough, marinate it overnight."

• If you're loath to give up burgers and fries, whip up a lower-fat, lower-cholesterol version of this all-American treat. Substitute a whole-grain bun for a white-bread bun, and use low-fat or choles-terol-free mayonnaise and low-fat or nonfat cheese instead of regular mayo and American cheese. And put away your deep-fat fryer and opt for spiced, oven-baked home fries instead. Round out the meal with a side dish of baked beans without the salt pork—lots of fiber, virtually no fat.

• If you must have a fast-food burger, order a small burger without fixin's such as cheese, mayonnaise and special sauce, suggests Baker. On the side, opt for a salad with low-fat or nonfat dressing or a baked potato without sour cream or butter.

❧

# LOW-FAT AND NONFAT CHEESES

## *Slice Away Fat, Not Flavor*

If you grew up believing that the four food groups were as sacred as baseball and Mom's apple pie, you may be wondering: How did cheese, once considered an important part of a healthy diet, become so maligned?

If you're trying to lower your blood cholesterol, the answer is all too clear: Eating too much rich, creamy cheese can raise your blood cholesterol and clog your coronary arteries faster than you can say "double-cheese pizza."

But cheer up, cheese-o-philes: "Light" (or "lite") and low-fat cheeses can be just as tasty and versatile as their full-fat counterparts. You might even try nonfat cheeses, which don't contain a speck of fat. And while you may never mistake a low-fat or nonfat cheese for your favorite French Brie, you can make these products a tasty part of a low-fat, low-cholesterol diet. Here's how.

## Bypassing Fat City: The Basics

Cheese is little more than a concentrated form of milk. It takes about eight pounds of milk to create a single pound of most cheeses. In many full-fat cheeses, 60 percent or more of their calories come from fat, and one ounce of Cheddar, Swiss, Monterey Jack or Muenster contains eight to ten grams of fat. Just reading a cheese label with those kinds of numbers is enough to make your arteries slam shut!

The good news is that the dairy industry has responded to the public's demands for healthier cheese by introducing some products that get 10 percent or less of their calories from fat and contain two grams or less of fat per ounce. So if you can walk past the Camembert, the Brie and other exotic (and fatty) selections in the deli section of the supermarket and follow a few basic guidelines, you can still say "cheese" with a smile.

The key to choosing heart-healthy cheese, say experts, is to become a dedicated label reader. Select cheeses with low amounts of total fat and saturated fat and low percentages of calories from fat, advises Sheah Rarback, R.D., director of nutrition at the University of Miami School of Medicine's Mailman Center.

"Choose a cheese in which the percentage of fat is lower than the percentage of protein," says Gene Spiller, D.Sc., Ph.D., director of the Health Research and Studies Center in Los Altos, California, and author of *The Superpyramid Eating Program.* A product that is 20 percent fat and 15 percent protein, for example, should stay out of your shopping cart, says Dr. Spiller.

Also, when it comes to controlling blood cholesterol, a cheese's fat content is more important than its amount of dietary cholesterol, says Ruth Lowenberg, R.D., a dietitian in New York City. The American Heart Association recommends that adults eat less than 300 milligrams of dietary cholesterol per day. Don't be misled, however: A one-ounce serving of American cheese contains 26 milligrams of cholesterol but nine grams of fat—a hefty amount if you're trying to follow a low-fat diet.

## Low-Fat or Nonfat?

If you're looking to knock a few points off your blood cholesterol by slicing your intake of fatty cheese, you might try low-fat or nonfat cheeses. Here's how these products compare.

***Low-fat cheeses.*** At three grams or less of fat per ounce and about 20 to 50 percent less fat than full-fat cheeses, these products look and taste much like their higher-fat counterparts, says Alicia Moag-Stahlberg, R.D., a dietitian in Chicago and a spokesperson for the American Dietetic Association. Low-fat products even melt like their full-fat counterparts, making them perfect for sauces and toasted cheese sandwiches. "Most people are quite happy with low-fat cheeses," says Moag-Stahlberg. If you're already following a low-fat diet, you may want to select a low-fat cheese over a nonfat product, she says.

***Nonfat cheeses.*** These products contain the barest amount of fat, if any at all. But finding a nonfat cheese that tastes like the real thing can be tricky. Here's why. Whole-milk cheese gets its characteristic consistency, texture and flavor from butterfat. To make nonfat cheese, the dairy industry replaces butterfat with fat substitutes, milk solids or other ingredients. "Nonfat products tend to have different textures than low-fat cheeses," says Moag-Stahlberg. "They don't melt as well, either." What's more, nonfat cheeses tend to have very mild flavors—what some people might call bland.

But many people have learned to enjoy nonfat cheese. These folks' secret? Using a little culinary ingenuity. "If you're using a cheese that has more than 50 percent fat reduction by weight, you may need to find a creative way of preparing it," says Lowenberg, "combining it with other foods to give it more flavor."

## Tasty Tips for Cheese Junkies

The kind of cheese you choose—and the way you use it—can make all of the difference. These hints can help.

• Look for low-fat "impostors." Chances are there's a low-fat or nonfat alternative for your favorite type of full-fat cheese, including

---

## A TIP FROM THE FRENCH

Just can't give up your favorite full-fat cheese? You might try doing as the French—the world's most prolific cheese-eaters—do, says Audrey Cross, Ph.D., associate clinical professor at Columbia University's Institute of Human Nutrition in New York City.

"The French eat very high-fat cheeses," says Dr. Cross. "But they eat tiny amounts of them, along with a lot of bread and fruit. Americans tend to eat hunk after hunk of cheeses that aren't as satisfying, trying to attain some satisfaction.

"If we would eat foods that taste good, we'd eat less of them, because we'd be satisfied," continues Dr. Cross. "Try eating an ounce of your favorite cheese instead of five ounces of a variety that you don't enjoy as much. And eat the cheese with bread and a piece of fruit instead of with fatty crackers."

---

Cheddar (Healthy Choice Fat-Free, Cracker Barrel Light), mozzarella (Kraft Healthy Favorites, Alpine Lace Low Moisture Part-Skim), Swiss (Light 'N' Lively Singles, Kraft Light Naturals) and American (Weight Watchers Slices, Kraft Free Singles). "Do some taste testing," says Evelyn Tribole, R.D., a dietitian in Beverly Hills, California, and author of *Healthy Homestyle Cooking.* "You may find that there's a considerable difference in taste among brands of the same type of cheese."

• Try combining small amounts of a higher-fat cheese with a low-fat or nonfat product. "You might add cubes of low-fat mozzarella to a salad, then sprinkle the salad with blue cheese," says Lowenberg. "You'll get a wonderful cheesy flavor without using a large amount of the higher-fat cheese."

• Using condiments can give a nonfat cheese some extra zip. "If you're using a nonfat cheese in a sandwich, you may not be able to get away with adding just lettuce and tomato," says Lowenberg. "Try spreading on some horseradish or chutney, which will enhance the cheese's flavor."

• To make a delicious dip, blend low-fat cottage cheese with a dry salad-dressing mix, suggests Lowenberg. If a dip recipe calls for sour cream, substitute a mixture of low-fat cottage cheese and yogurt, she says.

• Substitute nonfat cream cheese for the full-fat product in no-bake cheesecakes and refrigerated desserts. Or toss nonfat cream cheese with hot pasta (along with your favorite herbs and spices) for a creamy, Alfredo-type sauce.

• Love the taste of creamy cheeses such as Brie? Try this mock Brie dish, suggests Sue Chapman, executive chef at Skylonda Fitness Retreat in Woodside, California: Mix one part Brie cheese, four parts nonfat cream cheese and some rosemary, shape into rounds and dip in bread crumbs. Then bake.

• The next time you make lasagna, substitute part-skim ricotta cheese for the whole-milk product. A half-cup of part-skim ricotta cheese contains 9.8 grams of fat, compared with 16.1 grams in the same amount of the whole-milk stuff.

• As mentioned previously, nonfat cheeses don't melt very well. So don't use these products to top casseroles, advises Tribole. "Nonfat cheese will look like toasted coconut," she says. "I'd use a low-fat cheese instead." Similarly, nonfat mozzarella works better baked into lasagna than on a pizza, she notes. But if you want to use a nonfat cheese in a sauce, "try shredding it very finely," Tribole suggests. "It will melt nicely."

<hr />

# LOW-FAT DIET

## *The Ultimate Eating Plan*

Studies published in medical and nutritional journals show that following a low-fat diet can help trim a bloated cholesterol level. But how low in fat is a low-fat diet? And how low should you go?

It depends on whom you ask—and perhaps on the health of your heart. The American Heart Association recommends that we consume less than 30 percent of our daily calories from fat, while other experts recommend a 25 percent fat limit. And for people with coronary heart disease, Dean Ornish, M.D., president and director of the Preventive

## WHAT THE DOCTOR ORDERS

How does a doctor defat his own diet? Ask James W. Anderson, M.D., professor of medicine and clinical nutrition at the University of Kentucky College of Medicine in Lexington and author of *Dr. Anderson's High-Fiber Fitness Plan*. Here's what his diet is like.

- For breakfast, Dr. Anderson often chooses hot oatmeal or oat bran with a banana and skim milk.
- At lunchtime, he frequently opts for raw vegetables, a glass of vegetable juice, fruit and a couple of oat bran muffins.
- For dinner, Dr. Anderson might select pasta, broiled fish or bean (not beef) burritos with a fruit cup for dessert. "If I'm dining out, I might order strawberries sprinkled with brown sugar," he says.
- On the rare occasions when Dr. Anderson finds himself in a fast-food restaurant, he orders a lower-fat selection, such as a grilled chicken fajita.
- At a Chinese restaurant, Dr. Anderson bypasses fatty fare such as egg rolls and sweet-and-sour chicken for lower-fat dishes such as wonton soup and plain steamed rice and vegetables.

Medicine Research Institute in Sausalito, California, who describes his program in his book, *Dr. Dean Ornish's Program for Reversing Heart Disease*, advocates a "reversal diet" that contains just 10 percent fat.

"Moderate changes in diet can produce moderate improvements in cholesterol," says Dr. Ornish. "But big changes can do quite a bit more. Our studies show that if you consume 10 percent fat and almost no dietary cholesterol, it's possible to reduce LDL cholesterol (the 'bad' kind) by an average of 40 percent—not 40 points, but 40 percent!"

Whether to curb your daily fat intake to 30 percent of calories, 10 percent or somewhere in between is up to you and your doctor to decide, says William P. Castelli, M.D., medical director of the Framingham Cardiovascular Institute, a wellness program at Metro West Medical Center in Framingham, Massachusetts. But virtually all experts agree on one point: Americans should eat less fat—particularly saturated fat, found in animal foods such as red meat, in cheese and butter and in tropical oils such as coconut, palm and palm-kernel oils.

The good news is, cutting fat doesn't doom you to diet hell. Supermarket shelves are bulging with tasty low-fat or nonfat products that, eaten in moderation, can take the sting out of low-fat eating. Here's how to have your nonfat cake and eat it, too.

## Eat Like Jack Sprat

How might paring your fat intake affect your cholesterol? Take a look at these studies.

In a government study conducted with George Washington University in Washington, D.C., 42 men with normal or moderately high cholesterol alternated between a high-fat diet (41 percent of calories from fat) and a low-fat diet (19 percent of calories from fat). When the men switched from the high-fat to the low-fat plan, almost 80 percent saw their total cholesterol plunge 20 or more points after six weeks.

In another study, James W. Anderson, M.D., professor of medicine and clinical nutrition at the University of Kentucky College of Medicine in Lexington and author of *Dr. Anderson's High-Fiber Fitness Plan,* and his colleagues found that when 47 people with moderately high cholesterol levels consumed a diet with a fat content of 25 percent of their total calories, they lowered their cholesterol by about 9 percent after a year. When a comparable group of 48 people incorporated about 25 grams of fiber into this low-fat diet, their cholesterol dropped 13 percent.

Yet cutting total dietary fat may not lower cholesterol unless you trim saturated fat in particular, according to researchers at Columbia University College of Physicians and Surgeons in New York City. These researchers put 48 men on a high-fat diet (37 percent of calories from fat, 16 percent of them from saturated fat). After three weeks, two-thirds of the men switched to one of two low-fat diets. Both of these diets got 30 percent of their total calories from fat. But the first low-fat diet contained 9 percent saturated fat, and the second diet, 14 percent saturated fat.

After seven more weeks, the men who consumed the diet containing 9 percent saturated fat saw their total cholesterol drop 7.5 percent. But the cholesterol of the groups following either the high-fat diet or the low-fat diet containing 14 percent saturated fat barely budged.

If you're like many people, the thought of giving up high-fat foods isn't a pleasant one. Yet defatting your diet doesn't have to hurt—and one study shows that many people actually prefer a low-fat diet once they get used to it. These strategies can help take the sting out of low-fat eating.

## The Basics

• Limit your consumption of red meat to small portions a few times a week, advises dietitian Marilyn Guthrie, R.D., manager of health promotion at Virginia Mason Medical Center in Seattle. "Start thinking of meat as a side dish," she says. "Have a salad as an entrée, along with a few slices of smoked turkey or lean beef. You'll get plenty of protein and iron but less dietary fat."

• Switch to skim milk from whole- or low-fat milk, advises Lisa Lauri, R.D., nutrition consultant at North Shore University Hospital in Manhasset, New York. You'll cut a considerable amount of fat, cholesterol and calories. But you don't have to go cold turkey, says Lauri. "First, drink a blend of whole milk and 2 percent milk," she suggests. "Then try drinking half 2 percent low-fat milk and half 1 percent low-fat milk. You can gradually wean yourself to skim milk."

• Prepare your favorite high-fat dishes with low-fat or nonfat products, suggests Mindy Hermann, a nutrition consultant in Mount Kisco, New York. Tasty stand-ins for fatty ingredients include nonfat yogurt for sour cream, egg substitute for whole eggs and reduced-fat or nonfat cheese for the real thing.

• Don't overdo nonfat sweets, advises Dr. Castelli. "Low-fat" and "cholesterol-free" cakes and pastries aren't necessarily low in calories, and your waistline could pay the price.

## Italian Delights

• The next time you make lasagna, substitute a mixture of extra-lean ground beef and ground turkey for high-fat sausage and nonfat ricotta cheese for the whole-milk variety, says Nancy Baggett, author of *100% Pleasure: The Low-Fat Cookbook for People who Love to Eat.*

• Can't give up stuffed manicotti? Use part-skim ricotta cheese or nonfat cottage cheese, says Barbie Casselman, a nutrition consultant in Toronto. "To further reduce the amount of cheese you use, mix the cheese with spinach," she suggests.

• Make your own low-fat pizza, suggests Casselman. While many gourmet pizzas forgo the cheese entirely, she notes, you might use a small amount of cheese (about two ounces) and substitute grilled vegetables such as zucchini, peppers and eggplant for the sausage and pepperoni.

### Defatting an Old Favorite

• Craving fried chicken? Dip skinless chicken breasts in a mixture of skim milk and egg whites, then roll them in flour seasoned with herbs and spices or in bread crumbs, says Marilyn Cerino, R.D., nutrition consultant at the Benjamin Franklin Center for Health of Pennsylvania Hospital in Philadelphia. "Then coat a no-stick pan with vegetable spray, add one teaspoon of olive or canola oil and flash-fry the chicken for 30 seconds on each side to crisp the outside," says Cerino. Bake the chicken at 400° for about five minutes, or until the meat is completely white with no hint of pink. "People are surprised at how tasty this 'fried' chicken is," says Cerino.

### A Trio of Tasty New Ideas

• Stuff stir-fried vegetables or chunks of fish into rice wrappers, used in Thai cuisine. "Soften the wrappers in hot water, add your favorite filling, wrap them up, and you're ready to eat," says Casselman. You can buy rice wrappers in Chinese grocery stores and specialty food stores, she says.

• Try roasting vegetables, says Hermann. Here's how: Cube the vegetables (Hermann suggests turnips, butternut squash and sweet potatoes), coat them with a small amount of olive oil and season them with thyme. Place the vegetables on a no-stick baking sheet and slow-roast them for a couple of hours. "The vegetables release their own juices, which helps keep them moist," says Hermann.

• Try vegetarian burgers. They've become popular among folks trying to eat less red meat, and many people find them quite tasty. "They're always in my freezer," says Dr. Anderson. "If I want a last-minute sandwich, I just pop one in my toaster oven and fix it like a burger." Top with nonfat garnishes such as sliced tomatoes, onions, lettuce and mustard—hold the cheese.

### Eating away from Home

• Defat fast-food meals, says Hermann. "For breakfast, you could order a nonfat muffin and a container of skim milk," she suggests.

"Order a salad for lunch or dinner." But beware: Some fast-food chains' salad dressings contain as much fat and more calories than a plain hamburger, says Hermann. So ask for low-calorie, low-fat dressing or use the higher-fat version sparingly, she advises. Nix the bacon bits, too.

• Order foods low-fat, and be as specific as possible when giving the server detailed preparation guidelines, advises Sue Chapman, executive chef at the Skylonda Fitness Retreat in Woodside, California. "If you say 'no butter,' the chef may think that lots of olive oil is okay," she says. "And if you say 'no oil,' he might sprinkle the dish with cheese. So say something very specific, such as 'No butter, oil or fat of any kind.'"

### The Secret to Living Low-Fat—And Loving It

• Don't let fat grams rule your life. Curbing your fat intake doesn't mean you can't indulge your "fat tooth" occasionally, says Janet Lepke, R.D., a dietitian in Santa Monica, California, and a spokesperson for the American Dietetic Association.

"You can eat your favorite foods within the framework of a low-fat diet," she says.

*See also* Desserts, Eggs, Lean Meat, Low-Fat and Nonfat Cheeses, Margarine, Skim Milk, Vegetables, Yogurt, part 4, part 5

∾❧∽

# MARGARINE

## *Avoid the Great Trans Wreck*

We ate 43 percent less butter in the 1980s than we did in the 1960s. About three of every four of us spread margarine on our morning toast. Most Americans, it seems, have gotten the message: If you're watching your cholesterol, abandon butter and make the switch to margarine.

Confident that we were doing our hearts a favor, many of us did just that. Then the news . . . well, spread that margarine might not be so great after all. There's some evidence to suggest that trans-fatty acids, a type of fat found primarily in margarine, raise "bad" LDL cholesterol, lower "good" HDL cholesterol and increase the risk of heart attack.

The jury is still out on the health risks posed by trans-fatty acids. But there is good news about margarine. Some experts, including the American Heart Association, still say that it's better to opt for margarine over butter. Why? Because butter has more artery-clogging saturated fat, which has been proven to elevate blood cholesterol and raise the risk of heart disease.

"Studies show that while both trans-fatty acids and saturated fat increase LDL cholesterol, saturated fat has a greater effect on cholesterol," says Alicia Moag-Stahlberg, R.D., a dietitian in Chicago and a spokesperson for the American Dietetic Association. Further, we consume far more saturated fat. "About 3 percent of our total calories come from trans-fatty acids, compared with 12 to 13 percent from saturated fat," says Moag-Stahlberg.

Don't slather margarine over every baked potato or piece of toast, though. Experts advise consuming all fats—margarine included—in moderation.

## The Pumped-Up Fat

Like butter, margarine is 100 percent fat. But the fat in margarine is primarily unsaturated, which is normally easier on your coronary arteries than saturated fat. Butter contains about seven grams of saturated fat per tablespoon; margarine, about two grams per tablespoon.

So what's the problem? Trans-fatty acids, a by-product of innovations in food technology. Margarine is made mostly from unsaturated oils—corn, canola and safflower, to name a few. Unsaturated oils are liquid at room temperature. To solidify these unsaturated oils, manufacturers pump them up with hydrogen in a chemical process called hydrogenation. "Hydrogenation makes fats harder," says Sheah Rarback, R.D., director of nutrition at the University of Miami School of Medicine's Mailman Center. "A stick margarine is more hydrogenated than a soft tub margarine, for example."

Hydrogenation also creates trans-fatty acids. Ironically, when unsaturated fatty acids are chemically combined with hydrogen, they become more saturated.

The margarine controversy began some years ago, when a Dutch study found that trans-fatty acids elevate cholesterol levels. Some experts noted that the people in the three-week study consumed about four times more trans-fatty acids than the average American. But subsequent studies added fuel to the trans-fat fire, suggesting that smaller levels of trans-fats could help clog coronary arteries.

Perhaps the most persuasive of these investigations was the Nurses' Health Study at Harvard Medical School, which analyzed the health habits of about 87,000 women. The study concluded that women who ate four or more teaspoons (or pats) of margarine a day were 66 percent more likely to develop heart disease than women who consumed less than one teaspoon of margarine a month.

But international studies show that societies that eat the most butter have higher heart attack rates, says William P. Castelli, M.D., medical director of the Framingham Cardiovascular Institute, a wellness program at Metro West Medical Center in Framingham, Massachusetts. On the other hand, he says, a highly regarded clinical trial called the Finnish Hospital Study found that people who ate margarine lowered their cholesterol by about 15 percent and cut their heart attack rates roughly in half over a six-year period compared with people who ate butter.

## Select the Healthiest Spread

Ready to get rid of your margarine and renew your love affair with butter? Not so fast. For now, say experts, your best bet is to cut back on saturated fat, including butter. If you're still using butter, switching to margarine can be a good start. "You will dramatically lower your intake of saturated fat and your intake of trans-fatty acids, since many margarines have lower levels of trans-fatty acids than butter," says Dr. Castelli.

But with so many varieties of margarine to choose from, picking a truly heart-healthy product can be tricky. These guidelines can help.

• First and foremost, select a margarine that contains no more than two grams of saturated fat per tablespoon, advises the American Heart Association. "Choose only margarines that list water as the first

---

# THE FULL SPREAD ON MARGARINE

Regular margarine. Diet margarine. Margarine-butter blends. What sets them all apart? More than you'd think. This guide, with the most healthful options leading the list, can help you sort out the spreads.

***Powdered butter.*** You can sprinkle this nonfat alternative over moist, hot foods such as vegetables and pasta.

***Diet margarine.*** These products, also known as light margarine, contain high amounts of water and weigh in at about half of the fat and calories of regular margarine. Also, they frequently contain fewer trans-fatty acids than butter.

***Regular margarine.*** These products get 100 percent of calories from fat, but the fat is primarily polyunsaturated. Also, most varieties are cholesterol-free.

***Vegetable oil spreads.*** These products typically contain less than 80 percent fat by weight. But according to some experts, they may not be any better than regular margarine.

***Margarine-butter blends.*** These products typically contain from 15 to 40 percent butter, so they are likely to have more saturated fat and cholesterol than regular margarine. "They should be avoided," says William P. Castelli, M.D., medical director of the Framingham Cardio-vascular Institute, a wellness program at Metro West Medical Center in Framingham, Massachusetts.

---

ingredient," advises Dr. Castelli. These products will be low in trans-fatty acids as well as in saturated fat, he explains. "And avoid margarine that lists partially hydrogenated vegetable oil as the first ingredient," he says.

• Avoid stick margarine; it tends to be highly hydrogenated. Opt for soft, tub-style margarine instead. "The softer the margarine, the lower its content of trans-fatty acids and saturated fat," says Alice H. Lichtenstein, D.Sc., assistant professor of nutrition at Tufts University in Medford, Massachusetts, and a scientist at the Jean Mayer USDA Human Nutrition Research Center on Aging in Boston.

• Select a brand with the highest percentage of polyunsaturated fat, advises Dr. Lichtenstein. You might opt for products made from safflower, sunflower, corn or soybean oil.

• If possible, select a liquid or semiliquid spread, particularly for cooking, says Dr. Lichtenstein. When she compared three different diets—a baseline diet with 35 percent of calories from fat, a corn oil margarine–enriched diet with 30 percent of calories from fat and a liquid corn oil–enriched diet with 30 percent of calories from fat—the liquid corn oil was found to cut LDL cholesterol by 17 percent compared with the baseline diet. The corn oil margarine cut LDL by 10 percent compared with baseline.

• Spare the spread altogether. "We've been raised to think that we should smear something on our toast," says Dr. Lichtenstein. "But if we eat tasty bread, we may not need to." Another option: Top your toast with a small amount of jelly or jam, which contains no saturated fat.

• Avoid products that contain *partially hydrogenated vegetable oil,* another term for trans-fatty acids. "In particular, watch out for fried foods, cakes and cookies," says Dr. Lichtenstein.

• Consume all fat in moderation, says Dr. Lichtenstein. "If you're concerned about obesity, heart disease and cancer, the point is to cut as much fat as possible out of your diet," she says.

✌

# MEAL FREQUENCY

## *Nibble Away at High Cholesterol*

It sounds too good to be true: being able to eat all day long and lower your blood cholesterol in the process. But there's some evidence that "grazing"—eating many small meals or snacks throughout the day rather than the more customary three squares a day—can help shave a few points off your cholesterol level.

But don't confuse eating more often with consuming more calories, say experts. Grazing on hot fudge sundaes and hero sandwiches will benefit neither your cholesterol level nor your shape. "We're recommending not that people eat more calories but that they divide their daily caloric intakes into smaller meals," says Elizabeth Barrett-Connor, M.D., professor and chair of the Department of Family Medicine at the University of California, San Diego.

The good news is, studies indicate that the cholesterol-lowering benefits of eating smaller, more frequent meals seem to take effect without changing your overall diet. How's that for a dream come true?

## It Pays to Graze

Grazing may be the natural way to eat, says Dr. Barrett-Connor. "We evolved from people who ate frequent, small meals when they could," she says. "Occasionally, they would get a big kill and gorge. But Americans gorge nearly every night—and that's an unhealthy way to eat."

The body manages smaller meals more efficiently, explains Sharon Edelstein, a research scientist at George Washington University in Washington, D.C. "Humans were meant to be grazers, and that's the way our bodies perform best," she says. "If you pound your body with a lot of food once or twice a day, you may be giving it too much to deal with. If you put food into your body more slowly, you'll process it more efficiently."

Dr. Barrett-Connor agrees. "Eating more meals consisting of less food is more physiologically efficient," she says. "If you throw large amounts of fat and calories at the body all at once, it won't be able to manage them as well. It's more than the body can metabolize." So fueling up only once or twice a day may make it easier for dietary fat to collect in the coronary arteries, leading to elevated cholesterol levels, says Dr. Barrett-Connor.

If you'd like more evidence that eating smaller portions may affect heart health, Marla Mendelson, M.D., assistant professor of medicine at Northwestern University Medical School in Chicago, suggests looking at countries that have lower incidences of cardiovascular disease than the United States, such as Japan and China. "The people in these countries eat smaller portions," says Dr. Mendelson. "This may aid the digestive process, so you're not completely overwhelming the mechanism in the liver with too much food and asking the liver to process it." Overloading the liver may eventually cause free-floating fat and cholesterol to be deposited in the arteries, she says.

## Four (or More) Meals Are Better Than One

Researchers found that when monkeys, rats and rabbits ate large, infrequent meals rather than small, frequent ones, their blood cholesterol increased. Multiple feedings resulted in reduced heart disease risk factors—and longer lives, says Dr. Barrett-Connor.

Studies conducted on humans appear to bear out the conclusions of the animal research. Edelstein and Dr. Barrett-Connor, along with other colleagues, studied the diets of more than 2,000 people. They found that the total cholesterol of individuals who ate four or more meals a day was almost nine points lower than those who reported eating one or two meals a day, says Dr. Barrett-Connor. Also, the frequent eaters' "bad" LDL cholesterol averaged six points lower than that of the infrequent eaters, she says. And while the grazers tended to consume more fat, calories and cholesterol than the two-meal group, their blood cholesterol was still lower, and they were less likely to be obese.

Researchers in New Zealand had 19 healthy men and women with normal blood cholesterol levels consume their usual low-fat diets—with one difference: These folks alternated between eating three meals a day and eating nine meals a day. They spent two weeks on each diet. When these individuals followed the nine-meal plan, their total cholesterol fell 6.5 percent, and their LDL cholesterol dropped 8.1 percent. If every 1 percent change in total cholesterol translates to a 2 percent change in the risk of coronary heart disease, wrote the researchers, "then theoretically, there could be a mean 13 percent reduction in the risk of coronary heart disease when meal frequency is increased from three to nine meals a day."

When Canadian researchers had seven men consume 17 small meals or snacks a day, these individuals' total and LDL cholesterol fell 8.5 percent and 13.5 percent, respectively. The researchers theorized that the smaller meals caused the body to produce less insulin, which in turn decreased levels of a certain enzyme needed by the liver to process cholesterol.

### Eat Like a Bird—All Day

Thinking of joining the graze craze? These tips can help.

• People who eat breakfast generally eat more meals a day than people who don't, says Dr. Barrett-Connor. "Breakfast-eaters also are more likely to snack throughout the day than people who diet all day long and eat gigantic dinners," she says. In fact, people who skip breakfast to "save" calories end up spending them—with interest—in the long run. "Their bodies store up fat for the famine they think is coming," says Dr. Barrett-Connor.

• Many weight-control experts recommend that people eat a small snack between meals and another snack before bedtime, says Dr. Barrett-Connor. Snacking between meals provides the body with the same amount of calories but is more physiologically efficient, she says. "Avoid foods high in fat or sugar—they have no nutritional value," advises Dr. Barrett-Connor. "Fruits and vegetables are great choices."

# MEDITERRANEAN DIET

## *Eat Like Zorba to Heal Your Heart*

Pasta redolent with garlic and drizzled with olive oil. Vegetable stew bursting with sun-ripened eggplant and seasoned with herbs. Fresh seafood and hearty bean salad. And hunks of crusty bread to sop up every last drop of sauce or vinaigrette.

Are you salivating yet? Well, go ahead and *mangia*, because eating like this can actually be good for your heart. Just ask the Mediterraneans. The folks in the countries along the Mediterranean Sea—Italy, Greece, southern France and Spain, to be exact—tend to be a little healthier and live a little longer than people in northern Europe and the United States. Consider these facts.

• According to the World Health Organization, French men and women have a lower than usual incidence of heart attack. So do Italians, especially Italian women.

• In 1990, 243 men and 132 women per 100,000 people in the United States died of heart disease, according to World Health Organization statistics. The same figures for Italy were 139 men and 64 women per 100,000; for Spain, 106 and 47; for Greece, 137 and 59; and for France, 91 and 40. Quite a comparison.

• On average, Greeks live three years longer than Americans (74.3 versus 71.6 years).

What makes the Mediterranean diet so healthy? First, individual components of traditional Mediterranean dishes—garlic, olive oil, grains, beans—have cholesterol-lowering powers of their own. And second, this diet brings together these components in a cuisine now respected for its healthy ways.

## Lessons from the Southern Rim

The first to pick up on the Mediterranean mystique was Ancel Keys, Ph.D., of the School of Public Health at the University of Minnesota in Minneapolis, who along with his colleagues launched the Seven Countries Study. Begun in the late 1950s, this benchmark study sought to prove a link between diet and coronary heart disease in almost 13,000 middle-age men throughout the Mediterranean, Northern Europe, Japan and the United States.

After a lengthy follow-up period, Dr. Keys, now professor emeritus of public health at the University of Minnesota, and his team discovered that men from Italy and Greece—especially Greece—died less often from coronary heart disease than men from Finland, northern Europe and the United States.

What Dr. Keys hypothesized decades ago has been embraced by a multitude of eminent medical experts: Diet and heart health are inextricably linked.

But what do Mediterranean people eat—or not eat—that seems to protect their tickers? "The specifics may vary from one Mediterranean country to another, but in general, these populations eat less red meat and more fish," says Barbara Levine, R.D., Ph.D., associate clinical

## THE MEDITERRANEAN DIET PYRAMID

The Harvard School of Public Health, the Oldways Preservational and Exchange Trust and the World Health Organization Regional Office for Europe have endorsed the Mediterranean Diet Pyramid. This dietary model, an alternative to the U.S. Department of Agriculture (USDA) Food Guide Pyramid, is modeled on the traditional diets of the Mediterranean region around 1960 (before heavy influences of other nations).

The first two levels of the Mediterranean pyramid and the USDA pyramid are similar. Breads, cereals and grains comprise the "base" of each model, while fruits and vegetables comprise the next largest segments.

Then the two plans diverge. The USDA pyramid recommends two to three servings of meat, poultry and fish (along with dried beans, eggs and nuts) per day, while the Mediterranean pyramid recommends that poultry and fish be consumed a few times a week and red meat only a few times a month.

Further, the USDA pyramid recommends that fats and oils be used "sparingly." The Mediterranean pyramid recommends the liberal use of olive oil virtually to the exclusion of all other fats, especially saturated fats such as butter and margarine.

professor of nutrition in medicine at Cornell University Medical College in New York City. Mediterraneans also eat fewer fat-laden dairy products and more fruits, vegetables and grains than Americans. "To eat like Mediterraneans, you'd consume half as much whole milk, cream and butter and 45 percent less red meat," says Dr. Levine. Further, Mediterraneans tend to drink more red wine, which when consumed in moderation can boost levels of HDL, the "good" cholesterol, and limit the risk of heart disease. (See *"Salut*—In Moderation" on page 136.)

"Mediterranean people are also more physically active than Americans," notes Audrey Cross, Ph.D., associate clinical professor at Columbia University's Institute of Human Nutrition in New York City. "They ride bicycles to work or walk when we might drive, which tends to decrease both their incidence of obesity and their rate of cardiovascular disease."

---

### *SALUT*—IN MODERATION

In Italy, France and Greece, a bottle of red wine is as much a part of a meal as the robust cuisine and the hearty laughter around the table. But if you don't drink, don't start for the sake of your heart, say experts.

"I advise people to limit their intakes of alcohol to seven drinks a week," says James W. Anderson, M.D., professor of medicine and clinical nutrition at the University of Kentucky College of Medicine in Lexington and author of *Dr. Anderson's High-Fiber Fitness Plan.* (A drink is frequently defined as 4 ounces of wine, 12 ounces of beer or 1½ ounces of liquor.)

Should you opt to enjoy an occasional glass of vino, no need to fret about the wine's year or its bouquet—or its color, for that matter. Red and white wine may be equally beneficial for raising "good" HDL cholesterol, according to Tom Watkins, Ph.D., laboratory director of the Kenneth L. Jordan Heart Foundation and Research Center in Montclair, New Jersey. And when it comes to wine's apparent heart-healthy benefits, he continues, an inexpensive California Chablis is just as good as the priciest French Bordeaux.

---

## A Prudent—But Not Spartan—Cuisine

Thus, a number of factors appear to contribute to the Mediterranean people's health and longevity. But perhaps the biggest reason for this region's notable dearth of heart disease, some experts theorize, is its reliance on monounsaturated rather than saturated fat.

The traditional Mediterranean diet averages 35 to 40 percent of total calories from fat. So does the typical American diet. But the American diet is laden with artery-clogging saturated fat, found in animal-derived foods such as red meat, in whole-milk dairy products and in processed convenience foods. Mediterranean cuisine, on the other hand, tends to be richer in artery-saving monounsaturated fat, particularly olive oil. In the Mediterranean region, the per capita consumption of olive oil has averaged as high as two to three tablespoons per day. The typical American, on the other hand, consumes about three tablespoons of olive oil every four months. But given the popularity of low-fat cooking and a cholesterol-conscious population, we might use more olive oil in the near future.

In an editorial in the *New England Journal of Medicine*, Walter Willett, M.D., Dr.P.H., professor of epidemiology and nutrition at the Harvard School of Public Health, and his colleague Frank M. Sacks, M.D., associate professor of medicine and nutrition, endorsed the traditional Mediterranean diet, saying that it's just as low in saturated fat and cholesterol as a typical low-fat diet. "The Mediterranean alternative—using monounsaturated fat as a major dietary component—appears to be at least as healthful" as following a low-fat diet, they wrote, and "may be an even better way to improve (blood cholesterol levels)." Further, they wrote, eating the Mediterranean way "will provide more variety and greater satisfaction to many." That's good news for those of us with higher-than-average cholesterol—and hearty appetites.

## Eat as in Rome—At Home

If you're used to a diet of beef and butter, the Mediterranean diet may seem a little . . . well, foreign. But many Americans have found that Mediterranean cuisine is as delicious and inexpensive as it is health promoting. Here's how to add the Mediterranean touch to your table.

• Eat less red meat. "In Italy, the focus of the meal is pasta, and meat is more of a side dish," says Wahida Karmally, R.D., director of nutrition at the Irving Center for Clinical Research at Columbia-Presbyterian Medical Center in New York City and a member of the American Heart Association's nutrition committee. "By following the Italian approach and consuming less meat, you can reduce your intake of saturated fat."

• Replace butter and other saturated fats with monounsaturated fat, particularly olive oil. Drizzle this fragrant oil over pasta, steamed vegetables and baked potatoes, for example. Or use it to sauté onions and vegetables. Better yet, use an olive oil cooking spray.

• Eat more fresh vegetables. They're packed with cholesterol-reducing soluble fiber and antioxidant vitamins, which experts speculate may help keep "bad" LDL cholesterol from a damaging chemical reaction called oxidation. (Oxidized LDL becomes stickier and clings to artery walls, experts theorize.) Prepare a French-style ratatouille (an eggplant-based vegetable stew) by simmering onions, eggplant, zucchini and tomatoes with herbs and spices. Serve with crusty French bread, sans butter.

• Consume more whole grains, advises James W. Anderson, M.D., professor of medicine and clinical nutrition at the University of Kentucky College of Medicine in Lexington and author of *Dr. Anderson's High-Fiber Fitness Plan.* Many varieties, such as barley and oats, are packed with soluble fiber. Try whole-wheat pasta rather than the white-flour variety, suggests Dr. Anderson. Or you might try combining seasoned vegetables with bulgur or couscous (which contains more fiber than white rice) to make a spicy Spanish-style pilaf.

• Eat more legumes. Chick-peas, lentils and white beans, mainstays of Mediterranean cuisine, are great sources of low-fat protein and are rich in soluble fiber. Try the classic Italian dish *pasta e fagioli* (pasta with beans) or enjoy a French-style white-bean salad.

• Use more garlic. Besides adding its distinctive flavor and aroma to foods, this aromatic herb may contain certain components that help lower cholesterol. Add minced garlic to pasta dishes, soups and stews, sauces and grilled fish. Or whip up a pot of garlic broth, a popular French staple. Peel and slice six cloves of garlic. Place them in a one-quart saucepan with two cups of water, one bay leaf, one tablespoon of olive oil and some fresh sage. Simmer for 15 minutes, strain into mugs and enjoy.

• Italians like to taste their pasta. So don't overload this inherently healthy dish with fatty sauces or toppings. "Use marinara sauce (a meatless tomato sauce) rather then heavy meat sauces and cheeses," advises Dr. Anderson. Or toss with lightly steamed vegetables—broccoli, zucchini, red peppers—and fresh basil and add a little Parmesan for pasta primavera.

• Don't overdo the olive oil. "Olive oil is a fat," stresses Tammy Baker, R.D., a nutritionist in Cave Creek, Arizona, and a spokesperson for the American Dietetic Association. "Just because it's a monounsaturated fat doesn't mean you should use a lot of it. Your best bet is to get 30 percent or less of your total calories from fat."

*See also* Alcohol, Antioxidants, Exercise, Fish, Garlic, Monounsaturated Fat, Olive Oil, Wine

෧ᴥ᥊ᵕᵎ

# MONOUNSATURATED FAT
## *All Fats Are Not Created Evil*

Back in the good old days, when there was a pork chop on every plate and butter on every baked potato, not many Americans worried about dietary fat. Times sure have changed. Virtually everyone now knows that eating too much fat is hard on the heart as well as on the hips.

But as you may have heard, one type of fat—monounsaturated fat—isn't so fiendish after all. Monounsaturated fat generally maintains or even raises heart-saving HDL cholesterol while it scuttles "bad" LDL cholesterol. The difference between saturated fat, which contributes to the waxy buildup in arteries, and artery-scrubbing monounsaturated fat is primarily a matter of chemistry. (More about this in a minute.)

Make no mistake, though: Monounsaturated fat is still fat, and doctors generally advise cutting back on all fat, including the monounsaturated kind. Still, it's nice to know that not all fat is strictly off-limits. Here's what you need to know about mono.

## Why Nuts Are Better Than Nachos

Why bake with canola oil rather than butter? Or snack on a handful of nuts rather than the same amount of chips? The answer lies in fats' chemical makeup.

All fats are made up of carbon, hydrogen and oxygen atoms. Saturated fat is found primarily in red meat, whole-milk dairy products and the tropical oils (coconut and palm oils). This type of fat is stuffed, or saturated, with the maximum amount of hydrogen atoms and is usually solid at room temperature. Unsaturated fat, which includes both monounsaturated fat (abundant in olive and canola oils, along with certain plant foods such as nuts and avocados) and polyunsaturated fat (plentiful in corn, sunflower and safflower oils) contain fewer hydrogen atoms. The less-dense unsaturated fats are usually liquid at room temperature.

Most foods contain varying amounts of saturated, polyunsaturated and monounsaturated fats. Most doctors would agree, though, that cholesterol-conscious folks would do well to cut back on foods laden with saturated fat. In fact, some doctors believe that the Mediterranean region's reliance on mono-rich olive oil, coupled with its limited consumption of saturated fat, contributes to the Mediterranean people's unusually healthy hearts and squeaky-clean arteries. Further, several physicians from Harvard School of Public Health, along with the World Health Organization Regional Office for Europe and the Oldways Preservational and Exchange Trust, have endorsed the traditional Mediterranean way of eating as a healthy alternative to the typical saturated fat–soaked American diet.

## These Oils Foil Blood Fats

Study after study points to monounsaturated fat's cholesterol-pounding power. In Spain, researchers put 78 men and women on a diet enriched with sunflower oil. After 12 weeks, these individuals switched to an olive oil–based diet. Total cholesterol hadn't budged in the men after an additional four months and had increased 9 percent in the women, who followed the diet for seven months. But hold on: The olive oil plan also significantly increased these folks' HDL cholesterol—by 17 percent in the men and 30 percent in the women.

In another study, researchers in Israel put 17 young men on one of two diets. The first group followed a diet rich in monounsaturated fat (olive oil, avocados and almonds). The second group consumed a carbohydrate-based diet. Both diets contained similar levels of saturated and polyunsaturated fats. After three months, the men consuming the mono-rich diet switched to the carbohydrate-rich plan, and vice versa.

After another 90 days, the researchers tested the men's blood cholesterol. The researchers' findings? When the men followed the mono-rich diet, their total cholesterol fell by nearly 8 percent, and their LDL levels plunged about 14 percent. No such beneficial changes occurred while the men were following the carbo-based plan.

## A Fat by Any Other Name

No doubt about it: Replacing the saturated fat in your diet with unsaturated oils can do your heart good. But don't go hog-wild even on monounsaturated fats, advise experts. "Don't pour them over foods," says Michael Klaper, M.D., health director at the Royal Atlantic Health Spa in Pompano Beach, Florida, and author of *Vegan Nutrition: Pure and Simple*. "I generally recommend using a tablespoon or two a day at most."

A little bit of oil can go a long way, however. You might drizzle a bit of olive oil on a crusty piece of Italian bread for lunch and use the remaining allotment on your salad at dinner. Or lightly coat a skillet with it. "Rather than pouring olive oil in the pan, just brush the bottom with a light coat of oil," suggests Dr. Klaper.

You may want to think twice before using peanut oil, however. While this oil is primarily monounsaturated, "some studies show that peanut oil may promote arterial disease, at least in rabbits," says Evelyn Tribole, R.D., a dietitian in Beverly Hills, California, and author of *Healthy Homestyle Cooking*.

The bottom line: "Don't increase your intake of monounsaturated fat. Decrease your consumption of saturated fat," advises Tribole. "And if you pay attention to food labels, it's so easy to cut back."

*See also* Canola Oil, Mediterranean Diet, Olive Oil, Polyunsaturated Fat

# MUSHROOMS

## *Take a Tip from the Japanese*

Stuffed, stir-fried or sautéed, mild or robust, mushrooms are both familiar and mysterious. While you may remember when smooth, creamy white button mushrooms routinely topped a T-bone, you've no doubt noticed more exotic fungi in the produce section of the local grocery store.

But mushrooms may be more than just another food fad or salad fixin'. Long believed by the Japanese to help prevent and treat cancer, mushrooms—namely, the common button mushroom and the rich-tasting shiitake mushroom—may also help lower cholesterol, according to several studies. Research to date on mushrooms' potential cholesterol-cutting powers has been limited but intriguing.

## The Magic of Mushrooms

Wouldn't have guessed that mushrooms might contain cholesterol-cutting powers? That's understandable; after all, these pungent vegetables are about 90 percent water. But the remaining 10 percent contains a mother lode of nutrients, including potassium, calcium, riboflavin, niacin and iron.

What's more, some mushrooms are rich in protein and contain all of the essential amino acids. Essential amino acids, which are necessary for life, can't be manufactured by our bodies; we have to obtain them from food. Mushrooms also contain phytochemicals, or plant substances that may help fight disease, according to Robert Beelman, Ph.D., professor of food science at Pennsylvania State University in University Park.

Since the late 1960s, researchers at the National Institute of Nutrition in Tokyo have conducted tests on the effectiveness of shiitake mushrooms on blood cholesterol. In one study, researchers had young women eat 90 grams of fresh shiitake mushrooms (about five mushrooms) a day. Their average cholesterol level declined 12 percent in a week. The researchers conducted a similar experiment with 30 people over age 60, and these individuals' cholesterol levels fell 9 percent in a week.

In another study, also conducted at the National Institute of Nutrition, researchers had people add 60 grams of butter a day to their diets. These butter-laden diets raised their cholesterol by 14 percent in a week. These folks then consumed 90 grams of shiitake mushrooms a day along with their butter-rich diets. After a week, their average cholesterol level dipped 4 percent.

# Fungi Power—Experts' Tasty Tips

While the jury is still out on mushrooms' power to lower choles-terol, these earthy-tasting vegetables can enliven almost any dish, from casseroles to stir-fries. Try these delicious suggestions. *Caution:* Never eat wild mushrooms.

• Select mushrooms with smooth, unblemished caps, because they're the freshest, says Mindy Hermann, R.D., a nutrition consultant in Mount Kisco, New York.

• Toss sautéed mushrooms with white or brown rice. And forgo the butter or margarine: You can sauté three to four cups of mush-rooms in a teaspoon of oil in a no-stick skillet on medium heat, says Nancy Baggett, author of *100% Pleasure: The Low-Fat Cookbook for People Who Love to Eat.*

• Add shiitake mushrooms to stews, vegetable dishes or pasta, suggests Faye Levy, author of *Faye Levy's International Vegetable Cookbook.*

• Use sautéed mushrooms as a topping for chicken, says Evelyn Tribole, R.D., a dietitian in Beverly Hills, California, and author of *Healthy Homestyle Cooking.* "Or fold them into an egg-white omelet," she says.

• Don't add mushrooms in the early stages of preparing a cooked dish, advises Connie Diekman, R.D., a dietitian in St. Louis and a spokesperson for the American Dietetic Association; they can become tough and flavorless. "Add mushrooms toward the end of cooking," she says. "You'll still get the flavor of the raw mushrooms, and they'll be slightly tender."

• Add finely diced mushrooms to tomato sauce, suggests Tribole. "If you chop them very finely, they actually take on the texture of ground beef," she says.

• For a unique main dish, serve grilled portobello mushrooms, suggests Mona Sutnick, R.D., Ed.D., a dietitian in Philadelphia and a spokesperson for the American Dietetic Association. "Portobellos are a meaty sort of mushroom, and their caps are four to seven inches across," she says. "A restaurant in Philadelphia grills them and serves them with polenta and herbs."

~❧~

# OATS

## *Brimming Bowls of Goodness*

**R**emember the oat bran craze of the late 1980s? Reacting to several encouraging medical studies—and resulting newspaper headlines—cholesterol-conscious people began eating oat bran by the bowlful. Food manufacturers, reacting to our sudden enthusiasm for all things oat bran, added it to just about everything. (Some bakeries were even selling oat bran doughnuts!)

Then as suddenly as it began, it seemed, our oat bran mania died, a casualty of more headlines. This time, they reported, a study had concluded that oat bran is no better at lowering blood cholesterol than white bread.

End of story? No. Oats do appear to cause a modest reduction in blood cholesterol, and experts say that oats can be a valuable part of a low-fat diet. But when it comes to lowering blood cholesterol, no one food is a magic bullet. Eating a diet low in fat—especially saturated fat—is still one of the best ways to lower your blood cholesterol, say experts.

### Stick with It

Oats contain lots of soluble fiber, the kind proven to reduce "bad" LDL cholesterol. "When you cook oats, they're sticky," says Kay Stanfill, R.D., adjunct assistant professor in the Department of Nutritional Sciences at the University of Oklahoma Health Sciences Center in Oklahoma City. "That sticky, gelatinous matter is soluble fiber."

Barley, beans and many fruits and vegetables also contain soluble fiber. But there is something unique about oats' cholesterol-busting ability, says James W. Anderson, M.D., professor of medicine and clinical nutrition at the University of Kentucky College of Medicine in Lexington and author of *Dr. Anderson's High-Fiber Fitness Plan.* "While oat bran and beans have roughly equivalent overall cholesterol-lowering effects, oat bran preserves HDL cholesterol (the 'good' kind) a little better," he says.

## The Proof Is in the Porridge

Researchers have conducted a number of studies on the association between consuming oat bran and lower blood cholesterol levels. Investigators at Northwestern University Medical School in Chicago divided 80 men and women with high cholesterol into two groups. The first group ate two servings (about two ounces per serving) of instant oats a day. The second group stuck to their normal eating habits. After eight weeks, the oat group's total cholesterol had declined by about 15 milligrams/deciliter.

At the University of Kentucky College of Medicine, 20 men with high cholesterol consumed diets supplemented with either oat bran or wheat bran, both of which were added to cereal and muffins. After three weeks, the total cholesterol of the men eating oat bran had fallen 12.8 percent, and their LDL cholesterol had declined 12.1 percent. The men who consumed wheat bran saw no such declines in cholesterol.

In an attempt to summarize the existing research on oat bran and cholesterol, researchers from all over the world, including the United States, pooled data from ten studies and 1,300 people. The researchers found that people who ate three grams of the soluble fiber found in oat bran a day (equal to about 1⅓ bowls of oat bran cereal) saw their blood cholesterol fall an average of nearly six milligrams/deciliter in three months or less. What's more, the individuals who began with the highest cholesterol readings (230 milligrams/deciliter or more) experienced the greatest decreases in blood cholesterol—an average decline of 16 milligrams/deciliter.

## Five Ways to Feel Your Oats

Want to add oat bran to your diet? These tips can help.

• Choose a whole-oat product, advises Stanfill. "Look for the words 'rolled oats,' 'steel-cut oats,' 'Irish oats' or 'oat bran,'" she says. Instant oatmeal probably isn't a whole-oat product, she adds.

• Top a bowl of oat bran or oatmeal with a low-fat, low-cholesterol topping such as skim milk, fresh fruit or even a dollop or two of nonfat flavored yogurt.

• Try adding a small amount of oat bran to other dishes, suggests Dr. Anderson. "You can mix oat bran or oatmeal into ground-meat dishes, casseroles and pancakes," he says.

• Bake your own oat bran muffins using low-fat ingredients, including skim milk, egg substitute and unsaturated oil instead of butter. Try using ¾ cup of oat bran for every ¼ cup of flour in a 12-muffin recipe. For extra-tasty muffins, try adding a small amount of crushed pineapple to the mix, suggests Dr. Anderson.

Be wary of store-bought oat bran muffins. "They can contain a lot of fat," says Robert J. Nicolosi, Ph.D., director of the Cardiovascular Disease Control Center at the University of Lowell in Massachusetts. "The ideal way to get fiber is through grains and cereals."

• Don't expect a bowl of oat bran to compensate for a fat-laden diet. "All of the soluble fiber in the world isn't going to compensate for eating too much saturated fat," notes Linda Van Horn, R.D., Ph.D., associate professor of preventive medicine at Northwestern University Medical School.

∾❈↲

# OLIVE OIL

## *The Leading Good-for-You Fat*

Olive oil: golden essence of the Mediterranean. Nectar of the gods. Cholesterol crusher.

This fragrant oil, touted by the great Greek physician Hippocrates as a natural remedy over 2,000 years ago, is brimming with monounsaturated fat, which tends to cut heart-threatening LDL cholesterol while it preserves—or even raises—heart-saving HDL cholesterol.

One study suggests that the monounsaturated fat in olive oil may actually change the chemical composition of HDL cholesterol, making it better at routing LDL. No wonder some heart experts have recommended substituting olive oil for the artery-clogging saturated fat that plagues the typical American diet.

But make no mistake: Drowning your food in olive oil will not protect your heart from the ravages of ribs, french fries and rocky road ice cream, maintain experts. Too much of any fat—even monounsaturated fat—can wreak havoc on your cholesterol level, not to mention your waistline.

The good news is, a little bit of olive oil yields a lot of flavor. What's more, you're likely to find that this golden oil tastes delicious on everything from corn on the cob to crusty peasant bread. Here's how to "Mediterraneanize" your menu and help protect your heart.

## The Mediterranean Miracle

Not surprisingly, people in the Mediterranean region, where most olive oil is produced and enthusiastically consumed, have reaped the greatest health benefits from olive oil—a phenomenon first proven by Ancel Keys, Ph.D., professor emeritus of public health in the School of Public Health at the University of Minnesota in Minneapolis. In the Seven Countries Study—a seminal study dating back to the 1950s—Keys discovered that while Italian, Greek and other Mediterranean men consumed almost as much dietary fat as Americans, they consumed most of that fat in the form of olive oil. Keys associated the Mediterraneans' consumption of monounsaturated fat, particularly olive oil, with their lower rates of heart disease.

More recent studies have reached similar conclusions about the cholesterol-busting powers of olive oil. Researchers at the Universidad Autonoma de Madrid in Spain had 21 pre- and postmenopausal women follow a high-fat diet for four months. For the first month of the study, the women ate a diet high in saturated fat (such as butter) and lower in polyunsaturated and monounsaturated fats. For the next six weeks, the women followed an olive oil–rich diet lower in saturated and polyunsaturated fats. And for six weeks after that, the women consumed a diet rich in sunflower oil (a polyunsaturated fat) and lower in monounsaturated and saturated fats.

The women's total and LDL cholesterol fell on both the olive oil and sunflower oil diets. But their HDL cholesterol increased only on the olive oil diet—and fell on the sunflower oil diet.

In another study, researchers at the University of Nijmegen in the Netherlands had 48 healthy people follow a high-fat diet. Then for five weeks, half of these folks followed a low-fat diet (22 percent of calories from fat). The other half consumed a high-fat diet (41 percent of calories from fat), but the fat came mostly from monounsaturates such as olive oil.

After a month, both groups' total cholesterol had fallen. But the HDL cholesterol of the folks on the low-fat diet had declined an average of 7.3 milligrams/deciliter, while HDL had actually increased 1.1 milligrams/deciliter in the people who followed the olive oil program.

## An Olive Oil Primer

When it comes to olive oil, a little goes a long way. "Compared with some other oils, olive oil is so flavorful that you can use less of it," says Barbara Levine, R.D., Ph.D., associate clinical professor of nutrition in medicine at Cornell University Medical College in New York City.

Olive oil connoisseurs categorize the flavor of olive oil as mild (with a light or buttery taste), semifruity (a stronger, more olivelike flavor) or fruity (oil with an intense olive flavor). And despite what you may have heard, the color of olive oil has nothing to do with its flavor. Like wine, olive oil gets its unique color, flavor and aroma from the olives used and the climate and soil conditions in which they were grown. So you may want to taste-test olive oil to find the variety and brand most pleasing to your palate.

Here's how to get more olive oil into your diet.

• Spread crusty bread with olive oil rather than butter, suggests Dr. Levine. Or rub a toasted slice of this hearty bread with a piece of garlic, then drizzle the bread with olive oil.

• Dress salads the Mediterranean way—with a small amount of extra-virgin olive oil and a little bit of vinegar, suggests Gene A. Spiller, D.Sc., Ph.D., director of the Health Research and Studies Center in Los Altos, California, and author of *The Superpyramid Eating Program*.

## VERSIONS OF VIRGINS

When it comes to olive oil, "refined" isn't a compliment. Confused? Relax: This guide can help you decipher the labels and select the perfect oil.

***Extra-virgin olive oil.*** Produced in limited quantities, extra-virgin oil is the best and most expensive grade of olive oil that money can buy. Most people use extra-virgin oil, which has an intense fruity or peppery flavor, to flavor foods after they've been cooked rather than as a cooking oil.

***Virgin olive oil.*** The flavor of this oil isn't as perfect as that of extra-virgin oil and is slightly more acidic.

***Olive oil.*** Most people use this blend of refined and virgin oils for cooking.

***"Light" olive oil.*** Perfect for baking, this extra-refined oil has little or no olive taste. But don't be fooled: Light olive oil contains the same amount of fat and calories as other oils.

• Brush corn on the cob with extra-virgin olive oil rather than butter or margarine, suggests Dr. Spiller.

• Add olive oil to sauces, marinades and any other dish in which you want a more robust flavor, says Tammy Baker, R.D., a nutritionist in Cave Creek, Arizona, and a spokesperson for the American Dietetic Association. You might bathe fresh garlic and spinach with a small amount of olive oil spray and sauté in a no-stick skillet, suggests Lynn Fischer, author of *Healthy Indulgences.* Spinach-lovers will enjoy this Sicilian-style dish, says Fischer.

• Bake or sauté fish in olive oil rather than butter, says Dr. Levine. "Olive oil expands in the pan, so you need much less of it," she says.

• Bake with olive oil. Yes, you read right. "People in Italy bake magnificent desserts with olive oil," says Dr. Levine. "You can substitute olive oil for butter, margarine or vegetable shortening in cakes, pies and other desserts." She suggests using a light variety, "so you won't taste olive oil in your dessert." (See "Versions of Virgins.")

• Don't cook with extra-virgin olive oil, advises Dr. Levine. "Heating this oil will accomplish only what's called perfuming the kitchen," she says. "That is, the olive oil goes into the air rather than into the food. Save extra-virgin oil for salads or for drizzling over pasta."

## Before You Get All Oiled Up

Don't forget that olive oil is still 100 percent fat and contains 120 calories per tablespoon. So overusing olive oil may cause you to gain weight—not a heart-smart move, say experts.

"Many people are drowning their foods in olive oil, thinking that they're doing themselves a service," says Karen Miller Kovach, R.D., chief nutritionist at Weight Watchers International in Jericho, New York. But it's better to substitute olive oil for saturated fats such as butter, says Kovach, than to add olive oil to an already high-fat diet.

Dr. Levine agrees. "Don't consume lots of olive oil or any other kind of oil. Anoint your food with a small amount of olive oil, like the Italians do."

*See also* Mediterranean Diet

# ONIONS

## *The Benefits of a Good Cry*

Sure, chopping onions may bring tears to your eyes or start your nose running like a leaky faucet. But those tears and sniffles might be worth it: The same compounds in onions that leave many of us helplessly weepy-eyed may also help wallop elevated blood cholesterol and bust up blood clots that can trigger a heart attack.

There's not yet conclusive proof that onions can help control cholesterol or prevent a heart attack. But investigators continue to be intrigued by the potential health benefits of this odoriferous bulb. In one study, researchers in India had ten men consume 3½ ounces of butter a day, which increased their cholesterol levels. The researchers then added about 2 ounces of juice from raw onions to the men's daily servings of butter. The onion extract prevented the expected rise in cholesterol from the butter. It also increased the men's clot-busting activity almost 16 percent, reducing their risk of heart attacks.

Another Indian study found that cholesterol levels were lowest among people who consumed over 600 grams of onions and 50 grams of garlic a week and highest among individuals who never touched the stuff.

Researchers in the Netherlands found that antioxidant constituents called flavonoids—found in many fruits and vegetables, including onions, tea and apples—reduced the risk of coronary heart disease and heart attack in elderly men, apparently by blocking the formation of clotting compounds in the blood and by interfering with the oxidation of "bad" LDL cholesterol, which leads to the buildup of plaque in the coronary arteries.

## Mild-Mannered Onion Power

Many people love the taste and smell of onions. But if you'd like to tone down their taste—or at least dry up your tears as you slice them—these tips are for you.

• Investigate sweet onions, suggests Connie Diekman, R.D., a dietitian in St. Louis and a spokesperson for the American Dietetic Association. There are several varieties of these mild-tasting onions, such as Vidalia, Walla Walla, Maui and Texas Spring Sweet. "Some people even eat them plain," says Diekman.

• Don't fry onions in oil or butter. Instead, "sauté" them in the microwave, suggests Barbie Casselman, a nutrition consultant in Toronto. Place a sliced onion in a microwave-safe bowl, along with a tablespoon or two of water. Cover the bowl with a plate. Then nuke the covered bowl for three to four minutes. "The onions will be as soft as if they had been sautéed in butter," says Casselman.

• To avoid shedding tears as you slice an onion, "hold it under cold water as you cut," suggests Diekman. Or refrigerate the bulb before you slice it, suggests Mona Sutnick, R.D., Ed.D., a dietitian in Philadelphia and a spokesperson for the American Dietetic Association. They're less pungent when they're chilled first, she says.

⊱✤⊰

# PECTIN

## *The King Fiber*

You may know it as the stuff that puts the jell in jelly. But pectin—a gummy substance found in most fruits and many vegetables—can help wallop elevated cholesterol as well, say experts.

There are two kinds of fiber: soluble and insoluble. Soluble fiber has been proven to help trounce blood cholesterol.

"Like other types of soluble fiber, pectin has the capacity to reduce blood cholesterol levels," says Thomas Bersot, M.D., associate professor of medicine at the University of California, San Francisco. "Pectin may interfere with the body's absorption of cholesterol, which helps lower blood cholesterol levels."

Pectin may also affect certain enzymes in the liver that produce cholesterol, says James J. Cerda, M.D., professor of medicine at the University of Florida College of Medicine in Gainesville.

"The more pectin you eat, the less cholesterol is produced by the liver," says Dr. Cerda.

## Staging a Plaque Attack

In one study, Dr. Cerda and his colleagues had 27 people considered to be at moderate to high risk for coronary heart disease consume either 15 grams of pectin each day (in capsule form) or a placebo each day for a month. Then for another four weeks, the people consuming the pectin took the placebos, and vice versa.

Researchers found that when these folks consumed the pectin supplements as opposed to the placebos, their total cholesterol dropped an average of 7.6 percent, and their "bad" LDL cholesterol plummeted about 10.8 percent.

In another study led by Dr. Cerda, 14 miniature pigs were fed a high-fat diet for more than a year—long enough for the pigs to develop plaque-clogged coronary arteries. Then for another nine months, half of the pigs continued on this same fatty diet plus 3 percent grapefruit pectin. The remaining seven pigs were fed the same diet but with no added pectin.

After nine months, the pectin had not significantly lowered the pigs' cholesterol levels. But the pectin had stopped the progression of, or reduced the extent of, the plaque buildup in the animals' coronary arteries and aortas. In fact, the coronary arteries of the swine who hadn't consumed pectin had narrowed an average of 45 percent, while the arteries of the pectin-fed pigs had narrowed only 24 percent.

## Getting Your Peck of Pectin

How much pectin might you have to eat to help send your cholesterol level south? A lot. "The therapeutic dose for water-soluble fibers such as pectin is 15 grams a day," says Dr. Cerda.

Here's how to get more pectin into your diet.

• Load up on fruits and veggies. Pectin-rich vegetables include carrots, lettuce, spinach, carrots, beets, brussels sprouts, cabbage, potatoes, onions and peas. Pectin-rich fruits include grapefruit, oranges, bananas, strawberries, peaches, apples, grapes and plums.

• Eat more grapefruit. Whether red, white or pink, grapefruit is one of the best sources of pectin around, suggests Dr. Cerda. "It's also high in vitamin C," he says.

• Eat the whole fruit or vegetable rather than drink its juice, suggests Martin Yadrick, R.D., a dietitian in Manhattan Beach, California, and spokesperson for the American Dietetic Association.

"Juice doesn't contain as much fiber as the fruit itself," says Yadrick. Bonus: You'll most likely feel more satisfied after eating a grapefruit or an apple than after downing a glass of juice.

*See also* Apples, Carrots

~❊~

# POLYUNSATURATED FAT

## *It's Rated Second Best*

As you may already know if you're trying to lower your cholesterol, most doctors advise replacing artery-clogging saturated fat, found primarily in animal products such as red meat and in dairy foods, with unsaturated fat, found mostly in plant foods. There are two types of unsaturated fat: monounsaturated and polyunsaturated. Monounsaturated fat is abundant in olive oil, canola oil, nuts and avocados. Polyunsaturated fat is found in corn oil, sunflower oil and safflower oil. The American Heart Association recommends that Americans consume no more than 10 percent of their calories from polyunsaturated fat.

Both monounsaturates and polyunsaturates lower "bad" LDL cholesterol. But polyunsaturates tend to lower "good" HDL cholesterol, too. So you may be wondering: If polyunsaturates lower the good stuff along with the bad stuff, is it better to opt for monos over polys?

Most doctors endorse unsaturated fat over saturated fat, period. "In general, highly polyunsaturated oils lower LDL cholesterol slightly better than monounsaturated oils," says Robert J. Nicolosi, Ph.D., director of the Cardiovascular Disease Control Center at the University of Lowell in Massachusetts. "But monounsaturated fat is a bit better at preventing reductions in HDL cholesterol. So it's somewhat of a wash. But it's fair to say that you should replace saturated fat with either monounsaturated fat or polyunsaturated fat."

Other doctors echo Dr. Nicolosi's assertion. "One reason that total and LDL cholesterol levels have declined in the United States in the past 30 years is that we're eating less saturated fat and more polyunsaturated fat," says Robert Rosenson, M.D., director of the Preventive Cardiology Center at Rush-Presbyterian-St. Luke's Medical Center in Chicago. What's more, says Dr. Rosenson, declines in HDL cholesterol that are associated with polyunsaturated fat may be more significant in people with low HDL cholesterol than for those with normal or high HDL cholesterol.

Studies comparing the effects of monounsaturates and polyunsaturates are continuing. In the meantime, follow the Golden Rule of cholesterol reduction: Consume all fats in moderation.


## How Polys Stack Up

Several studies that compared the effects of monounsaturated fat and polyunsaturated fat on blood cholesterol concluded that HDL cholesterol declines almost as much on a mono-rich diet as on a poly-rich diet.

Researchers at the University of Uppsala in Sweden studied 40 men and women who had high cholesterol or high triglycerides (another blood fat implicated in heart disease). These individuals ate either a polyunsaturate-enriched diet or a monounsaturate-enriched diet for three weeks. Both diets lowered total and LDL cholesterol. Further, HDL cholesterol dipped 7 percent on the monounsaturated diet and 12 percent on the polyunsaturated diet—a five-point difference that the researchers concluded was not statistically significant. The investigators' conclusion: Polyunsaturated fat and monounsaturated fat are interchangeable within a cholesterol-lowering diet.

The same team conducted another study in which 26 people with high cholesterol consumed two diets: one enriched with corn oil, the other enriched with olive oil. After about three weeks on each diet, these individuals' total and LDL cholesterol levels had declined. HDL cholesterol had also dropped by 9 percent on the corn oil diet and by 10 percent on the olive oil diet—again, not a statistically significant difference.

In other research, Christopher Gardner, Ph.D., of the Stanford Center for Research in Disease Prevention at Stanford University Medical Center in California, analyzed data from 14 independent studies that examined the effects of monos versus polys on cholesterol levels. Included in his review was a 1985 study suggesting that monounsaturates might be healthier than polyunsaturates because they reduce HDL cholesterol less. Dr. Gardner's study, called a meta-analysis, found no significant differences in cholesterol readings between the people who ate high levels of monounsaturated fat and those who consumed poly-rich diets.

"If you replace the saturated fat you get from animal products—such as meat and dairy foods—with unsaturated fat from plants and vegetables, you'll be in good shape," says Dr. Gardner. "When it comes to HDL and LDL cholesterol levels, it doesn't matter whether they're monounsaturated or polyunsaturated, as long as they're not saturated."

*See also* Canola Oil, Monounsaturated Fat, Olive Oil

❧

# POPCORN

## *The Four-Star Snack*

Ever wonder what makes popcorn pop?

The secret lies inside the popcorn kernel itself. When the kernel is exposed to heat, the moisture inside it begins to soften the starch within. As the internal temperature of each kernel rises, this moisture turns to steam and causes the kernel to explode, forcing the starch to expand. Voilà—the kernel bursts into a fluffy piece of popped corn.

That ping-ping-ping of kernels against saucepan lid, air popper or microwaveable bag will be heard billions of times in the United States this year. In an average year, we eat 18 billion quarts of popcorn!

Prepared in a heart-healthy manner, popcorn is a perfect antidote to a snack attack. "It's a high-carbohydrate, low-calorie and filling snack," says Karen Vartan, R.D., a dietitian in Chicago. What's more, half of the fiber in popcorn is soluble, the kind that can help knock points off your blood cholesterol level.

But popcorn is only as healthful as the way it's prepared. "Air-popped popcorn is the way to go," advises Lisa Lauri, R.D., nutrition consultant at North Shore University Hospital in Manhasset, New York. A typical serving (three cups) of air-popped popcorn contains

81 calories and just a trace of fat. Popcorn popped in oil and drenched in butter or margarine and salt, on the other hand, contains large amounts of total and saturated fat and sodium. So do many varieties of microwaveable and prepopped, ready-to-eat popcorn.

But more than a few of us believe that unless popcorn is bathed in butter and soaked with salt . . . well, it's just not popcorn. "There are two kinds of popcorn-eaters," says Vartan. "The first kind thinks that air-popped popcorn with nothing on it tastes perfectly acceptable. The second kind eats popcorn as a pleasure food, complete with butter or even chocolate. This kind of popcorn is as much a treat as premium ice cream." While there's nothing wrong with treating yourself to gourmet popcorn occasionally, says Vartan, indulging too often can help launch your intake of artery-clogging fat into orbit.

## Flavor without Fat

Here's how to make home-popped popcorn extra delicious and how to select heart-smart microwaveable or ready-to-eat popcorn.

• To add pizzazz to air-popped corn, lightly spray it with a vegetable oil cooking spray, such as Pam, and get creative with the seasonings. "Sprinkle the popcorn with some low-fat cheese—perhaps low-fat Cheddar, Monterey Jack or Swiss—along with some caraway or mustard seeds," suggests Vartan.

Other options? "Try sprinkling popcorn with Butter Buds, oregano, basil or sage," suggests Janet Lepke, R.D., a dietitian in Santa Monica, California, and a spokesperson for the American Dietetic Association.

• It's probably not the first popcorn topping that comes to mind, but Vartan suggests coating air-popped corn with dry sugar-free gelatin. "Spray the popcorn lightly with Pam, sprinkle on the gelatin and bake for five minutes at 350°," she says.

• If you buy microwaveable or ready-to-eat popcorn, opt for "light" varieties; they contain less fat and sodium. More and more brands, including Orville Redenbacher's, Jolly Time and Pop-Secret, are offering lower-fat products as well as their regular lines. Light popcorn isn't necessarily low-fat, however. So check the label for fat grams and the percentage of calories from fat.

Take note of the product's serving size, too. "Many people think that a bag is one serving, but each serving might actually be three cups," says Lauri. "There could be nine cups in a bag." So if you munch beyond the first three cups, you may be consuming more fat than you think.

• If you must pop your popcorn in oil, opt for canola oil. But make no mistake: Even popcorn popped in canola oil contains fat, notes Martin Yadrick, R.D., a dietitian in Manhattan Beach, California, and a spokesperson for the American Dietetic Association. "You'll consume less saturated fat if you use canola oil, but you'll still consume fat," says Yadrick. "So the trick is to use less oil when you make popcorn—or, even better, to air-pop."

## Pass on Movie Popcorn

If you're like a lot of people, watching the latest blockbuster without a big tub of buttered popcorn is just about unthinkable. But a few years ago, a study conducted by the Center for Science in the Public Interest (CSPI) painted a picture of movie popcorn more frightening than the latest flick from Stephen King.

The CSPI study found that a large tub of butter-flavored popcorn popped in coconut oil, which is 86 percent saturated fat, contains over 1,600 calories and nearly 130 grams of fat. That's as much fat as in eight Big Macs! Even a small tub (about five cups) of butter-flavored popcorn popped in coconut oil packs about 20 grams of fat total, 14 of them saturated.

Most likely, the "butter" is partially hydrogenated soybean oil, which is full of saturated fat and trans-fat, an unsaturated fat that raises cholesterol. The good news is, more and more movie chains are offering air-popped corn or are popping popcorn in canola oil. This unsaturated fat is easier on your coronary arteries than the more commonly used coconut oil, a highly saturated fat.

Why do most theaters use coconut oil? People seem to prefer it, says Yadrick. Also, coconut oil has a longer shelf life than unsaturated fats such as canola and corn oils, which may make coconut oil a more attractive choice to theater owners.

To avoid movie popcorn's sat-fat attack, consider taking your own air-popped corn to the theater. You might also suggest that the theater offer air-popped corn as well as the oil-popped kind. You never know.

# PSYLLIUM

## *This Natural Laxative Has Other Powers*

If you're like most people, you've taken a laxative now and then to get things moving again. But did you know that an ingredient in some laxatives can help lower blood cholesterol?

It's true: Several studies have shown that psyllium, an ingredient in some bulk-forming laxatives, can reduce moderately elevated blood cholesterol. That's because psyllium, derived from the seed husks of a plant with origins in India, is rich in soluble fiber, a gummy substance found in certain fruits and vegetables that has been shown to deflate cholesterol.

"Psyllium is a very good source of soluble fiber," says James W. Anderson, M.D., professor of medicine and clinical nutrition at the University of Kentucky College of Medicine in Lexington and author of *Dr. Anderson's High-Fiber Fitness Plan.* You'll find psyllium in supplement form, such as powders and wafers, as well as in some breakfast cereals.

Taking psyllium supplements to lower cholesterol may not be right for everyone. (More on that in a bit.) But generally speaking, teaming psyllium with a low-fat, low-cholesterol diet can help deflate total and "bad" LDL cholesterol.

## Psyllium Solutions

How does psyllium work? Some studies suggest that like other forms of soluble fiber, psyllium prevents the body from reabsorbing a digestive secretion called bile. If the small intestine contains soluble fiber, bile—which contains cholesterol—gets trapped in this gummy stuff and is excreted from the body. Without soluble fiber, the body reabsorbs bile and recycles the cholesterol it contains.

At the University of Kentucky, Dr. Anderson and his colleagues had 44 people following a low-fat, low-cholesterol diet eat either a psyllium-enriched breakfast cereal containing 2.9 grams of psyllium and 3 grams of soluble fiber per serving or a wheat bran cereal containing negligible amounts of soluble fiber. After six weeks, LDL cholesterol dropped nearly 13 percent in the people who ate the psyllium-enriched cereal but only 2.5 percent in the wheat bran group.

Researchers at the University of Cincinnati and Washington University School of Medicine in St. Louis put 118 people with elevated cholesterol (220 milligrams/deciliter or higher) on either a low-fat or a high-fat diet. Some of these individuals consumed five grams of psyllium (in sugar-free orange-flavored Metamucil) twice a day, just before breakfast and dinner. The others were given a placebo. After two months on the psyllium, LDL cholesterol fell 7.2 percent in the individuals following the low-fat diet and 6.4 percent in the individuals on the high-fat diet. The LDL cholesterol of the people who took the placebo didn't change.

## The Cereal Ingredient That Surprises Some

As mentioned previously, you can take psyllium as a powder mixed with water or juice, in wafer form or in a psyllium-containing breakfast cereal such as Bran Buds or FiberWise. "Bran Buds are a good choice," says Dr. Anderson. "They contain wheat bran, an insoluble fiber that promotes regularity and health of the colon, as well as soluble fiber, which lowers cholesterol."

If you choose to try a psyllium supplement, follow the recommended dosage on the label, advises Dr. Anderson. Also, for maximum effect, take psyllium with meals. In a study at the University of Toronto, people with mildly high cholesterol who ate Bran Buds for two weeks (one-third cup at breakfast and one-third cup at dinner) saw their cholesterol drop by 8 percent. But people who took psyllium powder, mixed with water, between meals had only a minor drop in cholesterol.

*Note:* There are some instances in which you should not consume this fiber. Don't use psyllium if you're taking certain prescription drugs. Too much psyllium can slow the absorption of heart medication and blood pressure medication, says Dr. Anderson.

Also, if you've had an allergic reaction to laxatives—or if you have any kind of allergy at all—consult your doctor before taking psyllium.

This fiber has caused anaphylaxis (a severe allergic reaction) in some people. Such a reaction is rare, however.

ᨠᨰᨠ

# SKIM MILK

## *It Does a Body Good*

On an airplane flight during which breakfast was served, Martin Yadrick, R.D., a dietitian in Manhattan Beach, California, and a spokesperson for the American Dietetic Association, asked the flight attendant if he could have some skim milk. "She said, 'No, not unless you order a special meal. But who can drink that stuff anyway? You may as well not drink milk at all!'" recalls Yadrick.

If that's the way you feel about skim milk, you're not alone. Many an adult, contemplating the switch from whole to skim milk, may feel like a kid who has just watched Mom heap broccoli on his plate.

Americans love milk. We dunk cookies in it, lavish it in sauces and crave its rich, creamy taste in ice cream, cheese and other dishes. Whole milk is a good source of calcium, which helps prevent osteoporosis, and is rich in protein, minerals and vitamins A and D.

If you're trying to lower your blood cholesterol, however, whole milk doesn't do a body good. One cup of whole milk contains eight grams of fat, 33 milligrams of cholesterol and 150 calories. One study concluded that Americans' passion for whole milk and whole-milk products such as cheese "probably contributes substantially to the population burden of coronary heart disease."

But don't assume you have to pass up milk entirely. One cup of skim milk contains only 0.4 gram of fat, four milligrams of cholesterol and 85 calories. What's more, skim milk contains all of the nutrients of whole milk, so you won't lose out on the calcium you need to maintain healthy bones.

Best of all, you don't have to give up the taste of coffee with milk, frothy milk shakes and rich, creamy sauces. You can make delicious dishes and desserts with skim milk. Read on to find out how.

## The Benefits of Moo Juice Lite

A number of studies have compared the effects of whole milk with those of skim milk on blood cholesterol. Here's what these studies have found.

Researchers at the University of Minnesota in Minneapolis and other institutions put eight healthy men on a low-fat diet that followed the guidelines of the American Heart Association. For six weeks of a three-month-long study, the men drank two to four cups of whole milk per day. For the other six weeks, they drank an equal amount of skim milk. The men's total cholesterol was 7 percent lower, and their "bad" LDL cholesterol was 11 percent lower, on the skim-milk diet than on the whole-milk plan.

These researchers noted that for every 1 percent reduction in total cholesterol, the risk of coronary heart disease drops 2 to 3 percent. Consequently, these experts proposed, healthy men with normal blood cholesterol who drink two to four cups of whole milk a day could slash their risk of coronary heart disease by about 14 percent if they switched from whole milk to skim milk.

Researchers at Kansas State University in Manhattan and Pennsylvania State University in University Park had 64 people supplement their diets with a quart of skim milk a day. After two months, people who began the study with total cholesterol of 190 milligrams/deciliter or above saw their total cholesterol decline 6.6 percent and their triglyceride levels drop almost 12 percent. The blood pressure of these men and women dropped as well, perhaps due to the calcium and potassium content of the skim milk.

## The Skinny on Low-Fat Milk

Using a couple of teaspoons of low-fat milk a day won't hurt you, say experts. But if every day you gulp down a couple of glasses of low-fat milk, which contains either 1 or 2 percent milk-fat, you're not trimming as much fat from your diet as you may think.

"Whole milk is 3½ percent milk-fat," notes Lisa Lauri, R.D., nutrition consultant at North Shore University Hospital in Manhasset, New York. So if your goal is to lower your blood cholesterol, she says, drinking 2 percent low-fat milk isn't the ideal choice.

Keep in mind, too, that water makes up most of the weight of milk. So once water is eliminated from the calculations, 2 percent low-fat milk contains 20 percent fat by weight. What's more, 2 percent low-fat milk gets 35 percent of its calories from fat, while only 5 percent of the calories in skim milk come from fat.

Still not convinced? Here's one more calculation that may help you make the switch to skim. If you drink two glasses of 1 percent low-fat milk every day for a year, you're swallowing four pounds of fat. Drinking the same amount of skim milk, on the other hand, provides less than one-tenth of a pound of fat.

## Fake Out Your Taste Buds

These tips can make the transition from whole or low-fat milk to skim milk practically painless.

• Drink skim milk from a frosted mug. For some reason, lowering the temperature enhances the taste.

• Don't feel you have to switch to skim milk right away. "Don't rush it," says Yadrick. "Use 2 percent low-fat milk for about a month, then move to 1 percent for the next month. Finally, make the jump to skim milk."

• Many people find it difficult to use skim milk on breakfast cereals, says Janet Lepke, R.D., a dietitian in Santa Monica, California, and a spokesperson for the American Dietetic Association. "So if you want to use 1 percent low-fat milk instead of skim on your cereal, it's no big deal," she says. (Consider making the switch to skim milk sometime down the road, though.)

• If you've always used half-and-half or straight cream in your coffee, "try mixing two teaspoons of a liquid nondairy creamer and two teaspoons of 1 percent low-fat milk," says Marilyn Cerino, R.D., nutrition consultant at the Benjamin Franklin Center for Health of Pennsylvania Hospital in Philadelphia. "This substitute looks and tastes rich."

• Love bathing your vegetables in a white cream sauce? "Mix a teaspoon each of margarine and flour, then heat for two minutes, slowly whisking in skim milk," suggests Cerino. "It makes a delicious sauce."

• If you're yearning for a rich, creamy milk shake, whip up a banana health shake, suggests Evelyn Tribole, R.D., a dietitian in Beverly Hills, California, and author of *Healthy Homestyle Cooking*. Blend one ripe banana, ¼ cup of nonfat dry milk, ½ cup of orange juice, one teaspoon of vanilla, a dash of nutmeg and five ice cubes until creamy. "In about a minute, you'll have made a delicious, refreshing drink containing only a trace amount of fat," says Tribole.

~❧~

# SMOKING CESSATION

## *How to Kick Butts*

If you smoke, there's a good chance that you've felt the scorch of social disapproval at least once. But make no mistake: Being hissed out of a restaurant can't begin to match the havoc smoking can wreak on your cholesterol level—and your heart. Consider the facts.

• Scientific evidence shows that smoking is a major contributing factor to elevated blood cholesterol and heart disease.

• Smokers tend to have less HDL cholesterol (the "good" kind) and higher total and LDL cholesterol (the "bad" stuff) than nonsmokers.

• Smokers who already have elevated cholesterol are more likely to develop coronary heart disease and suffer heart attacks than nonsmokers.

"If you smoke, quitting is almost certainly the best thing you can do for your cardiovascular system and for your overall health and quality of life," says John W. Zamarra, M.D., founding director of the cardiac rehabilitation program at Placentia-Linda Community Hospital in Brea, California.

There's more good news. Not only is smoking-related damage reversible, but it is possible to quit, no matter how many times you've tried in the past. In fact, one study found that people who can quit for just two weeks are likely to quit for good! Over three million Americans quit smoking every year. So can you—and you'll find lots of help along the way. Read on.

## Ground Zero for Your Arteries

Research has shown that smoking damages far more than the lungs; it's hard on the arteries, too. Smoking accelerates hardening of the arteries (arteriosclerosis) and leaves fatty deposits on artery walls (atherosclerosis). Further, cigarette smoke increases the level of carbon monoxide in the blood. This poisonous chemical robs cells of oxygen, injuring the lining of the arteries and allowing fatty material to pass from the bloodstream into the vessel walls.

One study examined the data from 54 earlier studies on the association between smoking and elevated blood cholesterol. This study found that smokers had significantly higher levels of total cholesterol, LDL cholesterol and triglycerides, as well as lower levels of HDL cholesterol.

Another study, conducted by investigators at the University of California, Berkeley, found that the effectiveness of a key enzyme known as lecithin-cholesterol acyl transferase (LCAT), which helps clear cholesterol from the blood, is "dramatically inhibited" by cigarette smoke. This enzyme is essential to allow cholesterol to pass from deposits in the cells into HDL cholesterol in your blood and eventually to your liver for excretion. "Cigarette smoke hits human plasma with a double whammy" and reduces both LCAT and HDL, says Mark R. McCall, Ph.D., of the University of California, Berkeley.

## Getting Ready to Stop

Quitting smoking isn't easy. But you can make it easier. These tips can help.

## PATCHING UP HDL

Sure, quitting smoking can increase "good" HDL cholesterol. But if you're using nicotine transdermal replacement (better known as the nicotine patch) to kick the habit, you may be wondering: Won't using a nicotine patch continue to keep HDL levels low? Maybe not, according to one study.

Researchers at the University of Minnesota Medical School in Minneapolis examined the effect of the nicotine patch in people who abstained from smoking. After six weeks, these folks' blood pressure, heart rates and "bad" LDL cholesterol dropped while their HDL cholesterol and triglycerides increased—even while they were using active nicotine patches.

But patches aren't magical, experts note. "People who expect nicotine patches to miraculously make them stop smoking will be disappointed," says Gary DeNelsky, Ph.D., director of the smoking cessation program at the Cleveland Clinic Foundation in Cleveland. "The patch should be used under a doctor's supervision as part of a comprehensive smoking cessation program."

• Keep a smoking journal for two weeks before you quit, suggest C. Richard Conti, M.D., and Diana Tonnessen in their book *Beating the Odds against Heart Disease and High Cholesterol.* Jot down the circumstances that most often prompt you to light up: during your coffee break, after dinner, while chatting on the phone, when you're feeling lonely or bored and so forth.

• After a week, review your journal, pinpointing circumstances that prompt you to smoke. Then list alternatives to smoking during those times. If your journal shows that you tend to smoke after meals, for example, brush your teeth or take a walk instead.

• Decide whether you want to quit smoking all at once—that is, "cold turkey"—or taper off. While you may decide to stop smoking gradually, there's evidence that most successful quitters go cold turkey.

• Pick a Quit Day and mark it on your calendar. Make it no later than one week away. Many experts suggest quitting on a weekend, when most people have better control of their time, surroundings and circumstances.

• Get yourself a buddy to help you make it through the quitting process. This person can be a nonsmoker, a former smoker or a smoker who will quit with you. Call this person when the going gets rough.

• Tell your family, friends and co-workers about your Quit Day. Letting people know about your decision to quit smoking will serve to help hold you to your resolve.

• Call or write your local chapter of the American Heart Association, the American Cancer Society or the American Lung Association, and ask for their free brochures and pamphlets on smoking cessation.

## A Quit Day Checklist

Here's what to do when your Quit Day dawns.

• Throw away all of your cigarettes and matches. Soak the cigarettes in water, so you can't scrounge them out of the trash.

• Hide all ashtrays. Better yet, get rid of them.

• Lay in a supply of healthy snacks such as celery, carrots, apples, sunflower seeds and air-popped popcorn. They'll keep your mouth and fingers busy without wreaking havoc on your shape.

• Take a long walk or visit a nonsmoking environment such as a library, museum or movie theater.

• Get your teeth cleaned to get rid of tobacco stains. Resolve to keep them that way.

• Avoid stressful situations and smoking environments (bars, for example). Spend as much time as possible in places where smoking isn't permitted.

What about withdrawal symptoms? Well, there's good news and bad news. Bad news first: About 80 percent of smokers experience such symptoms when they quit, from headaches and fatigue to nausea, diarrhea and constipation. Some people also feel anxious, depressed or irritable or have trouble sleeping. The good news: Withdrawal symptoms tend to subside in two to three days, after the nicotine has left your body, and will be gone—or nearly so—within a couple of weeks.

## Staying Off 'Em

Most people are capable of quitting smoking. The key is to not start again. Here are three ways to kick the habit for good.

• Be alert for "smoke signals." One study identified the four most likely relapse scenarios: during social drinking, after a meal, feeling anxious at work and feeling depressed or anxious while home alone.

• Learn a relaxation technique, such as deep breathing or progressive relaxation. If smoking helps you relax, "you're likely to feel more stressed when you quit smoking unless you have other ways to manage stress that aren't centered around cigarettes," says Dean Ornish, M.D., president and director of the Preventive Medicine Research Institute in Sausalito, California, and author of *Dr. Dean Ornish's Program for Reversing Heart Disease.*

• On an index card, list two or three of your most important reasons for quitting smoking. Stash the card in your pocket or purse, where you used to keep your cigarettes. Pull it out and go over the list often, particularly when you feel the urge to smoke.

*See also* Stress Management, Yoga

# SOY FOODS

## *From Fad to Phenomenon*

**W**hat a difference a few decades make! Once disdained as bland fare strictly for health nuts, tofu and other soy products are entering the mainstream. More and more regular folks are topping their pizzas with tofu, scarfing down soybean-based "meatless" burgers and franks—and discovering how succulent soy foods can be.

And not a moment too soon, it seems. Scientists studying the potential healing properties of soy have discovered a grab bag of health benefits. There's evidence that adding just a small amount of soy to your diet can help fight certain cancers, soothe menopausal symptoms, boost your immune system and, yes, lower blood cholesterol.

It's the people in Asian countries, who tend to consume soy-rich diets, who seem to have reaped most of soy's potential health benefits. The Japanese, for example, live longer than any other nationality in the world. What's more, Japanese men have the lowest rate of death from heart disease in the world, and Japanese women, the second lowest. The average Japanese person eats 50 to 80 grams (about two to three ounces) of soy food a day; the typical American, 5 grams a day.

Tofu is perhaps the most well known soy food. Like pasta, this soft, mild-tasting substance takes on the flavor of whatever it's cooked with. So tofu tastes equally good in the spiciest chili and the creamiest cheesecake—and in virtually any other dish.

---

## HOW TO SPEAK SOY

Don't know tofu from tempeh? Relax—this primer can help introduce you to some of the most common soy products.

***Isolated soy protein.*** A powdered form of soy protein found in powdered weight-loss drinks and other products.

***Meat analogs.*** These soy-based "meats" include cold cuts, bacon, sausage, franks and burgers.

***Soy flour.*** Made by flaking and grinding roasted soybeans. You can replace up to 20 percent of regular flour with soy flour. Also, use defatted soy flour; the regular variety is very high in fat.

***Soy milk.*** A creamy, milklike drink made from ground soaked soybeans and water. You can drink soy milk straight, pour it over cereal or substitute it for whole or skim milk in other dishes.

***Tempeh.*** Cakes of cooked, fermented soybeans, laced with a mold that gives tempeh its distinctive flavor. Tempeh is usually grilled, roasted, steamed or added to soups.

***Texturized soy protein.*** Made from soy flour, this is a meat substitute that is used to replace part or all of the meat in chili or hamburgers. You buy it in dry form and add water before use.

***Tofu.*** A creamy white, soft cake made from curded soy milk. Tofu can be sliced, diced or mashed and used in soups, stir-fries, casseroles and sandwiches.

But if tofu isn't to your liking, you can still enjoy your soy. That's because more and more supermarkets are carrying commercially prepared soy-based products, from cheese and yogurt to meat analogs (meat substitutes made from soy protein).

Of course, wolfing down tofu or soy-based breakfast "sausage" on top of a burgers-and-fries diet isn't likely to reduce your cholesterol. It works only as part of a low-fat, low-cholesterol diet. And according to experts, replacing a portion of the meat and dairy foods in your diet with their tasty soy impersonators can be a heart-smart move.

## The Joy of Soy

How might soy send cholesterol south? Experts aren't sure. One likely reason is that soy foods, while moderately high in fat, are still lower in fat—particularly artery-choking saturated fat—than meat and dairy products. So replacing animal protein with protein from soy products would theoretically lower blood cholesterol. "Soybeans also are fairly high in fiber," says Kristi A. Steinmetz, Ph.D., consulting nutritional epidemiologist in the Division of Epidemiology at the University of Minnesota in Minneapolis. "This could explain the lowering effect on blood cholesterol."

There are other theories, too. Some investigators speculate that a certain substance in soy, genistein, may help keep fatty plaques from clogging the arteries. Genistein is part of a group of compounds called phytoestrogens, plant substances that some researchers believe may help prevent certain types of cancer.

Yet other research suggests that soy may help the liver excrete cholesterol-rich bile acids, which aid in digestion. When the liver replaces these acids, it draws from the cholesterol circulating in the blood. Presto—your blood cholesterol sinks.

"More than 40 studies have shown that soy protein lowers blood cholesterol," says Herbert Pierson, Ph.D., vice-president of Preventive Nutrition Consultants in Woodinville, Wisconsin, and former project director of the Cancer Preventive Designer Food Project at the National Cancer Institute in Rockville, Maryland.

A team of researchers led by James W. Anderson, M.D., professor of medicine and clinical nutrition at the University of Kentucky College of Medicine in Lexington and author of *Dr. Anderson's High-Fiber Fit-*

*ness Plan*, analyzed 29 separate studies involving a total of 743 people that examined how soy protein affects blood cholesterol. Most of these studies were conducted with isolated soy protein (ISP) or texturized soy protein (TSP). ISP is a powdered form of soy protein and is often used in powdered weight-loss drinks and other products. TSP is a meat substitute made from soy flour and is often found in hot dogs, hamburgers and sausages. You can also buy TSP in dry form.

The investigators found that consuming 47 grams of soy protein per day instead of animal protein lowered total cholesterol by 9.3 percent, "bad" LDL cholesterol by 12.9 percent and triglycerides (another blood fat implicated in heart disease) by 10.5 percent.

Investigators at the University of Illinois at Urbana-Champaign had 25 men with high cholesterol follow a low-fat, low-cholesterol diet. The men were also assigned to one of four groups. For four consecutive four-week periods, the men substituted muffins made with 50 grams of soy protein for half of their normal protein intakes. The soy protein came from soy flour, ISP and soy fiber, ISP alone or nonfat dry milk alone.

The results? The ISP-only muffins lowered the men's total cholesterol by 12 percent and their LDL cholesterol by 11.5 percent. Since every 1 percent drop in total cholesterol results in a 2 percent reduction in the risk of coronary heart disease, these men lowered their risk by 24 percent! Some of the same investigators replicated these results in a later study, showing that even 25 grams of soy protein reduced total cholesterol in 21 men with high cholesterol.

## You'll Never Miss the Meat

Many supermarkets carry some soy-based products, from tofu (often found in the produce section) to commercially prepared "meat products" such as vegetable burgers. Finding ISP, TSP and tempeh may require a trip to the health food store. These tips can help you enjoy your soy.

• Mix mashed tofu with diced vegetables, herbs and spices and use it as a vegetable dip or sandwich filling.
• Add cubed tofu to stir-fried vegetables.
• Crumble tofu into spaghetti sauce or chili.

---

### A BEGINNER'S GUIDE TO TOFU

Want to give tofu a try? Follow these tips.

- Select low-fat or nonfat tofu. Regular versions can get anywhere from 30 to over 50 percent of their calories from fat.
- Select tofu curded with calcium sulfate. This variety contains 860 milligrams of calcium, compared with 258 milligrams of calcium in tofu curded with nigari (magnesium chloride).
- Buy tofu in sealed packages. Tofu that sits in water and is exposed to the open air has been found to contain high levels of bacteria.

---

- Pour soy milk over cereal or substitute it for whole milk in soups, cakes, puddings and other dishes that call for milk.
- Grill sliced tempeh, then top it with regular burger fixin's, suggests registered pharmacist Earl Mindell, Ph.D., professor of nutrition at Pacific Western University in Los Angeles and author of *Earl Mindell's Soy Miracle.*
- Add ISP to baked goods.

And for some great recipes that make the most of tofu, tempeh and other soy products, see Sensational Soy on page 371.

# STRESS MANAGEMENT

## *The No-Sweat Cure*

The hassles and headaches of everyday life eventually catch up with all of us. But stress can give you more than a yen to escape to an as yet undiscovered South Seas island. There's some evidence that chronic stress can elevate cholesterol and set the stage for coronary heart disease.

Fortunately, you can learn to reduce the stress in your life using a variety of simple techniques. What's more, learning to feel challenged by stress rather than overwhelmed by it can further reduce the effect of stress on your health, say experts. In other words, while you can't always control the sources of your stress, you can change the way you react to them.

Not every heart expert believes that stress causes elevated cholesterol. Stress does have an effect on cholesterol levels, although "it's not nearly as important a factor as diet," says Dean Ornish, M.D., president and director of the Preventive Medicine Research Institute in Sausalito, California, and author of *Dr. Dean Ornish's Program for Reversing Heart Disease.* Nevertheless, if you're following a low-fat, low-cholesterol diet and making other lifestyle changes that lower your risk of heart disease, why not give your response to stress a makeover, too? So unclench your jaw, count to ten and explore how keeping your cool might help keep the lid on cholesterol.

## The Stone Age Response

Ironically, the same physiological reaction to stress that helped our caveman ancestors outrun predators may play some role in modern man's (and woman's) proclivity for developing coronary heart disease. This reaction, called the fight-or-flight response, is your inborn red-alert system that readies your body to repel a threat—real or imagined.

During the fight-or-flight response, your body releases stress hormones such as cortisol and adrenaline into your bloodstream. These hormones speed up your breathing, increase your heart rate and accelerate the flow of blood to your arms and legs (the better to help you flee). But if your body triggers this inner alarm dozens of times a day, it can lay the foundation for heart disease.

"Stress seems to accelerate the depositing of plaque into the arteries independent of its effect on blood cholesterol," says Dr. Ornish. In other words, he says, the harmful part of stress has less to do with its effect on cholesterol than its effect on the arteries themselves.

"Stress can make your arteries constrict, which can reduce blood flow to the heart," says Dr. Ornish. "It can cause something called plaque hemorrhage, which is a rupture of the lining of the arteries that can lead to the arteries becoming obstructed. And stress can cause blood to clot faster, which can lead to a heart attack."

## Arterial Terrorists: Beef, Butter and . . . Burnout?

Think burgers and butter are your arteries' only enemies? Think again. Years ago, a well-known study demonstrated that accountants' blood cholesterol skyrocketed by as many as 100 points above their usual levels during tax season. Another study showed that students' blood cholesterol spiked during exams. Here are a few other studies linking stress with stratospheric cholesterol counts.

Researchers at the University of Pittsburgh had 44 healthy men and women either take a complicated computerized test to raise their stress levels or rest quietly for 20 minutes. Blood samples were taken before and after the test and the rest period. Those who took the test showed significant increases in total and "bad" LDL cholesterol.

Researchers in Israel studied 104 men between the ages of 24 and 68. These men didn't have cardiovascular disease, but they did have highly stressful jobs and were defined by the researchers as "burned out." (The study defined burnout as a mix of physical fatigue, mental exhaustion and other factors.) After controlling for age, weight and other factors, the researchers discovered that the total cholesterol of the most burned-out men was 14 percent higher than that of the most relaxed men. What's more, the most stressed-out men had significantly higher LDL cholesterol, the kind that wreaks the most cardiovascular damage.

Researchers at the Brown University Program in Medicine in Providence, Rhode Island, drew blood from 114 men and women, then administered two psychological tests used to measure anxiety and responses to it. After factoring in age, weight and smoking habits, the researchers found that men who repressed their feelings tended to have higher cholesterol than men who didn't. Interestingly, women who repressed negative emotions had lower total and LDL cholesterol than women who didn't. One researcher has suggested that emotional stress may exert a lower physiological toll on women than on men.

# Learning to Let Go

The bad news: There's no way to avoid stress. The good news: You can cope with stress in a more heart-healthy manner, say experts. "The impact of emotional stress has little to do with what's actually causing the stress and everything to do with how well you tolerate it," says David Bresler, Ph.D., a stress and imagery specialist at the Los Angeles Healing Arts Center. "Some people experience minimal stress and fall apart, while others face serious stress and don't have a problem with it."

So before you come apart at the seams, consider your cholesterol level and try these stress-busting tips.

• Breathe deeply. "Your breathing is a reflection of your mental state. It's a bridge between your mind and your body, and it can be used to change your frame of mind," says Dr. Ornish. "If you're feeling anxious, your breathing becomes more rapid and shallow. But consciously making yourself breathe more slowly and deeply can help calm you."

• Get some real exercise. According to experts, aerobic exercise, such as a brisk stroll, can help reduce the amount of stress-producing hormones barreling through your bloodstream. "Exercise is a great stress-reducing tool," says Peter O. Kwiterovich, Jr., M.D., professor of medicine and director of the Lipid Research and Atherosclerosis Unit at Johns Hopkins University School of Medicine in Baltimore and author of *The Johns Hopkins Complete Guide for Preventing and Reversing Heart Disease.* "I recommend regular aerobic exercise. Try to exercise a half-hour a day, three to four times a week."

• Don't spread yourself too thin—it's a major cause of stress, says James W. Anderson, M.D., professor of medicine and clinical nutrition at the University of Kentucky College of Medicine in Lexington and author of *Dr. Anderson's High-Fiber Fitness Plan.* "Schedule your time carefully and learn to say no when you need to," advises Dr. Anderson.

• Try turning a stressful situation into a challenge, suggests Dr. Bresler. "If your boss demands a report in two hours, for example, you can think 'This isn't fair' or 'I might get fired if I don't do a good job,'" he says. Thinking this way "can trigger fear and anger as well as

## AHHHH . . . TRY THIS RELAXING ROUTINE

Stress reduction techniques such as yoga and meditation have been shown to elicit the relaxation response. This physiological state lowers heart and breathing rates, slows brain waves and even lowers blood pressure in some people, according to Herbert Benson, M.D., chief of the Division of Behavioral Medicine at Deaconess Hospital in Boston, associate professor of medicine at Harvard Medical School and author of *The Relaxation Response*. Here's how to perform a stress reduction technique called progressive relaxation.

1. Get comfortable. You can sit up or lie down, whichever you prefer.
2. Close your eyes.
3. Inhale gently and make a fist with your right hand. Hold the fist for 5 to 7 seconds, exhale and relax. Feel the tension drain from your hand and forearm, comparing the sensations of how your arm feels relaxed and how it feels tense. Rest for about 45 seconds, then repeat a second time.
4. Tense and relax your left hand as you did with your right.
5. Repeat this exercise from your head to your toes, tensing and relaxing each muscle group in the following order: After your hands, tense and relax your biceps, facial muscles (frown, then relax), neck, upper back (pull your shoulders back as though trying to touch them together behind you), chest (try to pull your shoulders in front of you), stomach, thighs and calves.

the physiological responses associated with those emotions," says Dr. Bresler.

But if you choose to think "This is a real challenge! Let's see what I can accomplish in two hours," you can transform negative stress into the positive kind, says Dr. Bresler: "You can wrap the identical situation in a completely different package, which will influence how your body responds." As the saying goes, "Perception is reality."

*See also* Exercise, Yoga

❧

# TEA

## *Get It While It's Green*

If your day isn't complete without a cup (or two) of tea, you could be doing your heart a favor. Research indicates that tea, especially the variety known as green tea, may help ward off heart disease and reduce blood cholesterol levels.

Tea is the most widely consumed beverage in the world, second only to water. The United States ranks seventh in tea consumption, behind countries such as India and Russia.

Tea leaves are processed in a variety of ways to make three basic types of tea: black, green and oolong. Black tea, the kind that most Americans drink, is fermented—that is, the leaves are partially dried, crushed, allowed to sit for a few hours and then completely dried. Green tea, the variety most often consumed in Japan, Korea and China, is simply steamed, rolled and crushed. Oolong tea, which is partially fermented, is a cross between black and green tea. One cup of tea contains about 27 milligrams of caffeine, about one-third of the amount found in a cup of ground or roasted coffee.

It's green tea that has garnered the most scientific scrutiny—and according to some experts, it may have the most health benefits.

## The Muscle behind Tea

Many researchers credit compounds called polyphenols for tea's cardiovascular protection. Polyphenols act as antioxidants, chemicals that help gobble up free radicals. (Free radicals are cell-damaging compounds thought to accelerate aging and play a role in degenerative conditions such as heart disease and cancer.) Green tea is bursting with polyphenols. The fermentation process tends to alter or destroy the polyphenols in black and oolong teas, however.

Polyphenols may help hinder the oxidation of "bad" LDL cholesterol, says Robert J. Nicolosi, Ph.D., director of the Cardiovascular Research Center at the University of Lowell in Massachusetts. Oxidation is the chemical process that rusts metal and turns bananas brown and spotty—and makes LDL particles more likely to cling to artery walls. Polyphenols may play a role in keeping LDL from accumulating in the coronary arteries, says Dr. Nicolosi. "Polyphenols are reported to be much more active as antioxidants than vitamin E, for example," says Dr. Nicolosi. And one study suggests that the antioxidant properties in tea might also help prevent blood from clotting, which can lead to heart attacks, says Dr. Nicolosi.

Tea also contains flavonoids, antioxidant compounds that seem to short-circuit the process that leads LDL cholesterol to accumulate in the bloodstream. Dutch researchers who conducted a five-year study of 805 men ages 65 to 84 found that the men who ate the most flavonoids (also found in onions, apples and wine) were 50 percent less likely to have a first heart attack and die of heart disease than those who consumed the least.

## The Green Scene

Two other studies have found an association between green tea consumption and cholesterol reduction.

Japanese researchers investigated the link between green tea intake and cardiovascular and liver diseases in 1,371 men over age 40. These researchers found that as tea consumption rose, "good" HDL cholesterol increased, while triglyceride, total cholesterol and LDL cholesterol levels fell. In fact, total cholesterol in the men who drank ten or more cups of tea a day was about 6 percent less than in the men who drank three or fewer cups a day.

In another Japanese study of 1,300 men, researchers found that the greater the consumption of green tea, the lower the men's cholesterol. Men who drank two cups or less of tea a day had total cholesterol levels averaging 193 milligrams/deciliter. Those who drank between six and eight cups a day had an average cholesterol reading of 188 milligrams/deciliter. And the average cholesterol of men who drank nine or more cups a day was even lower—185 milligrams/deciliter.

## Teatime Tips

You want to wallop your blood cholesterol. Should you trade in your coffee mug for a teacup? And how much tea do you need to drink?

Since there is not yet conclusive proof that tea can lower cholesterol, there's no way to know how much tea might do the trick. There's some evidence that drinking a few cups of tea a day may give you a slight edge, however. If you enjoy black tea, avoid adding cream, half-and-half or whole milk—all are high in fat. Use skim or low-fat milk instead. Most people drink green tea without cream or sugar. You can find green tea in some large supermarkets and most health food stores and Asian groceries.

No amount of tea can compete with the benefits of an overall heart-healthy diet, however. So concentrate your cholesterol-cutting efforts on proven dietary strategies, such as reducing your intake of saturated fat and dietary cholesterol, advises Dr. Nicolosi.

Also, consume tea in moderation, especially if you're at risk for certain heart arrhythmias. "Caffeine is a stimulant and has a tendency to accelerate the heart rate," says Connie Diekman, R.D., a dietitian in St. Louis and a spokesperson for the American Dietetic Association. People taking medication to control tachycardia, for example, may want to avoid caffeine.

*See also* Coffee

&#10086;

# TELEVISION VIEWING

## *The Plight of the Couch Potato*

Perhaps the small screen that commands so much of our attention should carry a warning—"*Caution:* Frequent viewing may be hazardous to your health."

Okay, it's not fair to single out television as Public Health Enemy Number One. But some studies suggest that being a hard-core couch potato can be hard on the coronary arteries—and the cholesterol level.

It's not hard to see why. The more sitcoms, miniseries and movies of the week that you take in, say experts, the more likely you are to take in calories in the form of high-fat snacks. Eventually, those bowls of ice cream and bags of chips can help send cholesterol levels into orbit.

Further, studies have shown that the more people work their remotes, the less likely they are to work their bodies. "We have a limited amount of free time when we're not working, sleeping, eating or tending to other responsibilities," says Nathan D. Wong, Ph.D., associate professor and director of preventive cardiology at the University of California, Irvine. "If you're watching a lot of television, you're less likely to have time for exercise."

No one is suggesting that it's a sin to park yourself in front of the tube to enjoy your favorite soap or game show. But you might reflect on how your viewing habits may be affecting your health—and consider tuning in a bit less often. Read on.

## Prime Time for High Cholesterol

Americans watch a lot of television. In fact, only working and sleeping consume more of our time than watching the tube, says Larry A. Tucker, Ph.D., professor and director of health promotion at Brigham Young University in Provo, Utah. In fact, notes Dr. Tucker, the average household spends seven hours—almost one-third of the day—basking in the television's flickering light.

Dr. Tucker and his colleagues have conducted several studies on the connection between blood cholesterol levels and television viewing. In one study of nearly 12,000 adults, 22 percent of the folks who watched television for three or more hours a day had high cholesterol (240 milligrams/deciliter or greater). Of the individuals who watched less than an hour a day, however, only 14 percent had high cholesterol, even after researchers factored in age, gender, smoking, exercise habits and percentage of body fat.

What's more, experts say that as the plot thickens, so does the waistline. "Obesity and body fat are strongly related to high cholesterol levels," notes Dr. Tucker. "When people watch three, four and five hours of television a day, it tends to reflect a syndrome of poor health. These people are out of shape, they're overweight, and they may smoke."

Another of Dr. Tucker's studies—this one of 4,771 women—found that the women who watched television three to four hours a day were more than twice as likely to be obese as those who watched for less than an hour. The researchers didn't draw a cause-and-effect conclusion from this data but suggested a "dynamic model" in which watching television, lack of physical activity and snacking are interrelated and result in weight gain.

Further evidence that the small screen can have a big impact on health: Researchers at Tufts New England Medical Center in Boston and the Harvard School of Public Health identified inactivity, especially watching television, as a likely important cause of obesity. These experts also examined the viewing habits of staff and students at the Harvard School of Public Health. They discovered that 19.2 percent of the individuals who watched television three or more hours a day were obese, compared with only 4.5 percent of those who watched an hour or less a day.

## A Television Deprogramming Plan

Do you find yourself watching reruns for the third time? Then you may want to consider weaning yourself off the tube. These expert strategies can help.

• Track your viewing habits. "For a week, write down how many hours a day you sit in front of the television," says Robert Kubey, Ph.D., psychologist and professor in the Department of Communication at Rutgers University in New Brunswick, New Jersey. "Most people who do this are astonished at how much television they watch."

• List alternatives to the tube. "Make a list of all of the interesting and useful activities you can engage in other than watching television—walking, reading a good book, playing cards, whatever," suggests Dr. Kubey. "Post the list on your refrigerator or even on your television. Then instead of turning on the television after dinner, do something from your list." You might renew your interest in cross-word puzzles, crafts or jigsaw puzzles, for example.

• Tape, don't watch, your favorite shows, suggests Dr. Kubey. Why? So you can fast-forward through commercials. Dr. Kubey says he regularly tapes two-hour movies and watches them in an hour and 15 minutes, trimming 45 minutes off his tube time.

• Be aware of what—and how much—you're eating while you're watching television, advises Dr. Wong. Healthful treats include air-popped popcorn, rice cakes and a plate of raw fresh baby carrots.

• "Consume" television the way you consume high-fat foods: in moderation. "It's okay to binge on television once in a while," says Dr. Kubey. "But if your television habit interferes with real life, it's time to take control." You have nothing to lose but points off your cholesterol level.

❧

# TRIGLYCERIDE CONTROL

## *Taming the Forgotten Blood Fat*

Don't have a clue as to what your triglyceride reading is—or even what triglycerides are? You should. There's evidence to suggest that elevated triglycerides may predict coronary heart disease, particularly in women and in people with diabetes.

Triglycerides, one of the major fats carried in blood, transport fatty acids that are derived from food or manufactured in the liver. Like cholesterol, triglycerides are measured in milligrams/deciliter.

In the famed Framingham Heart Study, which has tracked the health of the residents of Framingham, Massachusetts, for more than a generation, "a high triglyceride level (150 milligrams/deciliter or higher) appears to be an especially strong predictor of coronary heart disease in people who have low HDL cholesterol (less than 50 milligrams/deciliter)," says William P. Castelli, M.D., medical director of the Framingham Cardiovascular Institute, a wellness program at Metro West Medical Center. What's more, "high triglycerides may play a more important role in women than in men," says Marla Mendelson, M.D., assistant professor of medicine at Northwestern University Medical School in Chicago. "Triglycerides are also higher in people with uncontrolled diabetes, which is itself a risk factor for heart disease."

Most experts agree that a high triglyceride level should not be ignored, especially if it's coupled with high LDL cholesterol (the "bad" kind) and low HDL cholesterol (the "good" kind).

## Conflicting Evidence

Triglycerides are essential to life. But consuming too many triglycerides can cause the body to make too much cholesterol. "There's an indirect relationship between high cholesterol and high triglycerides," says Frederic J. Pashkow, M.D., cardiologist at the Cleveland Clinic Foundation in Cleveland and author of *50 Essential Things to Do When the Doctor Says It's Heart Disease.* "Triglycerides in the liver can be remetabolized and reconfigured as LDL cholesterol. The LDL formed as part of this triglyceride metabolism tend to be small and dense—the ones that are particularly atherogenic and dangerous."

Some studies have concluded that there is no direct association between triglyceride levels and cardiovascular risk. But other research has shown a significant association between the two. Here's a sampling of those studies.

In the Framingham Heart Study, high triglycerides in association with low HDL cholesterol were found to be an independent predictor of coronary heart disease in men and women over age 50. "People with high triglycerides and low HDL have many other problems that together greatly increase the risk of heart disease and diabetes," says Dr. Castelli. "These people can be missed in cholesterol screenings because their levels of total and LDL cholesterol aren't high."

Researchers in Norway analyzed triglyceride levels in 24,535 middle-age women. These researchers found that as triglyceride readings increased, so did deaths related to coronary heart disease—as well as deaths from all causes. The researchers found no relationship between triglycerides and mortality in 25,058 men, however.

Researchers at Johns Hopkins University School of Medicine in Baltimore examined the relationship between cardiovascular disease and various blood fat measurements (total, HDL and LDL cholesterol and triglycerides) in about 1,400 women ages 50 to 69. Over a 14-year period, high triglycerides (over 200 milligrams/deciliter), particularly in combination with low HDL levels (under 50 milligrams/deciliter), were associated with an increased risk of dying of heart disease. These researchers concluded that elevated triglycerides are an independent predictor of death from cardiovascular disease in women. Further, the researchers recommended, "cholesterol-screening guidelines should be re-evaluated to reflect the importance of HDL and triglyceride levels in determining risk in women."

Finally, people with high triglyceride levels may have more problems than other folks in lowering their LDL cholesterol, according to a study conducted at the Alton Ochsner Medical Foundation in New Orleans. Researchers followed the progress of 313 people enrolled in a rehabilitation program following heart trouble. All of these individuals had high cholesterol, and 39 had elevated triglycerides. The group was put on a low-fat, low-cholesterol diet for three months.

By the end of the study, the group as a whole had significant im-

---

### SERVE UP SOME SALMON

Can the cholesterol-lowering omega-3 fatty acids in fatty fish such as salmon and albacore tuna help lower elevated triglycerides? According to some experts, the answer is yes.

"Studies have shown that these omega-3's can lower triglycerides as well as cholesterol," says James W. Anderson, M.D., professor of medicine and clinical nutrition at the University of Kentucky College of Medicine in Lexington and author of *Dr. Anderson's High-Fiber Fitness Plan.* "I recommend eating fish about twice a week. But you need to prepare the fish properly—broil or steam the fish rather than fry it."

Fish oil can help lower triglycerides as well, according to William P. Castelli, M.D., medical director of the Framingham Cardiovascular Institute, a wellness program at Metro West Medical Center in Framingham, Massachusetts. Research conducted at Oregon Health Sciences University in Portland, says Dr. Castelli, showed that only fish oil lowered triglycerides to under 500 milligrams/deciliter in people whose triglycerides topped 1,000 miligrams/deciliter. "As little as three to four grams of fish oil a day may be all that's needed," he says.

---

### WHAT'S YOUR LEVEL?

Like cholesterol, triglycerides are measured in milligrams/deciliter. Here are the National Cholesterol Education Program's guidelines for triglyceride levels.

| | |
|---|---|
| 200 | Borderline high |
| 400 | High |
| 1,000 | Very high |

---

provements in total, LDL and HDL cholesterol. But the people with high triglyceride levels had no significant improvement in LDL cholesterol or in the ratio of LDL to HDL. According to the researchers, people with high triglycerides may need more aggressive nondrug treatment to improve their cholesterol profiles.

## Cutting These Fats Down to Size

"Ideally, your triglyceride level should be below 150 milligrams/deciliter," says Dr. Castelli. "People with coronary heart disease should probably have triglyceride levels below 100 milligrams/deciliter."

Most experts advise taking steps to lower high triglycerides, especially if you have low HDL cholesterol or high LDL cholesterol. "A high triglyceride level is a warning sign in many patients who have a predisposition for coronary heart disease," says Peter O. Kwiterovich, Jr., M.D., professor of medicine and director of the Lipid Research and Atherosclerosis Unit at Johns Hopkins and author of *The Johns Hopkins Complete Guide for Preventing and Reversing Heart Disease.* "It needs to be taken care of."

Fortunately, say most doctors, you can usually lower a high triglyceride level with lifestyle changes. Here are some of the most common triglyceride-lowering strategies.

• Lose weight. "Triglycerides respond very well to weight reduction," says Dr. Kwiterovich. "Losing as little as five to ten pounds will significantly lower your triglycerides."

• Avoid alcohol. While studies have shown that a drink or two a day can help raise HDL cholesterol, alcohol can actually raise triglycerides by lowering the concentration of an enzyme used to break them down. "Even having a glass of wine with dinner every night can substantially raise triglycerides in people who are overweight or who have hereditary triglyceride problems," says Thomas Bersot, M.D., associate professor of medicine at the University of California, San Francisco.

• Avoid refined carbohydrates and sugars. Partially refined carbohydrates, including white flour and white rice, refined sugars such as those in candy and even some high-sugar fruit juices such as orange juice will raise triglycerides in some people, says Dr. Castelli. "Switching to complex carbohydrates, such as whole-wheat bread, brown rice, barley and rolled oats, can help lower triglycerides," he says.

• Exercise. "Walking just two miles a day can dramatically lower your triglycerides and raise your HDL cholesterol," says Dr. Castelli.

• Consider medication. If all else fails, your doctor may advise medication to help lower very high triglycerides, says Dr. Bersot. All drugs have potentially adverse effects. So discuss any possible downside to the use of medication, says Dr. Castelli.

∼✿∽

# VEGETABLES

## *Recapture Your Salad Days*

For many of us, hating vegetables was as much a part of childhood as climbing trees or playing with dolls. Fortunately, most of us outgrew this disdain. As adults, we not only acquired a taste for beans, broccoli and bok choy, we began to appreciate their health benefits, too.

Vegetables are virtually nonfat, a boon if you're on a cholesterol-lowering program. "As you add more vegetables to your diet, you tend to consume less fat," says Martin Yadrick, R.D., a dietitian in Manhattan Beach, California, and a spokesperson for the American Dietetic Association. Vegetables are also loaded with fiber—both the insoluble kind, which promotes regularity and may lessen the risk of colon cancer, and the soluble variety, which helps trounce blood cholesterol levels. Soluble fiber is found in many of our favorite vegetables, including peas, corn and potatoes.

Best of all, veggies are so low in calories that you can eat virtually as many juicy beefsteak tomatoes, crisp snow peas and colorful red, orange and yellow peppers as you wish. "Americans like to eat lots of food," says Janet Lepke, R.D., a dietitian in Santa Monica, California, and a spokesperson for the American Dietetic Association. "When people eat less, they tend to feel deprived. But you can eat a lot of vegetables and feel good about it."

There's only one catch: You can cancel all of these benefits if you're in the habit of drowning your vegetables in butter, cream sauce or cheese sauce or loading them with salt. But you don't have to do without flavor. Using herbs, spices and condiments can transform a naked baked potato or plain green beans into veritable veggie delights. And your heart will thank you.

## Greens, Glorious Greens

Some of the most compelling studies of the cholesterol-lowering benefits of vegetables (and fruits) were conducted in India. In one study, researchers put over 600 people at risk for coronary heart disease on a low-fat, low-cholesterol diet. Half of these individuals were instructed to increase their intakes of fruits and vegetables to 400 or more grams (about five servings) a day; the others were not. After 12 weeks, the total cholesterol of the folks who ate the most fruits and vegetables dropped an average of 6.5 percent, and their "bad" LDL cholesterol dropped 7.3 percent. What's more, these folks' heart-healthy HDL cholesterol rose 5.6 percent. The total and LDL cholesterol of those who didn't eat the extra roughage remained the same.

In another Indian study, researchers put 400 people who had previously had heart attacks on a low-fat, low-cholesterol diet. As in the first study, half of these people were instructed to eat lots of fruits and vegetables; the other half were not. After three months, the total cholesterol of those who maxed out on fruits and vegetables plunged 27 points, from 226 to 199 milligrams/deciliter. Cholesterol readings in the control group fell, too, but less dramatically—14 points, from 229 to 215 milligrams/deciliter.

## A Bumper Crop of Produce Pointers

You don't have to be a vegetarian to appreciate perfectly steamed asparagus or a fresh ear of corn. "There are lots of ways to enhance vegetables without using rich, fatty sauces," says Lisa Lauri, R.D., nutrition consultant at North Shore University Hospital in Manhasset, New York. These strategies can help maximize vegetables' nutrients—and flavors.

• Choose fresh or frozen vegetables over canned; they taste better and contain more nutrients. If you opt for frozen, read the package to make sure the product doesn't contain added salt or fat.

• Steam rather than boil vegetables, advises Los Angeles dietitian Bettye Nowlin, R.D., spokesperson for the American Dietetic Association. "Steamed vegetables are ready to eat in five minutes and retain most of their nutrients," she says. "They're nice and crunchy, too."

• Top baked potatoes and steamed vegetables with a blend of nonfat yogurt, garlic, a sprinkling of "light" salt and a dash each of curry and cayenne pepper. Delicious.

• Season vegetables with rice vinegar or another flavored vinegar, suggests Tammy Baker, R.D., a nutritionist in Cave Creek, Arizona, and a spokesperson for the American Dietetic Association. "You'll add flavor and avoid the butter dish," she says.

• Liven up cooked vegetables with herbs and spices, says Lauri. "Dill tastes wonderful on carrots," she says. You might also top a baked potato with chives, bring out the flavor of fresh green beans with garlic and rosemary or dust a sweet potato with ginger.

• At your next barbecue, pass up the ribs and grill up some vegetables. "Marinate sliced eggplant in low-sodium teriyaki sauce, ginger and garlic, then barbecue it," suggests Lepke. "It tastes delicious over rice." Try grilling big slices of mushrooms, peppers and zucchini, too. You can find suitable skewers or racks wherever grill accessories are sold, so food doesn't fall into the coals or burners.

• Want to make a low-fat cream sauce for vegetables? Blend a teaspoon each of low-fat margarine and flour, then heat for two minutes while slowly whisking in skim milk, suggests Marilyn Cerino, R.D., nutrition consultant at the Benjamin Franklin Center for Health of Pennsylvania Hospital in Philadelphia. Add seasonings appropriate to the vegetables.

• Prepare vegetables with flair, says Michael Klaper, M.D., health director of the Royal Atlantic Health Spa in Pompano Beach, Florida, and author of *Vegan Nutrition: Pure and Simple.* "You don't have to eat dry, plain vegetables. Have some fun with them. When you make pasta primavera, for example, use lots of green and yellow vegetables. Top rice or noodles with Chinese-style stir-fried vegetables. If you like East Indian cuisine, learn to make a vegetable curry."

• Don't shower vegetables with salt. A high-sodium diet may contribute to high blood pressure, which is no better for your heart than high cholesterol. "Cutting down on salt is like reducing the fat in your diet," says Neal Barnard, M.D., president of the Physicians Committee for Responsible Medicine in Washington, D.C. "You get used to it. So squirt a little lemon juice on your broccoli instead of salting it. It can make all of the difference in the world."

# VEGETARIAN DIET

## *Simple, Nutritious and Tasty, Too*

If the phrase "vegetarian diet" makes you think of alfalfa sprouts and tofu, it's time to update your thinking: Vegetarian cuisine is hot. Spurred in part by public recognition of its health benefits and by its new emphasis on elegance, ease of preparation and flavor, the meatless way of eating is surfing a renewed popularity unprecedented since the first wave of vegetarianism in the 1970s.

In fact, you may even consider yourself part of a new breed of vegetarian—the part-time vegetarian, who enjoys meatless meals prepared with pastas, grains and beans a few times a week.

In general, a vegetarian diet is low in fat and dietary cholesterol and high in fiber. In fact, a considerable amount of scientific evidence suggests that vegetarians are less likely to develop a number of chronic diseases, including coronary heart disease.

A vegetarian diet can provide your body with all of the nutrients that it needs, as long as you follow a few basic guidelines. Going vegetarian can also be delicious—and far easier than you might think.

## Moving Away from Meat

Study after study suggests that vegetarianism and good heart health go hand in hand. Perhaps the best-known of these studies is the Lifestyle Heart Trial, led by Dean Ornish, M.D., president and director of the Preventive Medicine Research Institute in Sausalito, California, and author of *Dr. Dean Ornish's Program for Reversing Heart Disease.* In this study, Dr. Ornish and his colleagues placed 28 people with coronary atherosclerosis (fatty plaques in the arteries) on a low-fat vegetarian diet for a year. The diet derived about 10 percent of its calories from fat. To put this figure in perspective, the typical American diet gets about 37 percent of its calories from fat. These 28 individuals also quit smoking, engaged in moderate exercise, including walking, and performed stress management techniques such as meditation and yoga.

Another group of 20 people with arterial plaques were treated in the usual manner: Some took cholesterol-lowering drugs and all, on average, ate a diet deriving 30 percent of its calories from fat, a standard recommendation for people who want to lower their cholesterol.

After a year, it was found that the arteries of 82 percent of the people who followed the low-fat vegetarian diet were less clogged than they had been before the study began. The drug-treatment group ended up with arteries that were more clogged. And—get this—the people whose arteries were the most closed to begin with showed the greatest improvement.

Researchers from the American Health Foundation in New York City compared the cholesterol levels of Seventh-Day Adventists who were vegans with those of people who ate the typical American diet. Vegans (pronounced VEE-gans), the strictest of all vegetarians, don't eat any foods from animal sources, including fish, poultry, dairy products and eggs. The researchers found that the Adventists' average total cholesterol was 25 percent lower and their average LDL cholesterol (the "bad" kind) was 38 percent lower.

In an 11-year study of over 1,900 vegetarians, researchers in Germany found that death from all causes was cut by one-half compared with the general population, while deaths from heart disease were reduced by one-third. Nondietary factors may have contributed to the vegetarians' longevity, said the researchers, who noted that most vegetarians are nonsmokers and are rarely overweight.

Researchers in China compared the cholesterol levels of 55 young Chinese Buddhist vegetarians with those of 59 Chinese medical students who ate both animal and vegetable substances. It was found that the vegetarians, who had been eating meatless diets for at least two years, consumed an average of 7 percent less fat, 3 percent less protein and 10 percent more carbohydrates than the students. Further, the students had significantly higher blood cholesterol levels—about 25 points higher in men and 36 points higher in women.

## Ready for Veggies? Read This First

A vegetarian diet isn't automatically healthy. A steady diet of pizza, potato chips and chocolate cream pie may satisfy your taste buds, but not your body's need for vitamins and minerals. Here's how to make sure you get the nutrients you need without the fat and cholesterol you don't.

If you're on a vegetarian diet that allows dairy products, eat the low-fat or nonfat varieties. Whole-milk cheese and whole milk are loaded with saturated fat, which can send your blood cholesterol skyward.

Also, when you dine out, make it clear that you want your food prepared with little or no fat. "A single serving of pasta primavera

## WHAT KIND OF VEGETARIAN ARE YOU?

There are several types of vegetarians, all of whom eat fruits, vegetables, grains and legumes. But some vegetarians eat dairy products and eggs, while others don't. Some people even qualify as part-time vegetarians, who eat meatless meals made with pastas, beans and grains several times a week. Here's a rundown of the most common types of vegetarians.

- Semivegetarians eat poultry, fish and dairy products.
- Lacto-ovo-vegetarians eat both dairy products and eggs.
- Lacto-vegetarians eat dairy products but not eggs.
- Ovo-vegetarians eat eggs but not dairy products.
- Vegans don't eat poultry, fish, dairy products or eggs.

might contain four tablespoons of butter," explains Sue Chapman, executive chef at the Skylonda Fitness Retreat in Woodside, California.

Most important, make sure your diet contains adequate amounts of key nutrients. A vegetarian diet may fall short in protein, vitamin $B_{12}$, iron, zinc and calcium.

"If you go on a vegetarian diet, you must educate yourself on how to get enough nutrients," says William P. Castelli, M.D., medical director of the Framingham Cardiovascular Institute, a wellness program at Metro West Medical Center in Framingham, Massachusetts.

- If you omit all animal products from your diet, you may fall short in protein or vitamin $B_{12}$. So make sure your diet emphasizes protein-rich plant foods such as beans, peas and nuts.

Also, eat cereals fortified with vitamin $B_{12}$ (a nutrient found naturally only in animal foods). If you give up only meat and not eggs or dairy foods, you'll be more likely to get the vitamin $B_{12}$ you need, however.

- If you give up meat, you may also give up plenty of iron, zinc and calcium. You can get more of these vital nutrients by eating tofu, beans, peas and orange juice fortified with calcium.

*See also* Beans, Complex Carbohydrates, Fiber, High-Fiber Cereals, Oats, Vegetables

# WALKING

## *The Ultimate Exercise*

Walking is man's best medicine," said the Greek physician Hippocrates. If the good doctor were around today, he'd add that regular constitutionals can benefit women, too. In fact, walking is good medicine for virtually everyone, no matter what their age or level of fitness. Studies have shown that walking can help improve your cholesterol profile as well as lower blood pressure, reduce the risk of heart attack and stroke and control diabetes. "Walking may be the best medicine, because you can do it forever," says William P. Castelli, M.D., medical director of the Framingham Cardiovascular Institute, a wellness program at Metro West Medical Center in Framingham, Massachusetts.

"It's thought that much of exercise's ability to reduce the risk of heart disease comes from its ability to increase HDL cholesterol," says James Rippe, M.D., director of the Center for Clinical and Lifestyle Research at Tufts University School of Medicine in Boston and co-author of *Dr. James Rippe's Complete Book of Fitness Walking*. HDL cholesterol, the "good" kind, helps escort "bad" LDL cholesterol out of the body.

What's more, you don't need to own a closetful of expensive gear to reap the benefits of this simple yet effective exercise, say experts. "Walking is convenient and easy to do and requires no special equipment," says Darlene A. Sedlock, Ph.D., associate professor of kinesiology at Purdue University in West Lafayette, Indiana. "You can just step out your back door and go."

## Step Lively to Stay Heart-Healthy

There's a significant amount of evidence to suggest that walking can promote heart health. Here are a few of those studies.

Investigators at the Institute for Aerobics Research in Dallas gave treadmill tests to more than 13,000 people and followed these individuals' fitness levels for eight years. They discovered that folks who walked for a half-hour a day had reduced levels of premature death nearly as impressive as those of people who ran 30 to 40 miles a week.

Researchers at Brigham Young University in Provo, Utah, examined how walking affected the cholesterol levels of over 3,600 people. The ratios of total cholesterol to HDL cholesterol in folks who walked for 2½ to 4 or more hours per week were less likely to be elevated (a ratio of five or higher) than the ratios of those who didn't exercise regularly, according to Larry A. Tucker, Ph.D., professor and director of health promotion at Brigham Young.

Regular brisk walking increased HDL cholesterol in ten sedentary women who took part in a British study. These women (average age 47) followed a walking regimen for three months. Not only did brisk walking increase their HDL, but when researchers retested the women after six months of not walking, they discovered that the women's cardiovascular gains were lost.

Walking may also help stomp high levels of triglycerides (another blood fat implicated in heart disease) by stimulating an enzyme that carries triglycerides out of the blood, according to researchers at Baylor College of Medicine in Houston. These researchers had one group of 12 people take a single 2-hour walk. A second group didn't exercise at all. Then 15 hours later, all of these individuals ate a high-fat meal. After eating, the walkers' triglyceride readings were 31 percent lower than those of the nonexercisers.

## How Fast? How Far?

You don't have to power-walk to prevent heart disease and promote health. Walking briskly for two miles every day, or nearly every day, is a great way to accumulate the half-hour of physical activity a day recommended by experts convened by the Centers for Disease Control and Prevention in Atlanta and the American College of Sports Medicine. What's more, when it comes to walking, speed doesn't determine effectiveness, say many experts.

Researchers at the Institute for Aerobics Research had 59 women walk three miles a day, five days a week, for six months. But each group walked at varying speeds. The first group of women walked a mile in 12 minutes. The second group walked a mile in 15 minutes. And the third group took 20 minutes to walk a mile. The fastest group of women had more impressive improvements in their overall fitness than the slowest group. But the HDL levels of all three groups jumped an average of 6 percent.

What about distance? Don't walk too far too fast, advises Ann Marie Miller, director of fitness and health services at the 92nd Street Y for Health, Fitness and Sport in New York City. "Walk a comfortable distance at a comfortable pace," she says. Other experts concur. "You should be able to carry on a conversation while you walk," says exercise physiologist Peter Snell, Ph.D., assistant professor of internal medicine at the University of Texas Southwestern Medical Center at Dallas. "If you can't talk without gasping for breath, slow down." Dr. Rippe concurs. "Give yourself time to make progress," he says.

The bottom line? Speed and distance are less important than consistency, say experts. "It's more important to walk at a comfortable pace on a regular basis," says Dan Rench, R.N., program director for cardiovascular rehabilitation at the Indiana Heart Institute at St. Vincent Hospital in Indianapolis. "If walking is fun, you'll probably stick with it."

## Ready, Set, Walk!

Ready to hit the road? These expert tips can help you keep pace.

• Invest in a good pair of walking shoes. While you don't need hundred-dollar footwear, "you need more than ordinary tennis shoes for walking," says Dr. Rippe. The shoe you choose should be lightweight and padded at the heel and tongue as well as have an absorbent lining. Also, the shoe should bend easily across the ball of your foot and feature an uptilted sole to enhance your natural walking motion.

• Find a walking buddy, suggests Miller. Invite a co-worker to take a "walk break" instead of a coffee break, then take a 15-minute stroll. You might even ask your spouse to share your walk before or after work.

- Walk with the weather in mind. In hot weather, wear loose-fitting, lightweight clothes, advises Dr. Rippe. And try to walk in the early morning or early evening, when the heat is less intense. Drink lots of water before and during your walk.
- In cold weather, dress in light layers that you can easily remove as your body warms up. "And watch your footing—your path could be icy and hazardous," says Miller. In truly stormy weather, climb up and down the stairs at home. *Caution:* If you have heart disease, diabetes, asthma or other health conditions, consult your doctor before walking in cold weather.
- Join a local walking club, suggests Miller. If you can't find one, consider starting your own.
- Forge new paths. Explore the grounds of a nearby botanical garden on foot. Or buy a book of local walking tours and hit the road.
- Imagine success. Visualize yourself on a brisk walk, feeling refreshed, positive and healthy. After all, a true power walk has just as much to do with the way you feel inside as with the speed of your stride.

*See also* Exercise

# WALNUTS

## *Modern Benefits from an Ancient Food*

In the early days of Rome, walnuts were considered a food fit for the gods and were named *Juglans regia* in honor of Jupiter. Not a bad endorsement. These days, however, we're more likely to bemoan the walnut's high content of fat and calories than to treat ourselves to this divinely delicious nut.

It's true that an ounce of walnuts contains about 180 calories and 17 grams of fat. But hold on: Eaten in moderation, walnuts may actually help lower your blood cholesterol without sabotaging your waistline.

How can the fat-laden walnut whittle down cholesterol? The answer lies in the type of fat this nut contains. Seventy percent of the fat in walnuts is polyunsaturated, which is gentler on your heart than the artery-plugging saturated fat found in red meat, cheese and butter. In fact, one study of the walnut notes that this nut's ratio of polyunsaturated to saturated fat is 7 to 1—"one of the highest among naturally occurring foods," the study states.

Walnuts are also rich in linolenic acid. This omega-3 fatty acid, also found in canola oil, is similar to the cholesterol-lowering omega-3's found in fatty fish.

## A Nutty Way to a Healthier Heart

Two studies conducted at Loma Linda University in California indicate that walnuts can help put the crunch on elevated cholesterol levels.

Researchers at Loma Linda first studied the lifestyles and diets of 31,208 Seventh-Day Adventists, searching for possible reasons why these individuals' rates of heart disease and some cancers were lower than in other Americans. One of the researchers' findings: The Adventists who ate nuts (including peanuts and almonds as well as walnuts) five or more times a week were about half as likely to have a heart attack or to die from heart disease as those who ate nuts less than once a week.

And despite the fact that nuts are high in fat and calories, the most enthusiastic nut munchers in the study were not the heaviest. "The people who ate nuts five or more times a week were significantly thinner than those who didn't eat nuts at all," says Gary E. Fraser, M.D., Ph.D., professor of medicine at Loma Linda University School of Public Health. "These people ate nuts a small handful—about two ounces—at a time. They weren't sitting in front of the television with a can of nuts." In fact, being a couch potato is more likely to make you fat than eating certain foods, the study notes.

While this first study showed an association between nut consumption and heart health, it didn't prove a direct cause-and-effect relationship. So the Loma Linda researchers conducted a second study that examined the cholesterol-curbing effects of walnuts alone.

In this study, the researchers put 18 men with normal cholesterol on one of two low-fat diets. Half of the men followed a low-fat, low-cholesterol control diet. The second group of men ate the same diet but also consumed three ounces of walnuts a day (20 percent of calories from walnuts). At the midpoint of the two-month study, the men switched diets.

The men's total cholesterol averaged 182 milligrams/deciliter on the control diet but plunged to 160 milligrams/deciliter on the walnut diet. Further, the men's "bad" LDL cholesterol plummeted from 112 milligrams/deciliter on the control diet to 94 milligrams/deciliter on the walnut plan, a 16.3 percent drop. "This was a small study of 18 young men," says Dr. Fraser. "But we carefully controlled their diets and clearly documented that the walnut period was associated with a substantial decline in blood cholesterol."

The drops in cholesterol were mostly the work of walnuts' high content of polyunsaturated fat, says Dr. Fraser. But the reductions were "substantially larger than we would have predicted," he adds. "So it raises the question of some additional factor" in walnuts that may help deflate cholesterol levels, he says.

## Grab a Handful of Heart Protection

The second Loma Linda study concluded that eaten in moderation, walnuts can be part of a cholesterol-lowering diet. But don't go overboard, says Mary Donkersloot, R.D., a dietitian in Beverly Hills, California, a spokesperson for the California Dietetic Association and author of *The Fast Food Diet.* "I'm hesitant to look at any food as a magic bullet," says Donkersloot. "It's one thing to add walnuts to a Waldorf salad, another to sit down and eat a bag of walnuts."

Translation: Eat walnuts in place of, not in addition to, other fats—especially saturated fats. Try these nutty serving suggestions.

• Sprinkle chopped shelled walnuts over steamed brussels sprouts or baked sweet potatoes.

• Toss a small amount of chopped walnuts into a salad. "The nuts will add flavor, texture and vitamin E," says Donkersloot.

• Add chopped walnuts to pancake batter, suggests John Phillip Carroll, a chef in San Francisco and recipe author of *California the*

---

## LITTLE-KNOWN WALNUT HINTS

If you don't do much baking, you may not know much about how to shell, store or otherwise prepare walnuts, either. These simple hints can help.

- If you hate to crack walnuts, buy the preshelled kind. They're just as fresh and flavorful as the unshelled variety, says John Phillip Carroll, a chef in San Francisco and recipe author of *California the Beautiful Cookbook*.
- Refrigerate walnuts if you plan to use them within a few months, says Carroll. Otherwise, freeze the nuts. "Just wrap the walnuts well, so they won't absorb that freezer taste," advises Carroll.
- To get rid of walnuts' sometimes astringent aftertaste, which is caused by the tannin in the nuts' dry, papery skins, drop the nuts in boiling water for a minute or two (a process called blanching). Or simply add walnuts at the end of a recipe, says Carroll. "If the nuts sit in food for a while, their acidity may leach out," he says.

---

*Beautiful Cookbook.* Use about ¼ cup of walnuts in a recipe that yields about eight three-inch pancakes. "You might also add ¼ cup of mashed ripe banana and 1½ cups of berries," suggests Carroll. To further reduce fat and cholesterol, prepare the batter with nonfat milk and egg substitute.

- If you have a food processor, make walnut sprinkles, suggests Carroll. These crispy fixin's can add flavor and crunch to a variety of foods. Mix 1 cup of ground shelled walnuts with ½ cup of bread crumbs. Then bake at 325° for about 15 minutes, or until the sprinkles are crisp and golden brown. Stir in ¼ teaspoon of cayenne pepper and one tablespoon of paprika, then cool. Use the sprinkles on salads, soups or pasta, in place of Parmesan cheese.

To make sweet, spicy sprinkles, replace the cayenne and paprika with two tablespoons of sugar and ½ teaspoon each of cinnamon and nutmeg. Stir these sprinkles into low-fat or nonfat yogurt, suggests Carroll.

~✤~

# WEIGHT LOSS

## *Drop Pounds, Drop Cholesterol*

Trying to scale down your cholesterol? Then chances are good that you're trying to scale down, period. "Being 20 to 30 percent over your ideal weight and having high cholesterol frequently go hand in hand," says John W. Zamarra, M.D., founding director of the cardiac rehabilitation program at Placentia-Linda Community Hospital in Brea, California.

What's more, carrying excess poundage tends to deflate the body's level of "good" HDL cholesterol, which helps whisk the "bad" cholesterol, called LDL, out of the body. "People who are overweight generally have low HDL cholesterol, often accompanied by elevated total and LDL cholesterol," says Dr. Zamarra.

But chin up: Dropping those extra pounds can help you take control of your cholesterol level. Further, shedding even a few pounds—5 to 10 percent of your initial weight—can significantly improve cholesterol levels, according to one study.

This chapter explains why excess pounds can push cholesterol over the top—and why losing them can help. You'll also find tips that can help you lose inches from your waistline and trim points from your cholesterol level.

## Love Handles? Check Your Cholesterol

Numerous studies have made a connection between body weight, elevated cholesterol levels and risk of coronary heart disease.

Using data from the second National Health and Nutrition Examination Survey, researchers from the University of Texas Health Science Center at Dallas Southwestern Medical School and other institutions examined the association between excess body weight and high blood cholesterol levels. These researchers conducted two separate studies: one on men, the other on women. Both studies reached the same conclusion: Excess body weight is associated with higher levels of total and LDL cholesterol and lower levels of HDL cholesterol in White men and women, whatever their ages.

Perimenopausal and menopausal women had lower HDL cholesterol and higher total and LDL cholesterol than premenopausal women, regardless of their weight. What's more, researchers discovered a stronger connection between body weight and triglyceride levels than between body weight and cholesterol. Triglycerides, another type of blood fat, are now established as an independent risk factor for coronary heart disease in men and women, says William P. Castelli, M.D., medical director of the Framingham Cardiovascular Institute, a wellness program at Metro West Medical Center in Framingham, Massachusetts.

## Weigh In for the Last Time

Losing weight is one thing; keeping it off, quite another. But it can be done. These tips can help you shed those pounds—permanently.

• Work that body. There's no way around it, experts say. "The only way to lose weight is to burn more calories than you consume—not just today or this week but on a regular basis," says Leonard Doberne, M.D., an endocrinologist in private practice in Mount View, California.

• More important, regular exercise can also maintain or even raise HDL cholesterol. While cutting back on dietary fat and cholesterol can often lower total blood cholesterol levels about 15 percent, it also tends to reduce HDL cholesterol, notes Dr. Doberne. "So the ratio of total cholesterol to HDL cholesterol, which appears to be of primary importance, is not always much improved," he says. "Exercise is the best way we know to raise HDL. That's why a weight-loss program aimed at improving the cholesterol ratio should include exercise."

• Avoid crash diets. They tend to slow the metabolism until the body kicks in to survival mode and starts storing fat like crazy, says Peg Jordan, R.N., in her book *How the New Food Labels Can Save Your Life.* Worse, once you start eating normally again, your metabolism is still sluggish. So any pounds you may have lost quickly return.

• Cut the fat. Eating fatty foods such as processed lunchmeat, fried snacks and butter is the fastest route to weight gain, says Dr. Zamarra.

---

## EAT MORE AT HIGH NOON, LESS LATER ON

It's common knowledge that what we eat affects our weight. But so can when we eat it, according to Deepak Chopra, M.D., in his book *Perfect Weight.*

According to Ayurveda, the ancient Indian system of natural medicine, the body's "digestive fire" burns strongest at midday. Because digestion is stronger during this time, the body converts food into energy more efficiently, says Dr. Chopra. And in fact, many health professionals here in the West suggest eating a bigger breakfast and lunch and a lighter evening meal.

Make lunch your largest meal of the day and eat at approximately the same time each day, preferably between 12:00 and 12:30 P.M., suggests Dr. Chopra. "This one very simple change will make a profound difference in your metabolism," according to Dr. Chopra.

---

"Fat contains nine calories per gram, more than twice as many as carbohydrates and protein, which have only four. You don't have to eat a lot of fatty foods to consume lots of calories."

• Eat more complex carbohydrates—whole grains, legumes, vegetables and fruits, recommends dietitian Deralee Scanlon, R.D., author of *Diets That Work.*

Why? Because the body expends more calories digesting and metabolizing complex carbohydrates. To transform 100 calories of carbohydrates into stored body fat, the body must use up 23 calories. But the body uses only 3 calories to convert 100 calories of dietary fat into body fat.

• Foods high in complex carbohydrates tend to be higher in fiber and lower in calories and fat. It's likely that these foods also are more filling and take longer to chew—two qualities that can help you reduce the amount you eat.

• Slow down. It takes about 20 minutes for your brain to let your body know that you've eaten enough, says Scanlon. If you eat quickly, you're likely to eat more than you want.

If you rush through your meals like the Road Runner in the cartoon, Dr. Zamarra suggests you try these tips.

• Eating in a calm, settled atmosphere. A noisy, frenzied environment tends to make you eat faster—and more.

- Before you pick up your fork, close your eyes and take a few deep breaths. "This can help you eat at a slower, more leisurely pace," says Dr. Zamarra.

*See also* Complex Carbohydrates, Cooking, Exercise, Low-Fat Diet, Walking, part 4

಄಄಄

# WHEAT GERM

## *Sprinkle It On, Mix It In*

**W**ant to help your favorite "fiberful" cereal pack even more of a cholesterol-walloping punch? Sprinkle it with wheat germ. Several studies have associated this crunchy, nutty-tasting grain product with reduced cholesterol levels.

Nearly 80 percent of the fat in wheat germ—the sprouting part of the wheat kernel—is unsaturated, the kind proven to help reduce "bad" LDL cholesterol, says Mindy Hermann, R.D., a nutrition consultant in Mount Kisco, New York. Further, wheat germ is brimming with vitamin E.

Some researchers believe that this vitamin hinders oxidation, the process by which LDL cholesterol gums up artery walls. Wheat germ is also rich in folate, a B vitamin vital to the production of new blood cells, and magnesium, which may help protect your heart, arteries and blood pressure.

And if you think the only way to use wheat germ is to sprinkle it on your cereal, think again. You can sprinkle this versatile substance into virtually any dish, from salads to home-baked treats. Read on.

## Phytosterols: Your Arteries' Best Friend

How might wheat germ lower cholesterol? Experts aren't sure. But one theory involves phytosterols, certain chemicals found in wheat germ and other plants, says Fred Shinnick, Ph.D., a biochemist for the

Quaker Oats Company in Barrington, Illinois. "Phytosterols may prevent the intestinal absorption of cholesterol," theorizes Dr. Shinnick.

Still another theory suggests that some component of wheat germ plays a role in the activity of apolipoprotein B, a protein molecule involved in the transport of blood fats. A defect in apolipoprotein B receptors may lead to higher cholesterol levels, says Dr. Shinnick.

"There may be other factors at work, too," says Dr. Shinnick. Other nutrients and molecules in wheat germ may inhibit the process by which cholesterol plugs the coronary arteries, for example.

Researchers at the National Institute of Health in France had 19 people with high cholesterol add 20 grams (less than three tablespoons) of either raw or partially defatted wheat germ to their normal diets every day for a month. Researchers then increased the amount of wheat germ to 30 grams per day for the next 14 weeks. Throughout the study, these people consumed about 350 milligrams of cholesterol and 80 to 90 grams of fat per day.

After the additional 14 weeks, the total cholesterol of the folks consuming the raw wheat germ had fallen 7.2 percent—a potential 15 percent decrease in their risk of coronary heart disease—and their LDL cholesterol had plunged 15.4 percent. Their triglycerides, another indicator of heart disease risk, fell 11.3 percent. The people consuming the partially defatted wheat germ saw their total cholesterol fall 9.8 percent, but the effects of the defatted variety tapered off by the end of the study.

In another study conducted by the same French researchers, ten people with high cholesterol levels consumed 30 grams of wheat germ a day for a month. They followed their usual diets for a month before and after participating in the wheat germ plan. These individuals saw their total cholesterol levels fall about 8 percent (from an average of 301 to 275 milligrams/deciliter) while consuming the wheat germ. What's more, their triglyceride levels plummeted nearly 34 percent.

## Add Crunch to Your Diet

You can use wheat germ to add flavor—and crunch—to virtually any dish, from cereal to meat loaf. "Wheat germ has an appealing nutty taste," says Hermann. "And it's so versatile that you can use it in almost anything." Here are some ways to add this crunchy delight to your diet.

• The next time you make muffins, substitute ½ cup of wheat germ for ½ cup of the flour, suggests dietitian Sarah Murphy, R.D., a scientist for the Quaker Oats Company. "Because wheat germ is so nutrient-dense, you'll give your muffins a real nutrition boost." *Note:* Wheat germ tends to absorb moisture in baked goods, so add one to two tablespoons of water per ¼ cup of wheat germ.

• Try using wheat germ in cake and bread mixes, too, says dietitian Sharon Landvik, R.D., manager of the Vitamin E Research and Information Service in Chicago. Replace no more than one-third of the flour with wheat germ, however. It doesn't contain much gluten, the stuff that helps bread rise.

• "Sprinkle wheat germ on cold or hot cereal," says Hermann. "You can add the wheat germ while hot cereal is cooking or just before eating. You might also add cinnamon, raisins and skim milk." Or mix wheat germ into low-fat or nonfat yogurt or low-fat or nonfat vanilla, rice or tapioca pudding.

• Sprinkle wheat germ on tossed salads, suggests Hermann. Or try topping cooked vegetables with a blend of wheat germ and a drop of olive oil.

• Mix a small amount of wheat germ into meat loaf, suggests Hermann. "But make sure you're using lean beef," she says. "Otherwise, the benefits of using wheat germ may be outweighed by the high-fat beef."

# WINE

## *Research Worthy of a Toast*

Imagine: You live in Paris, where the bread is fresh, the Brie is creamy, and the croissants are butter-soaked. Nevertheless, like other French men and women, your heart attack risk is less than half of the rate of your American *amis*.

Welcome to the French paradox.

This mysterious phrase refers to the fact that in some regions of France, people consume high-fat diets bursting with artery-clogging saturated fat and have high blood cholesterol, high blood pressure and smoking habits similar to those of Americans. Yet these folks have lower rates of coronary heart disease. Why do the French seem to get away with indulging in less-than-perfect health habits?

Many researchers believe that it may in part be the amount of wine the French consume. Studies here and abroad have found that people who consume moderate amounts of alcohol (even just one drink per day), as the French tend to do, have lower rates of coronary heart disease.

Experts aren't sure how wine might benefit the heart. But they do know that drinking wine (and other alcoholic beverages) in moderation tends to boost "good" HDL cholesterol. There's also evidence that alcohol increases the body's stores of a substance that helps keep the blood from clotting.

But questions remain. Some researchers question whether it's the alcohol or other substances in wine—such as antioxidants, "supernutrients" such as vitamins C and E that have already been linked to a reduction in risk of heart disease and cancer—that exert the heart-healthy effects. And most experts agree: If you don't drink, don't start. Here's what is known about wine and blood cholesterol.

## To Your Health

Numerous studies have linked moderate alcohol intake with a low incidence of coronary heart disease.

Researchers in France analyzed data from 17 countries, including France. They concluded that despite the French population's high intake of saturated fat, the high rate of wine consumption may offset this dietary liability. The researchers noted that people in Toulouse, France, consume about 38 grams of alcohol per day (34 grams of it as wine), compared with a much lower intake in Stanford, California. Further, the death rate among men from heart disease is 57 percent lower in Toulouse than in Stanford. But the researchers noted that alcohol "is a drug that, studies suggest, should be used regularly but only at moderate doses of about 20 to 30 grams per day." At this level

## WHAT'S BETTER FOR YOUR HEART— BEAUJOLAIS OR CHARDONNAY?

Which wine is better for the heart—red or white? It depends on whom you ask.

French researchers gave rats white wine, red wine or 6 percent ethanol. At first, all three groups of rodents showed about a 70 percent reduction in the clumping of blood platelets (which helps form blood clots). But when the rats were deprived of alcohol for 18 hours, the platelet-clotting response increased 46 percent in the white wine group and 124 percent in the ethanol group. But the red wine–drinking rats showed a desirable 59 percent drop in clotting response.

"The platelets of the rats drinking red wine did not exhibit the rebound effect observed hours after alcohol drinking, eventually associated with sudden death and stroke in humans," wrote the researchers.

A study by researchers at the Kenneth L. Jordan Heart Foundation and Research Center in Montclair, New Jersey, on the other hand, found that white wine may be more beneficial than red.

The researchers had 20 men and women with high cholesterol consume 180 milliliters of either red or white wine every day for a month. The subjects then switched to the other type of wine for another month. These individuals ate whatever they wanted. While neither group had significant changes in total or "good" HDL cholesterol, the white wine lowered "bad" LDL cholesterol from 167 to 155 milligrams/deciliter. The researchers also found that both groups' blood showed a decreased clotting response.

And investigators at the Kaiser Permanente Medical Care Program in Oakland, California, analyzed both red wine drinkers and white wine drinkers and found that both groups have lower risks of coronary heart disease.

The upshot? "Classically, red wine has been thought to be more preventive than white wine, and there's some persuasive evidence in support of red wine—and that it probably has a more complex effect within the body," says Dr. Pashkow.

But not every expert agrees that red wine is a better cholesterol buster. "There's no difference (between red and white wine)," says William P. Castelli, M.D., medical director of the Framingham Cardiovascular Institute, a wellness program at Metro West Medical Center in Framingham, Massachusetts. "All of the scientific evidence points to either one as helping to lower the risk of developing coronary heart disease."

of consumption, the researchers said, "the risk of coronary heart disease can be decreased by as much as 40 percent."

Drinking wine and other alcoholic beverages may also boost levels of tissue-type plasminogen activator, or tPA. This substance, found naturally in the body, helps keep blood from clotting. In a study of over 600 men, those who reported drinking two or more drinks per day had 35 percent more tPA in their blood than men who said they rarely or never drank.

## Can Wine "Rustproof" Your Arteries?

Some researchers theorize that it's the antioxidants in wine, not the alcohol, that cause the beneficial effect. Some studies have shown that red wine has a potent antioxidative capacity and has reduced the oxidation of "bad" LDL cholesterol in test tubes. (Oxidation is a chemical process that appears to increase the likelihood of LDL cholesterol collecting in the arteries.)

"Red wine contains antioxidants," says Peter O. Kwiterovich, Jr., M.D., professor of medicine and director of the Lipid Research and Atherosclerosis Unit at Johns Hopkins University School of Medicine in Baltimore and author of *The Johns Hopkins Complete Guide for Preventing and Reversing Heart Disease.* (So does white wine.) These antioxidant compounds may hinder the buildup of fatty deposits in the coronary arteries, says John D. Folts, Ph.D., director of the University of Wisconsin Coronary Artery Thrombosis Research and Prevention Lab at the University of Wisconsin Hospital and Clinics in Madison. "This antioxidation process slows the rate of LDL deposition in the coronary arteries," says Dr. Folts.

One compound that has gotten a lot of attention is resveratrol, a fungus-fighting compound found in the skin of grapes. Rat studies have shown that purified resveratrol appears to lower cholesterol, and one study has theorized that resveratrol may be the active ingredient in wines that reduces blood cholesterol.

Researchers at the University of California, Davis, drew blood samples from a group of people with normal cholesterol levels. After removing the LDL cholesterol from the blood samples, the researchers then mixed the LDL with phenolic compounds drawn from red wine. The researchers found that these phenolic compounds reduced the oxidation of LDL cholesterol by 60 to 98 percent.

A separate study, conducted at Queen Elizabeth Hospital in Birmingham, England, provided the first evidence that red wine seems to enhance antioxidant activity in the blood. Researchers had ten people consume two lunches over two days. At one of the lunches, each person drank a glass of red wine. At the other lunch, they drank no wine. A half-hour after each meal, each volunteer gave the first of several blood samples taken over four hours. After the wine meal, the antioxidant levels in the people's blood rose, reaching a peak after 90 minutes. More significantly, their antioxidant levels were higher than those shown to inhibit oxidation of LDL cholesterol in test-tube experiments. After the wine-free meal, these individuals' blood showed little change in antioxidant activity.

## Before You Imbibe

A bottle of Bordeaux isn't a magic bullet against clogged arteries, says William P. Castelli, M.D., medical director of the Framingham Cardiovascular Institute, a wellness program at Metro West Medical Center in Framingham, Massachusetts. And some experts feel that wine shouldn't be touted as a cholesterol buster at all. One study concluded that "the protective effects of alcohol come at the cost of life-shortening alcohol abuse by large numbers of people." And other studies note that while a moderate amount of alcohol may have a protective effect, risk increases with the amount consumed.

The bottom line? If you don't drink, don't start, says Frederic Pashkow, M.D., cardiologist at the Cleveland Clinic Foundation in Cleveland and author of *50 Essential Things to Do When the Doctor Says It's Heart Disease*. "There are other ways besides drinking to improve your cholesterol profile, including reducing the fat in your diet and getting regular exercise," says Dr. Pashkow. "Nevertheless, if you're already having a drink a day, and your doctor says it's okay, then it's fine to continue to drink in moderation."

"In my view, a day without a glass of wine is a terrible day!" says Dr. Castelli. "But you can't overdo it. Have your glass—and that's it."

*See also* Alcohol, Grape Juice

ᴥ⚘↝

# YOGA

## *The Great Stress Reducer*

If the word *yoga* makes you think of turbaned East Indian yogis or spaced-out hippies chanting in incense-clouded rooms, take a new look at this centuries-old discipline. In recent years, yoga has cast off its counterculture image and gone mainstream.

More and more Americans are embracing yoga, a form of active meditation that originated in India 4,000 years ago, to banish back pain, relieve arthritis and increase their strength and flexibility. Others use yoga as a natural tranquilizer to help soothe emotional stress. "Practicing yoga can help you enter what some people call inner state, in which the mind becomes more tranquil," says Michael Lee, director of Phoenix Rising Yoga Therapy in Housatonic, Massachusetts. Westerners are most familiar with hatha yoga, which focuses on breathing and on assuming a series of poses, or *asanas.*

And if you think you have to twist yourself into a pretzel to reap the physical and mental benefits of yoga, think again. "Yoga postures can be very uncomplicated," says Christine Kaur, a yoga instructor in Los Angeles who has taught the discipline for over 20 years. "But even the simplest postures can produce tremendous health benefits." And one of these benefits may be a decrease in cholesterol levels, suggests F. J. Chandra, D.P.H., in *The Journal of the International Association of Yoga Therapists.*

### The Link to Cholesterol

While there's not much in the way of scientific proof that yoga can help curb cholesterol, there is evidence that stress can elevate cholesterol and may even damage the coronary arteries, setting the stage for heart disease. Yoga has been shown to temporarily alter automatic bodily functions such as heartbeat and breathing. According to research led by Herbert Benson, M.D., chief of the Division of Behavioral Medicine at Deaconess Hospital in Boston, associate professor of medicine at Harvard Medical School and author of *The Relaxation Response*, yoga can slow the heart rate, bring oxygen consumption and the breathing rate below resting levels and even reduce blood pressure in some people.

More directly, some studies have shown that stress management techniques such as yoga can reduce cholesterol levels, according to Dean Ornish, M.D., president and director of the Preventive Medicine Research Institute in Sausalito, California. Dr. Ornish includes the practice of yoga techniques, including breathing, meditation, visualization and progressive relaxation, in his program for people with heart disease. "The use of cholesterol-lowering drugs, while often helpful, is based on the presumption that cholesterol is the primary determinant of atherosclerosis," says Dr. Ornish, author of *Dr. Dean Ornish's Program for Reversing Heart Disease*. But Dr. Ornish says he has become increasingly convinced that other psychological factors, including emotional stress, can contribute to the development of heart disease.

And at least one study, while small, seems to support the theory that yoga can help deflate elevated cholesterol. Researchers in India had six healthy young men practice yoga breathing exercises each day. At the end of six months, their total serum lipids (blood fats such as cholesterol and triglycerides) reportedly fell dramatically.

## Do-It-Yourself Techniques

Interested in exploring the benefits of yoga for yourself? Consider enrolling in a yoga class, suggests Lee. To find a class, check the Yellow Pages under "Yoga Instruction" or see if your local YM/YWCA offers yoga instruction. Before you sign up for a class, though, make sure the instructor emphasizes yoga as a form of relaxation rather than as a form of spiritual enlightenment or rigorous exercise. Lee suggests sitting in on a class or two, so you can see the class—and the instructor—in action.

"Find an instructor you feel compatible with," suggests Lee. "Avoid instructors who believe that yoga has to 'hurt to work' or who are very results-oriented and believe that you have to reach a certain level of achievement." Finding the right yoga class is like trying on clothing—you have to find what fits.

In the meantime, try these simple stress-relieving postures. Lee suggests the following exercise.

1. While standing or sitting, place your arms behind your back and clasp your hands. If your hands don't meet comfortably, "cheat" by holding the ends of a towel.
2. Stretch upward and outward. Feel the stretch across your chest (but don't stretch so far that it hurts).
3. Take a deep breath. As you exhale, continue to stretch, opening up your chest and keeping your hands clasped.
4. Continue to take full, deep breaths, drawing air down into your belly and letting it out again. After several minutes, take one more breath and slowly unclasp your hands.

Kaur suggests this simple breathing exercise.

1. Sit comfortably in a chair or couch. Keep your spine fairly straight and your shoulders back and relaxed.
2. With your eyes closed, close off your right nostril with your right thumb and take 26 long, deep breaths through your left nostril. Then close off your left nostril with your left thumb and repeat the process, breathing through your right nostril. Let yourself become completely calm and try to enter a peaceful, focused state.

*See also* Stress Management

# YOGURT

## *A Low-Fat Treat with Culture*

Strictly speaking, yogurt can't lower blood cholesterol. But this custardlike concoction can help turn the tide on high-flying cholesterol levels. That's because low-fat yogurt (rather than the whole-milk variety) contains three grams or less of fat per cup, while the nonfat variety doesn't have a speck of fat at all. And as you'll see, there are lots of uses for "skinny" yogurt: The fruit-flavored kind makes a tasty snack, dessert or topping, while the plain variety stands in for high-fat ingredients in everything from dips to desserts.

And what is good for your cholesterol level is good for your bones, too. An excellent source of calcium, yogurt can help battle osteoporosis, the bone-thinning disease that preys on people later in life. One cup of low-fat or nonfat yogurt contains more calcium than a glass of milk and meets roughly one-third to one-half of your Daily Value for calcium (1,000 milligrams). What's more, yogurt contains very little lactose, a milk sugar that leaves some people unable to drink milk or eat other calcium-rich dairy products. So yogurt is a good source of calcium for these lactose-intolerant folks. Yogurt is brimming with protein and B vitamins, too.

Not all yogurt fits into a cholesterol-conscious diet, however. Avoid varieties that contain whole milk and sugar. Some brands of yogurt contain up to 350 calories and 11 grams of fat.

## Dips, Desserts and More

Whether you're craving a savory dip or a succulent dessert, yogurt can help fit the bill—deliciously. Try these suggestions.

• Top pancakes and waffles with low-fat or nonfat fruit-flavored yogurt instead of butter and syrup.

• For a tasty breakfast treat, stir a few tablespoons of wheat germ or high-fiber cereal into a cup of nonfat vanilla yogurt.

• To make a deliciously different dressing for chicken salad, blend vanilla low-fat or nonfat yogurt with nonfat mayonnaise, suggests Marilyn Cerino, R.D., nutrition consultant at the Benjamin Franklin Center for Health of Pennsylvania Hospital in Philadelphia.

• Create a creamy dip for raw vegetables or other low-fat snacks by mixing nonfat yogurt with nonfat sour cream, dill and garlic, says Janet Lepke, R.D., a dietitian in Santa Monica, California, and a spokesperson for the American Dietetic Association.

• Substitute nonfat plain yogurt for sour cream or buttermilk in homemade baked goods. "Drain the yogurt through a piece of cheesecloth or a coffee filter," suggests Cerino. "You'll end up with a nice, thick product that you can add to muffins and quick breads."

- Jazz up plain or vanilla yogurt with some chopped fresh fruit, suggests Lisa Lauri, R.D., nutrition consultant at North Shore University Hospital in Manhasset, New York.
- Whip up a frothy yogurt "smoothie" by blending nonfat plain or vanilla yogurt with fresh fruit or juice.
- If you're an ice cream maven, enjoy low-fat or nonfat frozen yogurt rather than premium ice cream, suggests William P. Castelli, M.D., medical director of the Framingham Cardiovascular Institute, a wellness program at Metro West Medical Center in Framingham, Massachusetts. You'll save yourself 30 or more grams of fat. It's possible to have too much of a good thing, however, and low-fat treats are no exception. "Some people eat twice as much frozen yogurt as ice cream and end up gaining weight," says Dr. Castelli. "So be aware of how much you're eating."

Most people with diabetes can eat foods that contain artificial sweeteners, says Lauri. But if you are pregnant and have diabetes (gestational diabetes), she recommends that you avoid products flavored with these substances just to be on the safe side. "Choose plain yogurt and mix in some fruit," suggests Lauri.

# PART III

# The 30/30 Menu Plan to Cut Cholesterol *Fast*

~✻~

# COUNTDOWN TO LOWER CHOLESTEROL

## *Drop 30 Points in 30 Days*

Your doctor has put you on notice: Your cholesterol level could pass for a decent bowling score, and if it doesn't shape up soon, you could be facing some serious health problems. You'd better start dropping points quick, you're told. The question is, how?

Well, you're in luck, because we have a menu plan that's perfect for you. Now don't let the word "plan" scare you off. While it has been developed and approved by nutrition experts, you won't be eating a steady diet of celery sticks and melba toast. Nor will you have to hunt down exotic ingredients and learn difficult cooking methods.

Instead, you're getting a full month's worth of daily menus that are as simple to prepare as they are satisfying to eat. You get complete meals for breakfast, lunch and dinner—plus snacks! And sticking to this plan will pay off handsomely: By the time you reach Day 30, you'll have shaved up to 30 points off your total cholesterol.

The menu plan was developed by nutritionist Anita Hirsch, R.D., of Allentown, Pennsylvania, and reviewed by Sonja L. Connor, R.D., research associate professor of clinical nutrition at the Oregon Health Sciences University in Portland. It provides about 2,000 calories a day, with 55 percent of calories from complex carbohydrates (starches), 20 percent from fat, 15 percent from protein and 10 percent from simple carbohydrates (sugars). And of the 20 percent of calories from fat, only about 5 percent come from saturated fat. The typical U.S. diet gets 37 percent of calories from fat, about 13 percent of those saturated.

As for cholesterol, this plan includes 150 milligrams a day, which is half of the American Heart Association's recommended limit of 300 milligrams a day. The plan also contains more fiber and less sodium than the typical U.S. diet. All the amounts specified in these menus are for one serving.

To reduce your cholesterol 30 points in 30 days, you have to follow the diet beginning on the opposite page to the letter. If you eat 30 percent of calories from fat, for example, your cholesterol may drop about 15 points in 30 days.

But if you think lowering your cholesterol while enjoying tasty, filling meals sounds too good to be true, you're in for a pleasant surprise. Sharon Faelten, a managing editor at Rodale Press in Emmaus, Pennsylvania, followed this very diet with amazing results.

Before she went on the diet, a cholesterol test showed that Faelten's total cholesterol was 238 milligrams/deciliter—borderline high, according to laboratory standards. After following this menu plan for the suggested 30 days, she took a follow-up test and found that her cholesterol had dropped 28 points to 210 milligrams/deciliter.

More important, the food tasted great, and there was plenty of it—three meals a day (including pizza, pasta and tacos) plus two snacks (from devil's food cookies to hot, chewy bake-and-eat pretzels).

"I was delighted that my cholesterol went down, and I had no trouble continuing the diet after the follow-up test," says Faelten. "As a bonus, I found I had more energy than ever. After staying up past 1:00 A.M. on a Friday, I had enough energy to get up before 7:00 A.M. to go hiking. Then I went home and started painting the bedroom."

It's a plan anyone can follow.

## Day 1

### Breakfast

¾ cup grape juice
1 cup oatmeal with ¼ cup raisins and ¼ cup skim milk
⅛ wedge cantaloupe

### Lunch

1 cup cooked pasta with ½ cup low-sodium marinara sauce
Tossed salad: 1 cup chopped romaine lettuce, ½ cup shredded carrots
   and ½ cup shredded red cabbage, dressed with 2 teaspoons canola
   oil, 2 tablespoons vinegar and a dash of sweet basil
Garlic bread: 2 slices toasted Italian bread, brushed with 2 teaspoons
   olive oil and rubbed with 1 clove fresh garlic

### Dinner

Fresh vegetable platter: ¼ cup cauliflower, ¼ green pepper, sliced, and
   ¼ cup chopped mushrooms
Vegetable dip: ¼ cup nonfat yogurt, flavored with 1 scallion, chopped
3 ounces broiled haddock
¾ cup steamed rice
1 cup steamed broccoli with ¼ teaspoon fresh ginger or a dash of dried
   ginger
½ cup cubed winter squash and ¼ cup crushed pineapple, sprinkled
   with nutmeg

### Snacks

2 ounces nonfat unsalted pretzels
1 apple, sliced and topped with ½ cup low-fat vanilla yogurt, 2 teaspoons wheat germ and 1 tablespoon slivered almonds

DAILY TOTALS: 1,932 CALORIES, 34 G. TOTAL FAT, 3.6 G. SATURATED FAT,
65 MG. CHOLESTEROL, 30 G. DIETARY FIBER, 1,457 MG. SODIUM.

## Day 2

### Breakfast

½ English muffin with 1 tablespoon strawberry spread and 1 teaspoon diet margarine

½ cup low-fat vanilla yogurt with 2 tablespoons wheat germ

1 orange

### Lunch

1 cup grape juice

Turkey sandwich: 1 ounce white-meat turkey on 2 slices whole-wheat bread with lettuce, tomato and 1 teaspoon mustard

Tossed salad: 3 cups chopped greens, 1 carrot, sliced, and ¼ cup garbanzo beans, dressed with 2 teaspoons olive oil and 2 tablespoons flavored vinegar

4 graham crackers

### Dinner

1 cup low-sodium minestrone soup

3 ounces lean roast beef

1 baked potato, topped with butter-flavored sprinkles and a dash of garlic powder

½ cup steamed brussels sprouts, topped with 1 tablespoon vinegar and a dash of dry mustard

2 slices Italian bread with 2 teaspoons diet margarine

1 cup canned peaches, in juice

### Snacks

½ bagel with 1 tablespoon low-fat cream cheese

1 pear

---

DAILY TOTALS: 1,982 CALORIES, 36 G. TOTAL FAT, 9 G. SATURATED FAT, 96 MG. CHOLESTEROL, 38 G. DIETARY FIBER, 1,796 MG. SODIUM.

## Day 3

### Breakfast

¾ cup orange juice
1 cup ready-to-eat raisin bran cereal with ½ cup skim milk
2 dried figs

### Lunch

Vegetable burger on whole-wheat bun with lettuce, tomato, onion and
    mustard
½ cup commercially prepared three-bean salad
1 carrot and 1 stalk celery, cut into sticks
½ cup low-fat coffee-flavored yogurt
1 tangerine or other fresh fruit

### Dinner

Tossed salad: 3 cups chopped romaine lettuce, 2 slices tomato,
    ½ carrot, sliced, 2 radishes and 2 slices cucumber, dressed with
    2 teaspoons olive oil and 2 tablespoons vinegar
3 ounces grilled or baked chicken breast, rubbed with fresh garlic and
    ½ teaspoon olive oil
1 cup steamed brown rice
Savory cabbage: ½ cup shredded cabbage and ¼ cup chopped onions,
    sautéed in 2 teaspoons olive oil, ½ teaspoon savory and ½ teaspoon
    dill
1 baked apple with 2 tablespoons maple syrup

### Snacks

3 nonfat devil's food cookies
2 cups air-popped popcorn with ½ teaspoon butter-flavored sprinkles

---

DAILY TOTALS: 1,969 CALORIES, 38 G. TOTAL FAT, 8.6 G. SATURATED FAT,
95 MG. CHOLESTEROL, 39 G. DIETARY FIBER, 1,909 MG. SODIUM.

## Day 4

### Breakfast

1½ cups ready-to-eat multigrain cereal with ½ cup skim milk, sprinkled with 5 almonds, chopped

½ red grapefruit

### Lunch

1 cup low-sodium split pea soup

1 toasted English muffin with 2 teaspoons diet margarine

¾ cup low-fat or nonfat strawberry yogurt with 1 teaspoon rice bran or wheat germ

### Dinner

Pork stir-fry: 1 ounce lean pork loin, 1 cup sliced bok choy, ½ cup snow peas, ¼ cup diced red peppers and ¼ cup diced celery, stir-fried in 1 teaspoon minced fresh garlic, 2 teaspoons canola oil and a dash of sesame oil

1½ cups steamed brown rice with a dash of poultry seasoning or sage

Tossed salad: 1 cup shredded romaine lettuce, ¼ cup chopped red onions and 2 radishes, dressed with 1 tablespoon lemon juice and 2 teaspoons olive oil

1 banana or other fresh fruit

### Snacks

1 cup grapes

1 bake-and-eat soft pretzel (2½ ounces, baked without salt)

DAILY TOTALS: 1,941 CALORIES, 40 G. TOTAL FAT, 6.8 G. SATURATED FAT, 33 MG. CHOLESTEROL, 25 G. DIETARY FIBER, 1,465 MG. SODIUM.

# Day 5

## Breakfast

1 English muffin with 2 teaspoons diet margarine

Breakfast blender drink: 1 cup skim milk and ½ cup fresh or unsweetened frozen strawberries, blended until frothy

## Lunch

Pita sandwich: 1 ounce cubed low-fat Cheddar cheese, ½ cup chopped spinach, tomato and onion, stuffed in a pita and dressed with 2 tablespoons nonfat dressing (your choice)

1 carrot and 1 stalk celery, cut into sticks

1 cup low-fat yogurt (your choice)

## Dinner

2 slices pizza (ask for half of the cheese)

Tossed salad: 3 cups chopped greens, ¼ cup broccoli, ¼ cup chickpeas, ¼ tomato, sliced, and 1 tablespoon chopped onions, dressed with 2 tablespoons nonfat dressing (your choice)

1 cup grapes

## Snacks

2 cups cooked pasta with ½ cup low-sodium marinara sauce

2 unsalted pretzels (2 ounces)

1 banana

DAILY TOTALS: 1,899 CALORIES, 28 G. TOTAL FAT, 7 G. SATURATED FAT, 50 MG. CHOLESTEROL, 26 G. DIETARY FIBER, 2,473 MG. SODIUM.

# Day 6

## Breakfast

¾ cup orange juice

Egg substitute, scrambled with 1 tablespoon skim milk in a no-stick pan

1 potato, sliced and sautéed with 1 tablespoon diet margarine, 2 tablespoons chopped onions and ½ clove fresh garlic, minced, in a no-stick pan

2 slices toasted whole-wheat bread with 2 teaspoons fruit spread

## Lunch

1 cup low-sodium lentil soup

Tossed salad: 3 cups chopped greens, ½ cup sliced carrots and ¼ cup sliced onions, dressed with 2 teaspoons olive oil and 1 tablespoon vinegar

1 toasted English muffin

## Dinner

Chicken fajita: 3 ounces chicken strips (prepared in a low-fat manner), ¼ cup mashed avocado, ¼ cup salsa, ¼ cup nonfat plain yogurt, 1½ teaspoons olive oil, 1 teaspoon lime juice and 1 teaspoon fresh cilantro in 1 flour tortilla

1½ cups steamed brown rice, flavored with 2 tablespoons salsa and ⅛ teaspoon chopped jalapeño peppers

10 low-fat tortilla chips (1 ounce)

## Snacks

1 cup fresh or canned chunked pineapple, in juice

1 carrot, cut into sticks, with ¼ cup commercially prepared nonfat herbed yogurt cheese

DAILY TOTALS: 1,902 CALORIES, 45 G. TOTAL FAT, 7.3 G. SATURATED FAT, 77 MG. CHOLESTEROL, 29 G. DIETARY FIBER, 1,717 MG. SODIUM.

## Day 7

### Breakfast

½ bagel with 1 tablespoon light cream cheese
1 cup low-fat vanilla yogurt with 2 teaspoons wheat germ
½ mango, cubed

### Lunch

2 ounces scallops, ½ cup chopped mushrooms, ¼ cup sliced onions,
    ¼ cup chopped celery and ¼ cup chopped green peppers, sautéed in
    1 teaspoon sesame oil, 1 tablespoon low-sodium soy sauce,
    1 clove fresh garlic, minced, and 1 teaspoon grated fresh ginger
2 cups steamed rice
1 fortune cookie

### Dinner

2 cups low-sodium vegetable soup
Tossed salad: 1 ounce flaked water-packed tuna, 4 cups chopped
    romaine lettuce, ¼ cup shredded carrots and 1 radish, dressed with
    1 teaspoon olive oil and 1 tablespoon vinegar
Baked pita crisps: 1 pita, brushed with 2 teaspoons olive oil and
    assorted herbs and spices and broiled and broken into pieces
1 cup fresh fruit (grapes, apples and oranges)

### Snacks

2 graham crackers with 1 tablespoon peanut butter and 1 cup skim
    milk
1 banana

DAILY TOTALS: 2,030 CALORIES, 40 G. TOTAL FAT, 10 G. SATURATED FAT,
61 MG. CHOLESTEROL, 25 G. DIETARY FIBER, 1,761 MG. SODIUM.

## Day 8

### Breakfast

¾ cup orange juice

1 cup oatmeal with ¼ cup raisins and ½ cup skim milk

1 slice toasted whole-wheat bread with 1 teaspoon diet margarine and 1 tablespoon apple butter

### Lunch

1 cup low-sodium tomato soup

¼ to ½ cup commercially prepared three-bean salad (add ¼ cup chopped red onions, basil and 2 tablespoons red wine vinegar)

2 slices rye bread with 2 teaspoons diet margarine

1 peach, nectarine or other fresh fruit

### Dinner

Bulgur salad: 1 cup cooked bulgur, 2 tablespoons parsley, ½ tomato, chopped, and 1 teaspoon lemon juice

Broiled skinless chicken breast

1 potato, baked, with 2 tablespoons nonfat sour cream and 2 teaspoons diet margarine

1 cup chopped spinach, sautéed in 1 teaspoon olive oil, ¼ cup chopped onions and 1 clove fresh garlic, minced

1 hard roll (2 ounces) with 1 tablespoon diet margarine

2 cups cubed watermelon or other fruit

### Snacks

2 cups air-popped popcorn with butter-flavored sprinkles and 1 teaspoon Parmesan cheese

1 fresh fig

DAILY TOTALS: 1,968 CALORIES, 41 G. TOTAL FAT, 7 G. SATURATED FAT, 84 MG. CHOLESTEROL, 41 G. DIETARY FIBER, 1,850 MG. SODIUM.

## Day 9

### Breakfast

¾ cup ready-to-eat fortified oat cereal with ½ cup skim milk
1 sliced banana

### Lunch

1 oat bran and raisin muffin (2 ounces)
1 cup low-fat yogurt (your choice)
1 orange, sliced

### Dinner

1 cup low-sodium vegetable soup (add ¼ cup white beans and 1 clove
  fresh garlic, minced, if desired)
3 ounces baked flounder
¼ cup chopped cabbage, sautéed in 2 teaspoons canola oil and ground
  red pepper (to taste) and served over 1 cup steamed rice
1 slice cornbread with 2 teaspoons diet margarine
1 baked apple with ½ teaspoon cinnamon and 2 teaspoons brown
  sugar

### Snacks

6 graham crackers with 1 tablespoon almond butter or peanut butter
½ cup skim milk

DAILY TOTALS: 1,748 CALORIES, 33 G. TOTAL FAT, 4 G. SATURATED FAT,
68 MG. CHOLESTEROL, 31 G. DIETARY FIBER, 1,273 MG. SODIUM.

## Day 10

### Breakfast

1 cup cooked oat bran cereal with 1 tablespoon rice bran or wheat germ

2 cups cubed honeydew, casaba or other melon

### Lunch

1 ounce applesauce muffin with 2 teaspoons diet margarine

½ cup 2 percent low-fat cottage cheese with 2 cups fresh fruit (your choice)

### Dinner

1 cup low-sodium vegetable juice

1 cup low-sodium green pea soup

Spinach salad: 2 cups spinach, ¼ cup sliced mushrooms, ¼ cup chopped red onions and 1 clove fresh garlic, minced, dressed with 2 teaspoons olive oil and 2 tablespoons vinegar

4 garlic breadsticks (4 ounces)

### Snacks

2 fig bars

1 orange

Fresh vegetable plate: 1 cup carrot sticks and ½ cup broccoli florets

Vegetable dip: 2 tablespoons commercially prepared nonfat herbed yogurt cheese

DAILY TOTALS: 1,796 CALORIES, 41 G. TOTAL FAT, 11 G. SATURATED FAT, 10 MG. CHOLESTEROL, 44 G. DIETARY FIBER, 1,985 MG. SODIUM.

## Day 11

### Breakfast

1 cup hot cereal with 1 tablespoon wheat germ and 2 tablespoons maple syrup

Fruit compote: 2 tablespoons prunes, 2 tablespoons figs and 2 tablespoons raisins, cooked in 2 tablespoons orange juice and 2 tablespoons water

### Lunch

1 cup low-sodium turkey vegetable soup

Tossed salad: 4 cups chopped romaine lettuce, dressed with 2 teaspoons olive oil and 2 tablespoons vinegar

2 slices toasted whole-wheat bread

1 cup low-fat yogurt (your choice)

### Dinner

3 ounces pork medallions in tomato sauce, served over 1 cup egg noodles

1½ cups steamed green beans and chopped carrots

2 slices rye bread with 2 teaspoons diet margarine

Streusel apple: 1 apple, baked with 1 tablespoon low-fat flavored yogurt, ½ tablespoon oats and 1 teaspoon brown sugar

### Snack

2 ounces low-sodium pretzel chips with mustard

---

DAILY TOTALS: 1,996 CALORIES, 41 G. TOTAL FAT, 7.2 G. SATURATED FAT, 122 MG. CHOLESTEROL, 32 G. DIETARY FIBER, 1,721 MG. SODIUM.

## Day 12

### Breakfast

1 cup ready-to-eat bran cereal with ½ cup skim milk
2 slices toasted whole-wheat bread with 2 teaspoons diet margarine
1 banana

### Lunch

½ grapefruit
Pasta salad: 1 cup cooked pasta, 1 ounce water-packed tuna, ½ cup
    snow peas, ½ cup frozen or canned plain artichoke hearts and
    2 scallions, chopped, dressed with 1 tablespoon low-fat mayonnaise,
    1 tablespoon vinegar, fresh basil and parsley
1 slice pumpernickel bread with 2 teaspoons diet margarine

### Dinner

Chicken kabobs: 2 ounces cooked cubed chicken breast with
    ¼ pepper, chunked, ½ tomato, chunked, 5 mushrooms, chunked,
    and ⅓ onion, chunked, marinated in 2 teaspoons olive oil,
    2 teaspoons lemon juice, 2 teaspoons low-sodium soy sauce,
    1 tablespoon chopped parsley, 1 clove fresh garlic, minced,
    ¼ chili pepper, minced, and ¼ teaspoon red-pepper flakes
1½ cups steamed brown and wild rice, tossed with thyme or parsley
1 frozen fruit bar

### Snacks

1 cup grapes
1 oat bran and raisin muffin (2 ounces)

---

DAILY TOTALS: 1,895 CALORIES, 33 G. TOTAL FAT, 5 G. SATURATED FAT,
65 MG. CHOLESTEROL, 38 G. DIETARY FIBER, 2,065 MG. SODIUM.

# Day 13

## Breakfast

4 four-inch buckwheat pancakes with 4 tablespoons maple syrup
Citrus salad: ¼ cup grapefruit sections and ½ cup orange sections

## Lunch

Egg drop soup: 1 cup hot low-fat chicken stock with 2 tablespoons egg substitute
Chicken teriyaki with vegetables (low-fat, low-calorie frozen entrée)
1½ cups steamed brown rice with chives
Wonton chips: 3 wonton wrappers, misted with no-stick cooking spray and baked
3 kumquats or ½ cup fresh or canned chunked pineapple, in juice

## Dinner

Omelet: ⅓ cup chopped mushrooms and ⅓ cup chopped onions, sautéed in 2 teaspoons olive oil and folded into ½ cup beaten egg substitute
2 slices toasted whole-wheat bread with 2 teaspoons diet margarine and 1 tablespoon strawberry spread
1 apple, sliced, with 1 tablespoon natural peanut butter

## Snacks

1 carrot, cut into sticks
2 slices melba toast with 1-ounce chunk low-fat Swiss cheese

DAILY TOTALS: 1,805 CALORIES, 42 G. TOTAL FAT, 11.4 G. SATURATED FAT, 123 MG. CHOLESTEROL, 32 G. DIETARY FIBER, 1,978 MG. SODIUM.

## Day 14

### Breakfast

¾ cup tropical fruit juice

2 whole-grain waffles, topped with ½ cup low-fat yogurt (your choice) and ½ cup blueberries

### Lunch

Turkey sandwich: 1 ounce low-fat turkey breast lunchmeat and 1 ounce light Swiss cheese on 2 slices rye bread with lettuce, tomato and 2 teaspoons mustard

1 carrot, cut into sticks

Curry dip: ¼ cup nonfat plain yogurt and ¼ cup nonfat mayonnaise, blended with ½ teaspoon curry and 1 clove fresh garlic, minced

### Dinner

3 ounces boneless, skinless chicken breast, poached with ¼ cup chopped onions, ¼ cup chopped carrots and 1 tablespoon parsley and served over 1 cup steamed chopped spinach

Hawaiian rice: 1 cup cooked brown rice with ½ cup snow peas, 4 pieces baby corn and ¼ cup water chestnuts, sautéed in 1 teaspoon peanut oil and ¼ teaspoon ground red pepper and tossed with ¼ cup drained chunked pineapple

1 sweet potato, baked or steamed (top with cinnamon, if desired)

½ mango, sprinkled with ¼ cup macadamia nuts

### Snack

1 slice cocoa angel food cake (¹⁄₁₂ cake) with ½ cup fresh raspberries

---

DAILY TOTALS: 2,108 CALORIES, 53 G. TOTAL FAT, 11 G. SATURATED FAT, 101 MG. CHOLESTEROL, 37 G. DIETARY FIBER, 2,228 MG. SODIUM.

## Day 15

### Breakfast

1 peach bran muffin (2 ounces)
1 cup skim milk
1 pear

### Lunch

1 cup low-sodium vegetable soup (add ¼ cup diced carrots and ¼ cup chopped kale, if desired)
Tossed salad: 2 cups chopped greens, 2 tablespoons chopped cabbage and ¼ cup diced celery, dressed with ¼ cup nonfat yogurt blended with 1 clove fresh garlic, minced
2 slices whole-wheat bread with 1 tablespoon natural peanut butter
1 cup grapes

### Dinner

2 ounces sliced lean roast beef
Mushroom barley: ⅓ cup chopped mushrooms, sautéed in 2 teaspoons olive oil and ¼ teaspoon thyme and added to 1 cup cooked barley
1 cup steamed sliced carrots
1 slice Italian bread with 1 teaspoon diet margarine
½ cup peaches with ½ cup pureed strawberry sauce

### Snacks

1 bake-and-eat soft pretzel (2½ ounces, baked without salt)
1 apple, sliced and sprinkled with cinnamon

---

DAILY TOTALS: 1,895 CALORIES, 40 G. TOTAL FAT, 9 G. SATURATED FAT, 108 MG. CHOLESTEROL, 49 G. DIETARY FIBER, 1,666 MG. SODIUM.

## Day 16

### Breakfast

1 English muffin with 2 teaspoons diet margarine, 1 tablespoon fruit spread and 1 teaspoon wheat germ

1 orange

### Lunch

1 potato, baked, with chives and 2 tablespoons nonfat sour cream

Spinach salad: 2 cups chopped spinach, ½ carrot, chopped, ¼ cup chopped mushrooms and ¼ cup chopped onions, dressed with 2 tablespoons low-fat dressing (your choice)

2 slices Italian bread with 1 tablespoon diet margarine

### Dinner

3 ounces grilled snapper

½ cup black beans with 4 tablespoons tomato salsa, served over 1 cup steamed rice

1 cup zucchini, sautéed in 2 teaspoons olive oil with ¼ cup chopped onions and 1 clove fresh garlic, minced

½ cup fresh blueberries and ¼ cup nonfat vanilla yogurt

### Snacks

2 oatmeal cookies (1 ounce each) with 1 cup skim milk

2 cups cubed watermelon

---

DAILY TOTALS: 1,809 CALORIES, 34 G. TOTAL FAT, 5.5 G. SATURATED FAT, 39 MG. CHOLESTEROL, 30 G. DIETARY FIBER, 1,823 MG. SODIUM.

## Day 17

### Breakfast

¾ cup orange juice

1 cup cooked bulgur with ¼ cup apricot nectar, 1 tablespoon chopped dried fruit bits, ¼ cup skim milk and 2 teaspoons oat bran

### Lunch

1 cup low-sodium vegetable soup

Roast beef sandwich: 1 ounce sliced lean roast beef on a 2-ounce hard roll with romaine lettuce, onion and 2 teaspoons mustard

Fresh veggie plate: 1 cup cauliflower florets, 1 carrot, cut into sticks, and 2 or 3 cherry tomatoes

2 tablespoons nonfat dressing (your choice)

### Dinner

Cheese and spinach lasagna (low-fat frozen entrée)

1 cup steamed broccoli with ¼ teaspoon basil

Garlic bread: 2 slices toasted Italian bread, brushed with 2 teaspoons olive oil and rubbed with 1 clove fresh garlic

Fruit plate: 1 kiwifruit, sliced, and 3 strawberries, sliced

2 reduced-fat cookies

### Snacks

2 cups air-popped popcorn with ¼ teaspoon of your choice of seasonings: curry powder, Worcestershire sauce, Parmesan cheese, dill or butter-flavored sprinkles

1 peach or other seasonal fruit

---

DAILY TOTALS: 1,726 CALORIES, 34 G. TOTAL FAT, 6.7 G. SATURATED FAT, 27 MG. CHOLESTEROL, 32 G. DIETARY FIBER, 2,212 MG. SODIUM.

## Day 18

### Breakfast

¾ cup grape juice
1 large shredded wheat biscuit with ½ cup skim milk
1 oat bran and blueberry muffin

### Lunch

1 cup low-sodium Manhattan clam chowder
1 slice toasted whole-wheat bread, topped with 1 ounce low-fat, low-sodium Cheddar cheese, ¼ cup sliced onions and 1 slice tomato and broiled
Tossed salad: 2 cups chopped greens, ¼ cup chopped mushrooms and ¼ cup shredded carrots, dressed with 2 tablespoons low-fat dressing (your choice)
½ cup fresh pineapple wedges

### Dinner

2-ounce chicken burger patty on a 1-ounce bun with lettuce, tomato and onion
Oven fries: 1 potato, thinly sliced and baked with garlic powder, Italian seasoning or other spices
1 cup canned or homemade baked beans, without salt
½ cup applesauce with a dash of cinnamon

### Snacks

½ cup low-fat frozen yogurt (your choice)
1 bake-and-eat soft pretzel (2½ ounces, baked without salt)
3 vanilla wafers

DAILY TOTALS: 1,939 CALORIES, 29 G. TOTAL FAT, 8.5 G. SATURATED FAT, 103 MG. CHOLESTEROL, 46 G. DIETARY FIBER, 2,203 MG. SODIUM.

## Day 19

### Breakfast

1 cup cooked oatmeal with 2 teaspoons rice bran and ½ cup skim milk
1 orange

### Lunch

Tacos: 1 ounce extra-lean ground beef, 8 tablespoons cooked lentils,
3 tablespoons stewed tomatoes, ¼ tomato, chopped, ½ cup chopped
lettuce, ½ ounce shredded low-sodium, low-fat Cheddar cheese,
2 tablespoons mashed avocado and 2 tablespoons nonfat sour
cream, layered in 2 taco shells
1 cup steamed rice (add 2 tablespoons salsa, if desired)

### Dinner

Beef stew: 2 ounces lean beef (bottom round), simmered in 1 cup
water with 1 cup chunked carrots, 1 cup chunked potatoes, ½ cup
sliced onions, 1 clove fresh garlic, minced, 2 tablespoons parsley,
1 teaspoon basil and 1 teaspoon savory
1 cup cooked barley or barley/rice mix, flavored with ¼ teaspoon marjoram, ¼ teaspoon chopped onions and ¼ teaspoon garlic powder
1 slice whole-wheat bread or low-sodium cornbread with 2 teaspoons
diet margarine

### Snacks

1 apple
2 ounces unsalted pretzels
2 cups air-popped popcorn with butter-flavored sprinkles

---

DAILY TOTALS: 1,870 CALORIES, 31 G. TOTAL FAT, 8 G. SATURATED FAT,
84 MG. CHOLESTEROL, 40 G. DIETARY FIBER, 737 MG. SODIUM.

## Day 20

### Breakfast

1 toasted bagel with 2 tablespoons nonfat cream cheese

1 baked apple with 1 teaspoon diet margarine and 1 tablespoon maple syrup

### Lunch

Tossed salad: 2 cups chopped greens with ¼ cup shredded carrots, ¼ cup diced celery, ¼ cup shredded cabbage, ¼ cup frozen or canned plain artichoke hearts and 1 tablespoon ground chili pepper (if desired), dressed with 2 tablespoons nonfat dressing (your choice)

6 whole-wheat crackers

1 cup fresh strawberries (or other seasonal fruit)

### Dinner

Greek salad: 4 cups chopped romaine lettuce, 1 ounce feta cheese, ¼ cup sliced mushrooms, ¼ cup chick-peas and 2 olives, dressed with 2 tablespoons lemon juice and 1 tablespoon olive oil

3 ounces haddock fillet

1 potato, chunked and roasted with 1 teaspoon rosemary

Ratatouille: ¼ cup tomato sauce, ½ cup chopped eggplant, ¼ tomato, chopped, ½ zucchini, sliced, and ¼ cup chopped celery, served over ½ cup cooked orzo

¼ cup hummus, spread over 1 pita bread

½ cup rice pudding with raisins

### Snacks

2 fresh or dried figs

½ cup nonfat yogurt (your choice)

1 orange

---

DAILY TOTALS: 1,940 CALORIES, 44 G. TOTAL FAT, 8.5 G. SATURATED FAT, 81 MG. CHOLESTEROL, 42 G. DIETARY FIBER, 2,486 MG. SODIUM.

## Day 21

### Breakfast

1 cup oatmeal with ½ cup sliced strawberries, 1 tablespoon brown sugar and ½ cup skim milk

2 slices toasted whole-wheat bread with 2 teaspoons diet margarine

### Lunch

Pizza: ¼ ready-made pizza crust, ¼ cup tomato sauce, 1 ounce part-skim mozzarella cheese, ¼ cup roasted red peppers, ½ teaspoon olive oil, ½ teaspoon hot-pepper flakes, ¼ cup chopped sweet green peppers, ¼ cup chopped sweet red peppers, ¼ cup cooked white beans and ¼ cup chopped spinach

1 carrot, cut into sticks

½ cup grapes

### Dinner

3 ounces lamb (loin chop)

Potato sauté: 1 potato, sliced, ¼ cup chopped mushrooms, ¼ cup chopped onions, 1 tablespoon parsley and 1 clove fresh garlic, minced, sautéed in ½ cup chicken stock

1 cup steamed brussels sprouts, seasoned with herbes de provence, savory or lemon juice

1 roll (2 ounces) with 2 teaspoons diet margarine

1 poached peach, sliced, with nutmeg and cinnamon

### Snacks

2 slices toasted cinnamon raisin bread

4 fig bars

---

DAILY TOTALS: 1,881 CALORIES, 39 G. TOTAL FAT, 10 G. SATURATED FAT, 98 MG. CHOLESTEROL, 29 G. DIETARY FIBER, 2,012 MG. SODIUM.

# Day 22

## Breakfast

¾ cup orange juice
1 cup ready-to-eat oat cereal with ½ cup skim milk
1 banana, sliced

## Lunch

1 cup chicken chow mein (low-calorie frozen entrée)
2 cups steamed white rice
1 fortune cookie or fresh fruit

## Dinner

3 ounces baked orange roughy
1 cup barley, topped with ½ cup chopped mushrooms and ¼ cup
  sliced onions sautéed in 2 teaspoons olive oil and ½ cup tomato
  salsa
1 cup steamed cauliflower

## Snacks

1 whole-grain waffle, topped with ½ cup frozen yogurt (your choice)
  and 2 tablespoons chocolate syrup
1 peach, sliced

---

DAILY TOTALS: 1,868 CALORIES, 23 G. TOTAL FAT, 6 G. SATURATED FAT,
66 MG. CHOLESTEROL, 27 G. DIETARY FIBER, 1,589 MG. SODIUM.

## Day 23

### Breakfast

1 bagel, topped with 2 tablespoons nonfat cream cheese mixed with
1 tablespoon chopped dates

1 orange

### Lunch

Salmon salad: 2 ounces canned red salmon, arranged on 2 cups
chopped romaine lettuce with 1 green onion, thinly sliced, and
¼ cup chopped mushrooms and dressed with 2 teaspoons olive oil
and 2 tablespoons vinegar

Cucumber and onion salad, dressed with ¼ cup nonfat plain yogurt
and dill

Garlic bread: 2 slices toasted Italian bread, brushed with 2 teaspoons
olive oil and rubbed with 1 clove fresh garlic

### Dinner

1 cup light cheese tortellini

½ cup tomato sauce

½ cup steamed green beans, flavored with ⅛ teaspoon olive oil, fresh
rosemary, grated lemon rind and butter-flavored sprinkles

3 soft breadsticks (1½ ounces total) with 2 teaspoons diet margarine

Mini fruit salad: ½ cup sliced apples and ¼ cup grapes, drizzled with
½ cup low-fat vanilla yogurt

### Snacks

Pronto pinto dip: ½ cup cooked pinto beans, mashed, with 2 tablespoons chunky salsa and 2 tablespoons nonfat sour cream

22 baked tortilla chips

DAILY TOTALS: 1,785 CALORIES, 42 G. TOTAL FAT, 8.3 G. SATURATED FAT,
86 MG. CHOLESTEROL, 25 G. DIETARY FIBER, 2,496 MG. SODIUM.

## Day 24

### Breakfast

1 cup oatmeal with 1 tablespoon brown sugar and ½ cup skim milk
1 tangerine (or other fruit in season)

### Lunch

1 cup low-sodium black bean soup
1 cup polenta with 1 cup stewed tomatoes (with onions) and ⅛ teaspoon ground chili pepper
½ cup grapes

### Dinner

Tossed salad: 2 cups chopped romaine lettuce, ¼ cup frozen or canned plain artichoke hearts and ¼ sweet red pepper, chopped, dressed with 2 teaspoons olive oil and 2 tablespoons vinegar
3 ounces roasted skinless chicken breast
Three-grain pilaf: ⅓ cup steamed rice, ⅓ cup steamed barley and ⅓ cup steamed buckwheat, tossed with ¼ cup diced onions, ¼ cup diced celery and ¼ cup diced mushrooms sautéed in chicken stock, ¼ teaspoon dried tarragon, ¼ teaspoon rosemary and ¼ teaspoon dry mustard
1 cup steamed sliced carrots and beets, dressed with 2 teaspoons olive oil, 2 teaspoons vinegar and ½ teaspoon basil

### Snack

2 rye crackers with 1 ounce low-fat mozzarella cheese

---

DAILY TOTALS: 2,201 CALORIES, 38 G. TOTAL FAT, 8.9 G. SATURATED FAT, 78 MG. CHOLESTEROL, 22 G. DIETARY FIBER, 1,485 MG. SODIUM.

## Day 25

### Breakfast

1 slice toasted whole-wheat bread with 2 teaspoons diet margarine
½ cup nonfat vanilla yogurt with 2 chopped dried figs and 2 teaspoons wheat germ

### Lunch

Chef's salad: 2 cups chopped mixed greens (romaine lettuce and spinach) with 1 ounce shredded nonfat Swiss cheese, 1 ounce julienne roasted turkey (without skin), ¼ cup sliced cucumbers, ¼ cup sliced radishes, ½ cup shredded carrots and 3 or 4 cherry tomatoes, dressed with 2 tablespoons nonfat dressing (your choice)
3 breadsticks (1¼ ounces each)
1 cup unsweetened applesauce with cinnamon

### Dinner

3 ounces broiled salmon
1½ cups white and wild rice with 2 teaspoons slivered almonds, 1 tablespoon sautéed diced onions, 2 teaspoons chopped parsley and a pinch of saffron
1 artichoke, dressed with 1 tablespoon lemon juice, 1 teaspoon olive oil, 1 tablespoon nonfat Parmesan cheese and butter-flavored sprinkles
¼ wedge cantaloupe

### Snack

Tropical shake: ½ cup skim milk, ½ cup orange juice, 1 banana and 5 strawberries, whipped until thick and frothy

DAILY TOTALS: 1,734 CALORIES, 32 G. TOTAL FAT, 6.9 G. SATURATED FAT, 80 MG. CHOLESTEROL, 34 G. DIETARY FIBER, 2,089 MG. SODIUM.

## Day 26

### Breakfast

¾ cup ready-to-eat raisin bran cereal with ½ cup skim milk
1 peach

### Lunch

1½ cups low-sodium turkey noodle soup
1 sweet potato, baked with 1 tablespoon maple syrup, cinnamon and
　　nutmeg
Spinach salad: 1 cup chopped spinach, ½ cup shredded carrots, ¼ cup
　　alfalfa sprouts and ¼ cup sliced onions, dressed with 2 teaspoons
　　olive oil and 2 tablespoons vinegar
1 pumpernickel roll (1 ounce) with 1 teaspoon diet margarine
Mixed fruit: ½ cup canned unsweetened pears, ¼ cup sliced apples,
　　¼ cup grapes, 1 dried fig, 2 tablespoons raisins

### Dinner

Vegetable lasagna (low-fat, low-calorie frozen entrée)
½ cup steamed sliced carrots with a dash of fresh or dried ginger
Garlic bread: 2 slices toasted Italian bread, brushed with 2 teaspoons
　　olive oil and rubbed with 1 clove fresh garlic
1 lemon sorbet bar

### Snacks

Tropical delight: ½ cup orange juice, 1 banana, sliced, and 1 table-
　　spoon slivered almonds, whipped until frothy
2 popcorn rice cakes

---

DAILY TOTALS: 1,874 CALORIES, 39 G. TOTAL FAT, 4.7 G. SATURATED FAT,
29 MG. CHOLESTEROL, 32 G. DIETARY FIBER, 2,215 MG. SODIUM.

## Day 27

### Breakfast

2 four-inch whole-grain pancakes
Scrambled eggs: ¼ cup egg substitute, scrambled with 1 tablespoon
  skim milk in a no-stick pan
1 ounce turkey sausage

### Lunch

Rice jambalaya: 1½ cups cooked rice with ¼ cup cooked diced ham,
  ¼ cup cooked cubed chicken breast, ¼ cup crushed tomatoes,
  ¼ cup diced celery, ¼ cup chopped onions, ¼ cup chopped green
  peppers and ¼ cup chopped mushrooms
2 buttermilk biscuits (¾ ounce each)
Fruit compote: 1 orange, sectioned, and 1 kiwifruit, sliced

### Dinner

Stuffed potato: 1 baked potato with 2 ounces low-fat Cheddar cheese,
  ½ cup steamed broccoli, ¼ cup chopped onions and 1 clove fresh
  garlic, minced
1 carrot, cut into sticks, with 1 tablespoon nonfat blue cheese dressing
½ cup nonfat pudding, made with skim milk

### Snacks

1 bake-and-eat soft pretzel (2½ ounces, baked without salt)
1 stewed apple, topped with ¼ cup nonfat vanilla yogurt and drizzled
  with honey

DAILY TOTALS: 1,727 CALORIES, 26 G. TOTAL FAT, 11 G. SATURATED FAT,
147 MG. CHOLESTEROL, 24 G. DIETARY FIBER, 2,401 MG. SODIUM.

## Day 28

### Breakfast

1 toasted bagel with 2 tablespoons nonfat cream cheese and 1 tablespoon strawberry spread

1 cup vanilla nonfat yogurt

½ cup mixed berries

### Lunch

3 ounces London broil (top round), marinated in ¼ teaspoon Worcestershire sauce, garlic and herbs and grilled

2 ears grilled corn on the cob with butter-flavored sprinkles

Veggie kabobs: ½ cup chunked mushrooms, ½ cup chunked onions and ½ cup chunked peppers, grilled on skewers and brushed with nonfat dressing (your choice)

2 breadsticks

2 cups cubed watermelon

### Dinner

Pita pizza: 1 pita bread, smothered with ¼ cup tomato puree, 2 ounces shredded nonfat or skim-milk mozzarella cheese, ⅓ cup sliced mushrooms, 1 clove fresh garlic, minced, and ¼ cup chopped onions

Tossed salad: 3 cups chopped greens, dressed with 2 tablespoons vinegar and 2 teaspoons olive oil

1 frozen fruit bar

### Snack

2 cups air-popped popcorn with butter-flavored sprinkles

---

DAILY TOTALS: 1,735 CALORIES, 38 G. TOTAL FAT, 14 G. SATURATED FAT, 121 MG. CHOLESTEROL, 29 G. DIETARY FIBER, 1,707 MG. SODIUM.

## Day 29

### Breakfast

1 cup ready-to-eat oat cereal with almonds, topped with 1 banana, sliced, and ½ cup skim milk

½ grapefruit

### Lunch

1 cup low-sodium chicken noodle soup

Ham and cheese sandwich: 1 ounce low-fat ham and 1 ounce low-fat American cheese on a 1-ounce hard roll with lettuce, tomato and mustard

1 carrot and 1 stalk celery, cut into sticks

Flavored sparkling water

### Dinner

Turkey tenders: 3 ounces white-meat turkey, sautéed with 2 teaspoons olive oil, ½ cup chopped kale, ¼ cup sliced mushrooms, ¼ cup chopped onions, ¼ cup sliced sweet peppers and ¼ cup chopped hot peppers and served over 1 baked potato

Pasta salad: 1 cup cooked macaroni, ¼ cup chopped zucchini, ¼ cup chopped onions and ¼ cup frozen or canned plain artichoke hearts, dressed with 2 tablespoons low-fat mayonnaise and sprinkled with basil and pepper

2 slices whole-wheat bread with 2 teaspoons diet margarine

### Snacks

1 apple

½ cup nonfat vanilla yogurt with 1 tablespoon chopped walnut topping

1 bake-and-eat soft pretzel (2½ ounces, baked without salt)

---

DAILY TOTALS: 1,959 CALORIES, 42 G. TOTAL FAT, 5 G. SATURATED FAT, 57 MG. CHOLESTEROL, 28 G. DIETARY FIBER, 2,020 MG. SODIUM.

## Day 30

### Breakfast

2 slices toasted raisin bread with ½ cup low-fat ricotta cheese
1 banana

### Lunch

1 cup low-sodium vegetarian chili, served over 1½ cups steamed rice
Carrot and raisin salad: ¼ cup shredded carrots and ¼ cup raisins,
    served on ½ cup chopped romaine lettuce with 2 tablespoons wal-
    nuts and dressed with 2 tablespoons nonfat yogurt and 1 tablespoon
    light mayonnaise
½ cup low-fat yogurt (your choice) with ½ cup raspberries

### Dinner

1 cup pasta
Red clam sauce: ¼ cup low-sodium stewed tomatoes, ¼ cup
    low-sodium tomato sauce, ¼ cup shredded carrots and 1½ ounces
    rinsed and chopped canned clams
1 slice Italian bread
2 almond biscotti or 1 nonfat cookie (your choice)

### Snacks

4 small gingersnap cookies (1 ounce total)
1 pear

DAILY TOTALS: 2,103 CALORIES, 37 G. TOTAL FAT, 10.5 G. SATURATED FAT,
76 MG. CHOLESTEROL, 28 G. DIETARY FIBER, 1,182 MG. SODIUM.

# PART IV

# What's Cooking in the No-Cholesterol Kitchen

# GREAT BEGINNINGS

## *Light Bites, Simple Snacks and Elegant Hors d'Oeuvres*

**W**hether it's because you're too busy to sit down to a full meal—let alone prepare one—or you've come down with a bad case of the "munchies," sometimes you want just a little something to eat. This is when you're most vulnerable to the convenience of a vending machine full of nutritionally nasty snacks or a half-empty tub of Triple Fudge Brownie ice cream that you decide to "just finish off." Sure, you end up with a full tummy—but you also come close to filling your daily quotas for fat and cholesterol in one sitting.

To navigate these dietary danger zones, you need to have more healthful alternatives on hand. The recipes that follow should do the trick. You can make them in just minutes (some you can even make ahead), so they're perfect for even the busiest schedule. And they'll satisfy your hunger pangs without sabotaging your heart-smart eating habits.

You can serve up cholesterol-free cuisine when entertaining, too. Party buffet tables are notorious fat traps: Spending a whole evening grazing on cocktail weenies and chips 'n' dip is just asking for trouble. But you don't have to resign yourself to carrot and celery sticks, either. Many of the recipes offered here make excellent hors d'oeuvres or appetizers—and they're sure to be crowd-pleasers.

## Portable Picks for Lunch on the Run

The recipes in this section make for quick-and-easy cholesterol-free lunches. Some, such as the Southwestern Red-Bean Chili, taste better after an overnight mellowing in the refrigerator.

## Southwestern Red-Bean Chili

*This spicy chili with a rich red color has plenty of beans— and is easy to make ahead in quantity and freeze for emergencies.*

      2  pounds mushrooms, sliced
      3  cups cooked and drained small red beans
      3  onions, coarsely chopped
      1  cup chopped celery
      1  cup chopped carrots
    ½  teaspoon olive oil
      1  teaspoon ground cumin
      1  teaspoon dried basil
      1  teaspoon chili powder (or to taste)
      8  ripe Italian tomatoes, chopped
      1  small can (about 2 ounces) green chilies, chopped
    ½  cup low-sodium soy sauce or tamari
    ½  cup non-alcoholic red wine
      3  tablespoons tomato paste
      4  cloves garlic, minced
      2  teaspoons ground red pepper (or to taste)

Coat a 6- to 8-quart heavy pot with no-stick spray. Add the mushrooms, beans, onions, celery, carrots, oil, cumin, basil and chili powder. Cover and cook over medium heat for 10 minutes, or until the onions are soft.

Add the tomatoes, chilies, soy sauce or tamari, wine, tomato paste, garlic and pepper. Increase the heat to high and bring to a boil. Lower the heat and simmer for at least 45 minutes (the flavors will improve the longer the chili simmers).

*Serves 6.*

PER SERVING: 264 CALORIES, 2.0 G. TOTAL FAT, 0.3 G. SATURATED FAT, 0 MG. CHOLESTEROL, 9.6 G. DIETARY FIBER, 871 MG. SODIUM.

# **Warm Cauliflower Salad**

*Adapted from a traditional Niçoise recipe, this warm, fragrant salad makes any lunchtime a sunny occasion. You may prepare it up to three days ahead; it will keep well in a tightly covered container in the refrigerator.*

1   large head cauliflower, broken into small pieces
⅓   cup chopped celery
3   tablespoons olive oil
1   tablespoon chopped sweet red peppers
1   tablespoon lemon juice
1   teaspoon Dijon mustard
½   teaspoon curry powder
¼   teaspoon ground cinnamon
¼   teaspoon herbal salt substitute

In a large steamer, steam the cauliflower until tender but still crisp, about 8 to 10 minutes.

In a large bowl, combine the celery, oil, peppers, lemon juice, mustard, curry powder, cinnamon and salt substitute. Add the warm cauliflower and toss to combine. Let stand for at least 5 minutes before serving.

*SERVES 4.*

PER SERVING: 132 CALORIES, 10.8 G. TOTAL FAT, 1.4 G. SATURATED FAT, 0 MG. CHOLESTEROL, 6.0 G. DIETARY FIBER, 99 MG. SODIUM.

# Noodles with Miso Sauce

*This creamy noodle dish tastes as if it were loaded with rich dairy cheese, but the flavor comes from tahini, a paste made from sesame seeds. The sauce keeps for a week in the refrigerator and is equally delicious hot or cold.*

⅓   cup water
½   cup thinly sliced mushrooms
3   tablespoons tahini
2   tablespoons minced scallions
1   tablespoon minced fresh parsley
2   tablespoons light miso
2   tablespoons hot water
2   cups cooked eggless noodles

In a large frying pan, heat the water until it's simmering. Add the mushrooms. Lower the heat, cover the pan and let the mushrooms cook for 5 minutes.

Stir in the tahini, heating until it becomes creamy. Remove the pan from the heat. Add the scallions and parsley.

In a small cup, combine the miso and hot water. Stir into the sauce. Add the noodles and toss well.

*SERVES 4.*

PER SERVING: 224 CALORIES, 7.8 G. TOTAL FAT, 0.1 G. SATURATED FAT, 0 MG. CHOLESTEROL, 0.5 G. DIETARY FIBER, 330 MG. SODIUM.

# Red Pepper Cornbread

*An ideal accompaniment to Southwestern Red-Bean Chili (page 252), this cornbread tastes especially good when it's warmed up. Using soy milk instead of dairy milk makes it a delicious variation of a traditional favorite.*

| | |
|---|---|
| 3 | cups coarse cornmeal |
| 2 | cups boiling water |
| ¼–½ | cup minced sweet red peppers |
| 3 | tablespoons olive oil |
| 1–3 | teaspoons herbal salt substitute |
| 1 | cup soy milk |
| 1 | tablespoon baking powder |

In a large bowl, mix together the cornmeal, water, peppers, oil and salt substitute. Let stand for 40 minutes. Stir in the milk and baking powder.

Preheat the oven to 400°.

Coat an 8″ × 8″ baking dish with no-stick spray. Place the empty dish in the oven for 1 minute, then remove (with hot pads) and pour in the batter. (Preheating the dish creates a crisp outer crust.)

Bake the cornbread for 30 to 40 minutes, or until a toothpick inserted in the center comes out clean. Let cool, then cut into squares.

*SERVES 9.*

PER SERVING: 200 CALORIES, 6.5 G. TOTAL FAT, 0.9 G. SATURATED FAT, 0 MG. CHOLESTEROL, 6.7 G. DIETARY FIBER, 128 MG. SODIUM.

**Morning-Glory Fruit Shake**

*Juicy, sweet Red Delicious apples give this shake a wonderful flavor, but feel free to use your own favorite variety.*

2  cups sliced bananas
2  cups sliced strawberries
2  cups chopped pineapple or papayas
1  cup chopped peeled apples
½  cup ice cubes
1  teaspoon honey

In a blender, combine the bananas, strawberries, pineapples or papayas, apples, ice cubes and honey. Puree on high speed until smooth. Serve immediately.

*SERVES 4.*

PER SERVING: 196 CALORIES, 1.3 G. TOTAL FAT, 0.3 G. SATURATED FAT, 0 MG. CHOLESTEROL, 5.3 G. DIETARY FIBER, 3 MG. SODIUM.

# Spiced Tempeh Sandwiches

*Tempeh is a great cholesterol-free substitute for beef. For these delicious sandwiches, it is cooked in a spicy marinade, then piled between slices of rye bread.*

1 pound tempeh
½ cup water
2 tablespoons low-sodium soy sauce or tamari
2 tablespoons apple juice
1 tablespoon honey
1 teaspoon minced garlic
1 teaspoon ground coriander
½ teaspoon grated fresh ginger
 Pinch of ground red pepper
4 slices rye bread
4 lettuce leaves or ½ cup radish sprouts
2 tomato or avocado slices

Cut the tempeh into 4 large pieces.

In a medium bowl, combine the water, soy sauce or tamari, apple juice, honey, garlic, coriander, ginger and pepper.

In a large no-stick frying pan over medium heat, lightly brown the tempeh on both sides. Add the marinade mixture and cook until the liquid evaporates. Remove from the heat. Slice each piece of tempeh in half horizontally to make it thinner.

Place on half of the bread slices. Add the lettuce or sprouts and tomatoes or avocados. Top with the remaining bread.

*Serves 2.*

---

Per serving: 677 calories, 20.3 g. total fat, 3.4 g. saturated fat, 0 mg. cholesterol, 18.6 g. dietary fiber, 957 mg. sodium.

# On the Lighter Side

These recipes are for those times when you don't have a huge appetite. They're sure to become family favorites for brunches, summer picnics and late-night suppers.

## Harvest Salad

*This bright and colorful salad combines raw vegetables and seeds, so you'll get a healthful dose of dietary fiber.*

| | |
|---|---|
| 1 | cup corn |
| 1 | cup chopped green cabbage |
| 1 | carrot, thinly sliced |
| 1 | stalk celery, diced |
| ⅓ | cup chopped sweet red peppers |
| 2 | tablespoons olive oil |
| ¼ | teaspoon salt |
| ½ | teaspoon ground black pepper |
| ¼ | cup water |
| 3 | tablespoons minced shallots |
| 2 | tablespoons lemon juice |
| 1 | tablespoon minced fresh dill |
| 1 | teaspoon Dijon mustard |

In a large bowl, combine the corn, cabbage, carrots, celery and red peppers.

In a small bowl, whisk together the oil, salt, ground pepper, water, shallots, lemon juice, dill and mustard. Pour over the vegetables. Let marinate for at least 1 hour before serving.

*SERVES 4.*

PER SERVING: 119 CALORIES, 7.0 G. TOTAL FAT, 0.9 G. SATURATED FAT, 0 MG. CHOLESTEROL, 2.4 G. DIETARY FIBER, 171 MG. SODIUM.

## Southwestern Bread Wraps

*A great light meal, these burritos can be rolled the night before and packed for a picnic or carried along for a quick bite while traveling. They use leftover Southwestern Red-Bean Chili (page 252). If desired, serve topped with sprouts, shredded lettuce, grated carrots, chopped tomatoes and sliced avocados.*

½  cup Southwestern Red-Bean Chili (page 252)
2  tablespoons Mexican salsa
1  teaspoon minced red onions
1  teaspoon minced fresh cilantro
½  clove garlic, minced
2  tortillas or chapatis

In a medium bowl, combine the chili, salsa, onions, cilantro and garlic. Mash with a potato masher or fork.

Spread on tortillas or chapatis and roll to enclose the filling. If desired, warm in a toaster oven or microwave before eating.

*SERVES 2.*

PER SERVING: 140 CALORIES, 1.2 G. TOTAL FAT, 0.2 G. SATURATED FAT, 0 MG. CHOLESTEROL, 3.1 G. DIETARY FIBER, 414 MG. SODIUM.

# Grilled Vegetables en Papillote

*Use aluminum foil or parchment paper (available in cookware stores) to wrap this savory vegetable mixture before cooking. This technique keeps fat and calories low and allows flavors to mingle in the moist packet.*

 2 cups broccoli florets
 1 red onion, thinly sliced
 1 cup thinly sliced carrots
 2 cloves garlic, minced
1½ teaspoons olive oil
 2 teaspoons chopped fresh tarragon
   Juice of ½ lime

In a large bowl, combine the broccoli, onions, carrots, garlic, oil, tarragon and lime juice. Let stand for 1 hour, stirring occasionally.

While the vegetables marinate, prepare a grill for cooking.

Cut aluminum foil or parchment paper into 4 circles about 10″ in diameter. Divide the vegetable mixture evenly among the circles. Fold into half-moon shapes, crimping the edges to seal.

Grill about 5″ to 6″ from medium-hot coals for about 10 minutes.

*Serves 4.*

---

PER SERVING: 59 CALORIES, 2.0 G. TOTAL FAT, 0.3 G. SATURATED FAT, 0 MG. CHOLESTEROL, 3.0 G. DIETARY FIBER, 23 MG. SODIUM.

---

# Mushroom Ragout on Rye Toast Triangles

*This recipe is so simple: Dried and fresh mushrooms are sautéed, then their juices are thickened into a rich sauce.*

1   ounce dried shiitake mushrooms
1   cup boiling water
½   cup apple juice
1   teaspoon olive oil
3   medium leeks, thinly sliced
2   cups mushrooms, thinly sliced
1   teaspoon minced garlic
1   cup nonalcoholic white wine
2   tablespoons arrowroot powder
    Herbal salt substitute (to taste)
    Ground white pepper (to taste)
4   slices rye bread

Place the dried mushrooms in a small bowl and cover with the boiling water. Let soak for 15 minutes, then drain. Cut off and discard the stems. Slice the caps into thin strips. Set aside.

In a large frying pan over medium-high heat, heat the apple juice and oil. Reduce the heat to medium and add the leeks. Sauté for 15 minutes, stirring frequently.

Add the soaked mushrooms, fresh mushrooms and garlic. Cook for 10 minutes, stirring frequently. Strain, reserving the cooking liquid (if any). Set the mushrooms aside. Return the liquid to the pan.

In a small bowl, combine the wine and arrowroot until dissolved. Pour the wine mixture into the pan. Bring to a boil and cook, stirring with a whisk, until the sauce thickens. Season with the salt substitute and pepper. Add the mushroom mixture to the sauce and heat through.

Meanwhile, toast the bread, then cut diagonally into quarters to form triangles. Place on a platter. Spoon the sauce over the toast.

*Serves 4.*

PER SERVING: 213 CALORIES, 2.8 G. TOTAL FAT, 0.4 G. SATURATED FAT, 0 MG. CHOLESTEROL, 3.4 G. DIETARY FIBER, 235 MG. SODIUM.

## Anytime Treats

You should have a few healthful snacks at the ready when the urge to munch strikes, so you're not tempted by the last cream-filled doughnut on your coffee break or one of those big and buttery soft pretzels at the local mall. These will quiet your stomach grumbles without guilt.

        **Hot Tomato Toddies**

*These are perfect for chilly evenings by the fire. You can even make them ahead and serve them hot from a thermos.*

> 6 cups low-sodium vegetable cocktail juice
> Juice of 1 lemon (about ¼ cup)
> Juice of 1 lime (about 2 tablespoons)
> ¼ teaspoon celery seeds
> Dash of hot pepper sauce or ¼ teaspoon ground red pepper
> 3 stalks celery, halved

In a 2-quart saucepan, combine the vegetable juice, lemon juice, lime juice, celery seeds and hot pepper sauce or red pepper. Bring to a boil over medium heat.

To serve, pour into mugs and add celery stalks for stirring.

*SERVES 6.*

PER SERVING: 13 CALORIES, 0.1 G. TOTAL FAT, 0 G. SATURATED FAT, 0 MG. CHOLESTEROL, 0.4 G. DIETARY FIBER, 25 MG. SODIUM.

## Oil-Free Potato Chips

*Paper-thin slices of red potatoes are baked until the moisture evaporates and the potatoes turn into crisp chips. The slicing is easiest if you use a food processor, but you can do it by hand, too.*

  1  pound red potatoes, well-scrubbed
     Herbal salt substitute (to taste)
     Ground black pepper (to taste)

Preheat the oven to 300°.

Lightly coat a large baking sheet with no-stick spray. Using a sharp knife or a food processor fitted with a thin slicing blade, cut the potatoes into paper-thin slices. Spread the potatoes on the baking sheet in a single layer. Sprinkle lightly with the salt substitute and pepper.

Bake until lightly browned and crisp, about 10 to 15 minutes.

*SERVES 10.*

PER SERVING: 44 CALORIES, 0.1 G. TOTAL FAT, 0.1 G. SATURATED FAT, 0 MG. CHOLESTEROL, 0 G. DIETARY FIBER, 2 MG. SODIUM.

## Savory Garlicky Popcorn

*Make up plenty of this crunchy cholesterol-free snack. With the delicious garlic flavor, nobody will miss the butter. The popcorn will keep for five days in a tightly covered container.*

2 tablespoons honey
2 tablespoons tomato paste
1 teaspoon garlic powder
¼ teaspoon chili powder
¼ teaspoon paprika
6 cups air-popped popcorn

Preheat the oven to 200°.

In a 1-quart saucepan, combine the honey, tomato paste, garlic powder, chili powder and paprika. Cook over medium heat, stirring frequently, until fragrant, about 3 minutes.

Place the popcorn in a large bowl. Drizzle with the honey mixture and toss to coat lightly.

Spread the popcorn on a large ungreased no-stick baking sheet. Bake for 15 minutes, stirring occasionally. Turn the oven off and let the mixture stand with the door closed for 1 hour, which helps the coating stick.

*MAKES 6 CUPS.*

---

PER CUP: 53 CALORIES, 0.1 G. TOTAL FAT, 0.1 G. SATURATED FAT, 0 MG. CHOLESTEROL, 0.7 G. DIETARY FIBER, 45 MG. SODIUM.

## Chili Tortilla Strips

*These chips will become favorites in your family. Crunchy and satisfying, they make great take-along snacks.*

6 large corn tortillas
2 teaspoons warmed olive oil
2 tablespoons chili powder
1 teaspoon ground cumin

Preheat the oven to 400°.

Lightly brush both sides of each tortilla with the oil. Using scissors, cut the tortillas into 1"-wide strips. Place in a single layer on a large ungreased baking sheet.

In a cup, mix the chili powder and cumin. Sprinkle over the strips. Bake for 15 to 20 minutes, or until crisp.

*Serves 6.*

PER SERVING: 79 CALORIES, 2.6 G. TOTAL FAT, 0.3 G. SATURATED FAT, 0 MG. CHOLESTEROL, 0.9 G. DIETARY FIBER, 67 MG. SODIUM.

## Ants on a Log

*A winner with kids, this snack is simple enough for them to make themselves. And it keeps for several days if tightly covered and refrigerated.*

3 stalks celery, halved
½ cup reduced-fat peanut butter
¼ cup raisins

Stuff the cavity of each celery stick with the peanut butter, then top with the raisins.

*Makes 6.*

PER STALK: 148 CALORIES, 8.1 G. TOTAL FAT, 1.7 G. SATURATED FAT, 0 MG. CHOLESTEROL, 1.2 G. DIETARY FIBER, 31 MG. SODIUM.

# Entertaining Eats

Whether you're planning an intimate get-together or a big celebra-tory bash, these goodies will start things off right. You can serve them buffet-style or as first-course appetizers. Either way, they're certain to whet your guests' appetites!

## Mushroom Kabobs

*These colorful Russian kabobs are first marinated in aromatic herbs and cholesterol-lowering olive oil, then broiled until golden.*

24 small mushrooms
2 teaspoons olive oil
½ teaspoon minced garlic
¼ teaspoon dried thyme
⅛ teaspoon ground red pepper (or to taste)
24 pineapple chunks

In a large bowl, combine the mushrooms, oil, garlic, thyme and pepper. Let marinate for 1 hour at room tem-perature.

Preheat the broiler.

Drain the mushrooms and reserve the liquid. On each of 6 bamboo or metal skewers, alternate 4 mushrooms with 4 pineapple chunks. Broil 3″ to 4″ from the heat until the mushrooms are lightly browned, about 3 minutes. Turn and broil 3 minutes more.

Serve hot with the reserved sauce.

*SERVES 6.*

PER SERVING: 30 CALORIES, 0.8 G. TOTAL FAT, 0.1 G. SATURATED FAT, 0 MG. CHOLESTEROL, 1.4 G. DIETARY FIBER, 1 MG. SODIUM.

# California Pizza Toasts

*The "crusts" for these miniature pizzas are actually slices of French bread. You can substitute another bread, if you like; just be sure it's made without dairy products. You can assemble the pizzas up to five hours ahead—simply cover them with plastic wrap and refrigerate.*

4   ounces soy mozzarella cheese, shredded
2   ounces soft tofu, drained
1   teaspoon minced garlic
¼   teaspoon dried oregano
¼   teaspoon dried basil
1   large baguette whole-wheat French bread
¼   cup tomato paste

Preheat the broiler.

In a food processor or blender, puree the cheese, tofu and garlic until smooth. Transfer to a bowl and stir in the oregano and basil.

Cut the bread diagonally into 20 (1″) slices. Spread each slice with a small amount of the tomato paste and top with a dollop of the cheese mixture. Place on a baking sheet.

Broil 3″ to 4″ from the heat for 1 minute, or until lightly browned. Serve hot.

*MAKES 20.*

---

PER PIZZA: 82 CALORIES, 0.9 G. TOTAL FAT, 0.2 G. SATURATED FAT, 0 MG. CHOLESTEROL, 0.3 G. DIETARY FIBER, 219 MG. SODIUM.

# Refrigerator Pickled Vegetables

*An overnight soak in marinade produces crisp, pickled vegetables that are great on a buffet with richer hors d'oeuvres.*

¼  cup rice-wine vinegar
¼  cup apple cider vinegar
1   umeboshi plum, mashed, or 1 teaspoon salt
1   tablespoon low-sodium soy sauce or tamari
1   teaspoon honey or maple syrup
1   large seedless cucumber, halved lengthwise and
    sliced into thin half-moons
1   cup radish halves
1   cup carrot sticks

In a jar with a tight-fitting lid, combine the rice-wine vinegar, apple cider vinegar, plum or salt, soy sauce or tamari, and honey or maple syrup. Add the cucumbers, radishes and carrots.

Cap the jar and shake. Place in the refrigerator and let marinate at least overnight. Remove the vegetables from the marinade and serve.

*MAKES 3 CUPS.*

PER CUP: 18 CALORIES, 0.2 G. TOTAL FAT, 0.1 G. SATURATED FAT, 0 MG. CHOLESTEROL, 0.7 G. DIETARY FIBER, 53 MG. SODIUM.

# Caper and Garlic Dip with Fresh Vegetables

*This creamy dip is a great partner for a platter of fresh vegetables. Be sure to choose a pepper with a flat bottom, so it can stand upright to serve as a container for the dip.*

1  large sweet red or green pepper
1  cup cherry tomatoes
1  cup broccoli florets
1  cup whole snow peas
2  small zucchini or yellow summer squash,
   sliced diagonally
1  cup whole green beans
8  ounces mushrooms, halved
8  ounces soft tofu, drained
1  tablespoon capers, drained
1  tablespoon stone-ground mustard
2  teaspoons minced fresh tarragon or
   1 teaspoon dried
2  teaspoons minced chives or scallions
2  teaspoons minced garlic

Cut the top off the pepper and discard the seeds and inner membrane. Place the pepper in the center of a large platter. Arrange the tomatoes, broccoli, snow peas, zucchini or squash, beans and mushrooms around it.

In a food processor or blender, puree the tofu until smooth. Transfer to a small bowl and stir in the capers, mustard, tarragon, chives or scallions, and garlic. Spoon the dip into the pepper. Serve at room temperature.

*SERVES 16.*

---

PER SERVING: 33 CALORIES, 0.8 G. TOTAL FAT, 0.1 G. SATURATED FAT, 0 MG. CHOLESTEROL, 1.3 G. DIETARY FIBER, 41 MG. SODIUM.

## Baked New Potatoes with Assorted Dips

*Here's a great serving idea for this appetizer: After baking the new potatoes, pile them into a wicker basket lined with a cloth napkin. Place the dips around the basket in colorful bowls.*

    20   unpeeled bite-size new potatoes
    ⅔    cup soft tofu, pureed until creamy
    ⅓    cup soy imitation bacon bits
    1    tablespoon lemon juice
    ¼    cup minced chives or scallions
    ¼    cup Dijon mustard
    1    cup chunky peanut butter
    1    teaspoon ground red pepper
    1    teaspoon low-sodium soy sauce or tamari

Preheat the oven to 350°.

Wash the potatoes, prick each once with a fork and place on a large ungreased baking sheet. Bake for 30 minutes, or until soft.

Meanwhile, in a small bowl, combine the tofu, bacon bits and lemon juice.

In another small bowl, combine the chives or scallions and mustard.

In a third bowl, combine the peanut butter, pepper, and soy sauce or tamari.

Place the warm potatoes on a platter and surround them with the dipping sauces.

*MAKES 20.*

PER POTATO: 250 CALORIES, 6.6 G. TOTAL FAT, 1.3 G. SATURATED FAT, 0 MG. CHOLESTEROL, 1.2 G. DIETARY FIBER, 108 MG. SODIUM.

## Sun-Dried-Tomato Pesto in Endive Spears

*This colorful pesto is served in spears of pale green endive for a striking presentation. The recipe abounds with garlic, known for its cholesterol-lowering properties.*

| | |
|---|---|
| 8 | ounces sun-dried tomatoes, well-drained |
| ¾ | cup fine cracker crumbs |
| 4 | cloves garlic, coarsely chopped |
| 1 | tablespoon apple juice |
| 2 | tablespoons pine nuts |
| 2 | bunches Belgian endive, separated into spears |
| | Fresh basil or cilantro |

In a food processor or blender, puree the tomatoes, crumbs, garlic and apple juice until smooth.

In a small frying pan over low heat, toast the pine nuts for 2 minutes, stirring continually. Add to the tomato mixture. Process until smooth.

Spread the pesto on the endive spears. Garnish with the basil or cilantro.

*Serves 12.*

Per serving: 90 calories, 1.0 g. total fat, 0.2 g. saturated fat, 0 mg. cholesterol, 1.6 g. dietary fiber, 27 mg. sodium.

# Miniature Stuffed Vegetables

*This pâté tastes just like chicken salad. It is spooned into cherry tomatoes and miniature cups made from thick slices of zucchini.*

12  large cherry tomatoes
2  large zucchini
8  ounces tempeh, cut into large chunks
2  tablespoons low-sodium soy sauce or tamari
¼  cup minced celery
3  tablespoons nonfat, cholesterol-free mayonnaise
2  tablespoons minced fresh parsley
1  tablespoon minced scallions
   Pinch of ground red pepper
   Pinch of dried dill
   Dill sprigs

Slice the tops off the cherry tomatoes and remove the insides using the small end of a melon scoop. Slice each zucchini crosswise into 8 pieces. With the melon scoop, make a shallow well in the center of each slice.

Coat a large frying pan with no-stick spray. Add the tempeh and sauté over medium-high heat until lightly browned, about 10 minutes. Add the soy sauce or tamari and mash the tempeh into a thick paste.

Transfer the mixture to a medium bowl and add the celery, mayonnaise, parsley, scallions, pepper and dried dill.

Spoon the mixture into the tomatoes and zucchini cups. Garnish with the dill sprigs.

*Makes 28.*

---

Per stuffed tomato or zucchini: 21 calories, 0.7 g. total fat, 0.1 g. saturated fat, 0 mg. cholesterol, 0.8 g. dietary fiber, 60 mg. sodium.

# Asian Nut Balls

*A savory, rich flavor weaves through these unusual hors d'oeuvres, which are made from an assortment of ground nuts seasoned with low-sodium soy sauce or tamari and nutritional yeast.*

1¼ cups finely ground, unsalted nuts, such as almonds, walnuts or cashews
2 cups cooked short-grain brown rice
½ cup grated onions
3 tablespoons nutritional yeast
1 tablespoon low-sodium soy sauce or tamari
1 tablespoon dried basil
1 teaspoon ground caraway seeds
1 teaspoon dried sage
½ cup prepared hot Chinese mustard

Preheat the oven to 350°.

In a large bowl, combine the nuts, rice, onions, yeast, soy sauce or tamari, basil, caraway and sage. Form into 1″ balls, adding a little water if needed for the mixture to hold together.

Place on an ungreased baking sheet and bake for 20 minutes. Serve hot with the mustard as a dip.

*MAKES 42.*

PER BALL: 39 CALORIES, 2.3 G. TOTAL FAT, 0.2 G. SATURATED FAT, 0 MG. CHOLESTEROL, 0.7 G. DIETARY FIBER, 53 MG. SODIUM.

# Simple Bean Spread on Rye Croutons

*This fiber-rich spread freezes well and will keep in the refrigerator for a week.*

    2   cups cooked and drained chick-peas or pinto beans
    3   cloves garlic
    2   teaspoons herbal salt substitute
    1   teaspoon lemon juice
    1   teaspoon ground cumin (or to taste)
  1–2   teaspoons water (optional)
    1   tablespoon minced fresh parsley
   20   slices round party-size rye bread

In a blender or food processor, puree the chick-peas or beans, garlic, salt substitute, lemon juice and cumin until smooth. (If needed to facilitate blending, add the water.) Transfer to a medium bowl. Stir in the parsley. Refrigerate overnight to let the flavors blend.

Preheat the oven to 250°.

Place the bread in a single layer on a large ungreased baking sheet. Bake for 20 minutes per side, or until crisp. Let cool for a few minutes. Spread with the bean mixture.

*SERVES 10.*

---

PER SERVING: 151 CALORIES, 2.3 G. TOTAL FAT, 0.3 G. SATURATED FAT, 0 MG. CHOLESTEROL, 1.2 G. DIETARY FIBER, 190 MG. SODIUM.

---

# Stuffed Mushrooms with Parsley Pesto

*Bypassing fatty cheeses and nuts, this pesto is a refreshing cholesterol-free alternative to traditional recipes. For variety, you can serve the pesto over hot pasta or as a spread on croutons or crackers.*

16 large mushrooms
 3 tablespoons minced onions
 2 teaspoons minced garlic
 1 teaspoon olive oil
 2 tablespoons fine rye bread crumbs
⅓ cup minced fresh basil
 2 tablespoons minced fresh parsley
½ teaspoon minced fresh oregano
   Herbal salt substitute (to taste)
   Ground black pepper (to taste)
   Shredded soy mozzarella cheese (optional)

Preheat the broiler.

Remove the stems from the mushrooms by wiggling them until they loosen. Mince the stems and set aside. Place the caps, round side up, on an ungreased baking sheet and broil 3″ to 4″ from the heat for 3 to 5 minutes, or until the mushrooms exude moisture. Set aside.

In a large frying pan over medium-high heat, sauté the onions and garlic in the oil for 5 minutes, stirring frequently to keep from browning. Add the minced mushroom stems and bread crumbs. Cook for 3 minutes.

Remove the pan from the heat and add the basil, parsley, oregano, salt substitute and pepper.

Lightly coat a shallow baking dish or jelly-roll pan with no-stick spray. Arrange the mushrooms in the dish, hollow sides up. Spoon the basil mixture into the caps. Sprinkle with a little cheese (if using).

Broil until the filling is hot and bubbling, about 3 to 5 minutes. Serve hot.

*Makes 16.*

PER MUSHROOM: 9 CALORIES, 0.6 G. TOTAL FAT, 0.1 G. SATURATED FAT, 0 MG. CHOLESTEROL, 0.6 G. DIETARY FIBER, 2 MG. SODIUM.

# Rice-Paper Vegetarian Spring Rolls

*Rice paper is traditionally used in Vietnamese and Thai cuisines as an alternative to deep-fried egg-roll wrappings.*

2   large carrots
2   tablespoons chopped scallion tops
1   tablespoon olive oil
1   tablespoon minced fresh tarragon or
    1 teaspoon dried
¼   teaspoon ground black pepper
16   rice-paper rounds, 6″ in diameter
2   cups cooked bean-thread noodles,
    snipped into 2″ pieces

Using a vegetable peeler, shave off long, thin slices of carrot. Place the carrots, scallions, oil, tarragon and pepper in a large bowl. Toss well and let stand for 1 hour.

Fill a large bowl with warm water. Dip each rice-paper round into the water until softened and translucent, about 10 seconds. Remove and let drain on a clean dish towel.

Place about 2 tablespoons of the noodles and about 2 tablespoons of the vegetable mixture along the lower edge of each piece of rice paper, about 1″ from the edge. Fold the bottom of the paper over the filling; fold in both sides over the filling. Roll the bundle into a cylinder.

Place the rolls on a plate and cover with plastic wrap. Chill for 30 minutes. Serve cold.

*Makes 16.*

---

PER ROLL: 55 CALORIES, 0.9 G. TOTAL FAT, 0.1 G. SATURATED FAT, 0 MG. CHOLESTEROL, 0.3 g. DIETARY FIBER, 4 MG. SODIUM.

# THE GOODNESS
# OF GREENS

## *Salads Turn Over a New Leaf*

**A**mong the generations of folks raised on meat and potatoes, the salad earned a reputation as the classic diet food. It seemed as if sitting down to a plateful of lettuce was the price folks had to pay for indulging their taste buds once too often and packing on some extra pounds.

Of course, this was all B.S.B.: before salad bars. These refrigerated feeding troughs made salads fashionable. People seem to love bellying up to the bar to pile their plates with all sorts of greens, toppings and condiments. And since it's a salad, it's naturally healthy and low in calories, fat and cholesterol.

Ah . . . the salad bar booby trap. Just because something is perched amidst bowls of broccoli, cauliflower and cherry tomatoes doesn't necessarily mean that it's good for you. Salad dressings, the worst offenders, can get 80 to 90 percent of their calories from fat. But there are more innocent-looking culprits, too: pasta salad, croutons, even cottage cheese if it's not low-fat.

Still, when it comes to dining out, salad bars can be your best bet for a healthful meal. You just have to know what to look for. Generally, you're safe if you stick to the stuff you'd find in the produce aisle of your grocery store—as long as it's not floating in mayonnaise. And choose nonfat or low-fat dressing, but be aware that the usual serving size is just two tablespoons.

Even better, you can make your own salads at home. They're super-easy when time is at a premium, and with the right mix of ingredients, they're hearty enough to satisfy even the biggest appetite. Plus, by choosing what goes into the salad bowl, you know that everything is fresh and healthful.

## Fix 'Em Fast

With the wide variety of produce available these days, you can create all sorts of salads with exciting flavors and textures. The recipes in this section feature some ingredients not usually found in salads, such as kiwifruit, eggplant and squash. But don't let the gourmet quality of these salads fool you: They can be prepared in just minutes.

### Chinese Vegetable Salad with Kiwifruit

*This salad may discolor if it stands too long, so plan to eat it soon after you make it.*

| | |
|---|---|
| 1 | cucumber |
| ½ | head green cabbage, thinly sliced |
| 2 | cups chow mein noodles (optional) |
| ½ | cup peeled and sliced fresh kiwifruit |
| ¼ | cup chopped fresh cilantro |
| ½ | cup rice-wine vinegar |
| ⅓ | cup honey |
| 1 | teaspoon sesame seeds |
| 1 | tablespoon grated onions |
| 1 | tablespoon low-sodium soy sauce or tamari |
| 1 | tablespoon grated fresh ginger |
| 1 | tablespoon dark sesame oil |
| 1 | teaspoon herbal salt substitute |

Peel the cucumber. Halve it lengthwise, remove the seeds and slice the flesh into thin half-moons. Place in a large bowl. Add the cabbage, noodles (if using), kiwi and cilantro. Mix well.

In a small bowl, whisk together the vinegar, honey, sesame seeds, onions, soy sauce or tamari, ginger, oil and salt substitute. Pour over the salad and mix well. Let marinate for 1 hour before serving.

*Serves 4.*

---

Per serving: 180 calories, 4.3 g. total fat, 0.6 g. saturated fat, 0 mg. cholesterol, 4.0 g. dietary fiber, 165 mg. sodium.

# Herbed Red-Potato Salad

*Just a drizzle of cholesterol-free mayonnaise makes this potato salad as creamy as the deli version, but without the cholesterol.*

3 cups small unpeeled red potatoes
2 tablespoons cholesterol-free mayonnaise
1 tablespoon olive oil
1 tablespoon chopped pimentos
2–3 teaspoons Dijon mustard
½ teaspoon lemon juice
½ teaspoon herbal salt substitute
⅓ cup chopped celery
⅓ cup diced green apples, such as Granny Smith
1 tablespoon minced fresh chives
¼ teaspoon ground black pepper

Quarter the potatoes and steam over boiling water until tender, about 20 minutes.

In a large bowl, whisk together the mayonnaise, oil, pimentos, mustard, lemon juice and salt substitute. Add the warm potatoes and toss well to coat. Let marinate for at least 1 hour.

Before serving, add the celery, apples, chives and pepper. Taste for seasoning and add more lemon juice, salt substitute or pepper, if needed.

*SERVES 4.*

PER SERVING: 245 CALORIES, 8.8 G. TOTAL FAT, 1.0 G. SATURATED FAT, 0 MG. CHOLESTEROL, 3.5 G. DIETARY FIBER, 90 MG. SODIUM.

## Marinated Mushrooms

*A traditional Ukrainian recipe, these marinated mushrooms can be prepared up to three weeks in advance and refrigerated. Toss them in a salad for a flavor boost.*

  ½   cup water
  ½   cup lemon juice
  1   tablespoon olive oil
  1   bay leaf, crushed
  2   cloves garlic, minced
  6   whole black peppercorns
  ½   teaspoon herbal salt substitute
  2   cups small mushrooms, stems trimmed

In a 1-quart saucepan, combine the water, lemon juice, oil, bay leaf, garlic, peppercorns and salt substitute. Bring to a boil over medium-high heat.

Place the mushrooms in a large bowl. Pour the hot marinade over them. Cover and refrigerate for 2 days. Drain and remove the bay leaf before serving.

*Serves 6.*

Per serving: 33 calories, 2.4 g. total fat, 0.3 g. saturated fat, 0 mg. cholesterol, 0.4 g. dietary fiber, 2 mg. sodium.

## Grilled-Eggplant Salad with Teriyaki Marinade

*The teriyaki marinade was originally developed for chicken, but it pairs just as well with eggplant for a delicious grilled salad.*

½  cup low-sodium soy sauce or tamari
1  tablespoon safflower oil
2  tablespoons light molasses
2  tablespoons grated fresh ginger
6  cloves garlic, minced
1  medium eggplant, cut into 1" × ½" strips
1  sweet red pepper, thinly sliced
1  cup thinly sliced cucumbers
   Red-leaf lettuce, separated into leaves

In a large bowl, combine the soy sauce or tamari, oil, molasses, ginger and garlic. Add the eggplant and toss well to combine. Cover and let marinate at room temperature for at least 2 hours, or overnight.

Preheat a broiler or stove-top grill.

Remove the eggplant slices from the marinade and place on a broiler pan or directly on the grill. (Reserve the marinade.) Broil or gill, turning once, until lightly browned on both sides.

Transfer to a large bowl. Add the peppers and cucumbers. Drizzle with 2 tablespoons of the reserved marinade. Toss well. Spoon onto a platter lined with the lettuce leaves and serve warm.

*Serves 4.*

PER SERVING: 136 CALORIES, 3.9 G. TOTAL FAT, 0.4 G. SATURATED FAT, 0 MG. CHOLESTEROL, 1.2 G. DIETARY FIBER, 1,062 MG. SODIUM.

# Gingered Cucumber and Squash Salad

*A light sweet-and-sour dressing anoints this refreshing warm-weather salad. The vegetable combination can be marinated from early morning to dinnertime—just add the lettuce right before serving.*

1½  teaspoons honey
4   teaspoons rice-wine vinegar
1   teaspoon low-sodium soy sauce or tamari
1   teaspoon dark sesame oil
2½  cups thinly sliced seedless cucumbers
⅓   cup julienned sweet red peppers
1   cup thinly sliced zucchini or yellow squash
4   cups torn leaf lettuce

In a large salad bowl, whisk together the honey, vinegar, soy sauce or tamari, and oil. Add the cucumbers, peppers and squash. Toss well and let marinate for at least 30 minutes. Add the lettuce, toss again and serve.

*Serves 4.*

Per serving: 49 calories, 1.5 g. total fat, 0.2 g. saturated fat, 0 mg. cholesterol, 1.4 g. dietary fiber, 51 mg. sodium.

## Chinese Picnic Coleslaw

*Bright with mandarin orange slices, this salad is an excellent side dish for picnics and parties.*

4 cups shredded napa (Chinese) cabbage
1 cup drained canned mandarin oranges
½ cup sliced water chestnuts
½ cup sliced seedless cucumbers
¼ cup drained canned litchi nuts
2 tablespoons minced fresh parsley
2 tablespoons nonfat, cholesterol-free mayonnaise
1 tablespoon lime juice
1 tablespoon Dijon mustard
1 teaspoon dark sesame oil
1 teaspoon safflower oil
1 teaspoon grated fresh ginger

In a large salad bowl, combine the cabbage, oranges, water chestnuts, cucumbers, litchi nuts and parsley.

In a small bowl, whisk together the mayonnaise, lime juice, mustard, sesame oil, safflower oil and ginger. Pour over the vegetables and toss well.

*Serves 6.*

Per serving: 55 calories, 1.8 g. total fat, 0.2 g. saturated fat, 0 mg. cholesterol, 0.9 g. dietary fiber, 109 mg. sodium.

## Miso Marinade for Vegetables

*Steep firm leftover vegetables—green or red peppers, cucumbers, cherry tomatoes, cabbage—in this marinade overnight. They'll taste delicious.*

⅓ cup light-colored miso paste
3 tablespoons rice-wine vinegar
3 tablespoons water
1 tablespoon dark sesame oil
2 scallions, minced
¼ teaspoon ground red pepper
4 cups chopped vegetables

In a large bowl, whisk together the miso, vinegar, water, oil, scallions and pepper. Add the vegetables and toss well to combine. Cover and let stand at room temperature for at least 1 hour, or overnight.

*Serves 4.*

PER SERVING: 117 CALORIES, 5.1 G. TOTAL FAT, 0.7 G. SATURATED FAT, 0 MG. CHOLESTEROL, 2.8 G. DIETARY FIBER, 839 MG. SODIUM.

## Three-Sprout Salad with Lemon Dressing

*This recipe calls for chick-pea, wheat-berry and radish
sprouts, but feel free to experiment with other combinations.*

1 cup chick-pea sprouts
1 cup wheat-berry sprouts
½ cup radish sprouts
1 large tomato, diced
¼ cup chopped scallions
¼ cup chopped fresh parsley
1 clove garlic, minced
3 tablespoons olive oil
2 tablespoons lemon juice
2 cups torn red-leaf lettuce
   Herbal salt substitute (to taste)
   Ground black pepper (to taste)

In a large salad bowl, combine the chick-pea sprouts,
wheat-berry sprouts, radish sprouts, tomatoes, scallions,
parsley and garlic.

In a cup, combine the oil and lemon juice. Pour over
the salad. Toss well and let marinate for 20 minutes.

Add the lettuce and toss again. Season with the salt
substitute and pepper.

*SERVES 4.*

PER SERVING: 123 CALORIES, 4.0 G. TOTAL FAT, 0.5 G. SATURATED FAT,
0 MG. CHOLESTEROL, 3.3 G. DIETARY FIBER, 16 MG. SODIUM.

# Make It a Meal

Salads have traditionally been relegated to a supporting role at mealtime. We even serve them on separate plates, a visual cue that they're something other than the main course. Yet with the right mix of ingredients, they can be just as filling and satisfying as an entrée of meat, poultry or pasta. And they're a great main-dish alternative when you want something light.

The salads presented here are meals in themselves. In smaller portions, they can serve as side dishes.

      **Pasta and Corn Salad with Red Sauce**

*This salad is a perfect choice for your next picnic. It's also a great way to use up leftover cooked pasta.*

   2   cups cooked pasta
   1   cup cooked corn
   1   cup chopped tomatoes
   2   tablespoons olive oil
   ¼   cup diced green peppers
   ¼   cup balsamic vinegar
   1   tablespoon lemon juice
   1   teaspoon dried basil
   ¼   teaspoon salt
   ½   teaspoon ground black pepper

In a large bowl, combine the pasta, corn, tomatoes, oil, green peppers, vinegar, lemon juice and basil. Let marinate for 10 minutes. Season with the salt and ground pepper.

*Serves 4.*

---

Per serving: 218 calories, 7.4 g. total fat, 1.0 g. saturated fat, 0 mg. cholesterol, 2.9 g. dietary fiber, 11 mg. sodium.

## Orange Salad with Walnuts

*This fruity salad combines the visual appeal of bright oranges with the contrasting textures of walnuts and crisp onions.*

4   large navel oranges, peeled, sectioned and cut into bite-size pieces
3   tablespoons lemon juice
2   tablespoons orange juice
1   tablespoon honey
2   teaspoons olive oil
1   teaspoon ground cinnamon
2   cups torn romaine lettuce
½   cup thinly sliced red onions
1   tablespoon chopped toasted walnuts
2   teaspoons chopped fresh mint

In a large bowl, combine the oranges, lemon juice, orange juice, honey, oil and cinnamon. Let marinate for 40 minutes at room temperature, stirring occasionally.

Add the lettuce, onions, walnuts and mint. Combine well.

*Serves 6.*

Per serving: 96 calories, 2.4 g. total fat, 0.3 g. saturated fat, 0 mg. cholesterol, 2.5 g. dietary fiber, 3 mg. sodium.

## Basque Bean Salad

*In the Basque Pyrenees, meals are hearty and satisfying—just like this salad, which combines savory beans and vegetables with a balsamic dressing.*

2 cups dried Great Northern beans, rinsed well and soaked overnight
5 cups Vegetable Stock (page 316)
1 cup nonalcoholic white wine
1 medium onion, diced
½ cup minced fresh parsley
½ cup diced sweet red peppers
½ cup diced celery
½ cup balsamic vinegar
3 tablespoons olive oil
2 tablespoons Dijon mustard
2 teaspoons minced garlic
1 teaspoon herbal salt substitute

Drain the soaked beans. Place in a 3-quart saucepan. Add the stock, wine and onions. Bring to a boil over high heat. Cover the pot, reduce the heat to medium and simmer for 2 hours, or until the beans are tender.

Drain the beans and onions and place in a large bowl. (Reserve any leftover liquid for another use.)

Add the parsley, peppers, celery, vinegar, oil, mustard, garlic and salt substitute. Toss well. Serve warm.

*SERVES 6.*

PER SERVING: 319 CALORIES, 8.0 G. TOTAL FAT, 1.2 G. SATURATED FAT, 0 MG. CHOLESTEROL, 10.9 G. DIETARY FIBER, 90 MG. SODIUM.

## Mango Salad with Curry Dressing

*This tropical salad can be presented as a simple one-course luncheon or as an elegant first course.*

| | |
|---|---|
| 6 | ounces soft tofu, drained and crumbled |
| 1 | tablespoon honey |
| 1 | tablespoon lime juice |
| 1 | teaspoon lemon juice |
| 1 | teaspoon curry powder |
| 1 | teaspoon olive oil |
| ⅛ | teaspoon ground white pepper |
| 5 | cups torn romaine lettuce |
| 1 | cup cubed, peeled mango |
| 2 | tablespoons minced red onions |

In a blender, combine the tofu, honey, lime juice, lemon juice, curry powder, oil and pepper. Blend at high speed for 1 minute.

In a large bowl, combine the lettuce, mango and onions. Add the dressing and toss well.

*Serves 6.*

Per serving: 70 calories, 2.0 g. total fat, 0.3 g. saturated fat, 0 mg. cholesterol, 1.8 g. dietary fiber, 13 mg. sodium.

## Mexican Rice Salad with Roasted Peppers

*This salad combines a cheery mix of bright vegetables,
the delicious barbecue flavor of roasted peppers and high-
fiber nutrition from three different kinds of rice.*

| | |
|---|---|
| 3 | large sweet red peppers, seeded and halved |
| 1 | jalapeño pepper, seeded and halved |
| 1 | cup cooked short-grain brown rice |
| 1 | cup cooked basmati rice |
| 1 | cup cooked wild rice |
| ½ | cup minced fresh parsley |
| ¼ | cup olive oil |
| ¼–¾ | cup diced yellow squash |
| 3 | tablespoons lemon or lime juice |
| ½ | teaspoon ground cumin |
| ½ | teaspoon minced garlic |
| ¼ | teaspoon ground red pepper (or to taste) |
| ¼ | teaspoon ground black pepper |
| ¼ | teaspoon dried oregano |

Preheat the broiler.

Cover a baking sheet with aluminum foil. Place the red
peppers and jalapeño peppers on the foil, cut side down.
Broil about 3″ from the heat for about 15 minutes, or until
the skins blacken. Transfer to a brown paper bag. Close
the bag and let the peppers steam (in their own heat) for
20 minutes, so the skins will slip off easily. Remove the
skins, pat the peppers dry on paper towels, then slice into
thin strips.

Place the peppers in a large bowl. Add the brown rice,
basmati rice, wild rice, parsley, oil, squash, lemon or lime
juice, cumin, garlic, ground red pepper, black pepper and
oregano. Toss well to combine.

*Serves 4.*

Per serving: 334 calories, 15.1 g. total fat, 1.9 g. saturated fat,
0 mg. cholesterol, 4.9 g. dietary fiber, 34 mg. sodium.

# Southwestern Corn and Barley Salad

*A satisfying combination of chewy cooked barley and corn kernels, this salad can be made ahead for a carry-along lunch.*

3 cups cooked barley
2 cups cooked corn
¾ cup diced sweet red peppers
¾ cup chopped scallions
½ cup diced green peppers
¼ cup minced red onions
¼ cup lemon juice
2 tablespoons olive oil
2 tablespoons rice-wine vinegar
¼ teaspoon salt
½ teaspoon ground black pepper
1 tablespoon minced fresh cilantro
2 teaspoons herbal salt substitute

In a large bowl, combine the barley, corn, red peppers, scallions, green peppers, onions, lemon juice, oil, vinegar, salt, ground pepper, cilantro and salt substitute. Let marinate for 1 hour before serving. Adjust the seasonings as needed.

*Serves 6.*

PER SERVING: 205 CALORIES, 5.1 G. TOTAL FAT, 0.7 G. SATURATED FAT, 0 MG. CHOLESTEROL, 6.8 G. DIETARY FIBER, 98 MG. SODIUM.

# Warm Chopped-Vegetable Salad

*Paired with crusty bread and hot soup, this salad is great cold-weather fare.*

    1   carrot, thinly sliced
    1   cup diced sweet red peppers
    1   cup chopped broccoli
    ½   cup diced celery
    1   cup nonalcoholic white wine
    1   tablespoon apple juice
    2   tablespoons olive oil
    2   tablespoons rice-wine vinegar
    1   tablespoon Dijon mustard
    1   teaspoon lemon juice
        Herbal salt substitute (to taste)
        Ground black pepper (to taste)

In a 2-quart saucepan, combine the carrots, peppers, broccoli and celery. Add the wine and apple juice. Bring to a boil over medium-high heat. Cover the pan, reduce the heat to medium and simmer for 5 minutes. Strain the vegetables and place in a large bowl. Discard the liquid.

In a small bowl, whisk together the oil, vinegar, mustard and lemon juice. Pour over the vegetables. Season with the salt substitute and pepper. Serve warm.

*Serves 4.*

---

PER SERVING: 103 CALORIES, 7.3 G. TOTAL FAT, 1.0 G. SATURATED FAT, 0 MG. CHOLESTEROL, 2.5 G. DIETARY FIBER, 79 MG. SODIUM.

---

## Cashew and Bean Salad

*Cashews add crunch and protein to this winter salad, while fiber-rich beans contribute their cholesterol-cutting power. Use small red beans for a pleasing color contrast with the green broccoli.*

  1  cup ice water
  ¼  cup thinly sliced red onions
1½  cups broccoli florets
1½  cups cauliflower florets
  1  cup cooked small red beans, such as adzuki
  3  tablespoons olive oil
  ¼  teaspoon salt
  ½  teaspoon ground black pepper
     Juice of 1 large lemon
  1  tablespoon apple cider vinegar
  1  tablespoon low-sodium soy sauce or tamari
  1  teaspoon dry mustard
  1  teaspoon dried basil
  1  tablespoon chopped toasted cashews

In a small bowl, combine the ice water and onions. Let stand for 15 minutes (this will take the bite out of the onions).

Steam the broccoli and cauliflower for 5 minutes, then drain and place in a large bowl. Add the beans.

In a small bowl, whisk together the oil, salt, pepper, lemon juice, vinegar, soy sauce or tamari, mustard and basil. Pour over the vegetables and mix well.

Drain the onions. Add the onions and cashews to the salad right before serving.

*Serves 4.*

---

PER SERVING: 191 CALORIES, 11.8 G. TOTAL FAT, 1.6 G. SATURATED FAT, 0 MG. CHOLESTEROL, 3.9 G. DIETARY FIBER, 288 MG. SODIUM.

---

# Bulgur Wheat Salad with Apricots

*Apricots make this a surprisingly sweet salad, colorful and rich tasting. And it's full of insoluble fiber, the kind that helps prevent colon cancer and digestive problems.*

1 cup bulgur
⅔ cup boiling water
1 small tomato, chopped
¼ cup chopped sweet red peppers
¼ cup chopped dried apricots
¼ cup chopped fresh mint
½ red onion, minced
2 tablespoons olive oil
5 sprigs parsley, chopped
Juice of ½ lemon

In a small bowl, combine the bulgur and water. Cover with a plate and let stand for 25 minutes, or until the water is absorbed. Fluff with a fork.

Meanwhile, in a large bowl, combine the tomatoes, peppers, apricots, mint, onions, oil, parsley and lemon juice. Toss well to combine.

Add the warm bulgur and combine well.

*Serves 4.*

---

Per serving: 222 calories, 7.5 g. total fat, 1.0 g. saturated fat, 0 mg. cholesterol, 9.7 g. dietary fiber, 12 mg. sodium.

## Salads in the Spotlight

Except for standbys such as coleslaw and macaroni salad, you don't often see salads on a party buffet. But each of the following selections will surely stand out in any spread. You just might be surprised at how fast the bowl empties! And as a bonus, most of these recipes can be prepared in advance, requiring only last-minute garnishing.

### Spicy Chinese Noodles

*This salad gets its kick from ground red pepper. You can go hotter or milder by adjusting the amount of pepper you use.*

6 ounces whole-wheat or buckwheat pasta
⅓ cup diced sweet red peppers
¼ cup chopped scallions
¼ cup low-sodium soy sauce or tamari
2 tablespoons dark sesame oil
1 tablespoon grated fresh ginger
1 tablespoon chopped macadamia nuts
1 tablespoon minced garlic
1 tablespoon minced fresh cilantro
1 teaspoon ground red pepper (or to taste)
½ teaspoon honey

In a large pot of boiling water over medium-high heat, cook the pasta for 8 minutes, or until tender. Drain well. Place in a large bowl.

Add the red peppers, scallions, soy sauce or tamari, oil, ginger, nuts, garlic, cilantro, ground red pepper and honey. Toss well. Let the salad marinate for 1 hour before serving.

*SERVES 4.*

PER SERVING: 259 CALORIES, 9.1 G. TOTAL FAT, 1.3 G. SATURATED FAT, 0 MG. CHOLESTEROL, 2.1 G. DIETARY FIBER, 534 MG. SODIUM.

# Lemon-Rice Salad

*Perfect for a picnic, this salad can be prepared two days ahead of time.*

½  cup Tofu-Mayonnaise Dressing (page 300)
1  tablespoon low-sodium soy sauce or tamari
2  tablespoons lemon juice
3  cups cooked long-grain brown rice
½  cup chopped scallions
½  cup diced green peppers
¼  cup minced fresh parsley
¼  cup diced celery
1  lemon, thinly sliced

In a large bowl, mix the dressing, soy sauce or tamari, and lemon juice. Add the rice, scallions, peppers, parsley and celery. Let marinate for at least 30 minutes. Garnish with the lemon slices just before serving.

*Serves 4.*

PER SERVING: 206 CALORIES, 2.3 G. TOTAL FAT, 0.4 G. SATURATED FAT, 0 MG. CHOLESTEROL, 3.7 G. DIETARY FIBER, 175 MG. SODIUM.

## Winter Pear and Spinach Salad with Balsamic Vinegar

*An elegant first course for a dinner party, this recipe was inspired by a salad tasted at the famous Greens Restaurant in San Francisco.*

4 cups torn spinach
2 large Bosc pears, thinly sliced
2 tablespoons minced red onions
6 tablespoons balsamic vinegar
6 tablespoons water
1 tablespoon olive oil
1 teaspoon Dijon mustard
1 clove garlic, minced

Place the spinach leaves on a large platter or individual salad plates. Arrange the pears on the spinach in a fan pattern. Sprinkle with the onions.

In a small bowl, whisk together the vinegar, water, oil, mustard and garlic. Drizzle over the salad. Serve immediately.

*SERVES 8.*

PER SERVING: 55 CALORIES, 2.0 G. TOTAL FAT, 0.3 G. SATURATED FAT, 0 MG. CHOLESTEROL, 1.7 G. DIETARY FIBER, 33 MG. SODIUM.

## TEN OIL-FREE SALAD DRESSINGS

Salad dressing can sabotage the natural goodness of your salad by coating it with calories, fat and cholesterol. Here are some more healthful alternatives that you can make yourself; they have a fraction of the fat of most store-bought varieties.

### Shiitake Mushroom Dressing

1 cup water
½ ounce dried shiitake mushrooms
½ cup white-wine vinegar
½ cup nonalcoholic white wine
2 teaspoons dried oregano
1 teaspoon ground black pepper
2 cloves garlic, minced
¼ teaspoon ground cloves

In a 1-quart saucepan, bring the water to a boil. Add the mushrooms and simmer for 20 minutes. Drain. Remove and discard the stems. Finely chop the mushroom caps.

Place the chopped mushrooms in a blender container. Add the vinegar, wine, oregano, pepper, garlic and cloves. Blend for 30 seconds.

*MAKES ABOUT 2 CUPS.*

PER 2 TABLESPOONS: 5 CALORIES, <0.1 G. TOTAL FAT, <0.1 G. SATURATED FAT, 0 MG. CHOLESTEROL, 0.1 G. DIETARY FIBER, 1 MG. SODIUM.

## Red Ranch Salad Dressing

1½  cups chopped, steamed beets
1½  cups chopped, steamed carrots
½  cup water
¼  cup lemon juice
2  tablespoons dried dill
1  teaspoon herbal salt substitute

In a blender, combine the beets, carrots, water, lemon juice, dill and salt substitute. Blend at high speed until smooth, about 2 minutes.

*Makes about 3½ cups.*

PER 2 TABLESPOONS: 8 CALORIES, 0.1 G. TOTAL FAT, 0.1 G. SATURATED FAT, 0 MG. CHOLESTEROL, 0.5 G. DIETARY FIBER, 9 MG. SODIUM.

## Lemon-Rosemary Dressing

8  ounces soft tofu, drained and crumbled
1  cup tomato juice
½  cup lemon juice
½  teaspoon ground rosemary
¼  teaspoon dried oregano

In a blender, combine the tofu, tomato juice, lemon juice, rosemary and oregano. Blend at high speed until smooth, about 2 minutes.

*Makes about 2½ cups.*

PER 2 TABLESPOONS: 11 CALORIES, 0.4 G. TOTAL FAT, 0.1 G. SATURATED FAT, 0 MG. CHOLESTEROL, 0.1 G. DIETARY FIBER, 46 MG. SODIUM.

*(continued)*

## TEN OIL-FREE SALAD DRESSINGS—CONTINUED

### Tofu-Mayonnaise Dressing

8 ounces soft tofu, drained and crumbled
3 tablespoons grated onions
2 tablespoons lemon juice
2 tablespoons rice-wine vinegar
2 tablespoons water
1 tablespoon Dijon mustard
2 teaspoons apple juice concentrate
1 heaping teaspoon minced garlic
1 teaspoon ground white pepper

In a blender, combine the tofu, onions, lemon juice, vinegar, water, mustard, concentrate, garlic and pepper. Blend at high speed until smooth, about 2 minutes.

*MAKES ABOUT 1⅓ CUPS.*

PER 2 TABLESPOONS: 22 CALORIES, 0.9 G. TOTAL FAT, 0.1 G. SATURATED FAT, 0 MG. CHOLESTEROL, 0.1 G. DIETARY FIBER, 27 MG. SODIUM.

### Cucumber-Dill Dressing

1½ cups diced, peeled cucumbers
1 tablespoon herbal salt substitute
2 teaspoons minced fresh dill
2 teaspoons lemon juice
2 teaspoons minced red onions

In a blender, combine the cucumbers, salt substitute, dill, lemon juice and onions. Blend at high speed until smooth, about 1½ minutes.

*MAKES ABOUT 1¾ CUPS.*

PER 2 TABLESPOONS: 3 CALORIES, 0.1 G. TOTAL FAT, 0.1 G. SATURATED FAT, 0 MG. CHOLESTEROL, 0.1 G. DIETARY FIBER, 2 MG. SODIUM.

## Mustard Dressing with Garlic

¼  cup balsamic vinegar
¼  cup water
2  teaspoons Dijon or stone-ground mustard
2  teaspoons lemon juice
2  tablespoons minced garlic
1  tablespoon minced red onions
1  teaspoon minced fresh parsley

In a small bowl, whisk together the vinegar, water, mustard and lemon juice. Stir in the garlic, onions and parsley.

*MAKES ABOUT ¾ CUP.*

PER 2 TABLESPOONS: 22 CALORIES, 0.1 G. TOTAL FAT, 0.1 G. SATURATED FAT, 0 MG. CHOLESTEROL, 0.2 G. DIETARY FIBER, 25 MG. SODIUM.

## Tomato-Tarragon Dressing

1¼  cups low-sodium vegetable cocktail juice
½  cup grated onions
¼  cup white-wine vinegar
1  teaspoon Dijon mustard
1  teaspoon dried tarragon
1  clove garlic, chopped
2  teaspoons minced fresh parsley

In a blender, combine the juice, onions, vinegar, mustard, tarragon and garlic. Blend at high speed until smooth, about 1 minute. Stir in the parsley.

*MAKES ABOUT 2 CUPS.*

PER 2 TABLESPOONS: 7 CALORIES, 0.1 G. TOTAL FAT, 0.1 G. SATURATED FAT, 0 MG. CHOLESTEROL, 0.1 G. DIETARY FIBER, 9 MG. SODIUM.

*(continued)*

## TEN OIL-FREE SALAD DRESSINGS—CONTINUED

### Sweet Dill Dressing

¼  cup rice-wine vinegar
2  tablespoons apple juice concentrate
2  tablespoons water
1  tablespoon lemon juice
½  teaspoon Dijon mustard
¼  cup minced red onions
2  tablespoons minced fresh dill
2  tablespoons minced fresh parsley

In a small bowl, whisk together the vinegar, concentrate, water, lemon juice and mustard. Add the onions, dill and parsley.

*Makes about 1¼ cups.*

PER 2 TABLESPOONS: 9 CALORIES, 0.1 G. TOTAL FAT, 0.1 G. SATURATED FAT, 0 MG. CHOLESTEROL, 0.1 G. DIETARY FIBER, 5 MG. SODIUM.

### Tofu-Dill Dressing

4  ounces soft tofu, drained and crumbled
½  cup water
¼  cup minced fresh dill or 2 tablespoons dried
¼  cup minced fresh watercress (optional)
2  tablespoons lemon juice
1  tablespoon rice-wine vinegar
1  teaspoon Dijon mustard
1  teaspoon ground white pepper

In a blender, combine the tofu, water, dill, watercress (if using), lemon juice, vinegar, mustard and pepper. Blend at high speed until smooth, about 2 minutes.

*MAKES ABOUT 1¼ CUPS.*

PER 2 TABLESPOONS: 10 CALORIES, 0.4 G. TOTAL FAT, 0.1 G. SATURATED FAT, 0 MG. CHOLESTEROL, 0.1 G. DIETARY FIBER, 10 MG. SODIUM.

## Vinegar-Herb Dressing

2 ounces soft tofu, drained and crumbled
½ cup water
¼ cup red-wine vinegar
2 teaspoons lemon juice
1½ teaspoons dried oregano
1½ teaspoons herbal salt substitute
1 teaspoon dried tarragon
1 teaspoon dried basil
¼ teaspoon Dijon mustard
¼ teaspoon ground black pepper
¼ teaspoon garlic powder
⅛ teaspoon vanilla

In a blender, combine the tofu, water, vinegar, lemon juice, oregano, salt substitute, tarragon, basil, mustard, pepper, garlic powder and vanilla. Blend at high speed until smooth, about 1 minute.

*MAKES ABOUT 1 CUP.*

PER 2 TABLESPOONS: 10 CALORIES, 0.3 G. TOTAL FAT, 0.1 G. SATURATED FAT, 0 MG. CHOLESTEROL, 0.1 G. DIETARY FIBER, 6 MG. SODIUM.

## Sweet Grapefruit, Orange and Kiwifruit Salad

*The tart/sweet combination of citrus, spinach and red onions blends well with the light olive oil and honey dressing.*

4   oranges, peeled and sectioned
2   large pink grapefruit, peeled and sectioned
2   kiwifruit, peeled and sliced
2   tablespoons honey or maple syrup
½   teaspoon ground nutmeg
½   teaspoon ground cinnamon
3   cups torn spinach
¼   red onion, thinly sliced
2   tablespoons olive oil
    Herbal salt substitute (to taste)
    Ground black pepper (to taste)

In a large bowl, combine the oranges, grapefruit and kiwis. Add the honey or maple syrup, nutmeg and cinnamon. Toss to combine. Let stand for 15 minutes.

In a medium bowl, toss together the spinach, onions and oil. Season with the salt substitute and pepper.

To serve, arrange a small mound of the greens on a plate and top with the fruit mixture.

*SERVES 6.*

---

PER SERVING: 153 CALORIES, 5.0 G. TOTAL FAT, 0.7 G. SATURATED FAT, 0 MG. CHOLESTEROL, 5.0 G. DIETARY FIBER, 24 MG. SODIUM.

# Ratatouille Salad in Lettuce Cups

*This salad is a surprisingly delicious combination of cooked and crunchy vegetables.*

    1   large onion, chopped
    2   large cloves garlic, minced
    ¼   cup apple juice
    4   cups chopped eggplant
    2   cups chopped zucchini
    1   teaspoon dried basil
    1   teaspoon dried oregano
    1   teaspoon herbal salt substitute
    2   cups chopped sweet red peppers
    3   large tomatoes, chopped
        Lettuce leaves

In a large heavy frying pan over medium-high heat, sauté the onions and garlic in the apple juice for 5 minutes, or until the onions are soft but not browned.

Add the eggplant, zucchini, basil, oregano and salt substitute. Cover the pan, reduce the heat to low and simmer the mixture for 15 minutes.

Add the peppers and tomatoes. Cook for 2 minutes, stirring frequently. Remove from the heat and transfer to a heatproof bowl. Chill for 20 minutes.

To serve, line individual plates with the lettuce leaves. Spoon on the salad.

*SERVES 6.*

---

PER SERVING: 78 CALORIES, 0.7 G. TOTAL FAT, 0.1 G. SATURATED FAT, 0 MG. CHOLESTEROL, 3.1 G. DIETARY FIBER, 11 MG. SODIUM.

## Green Rice and Avocado Salad

*Of Spanish origin, this unusual salad combines parsley and avocado with steamed basmati rice, creating a bright green-and-white dish that is as appealing to the eye as to the palate.*

2½ cups cooked basmati rice
½ cup diced avocados
½ cup sliced mushrooms
⅓ cup minced fresh parsley
¼ teaspoon minced garlic
¼ cup Vinegar-Herb Dressing (page 303)
½ cup tomato wedges
¼ cup julienned sweet red peppers

In a large bowl, combine the rice, avocados, mushrooms, parsley and garlic. Add the dressing and toss well. Let marinate for 1 hour. Before serving, garnish with the tomatoes and peppers.

*SERVES 4.*

PER SERVING: 192 CALORIES, 5.6 G. TOTAL FAT, 0.7 G. SATURATED FAT, 0 MG. CHOLESTEROL, 1.4 G. DIETARY FIBER, 37 MG. SODIUM.

## Green and White Bean Salad

*This creation adds color to any party menu. If fresh green beans are hard to find, you can substitute frozen ones instead; just thaw and add to the salad as directed.*

  3  cups sliced (1″) green beans
  1  cup cooked white beans, such as Great Northern or navy
 ⅓  cup minced fresh parsley
  2  tablespoons olive oil
  3  tablespoons lemon juice
  2  teaspoons Dijon mustard
  2  shallots, minced
 ½  teaspoon herbal salt substitute
 ¼  teaspoon dried sage
     Ground black pepper (to taste)

In a large bowl, combine the green beans, white beans, parsley, oil, lemon juice, mustard, shallots, salt substitute, sage and pepper. Let marinate for at least 1 hour. Serve at room temperature.

*SERVES 6.*

---

PER SERVING: 109 CALORIES, 4.9 G. TOTAL FAT, 0.7 G. SATURATED FAT, 0 MG. CHOLESTEROL, 2.6 G. DIETARY FIBER, 29 MG. SODIUM.

## Peanutty Pasta Salad

*This salad is quite spicy if you use the full amount of ground red pepper. If your taste runs a little milder, adjust the amount of pepper accordingly.*

| | |
|---|---|
| 4 | cups cooked whole-wheat linguine or rotelle (spirals) |
| 1 | cup sliced green beans |
| 1 | sweet red pepper, cut into strips |
| 1 | large cucumber, sliced |
| 6 | scallions, sliced |
| 1 | tablespoon chopped unsalted roasted peanuts |
| ¼ | cup olive oil |
| 2 | tablespoons reduced-fat chunky peanut butter |
| ¼ | cup water |
| 3 | tablespoons low-sodium soy sauce or tamari |
| 2 | tablespoons lemon juice |
| ¼–1 | teaspoon ground red pepper |
| ¼ | teaspoon ground cumin |
| ⅛ | teaspoon ground turmeric |

In a large bowl, combine the linguine or rotelle, beans, red peppers, cucumbers, scallions and peanuts.

In another bowl, whisk together the oil, peanut butter, water, soy sauce or tamari, lemon juice, ground red pepper, cumin and turmeric. Pour over the salad and mix well. Let marinate for 1 hour before serving.

*Serves 6.*

Per serving: 271 calories, 12.6 g. total fat, 1.8 g. saturated fat, 0 mg. cholesterol, 3.3 g. dietary fiber, 272 mg. sodium.

# SOUP'S ON!

## Savor It by the Spoonful

**W**hen it comes to comfort foods, few can hold a candle to good old-fashioned soup. There's just something about its gentle warmth and inviting aroma that can soothe and relax you from head to toe. Nothing is better at taking the chill off a bitter winter's day or at nursing you through a bout of the flu. And it's an ideal remedy for a grumbling stomach: It satisfies hunger but isn't laden with calories, fat or cholesterol.

In fact, research has shown that soup may help folks lose weight by acting as a natural appetite suppressant. One study, from Johns Hopkins University in Baltimore, showed that people who had soup before their meals ate 25 percent fewer calories of the main course than people who had cheese and crackers as an appetizer.

With all of soup's virtues, it seems like perfect fare for the cholesterol-conscious. But before you help yourself to a bowlful, be aware of these caveats: First, soup—especially canned varieties and powdered mixes—can contain astronomically high amounts of sodium. Just one serving of condensed chicken noodle soup (the kind you add water to) contains 1,106 milligrams of sodium, nearly half of the 2,400-milligram daily limit that most experts recommend. Second, cream soups can be exceptionally high in fat. A serving of condensed cream of mushroom soup, for example, gets 62 percent of its calories from fat.

If you prefer the convenience of store-bought soups, be sure to read labels before you buy. But nutrition-wise, you may be better off making your own. If you think you have to spend an entire afternoon watching a pot boil and simmer, you're in for a pleasant surprise: The recipes that follow can be whipped up in just minutes.

# The Cream of the (Low-Fat) Crop

Milk gives cream soups their characteristic thick consistency and rich taste. It also contributes a hefty helping of fat. But with the right ingredients and some culinary trickery, you can create slimmed-down versions of the originals that have all of the flavor but much less of the fat. The following recipes show you how.

   **Carrot Bisque**

*Carrots always lend a rich, autumnal color to pureed soups. Here they are seasoned with a delicious mixture of apple juice, orange and ginger.*

½  cup minced onions
¼  cup apple juice
1  tablespoon olive oil
8  large carrots, chopped
1  tablespoon grated fresh ginger
3  cups Garlic Broth (page 316)
1  cup minced scallions
1  tablespoon minced garlic
1  tablespoon orange juice concentrate
2  tablespoons minced fresh cilantro

In a 3-quart saucepan over medium-high heat, sauté the onions in the apple juice and oil for 10 minutes, stirring frequently to prevent browning. Add the carrots and ginger. Cook for 5 minutes, stirring occasionally.

Add the broth, scallions and garlic. Bring to a boil, lower the heat to medium and cover the pan. Simmer for 20 minutes, or until the carrots are tender.

Remove from the heat. Let cool for 10 minutes. Working in batches, puree the soup in a blender or food processor. Return the soup to the pot and add the juice concentrate. Heat through. Serve garnished with the cilantro.

*SERVES 6.*

PER SERVING: 93 CALORIES, 2.6 G. TOTAL FAT, 0.4 G. SATURATED FAT, 0 MG. CHOLESTEROL, 3.2 G. DIETARY FIBER, 36 MG. SODIUM.

# Hungarian Cream of Potato Soup

*Pureed cooked potatoes are one secret for making nondairy cream soups that taste as good as they look. What makes this concoction Hungarian? The substantial dose of paprika, a mild red pepper.*

| | |
|---|---|
| 1 | cup diced onions |
| ½ | cup nonalcoholic white wine |
| 2 | cups diced red potatoes |
| ½ | cup diced carrots |
| 1 | tablespoon paprika |
| 2 | cloves garlic, minced |
| ½ | teaspoon dried thyme |
| 3 | cups Vegetable Stock (page 316) |
| | Herbal salt substitute (to taste) |
| | Ground white pepper (to taste) |
| 1 | tablespoon chopped chives |

In a 3-quart saucepan over medium-high heat, sauté the onions in the wine for 10 minutes, stirring frequently to prevent browning.

Add the potatoes, carrots, paprika, garlic and thyme. Sauté for 5 minutes, stirring frequently. Add the stock, bring to a boil, then lower the heat to medium. Cover the pot and simmer the soup for 20 minutes, or until the potatoes are very tender.

Remove from the heat and let cool for 10 minutes. Working in batches, puree the soup in a blender or food processor. Return the soup to the pot, heat through and season with the salt substitute and pepper. Serve garnished with the chives.

*Serves 4.*

Per serving: 132 calories, 0.4 g. total fat, 0.1 g. saturated fat, 0 mg. cholesterol, 2.8 g. dietary fiber, 14 mg. sodium.

# Butternut Squash Soup with Five Spices

*Orange winter squash makes this visually stunning soup perfect for a chilly winter's day. Serve it topped with grated lemon rind to complement the five spices.*

½  cup chopped onions
2  tablespoons minced garlic
1  tablespoon grated fresh ginger
⅓  cup apple juice
1  tablespoon olive oil
4  cups cubed butternut squash
2  cups Vegetable Stock (page 316)
1  tablespoon lemon juice
½  teaspoon ground coriander
½  teaspoon ground nutmeg
¼  teaspoon ground cumin
¼  teaspoon ground cinnamon
1  tablespoon grated lemon rind

In a 3-quart saucepan over medium-high heat, sauté the onions, garlic and ginger in the apple juice and oil for 10 minutes, stirring frequently to prevent browning. If the vegetables stick, add a small amount of stock.

Add the squash and stock. Bring to a boil. Reduce the heat to medium, cover the pot and simmer for 25 minutes.

Remove from the heat. Let cool for 10 minutes. Working in batches, puree the soup in a blender or food processor. Add the lemon juice, coriander, nutmeg, cumin and cinnamon.

Cover tightly and refrigerate overnight to develop flavors. Heat through and serve garnished with the lemon rind.

*Serves 4.*

PER SERVING: 162 CALORIES, 3.9 G. TOTAL FAT, 0.6 G. SATURATED FAT, 0 MG. CHOLESTEROL, 4.4 G. DIETARY FIBER, 13 MG. SODIUM.

# Tahini Creamed Vegetable Soup

*Tahini, a silky paste made from ground sesame seeds, mimics the creaminess of milk in this recipe. It tends to separate when boiled, though, so be especially careful if you reheat any leftover soup.*

    1  onion, chopped
    2  cloves garlic, minced
    ¼  cup nonalcoholic white wine
    2  cups chopped carrots
    1  cup chopped celery
    ¼  cup chopped fresh parsley
    4  cups Vegetable Stock (page 316)
    2  teaspoons curry powder
    3  tablespoons tahini
       Low-sodium soy sauce or tamari (to taste)

In a 3-quart saucepan over medium-high heat, sauté the onions and garlic in the wine for 10 minutes, stirring frequently to prevent browning.

Add the carrots, celery, parsley and ½ cup of the stock. Cook for 10 minutes. Add the remaining stock and curry powder; bring to a boil. Lower the heat to medium and simmer, uncovered, for 20 minutes.

Remove from the heat. Let the soup cool for 10 minutes. Working in batches, puree the soup with the tahini in a blender or food processor. (If necessary to facilitate blending, add a little more stock.) Season with the soy sauce or tamari.

*Serves 4.*

---

PER SERVING: 130 CALORIES, 7.5 G. TOTAL FAT, <0.1 G. SATURATED FAT, 0 MG. CHOLESTEROL, 3.4 G. DIETARY FIBER, 50 MG. SODIUM.

## Dairyless Cream of Spinach Soup

*Thickened with a mixture of cooked oats and vegetables, this soup has all the flavor of the original with just a fraction of the fat.*

|   |   |
|---|---|
| 1 | cup minced onions |
| ¼ | cup chopped scallions |
| ¼ | cup apple juice |
| 2 | teaspoons olive oil |
| 2 | cups chopped spinach |
| ¼ | cup chopped fresh parsley |
| ¼ | cup chopped celery |
| 4 | cups Garlic Broth (page 316) |
| ⅓ | cup rolled oats |
| 1 | teaspoon herbal salt substitute |
| ¼ | teaspoon dried thyme |
| ¼ | teaspoon ground white pepper |

In a 3-quart saucepan over medium-high heat, sauté the onions and scallions in the apple juice and oil for 5 minutes, stirring frequently. Add the spinach, parsley and celery. Cook for 5 to 7 minutes, stirring occasionally.

Add the broth, oats, salt substitute, thyme and pepper. Bring to a boil, then lower the heat to medium. Cover and simmer for 20 minutes.

Remove from the heat. Let the soup cool for 10 minutes. Working in batches, puree in a blender until thick and smooth. Return to the pot. Reheat.

*SERVES 6.*

PER SERVING: 59 CALORIES, 2.0 G. TOTAL FAT, 0.3 G. SATURATED FAT, 0 MG. CHOLESTEROL, 1.7 G. DIETARY FIBER, 24 MG. SODIUM.

# Red Pepper Cream Soup with Thyme

*Paired with crusty black bread and a tossed green salad, this soup makes a complete meal.*

5  large sweet red peppers, seeded and halved
1  large onion, chopped
1  tablespoon olive oil
6  cups Vegetable Stock (page 316)
1  large russet potato, chopped
1  teaspoon minced garlic
½  teaspoon dried thyme
   Herbal salt substitute (to taste)
   Ground black pepper (to taste)

Preheat the broiler.

Cover a baking sheet with aluminum foil. Place the red peppers on the foil, cut side down. Broil about 3″ from the heat for about 15 minutes, or until the skins blacken. Transfer to a brown paper bag. Close the bag and let the peppers steam (in their own heat) for 20 minutes, so the skins will slip off easily. Remove the skins and pat the peppers dry with paper towels.

In a 3-quart saucepan over medium-high heat, sauté the onions in the oil for 5 minutes, stirring frequently to prevent browning. Add the stock, potatoes, garlic and thyme. Bring to a boil, then lower the heat to medium and simmer, uncovered, for 20 minutes.

Add the peppers and remove the soup from the heat. Let cool for 10 minutes. Working in batches, puree the soup in a blender or food processor. Return to the pot, season with the salt substitute and pepper and heat through.

*SERVES 6.*

PER SERVING: 119 CALORIES, 3.0 G. TOTAL FAT, 0.3 G. SATURATED FAT, 0 MG. CHOLESTEROL, 4.4 G. DIETARY FIBER, 2.4 MG. SODIUM.

## BASIC SOUP STOCKS

Many of the recipes in this chapter use one of these two stocks. They're indispensable for no-cholesterol cooking. Be sure to use vegetables with mild flavors, such as carrots, potatoes, onions and celery.

### Vegetable Stock

4 cups water
1 cup chopped vegetables

In a 2-quart saucepan, combine the water and vegetables. Bring to a boil over medium-high heat. Reduce the heat to the lowest setting and simmer the stock, uncovered, for 2 hours. Strain before using.

*MAKES ABOUT 2¼ CUPS.*

PER CUP: 3 CALORIES, 0.1 G. TOTAL FAT, 0.1 G. SATURATED FAT, 0 MG. CHOLESTEROL, 0.2 G. DIETARY FIBER, 0 MG. SODIUM.

### Garlic Broth

4 garlic heads
6 cups water
2 cups chopped vegetables
3 sprigs parsley
2 bay leaves, crushed

Separate the garlic heads into individual cloves, but don't peel them. Place in a 3-quart saucepan. Add the water, vegetables, parsley and bay leaves. Bring to a boil over high heat, then reduce the heat to low and simmer for 2 hours. Strain.

*MAKES ABOUT 3¾ CUPS.*

PER CUP: 9 CALORIES, 0.1 G. TOTAL FAT, 0.1 G. SATURATED FAT, 0 MG. CHOLESTEROL, 0.2 G. DIETARY FIBER, 1 MG. SODIUM.

## Winter Warm-Ups

When Jack Frost starts nipping at your nose, you can give him the slip by sipping spoonfuls of hot, hearty soup. The following recipes make superb wintertime fare—perfect after shoveling snow or a long walk in biting wind. Best of all, these soups freeze beautifully, so you can always have some on hand for quick reheating.

### Escarole Soup with Orzo

*Orzo is a tiny pasta shaped like rice. It lends a chewy texture to this exuberant Mediterranean soup.*

     3   cups chopped onions
     2   tablespoons olive oil
     1   pound escarole, cut into bite-size strips
     1   tablespoon chopped garlic
    5–6  cups Vegetable Stock (page 316)
     ¾   cup orzo
         Herbal salt substitute (to taste)
         Ground black pepper (to taste)
     ¾   cup fine rye bread crumbs

In a 3-quart saucepan over medium-high heat, sauté the onions in the oil, stirring frequently, until limp and transparent but not browned, about 5 to 7 minutes. Add the escarole and garlic; cook until the escarole wilts.

Reduce the heat to medium-low. Add the stock. Simmer, uncovered, for 20 minutes.

Add the orzo and cook for 10 minutes, or until the pasta is tender. Season with the salt substitute and pepper.

Before serving, toast the bread crumbs in a small dry frying pan over medium heat until lightly browned. Spoon over each serving of soup.

*Serves 4.*

Per serving: 321 calories, 8.3 g. total fat, 1.2 g. saturated fat, 0 mg. cholesterol, 5.3 g. dietary fiber, 74 mg. sodium.

## Beet Soup with Orange Juice and Green Onions

*The unusual combination of fresh beets and orange juice gives this soup its distinctive flavor. If you have the time, let the soup sit overnight in the refrigerator, so its flavors can deepen.*

|       |                                       |
|-------|---------------------------------------|
| 1     | onion, chopped                        |
| 2     | cloves garlic, minced                 |
| ⅓     | cup apple juice                       |
| 1     | tablespoon olive oil                  |
| 4     | cups Vegetable Stock (page 316)       |
| 2½    | cups chopped unpeeled beets           |
| ½     | cup orange juice                      |
| ¼–½   | teaspoon ground cumin                 |
| 2     | tablespoons minced scallions          |
| 2     | tablespoons minced fresh parsley      |

In a 3-quart saucepan over medium heat, sauté the onions and garlic in the apple juice and oil for 10 minutes, stirring frequently to prevent browning. Add the stock and beets. Bring to a boil. Lower the heat and simmer, uncovered, for 30 minutes, or until the beets are tender.

Remove from the heat. Let cool for 10 minutes. Working in batches, puree the soup in a blender or food processor.

Return the soup to the pot. Add the orange juice and cumin. Heat through. Just before serving, stir in the scallions and parsley.

*Serves 4.*

---

PER SERVING: 112 CALORIES, 3.7 G. TOTAL FAT, 0.5 G. SATURATED FAT, 0 MG. CHOLESTEROL, 1.2 G. DIETARY FIBER, 70 MG. SODIUM.

---

# Ann's Sweet Potato Soup

*The often-overlooked sweet potato takes center stage in this stunning soup, which makes a great alternative to candied yams at Thanksgiving.*

⅔ cup minced onions
1 tablespoon olive oil
1 carrot, sliced thinly
1 large sweet potato, diced
1 russet potato, diced
⅓ cup chopped celery
3 cups Garlic Broth (page 316)
2 bay leaves, crushed and wrapped
 in a piece of cheesecloth
¼ teaspoon ground nutmeg
1 tablespoon minced fresh chives

In a 3-quart saucepan over medium-high heat, sauté the onions in the oil for 5 minutes, stirring frequently to prevent browning. Add the carrots, sweet potatoes, russet potatoes and celery. Cook for 5 minutes.

Add the broth, bay leaves and nutmeg. Bring to a boil, then lower the heat to medium and simmer, uncovered, for 20 minutes. Discard the bay leaves.

Remove from the heat. Let the soup cool for 10 minutes. Working in batches, puree the soup in a blender or food processor. Return it to the pot, heat through and serve garnished with the chives.

*Serves 4.*

Per serving: 116 calories, 3.6 g. total fat, 0.5 g. saturated fat, 0 mg. cholesterol, 2.5 g. dietary fiber, 21 mg. sodium.

# Szechuan Hot-and-Sour Soup

*Traditional hot-and-sour soup gets its distinctive aroma and flavor from dried shiitake mushrooms. Soak them ahead of time to create a rich broth, which can then be added to the simmering soup.*

6   cups Vegetable Stock (page 316)
2   ounces dried shiitake mushrooms
1   teaspoon dark sesame oil
½   cup chopped scallions
1   teaspoon grated fresh ginger
6   ounces firm tofu, cut into 1″ squares
2   tablespoons arrowroot powder
¼   cup apple juice
    Juice of 1 lemon
2   tablespoons low-sodium soy sauce or tamari
½   teaspoon ground red pepper
    Ground black pepper (to taste)

In a 2-quart saucepan, bring the stock to a boil. Remove from the heat, add the mushrooms and let stand for 30 minutes. Strain, reserving the liquid. Remove and discard the mushroom stems. Slice the caps into thin strips.

In a 3-quart saucepan over medium-high heat, heat the oil. Add the scallions and ginger; sauté for 2 minutes. Add the tofu and cook for 1 minute. Add the stock and mushrooms.

In a small bowl, dissolve the arrowroot in the apple juice, lemon juice and soy sauce or tamari. Add to the soup and cook, stirring, until the soup thickens slightly. Add the red pepper and black pepper.

*Serves 8.*

---

Per serving: 77 calories, 2.6 g. total fat, 0.4 g. saturated fat, 0 mg. cholesterol, 1.4 g. dietary fiber, 136 mg. sodium.

# Fennel Soup Italian-Style

*Raw fennel has a sharp licorice taste. Here it is simmered to bring out a milder flavor.*

| | |
|---|---|
| 1 | large onion, chopped |
| ½ | cup diced celery |
| 2 | cloves garlic, minced |
| 1 | teaspoon olive oil |
| 2 | tablespoons nonalcoholic white wine |
| 4 | cups Vegetable Stock (page 316) |
| 1 | large head fennel, diced |
| 1 | cup diced small red potatoes |
| 1 | teaspoon herbal salt substitute |
| ½ | teaspoon ground black pepper |
| ⅓ | cup chopped sweet red peppers |

In a 3-quart saucepan over medium-high heat, sauté the onions, celery and garlic in the oil and wine for 10 minutes, stirring occasionally to prevent browning.

Add the stock, fennel and potatoes. Bring to a boil. Cover the pan, lower the heat to medium and simmer for 40 minutes. Add the salt substitute and black pepper. Serve garnished with the red peppers.

*SERVES 4.*

PER SERVING: 144 CALORIES, 7.0 G. TOTAL FAT, 0.9 G. SATURATED FAT, 0 MG. CHOLESTEROL, 2.2 G. DIETARY FIBER, 31 MG. SODIUM.

# Mediterranean Pesto Soup

*This version of a traditional Mediterranean soup uses an unusual blend of fresh parsley and spinach in place of the more traditional fresh basil, which can be hard to find in winter months.*

### Soup

¼   cup nonalcoholic red wine
1   teaspoon safflower or olive oil
6   scallions (including greens), thinly sliced
4   cups Vegetable Stock (page 316)
2   large carrots, diced
1   cup canned Italian tomatoes, with their liquid
1   cup diced russet potatoes
1   cup peeled and cubed winter squash
½   cup chopped celery leaves
½   cup pastina or other small pasta
⅓   cup chopped leeks
2   tablespoons tomato paste
⅛   teaspoon saffron threads
1   teaspoon ground black pepper
1   teaspoon herbal salt substitute

### Pesto

½   cup chopped spinach
½   cup minced fresh parsley
¼   cup chopped walnuts or pine nuts
3   cloves garlic, minced
2   teaspoons olive oil
1   teaspoon dried basil
1   teaspoon miso
6   thick slices whole-grain bread

*To make the soup:* In a 3- or 4-quart saucepan over medium heat, heat the wine and oil. Add the scallions and sauté until bright in color, about 1 minute. Add the stock, carrots, tomatoes, potatoes, squash, celery leaves, pastina, leeks, tomato paste and saffron. Bring to a boil.

Reduce the heat and simmer for 30 minutes, or until

the potatoes are soft. Add the pepper and salt substitute.

*To make the pesto:* In a blender or food processor, process the spinach, parsley, walnuts or pine nuts, garlic, oil, basil and miso into a thick paste.

To serve, spread the pesto on the bread. Place 1 slice in the bottom of each soup bowl. Ladle the soup over it.

*Serves 6.*

PER SERVING: 240 CALORIES, 7.0 G. TOTAL FAT, 0.8 G. SATURATED FAT, 0 MG. CHOLESTEROL, 2.7 G. DIETARY FIBER, 317 MG. SODIUM.

## Momma's Mock Chicken Soup

*Chicken soup with no chicken? You just might like this better than the real thing. The rich flavor comes from the garlic broth.*

4   cups Garlic Broth (page 316)
1   large carrot, diced
1   potato, diced
1   cup cubed winter squash
1   parsnip, diced
½   cup diced daikon radishes
3   cups chopped greens, such as spinach, parsley or mustard
     Light miso or low-sodium soy sauce or tamari (to taste)

In a 3-quart saucepan over medium-high heat, bring the broth to a boil. Add the carrots, potatoes, squash, parsnips and radishes. Cover, reduce the heat and simmer for 20 minutes, or until the potatoes are soft.

Add the greens and season with the miso or soy sauce or tamari.

*Serves 4.*

PER SERVING: 100 CALORIES, 0.5 G. TOTAL FAT, 0.1 G. SATURATED FAT, 0 MG. CHOLESTEROL, 4.5 G. DIETARY FIBER, 50 MG. SODIUM.

# Spinach and Wild Rice Soup

*Here's a hearty soup to enjoy after a day on the slopes or cross-country trails. It's especially good with Swedish rye bread.*

1 onion, chopped
1 large potato, diced
3 bunches spinach, destemmed and chopped
2 tablespoons olive oil
4 cups Vegetable Stock (page 316)
2 cups cooked wild rice
Herbal salt substitute (to taste)
Ground black pepper (to taste)

In a 3-quart saucepan over medium-high heat, sauté the onions, potatoes and spinach in the oil for 10 minutes, stirring frequently to prevent browning. Add the stock and bring to a boil.

Cover the pan, reduce the heat to medium and simmer for 20 minutes, or until the potatoes are tender.

Remove from the heat. Let cool for 10 minutes, then puree half of the soup in a blender or food processor. Return to the pot. Add the wild rice, heat through and season with the salt substitute and pepper.

*SERVES 6.*

---

PER SERVING: 158 CALORIES, 5.3 G. TOTAL FAT, 0.7 G. SATURATED FAT, 0 MG. CHOLESTEROL, 5.4 G. DIETARY FIBER, 116 MG. SODIUM.

## Tomato-Cilantro Soup

*The south-of-the-border influence is evident in this deliciously spicy concoction, lightly flavored with cilantro. For an unusual one-dish meal, serve it over hot pasta.*

2 onions, minced
2 cloves garlic, minced
¼ cup nonalcoholic red wine
1 teaspoon olive oil
4 cups chopped fresh tomatoes
1 cup diced sweet red peppers
¼ cup diced celery
2 tablespoons chopped canned green chilies
2 cups Garlic Broth (page 316)
2 tablespoons chopped fresh cilantro
½ teaspoon ground red pepper
¼ teaspoon ground cumin
  Herbal salt substitute (to taste)
  Ground black pepper (to taste)
  Fresh cilantro

In a 3-quart saucepan over medium-high heat, sauté the onions and garlic in the wine and oil for 10 minutes, stirring frequently to prevent browning. Add the tomatoes, red peppers, celery and chilies. Cook for 5 minutes.

Add the broth, cilantro, ground red pepper and cumin. Bring to a boil, then lower the heat and simmer for 45 minutes. Season with the salt substitute and pepper. Serve garnished with the cilantro.

*Serves 8.*

Per serving: 61 calories, 1.1 g. total fat, 0.1 g. saturated fat, 0 mg. cholesterol, 2.8 g. dietary fiber, 29 mg. sodium.

# Orange-Carrot Soup with Ginger

*With a spicy, exotic quality, this soup makes a great pre-lude to an entrée of curried vegetables or pasta.*

1 cup chopped onions
1 teaspoon safflower oil
4 cups Vegetable Stock or Garlic Broth (page 316)
2 cups chopped carrots
1 cup diced potatoes
3 cloves garlic, minced
¼ cup ground cashews
2 teaspoons grated fresh ginger
2 tablespoons apple juice
1 tablespoon orange juice concentrate

In a 3-quart saucepan over medium heat, sauté the onions in the oil until soft but not browned, about 5 minutes. Add the stock or broth, carrots, potatoes and garlic. Bring to a boil.

Cover, reduce the heat and simmer for 15 minutes, or until the carrots and potatoes are soft.

Remove from the heat and let cool for 10 minutes. Working in batches, puree the soup with the cashews in a blender or food processor until creamy.

Return the soup to the pot and reheat.

While the soup is reheating, in a small frying pan sauté the ginger in the apple juice for 3 minutes. Remove from the heat. Stir in the juice concentrate. Add to the soup and serve hot.

*SERVES 6.*

---

PER SERVING: 111 CALORIES, 3.6 G. TOTAL FAT, 0.6 G. SATURATED FAT, 0 MG. CHOLESTEROL, 2.7 G. DIETARY FIBER, 17 MG. SODIUM.

# Sweet Onion Soup

*If your market carries sweet Vidalia onions, be sure to try this fragrant soup. It's delicious served with crusty brown bread.*

| | |
|---|---|
| 4 | medium Vidalia onions, thinly sliced |
| ⅓ | cup nonalcoholic white wine |
| 2 | tablespoons minced garlic |
| 1 | tablespoon whole-wheat flour |
| 4–5 | cups Vegetable Stock (page 316) |
| 1 | tablespoon herbal salt substitute |
| 1 | teaspoon dried thyme |
| 1 | tablespoon low-sodium soy sauce or tamari |
| ¼ | cup minced scallions |

In a 3- or 4-quart saucepan over medium-low heat, sauté the onions in the wine, stirring frequently, for 25 minutes. The onions will begin to brown slightly and get very soft; be careful not to burn them. Add the garlic and flour. Cook, stirring, for 2 minutes. Add the stock, salt substitute and thyme.

Raise the heat to medium-high and bring the soup to a boil. Reduce the heat to low and simmer, uncovered, for 30 minutes. (Add additional stock if the soup becomes too thick.) Add the soy sauce or tamari. Serve garnished with the scallions.

*Serves 4.*

---

PER SERVING: 90 CALORIES, 0.4 G. TOTAL FAT, 0.1 G. SATURATED FAT, 0 MG. CHOLESTEROL, 3.3 G. DIETARY FIBER, 145 MG. SODIUM.

## Mushroom-Essence Soup

*This delicate consommé is made with a mixture of wild and domestic mushrooms simmered in nonalcoholic red wine.*

2   cups chopped onions
1   tablespoon olive oil
6   cups water
1   cup chopped mushrooms
1   cup chopped wild mushrooms, such as chanterelle
1   ounce dried shiitake mushrooms
¼   cup nonalcoholic red wine
2   sprigs parsley
    Herbal salt substitute (to taste)
    Ground black pepper (to taste)
2   tablespoons minced red onions
2   tablespoons minced scallions or chives
½   cup thinly sliced mushrooms

In a 3-quart saucepan over medium heat, gently sauté the onions in the oil for 15 minutes, stirring frequently to prevent browning. Add the water, chopped mushrooms, wild mushrooms, shiitake mushrooms, wine and parsley. Raise the heat to medium-high and bring the soup to a boil. Reduce the heat to medium-low and simmer, uncovered, for 45 minutes.

Place a colander over a large pot or bowl and line it with a double thickness of cheesecloth. Pour the soup into the colander and press the vegetables against it with the back of a wooden spoon to extract as much juice as possible.

Return the liquid to the pot and season it with salt substitute and pepper. Serve the soup garnished with red onions, scallions or chives, and mushrooms.

*Serves 4.*

PER SERVING: 96 CALORIES, 3.7 G. TOTAL FAT, 0.5 G. SATURATED FAT, 0 MG. CHOLESTEROL, 2.6 G. DIETARY FIBER, 5 MG. SODIUM.

# Hot Outside? Just Chill

When the heat is on in the summer months, probably the last thing you want for lunch or dinner is a piping-hot bowl of anything. But soup actually makes great summertime fare. With fruits and vegetables available in abundance, you have the ingredients for some colorful and refreshing creations. The secret is to serve them chilled.

The recipes that follow make the most of summer-fresh produce such as cantaloupe, strawberries and tomatoes. Be sure to pick the ripest, most vibrant fruits and vegetables that you can find, to give the soups the best color and flavor.

Most cold soups taste better when they've been refrigerated overnight, so try to prepare them ahead of time. They easily keep for two or three days when stored in tightly covered containers. Remember to stir well before serving.

## Two-Melon Soup

*Ripe cantaloupe and casaba melon give this soup wonderful flavor. Served in frosted glass bowls, it makes an elegant first course for a summer dinner party.*

    2  cups diced cantaloupe
    2  cups diced casaba melon
    ⅓  cup lime juice
    1  tablespoon honey
    3  tablespoons chopped fresh mint leaves

In a blender or food processor, puree the cantaloupe, casaba, lime juice, honey and 2 tablespoons of the mint leaves. Pour into a large bowl and chill for 20 minutes. Serve garnished with the remaining mint.

*SERVES 4.*

PER SERVING: 73 CALORIES, 0.4 G. TOTAL FAT, <0.1 G. SATURATED FAT, 0 MG. CHOLESTEROL, 1.6 G. DIETARY FIBER, 18 MG. SODIUM.

## Chilled Papaya-Pineapple Soup

*In Hawaii, this rich-tasting soup is garnished with small white orchids. Use fresh pineapple if it's available.*

- 4 cups cubed pineapple
- 3 cups diced papaya
  Juice of 2 oranges
  Juice of 1 lime
- 1 tablespoon honey
- ½ teaspoon ground nutmeg

In a blender or food processor, combine the pineapple, papaya, orange juice, lime juice, honey and nutmeg. Puree until smooth. Pour into a large bowl and chill for 30 minutes. Serve in tall glasses or frosted bowls.

*SERVES 4.*

---

PER SERVING: 151 CALORIES, 1.0 G. TOTAL FAT, 0.2 G. SATURATED FAT, 0 MG. CHOLESTEROL, 3.1 G. DIETARY FIBER, 5 MG. SODIUM.

---

## Chilled Leek and Potato Soup

*If available, new red potatoes or yellow Finnish potatoes are especially good in this delicate, creamy vichyssoise.*

- 1 yellow onion, finely chopped
- 1 teaspoon safflower oil
- 2 cups chopped potatoes
- 1 cup sliced leeks (white part only)
- 4 cups Vegetable Stock or Garlic Broth (page 316)
- 1 teaspoon herbal salt substitute
- ¼ teaspoon ground white pepper
- 2 tablespoons chopped fresh chives

In a 3-quart saucepan over medium-low heat, slowly sauté the onions in the oil until soft but not browned, about 5 to 7 minutes. Add the potatoes and leeks. Cook for 5 minutes; add a small amount of the stock or broth if the vegetables begin to brown.

Add the remaining stock and bring to a boil. Cover, reduce the heat and simmer for 15 to 20 minutes, or until the potatoes are soft. Add the salt substitute and pepper.

Remove from the heat and let cool for 10 minutes. In a blender, puree half of the soup until smooth. Combine with the remaining soup and chill for 2 hours. Serve garnished with the chives.

*SERVES 6.*

---

PER SERVING: 99 CALORIES, 1.0 G. TOTAL FAT, 0.1 G. SATURATED FAT, 0 MG. CHOLESTEROL, 2.0 G. DIETARY FIBER, 10 MG. SODIUM.

---

### Sweetheart Strawberry Soup

*This soup can be made with practically any combination of fruits in season. Traditionally, its base is yogurt or whipped cream, but this version tastes just as good without dairy products.*

2 cups sliced strawberries
2 cups chopped cantaloupe
½ cup chopped honeydew or casaba melon
1 cup pineapple juice
1 cup orange juice
1 cup apple juice
   Juice of 1 lemon
2 tablespoons honey
1 teaspoon chopped fresh mint
½ teaspoon ground nutmeg

In a blender or food processor, combine the strawberries, cantaloupe, honeydew or casaba, pineapple juice, orange juice, apple juice, lemon juice and honey until very smooth. Pour into a large bowl and chill thoroughly. Serve garnished with the mint and nutmeg.

*SERVES 6.*

---

PER SERVING: 124 CALORIES, 0.5 G. TOTAL FAT, <0.1 G. SATURATED FAT, 0 MG. CHOLESTEROL, 1.9 G. DIETARY FIBER, 9 MG. SODIUM.

---

# Chick-Pea and Tomato Gazpacho

*Gazpacho, the Spanish salad-soup, comes in many vari-
eties. Here's a delicious high-fiber version made with cooked
chick-peas and fresh tomatoes.*

  4   cups low-sodium vegetable cocktail juice
  3   cups diced tomatoes
  1   cup cooked chick-peas
  ½  cup diced green peppers
  ½  cup cooked corn
  ½  cup diced cucumbers
  ¼  cup minced red onions
  ¼  cup chopped fresh parsley
  2   tablespoons lime juice
  2   tablespoons rice-wine vinegar
  1   teaspoon honey
  1   teaspoon herbal salt substitute
  ½  teaspoon ground black pepper
  1   clove garlic, minced
  ¼  teaspoon ground red pepper
  ¼  teaspoon dried marjoram

In a large bowl, mix the vegetable juice, tomatoes,
chick-peas, green peppers, corn, cucumbers, onions, parsley, lime juice, vinegar, honey, salt substitute, black pepper, garlic, red pepper and marjoram. Chill overnight.

*SERVES 8.*

---

PER SERVING: 96 CALORIES, 0.9 G. TOTAL FAT, 0.1 G. SATURATED FAT,
0 MG. CHOLESTEROL, 2.3 G. DIETARY FIBER, 42 MG. SODIUM.

## "Souper"-Simple Meals

Because most soups can easily be frozen and reheated, they make great standbys for days when you just don't have the time or energy to prepare a big lunch or dinner. The recipes in this section produce soups that are meals in themselves, substantial and satisfying. Just make your favorites in advance, so you can serve them on a moment's notice.

### Simple Split-Pea Soup

*Here's an easy soup that can be made in double or triple batches, then frozen for "emergencies."*

> 1   cup minced onions
> 1   tablespoon olive oil
> 3   cups dried split peas, washed well
> 2   large carrots, grated
> 2   tablespoons nonalcoholic white wine
> 1   teaspoon herbal salt substitute
> 1   teaspoon dried marjoram
> ½   teaspoon ground rosemary
> 5   cups Vegetable Stock (page 316)

In a 3-quart saucepan over medium-high heat, sauté the onions in the oil for 5 minutes, stirring frequently to prevent browning. Add the split peas, carrots, wine, salt substitute, marjoram and rosemary. Sauté, stirring frequently, for 3 minutes. Add the stock.

Bring to a boil, then reduce the heat to medium-low and simmer, uncovered, for 45 minutes.

*Serves 6.*

Per serving: 381 calories, 3.5 g. total fat, 0.5 g. saturated fat, 0 mg. cholesterol, 5.2 g. dietary fiber, 26 mg. sodium.

# Fresh-Corn and Pepper Chowder

*When corn is in season, buy whole ears and scrape off the kernels with a sharp knife. Cooking the cobs gives extra flavor to the soup.*

| | |
|---|---|
| 5 | ears corn |
| 5 | cups Garlic Broth (page 316) |
| 1 | cup chopped onions |
| 1 | teaspoon olive oil |
| 1 | cup diced sweet red peppers |
| 1 | cup diced red potatoes |
| 2 | carrots, diced |
| 2 | stalks celery, diced |
| ¼ | cup whole-wheat pastry flour |
| 2 | tablespoons chopped canned green chilies |
| ½ | teaspoon ground black pepper |
| ¼ | teaspoon ground red pepper |
| 1 | tablespoon herbal salt substitute |
| 2 | tablespoons chopped fresh chives |

Remove the kernels from the corn cobs and set aside (you should have about 2½ cups). Place the cobs in a 3-quart saucepan. Add the broth and bring to a boil over medium-high heat. Reduce the heat and simmer for 1 hour. Discard the cobs and reserve the stock.

Wash and dry the pan. Add the onions and oil. Sauté over medium heat for 10 minutes, stirring frequently to prevent browning. Add the red peppers, potatoes, carrots and celery. Cook, stirring occasionally, for 10 minutes.

Add the flour and cook for 2 minutes, stirring frequently. Add the reserved stock and bring to a boil.

Cover, reduce the heat to medium and cook for 10 minutes. Add the reserved corn kernels. Cook for 10 minutes, or until the potatoes are very tender.

Remove from the heat and let the soup cool for 10 minutes. Working in batches, puree half of the soup in a blender or food processor. Return the soup to the pot.

Add the chilies, black pepper, ground red pepper and salt substitute. Heat through. Serve garnished with the chives.

*SERVES 6.*

PER SERVING: 178 CALORIES, 2.8 G. TOTAL FAT, 0.2 G. SATURATED FAT, 0 MG. CHOLESTEROL, 5.2 G. DIETARY FIBER, 54 MG. SODIUM.

## Greek Lentil Soup

*The vinegar in this tomato-based soup takes the common lentil to new heights of flavor.*

1   stalk celery, chopped
1   small carrot, chopped
1   small russet potato, chopped
½   onion, chopped
1   tablespoon olive oil
5   cups Vegetable Stock (page 316)
1   cup dried lentils, washed well
1   cup low-sodium tomato sauce
1   bay leaf, crushed and wrapped in cheesecloth
¼   cup nonalcoholic red wine
2   teaspoons red-wine vinegar
¼   teaspoon ground cinnamon
    Herbal salt substitute (to taste)
    Ground black pepper (to taste)

In a 3-quart saucepan over medium-high heat, sauté the celery, carrots, potatoes and onions in the oil for 10 minutes, stirring frequently. Add the stock, lentils, tomato sauce and bay leaf. Bring to a boil.

Lower the heat to medium and simmer the soup, uncovered, for 45 minutes, or until the lentils are soft. Add the wine, vinegar and cinnamon. Season with the salt substitute and pepper. Discard the cheesecloth before serving.

*SERVES 6.*

PER SERVING: 166 CALORIES, 2.7 G. TOTAL FAT, 0.4 G. SATURATED FAT, 0 MG. CHOLESTEROL, 1.6 G. DIETARY FIBER, 31 MG. SODIUM.

### Boston Bean Soup

*Lima or pinto beans are recommended for their richness and high fiber content. Be sure to allow time to presoak the beans overnight.*

| | |
|---|---|
| 2 | cups dried lima or pinto beans, washed well |
| 1 | large onion, coarsely chopped |
| ¼ | cup nonalcoholic white wine |
| 2 | tablespoons dark sesame oil |
| ⅓ | cup chopped celery |
| 4 | cloves garlic, minced |
| 6 | cups Vegetable Stock (page 316) |
| | Juice of 1 lemon |
| 1 | tablespoon molasses |
| 1 | tablespoon tomato paste |
| 1 | teaspoon ground cumin |
| 1 | teaspoon ground coriander |
| | Pinch of ground red pepper |
| 1 | teaspoon red-wine vinegar |
| | Herbal salt substitute (to taste) |
| | Ground black pepper (to taste) |

Place the beans in a large bowl and cover with cold water. Let stand overnight, then pour off the soaking water. Set the beans aside.

In a 3-quart saucepan over medium-high heat, sauté the onions in the wine and oil for 10 minutes, stirring frequently to prevent browning. Add the celery and garlic. Cook for 5 minutes.

Add the reserved beans, stock, lemon juice, molasses, tomato paste, cumin, coriander and red pepper. Bring to a boil, then reduce the heat to medium. Simmer, uncovered, for 2 hours, or until the beans are soft.

Add the vinegar. Season with the salt substitute and black pepper.

*Serves 6.*

---

Per serving: 272 calories, 5.1 g. total fat, 0.7 g. saturated fat, 0 mg. cholesterol, 12.2 g. dietary fiber, 44 mg. sodium.

# THE MAIN EVENT

## *Meet the New Stars on the Dinner Plate*

You've probably noticed the multi-tiered triangle that is showing up on food labels these days. It's called the Food Guide Pyramid, and it was developed by the U.S. Department of Agriculture to show folks what they should be eating for optimum nutrition. It's quite a departure from the four food groups that we grew up with. Meats and dairy products, once mainstays of the typical American diet, have essentially become side dishes. The place of honor on the dinner plate is now reserved for grains: bread, cereal, rice and pasta. According to the pyramid, we're supposed to consume 6 to 11 servings of these grain-based foods every day.

Following the new dietary guidelines ensures that our bodies have all the nutrients they need to fend off disease and function properly. Still, the promise of good health may not be enough to persuade everyone to swap a thick, juicy sirloin for a bowl of plain brown rice.

Truth is, there's nothing at all plain about grains. No other food can match their versatility; their flavors and textures nicely complement vegetables, poultry and seafood without being overpowering. And as long as you don't drench pasta and other grain-based foods in heavy, fatty sauces, you're guaranteed a healthful, fiber-rich meal.

And don't be put off by the recommended 6 to 11 servings a day. A serving equals just one-half cup of cooked pasta, rice or cereal; one slice of bread; or one ounce of ready-to-eat cereal.

The recipes that follow transform ordinary pasta, rice and other grains into extraordinary meals. You'll find an assortment of bean dishes, too. While the Food Guide Pyramid recommends just two to three servings of dry beans a day (a serving is about one-half cup cooked), these legumes make an excellent substitute for meat. They pack a protein punch, but with just a fraction of meat's calories, fat and cholesterol. And like grains, they can give your diet a fiber boost.

## Palate-Pleasing Pasta

Pasta isn't just spaghetti anymore. From needle-thin angel hair to tube-shaped ziti, it comes in enough shapes, sizes and even colors to suit everyone's preferences. Most varieties are cholesterol-free and get less than 10 percent of their calories from fat.

Of course, it's the sauce that gives pasta its flavor. Creamy concoctions and those laden with meat can drown pasta's natural goodness. For more healthful selections, sample some—or all—of the easy sauce recipes at the end of this section.

 ### Five-Vegetable Lasagna

*This recipe has three components: a rich-tasting vegetable sauté, a seasoned tofu mixture that replaces the usual cheese and a thick tomato sauce. You can make these parts ahead of time, then assemble them just before serving.*

     1   cup sliced onions
     2   teaspoons minced garlic
    ½   cup apple juice
     3   cups thinly sliced zucchini
    1½  cups chopped spinach
     1   cup sliced mushrooms
     1   cup chopped tomatoes
    ¼   cup minced fresh parsley
    12   eggless spinach lasagna noodles
    16   ounces firm tofu, well-drained and crumbled
     1   tablespoon honey
     1   tablespoon herbal salt substitute
     2   teaspoons dried basil
    1½  teaspoons dried oregano
    ½   teaspoon ground black pepper
     1   cup Salt-Free Tomato Sauce with Mushrooms (page 349)
    ⅓   cup toasted whole-wheat bread crumbs

In a large frying pan over medium-high heat, sauté the onions and garlic in the apple juice for 10 minutes, stirring frequently to prevent browning. Add the zucchini, spinach, mushrooms, tomatoes and parsley. Lower the heat to medium and cook for 15 minutes, stirring frequently. Remove from the heat and set aside.

In a large pot of boiling water over high heat, cook the noodles for 8 minutes. Drain and rinse with cold water. Set aside in a single layer.

In a small bowl, combine the tofu, honey, salt substitute, basil, oregano and pepper.

Preheat the oven to 350°.

Lightly oil a 9″ × 13″ baking pan. Spread half of the vegetable mixture in the bottom of the pan. Top with half of the tofu mixture and half of the noodles (overlap as needed to fit). Repeat the layers with the remaining vegetables, tofu and noodles.

Top with the tomato sauce. Sprinkle with the bread crumbs. Cover with foil and bake for 45 minutes. Uncover and bake for 15 minutes.

*Serves 6.*

PER SERVING: 339 CALORIES, 8.2 G. TOTAL FAT, 1.1 G. SATURATED FAT, 0 MG. CHOLESTEROL, 9.8 G. DIETARY FIBER, 71 MG. SODIUM.

# Saffron Orzo

*Orzo, a tiny rice-shaped pasta, turns harvest gold from the saffron in this recipe. Soaking the saffron threads in nonalcoholic white wine before combining them with the pasta makes the color spread more evenly.*

1½   cups orzo
¼   cup nonalcoholic white wine
⅛   teaspoon saffron threads
2   tablespoons minced onions
1   teaspoon minced garlic
1   teaspoon olive oil
2   tablespoons chopped chives

In a large pot of boiling water over high heat, cook the orzo until just tender, about 10 minutes. Drain and set aside.

In a small bowl, combine the wine and saffron. Let steep for 10 minutes.

While the saffron is steeping, in a large frying pan over medium heat, sauté the onions and garlic in the oil for 5 minutes, stirring frequently to prevent browning. Add the saffron and orzo.

Continue cooking and stirring for 5 minutes, or until the orzo has taken on a golden color. Sprinkle with the chives.

*SERVES 4.*

PER SERVING: 341 CALORIES, 2.7 G. TOTAL FAT, 0.4 G. SATURATED FAT, 0 MG. CHOLESTEROL, 0.1 G. DIETARY FIBER, 3 MG. SODIUM.

## Nona's Pasta with Beans

*The recipe for this dish comes straight from Venice.*

　1　cup chopped onions
1–1½　cups chopped tomatoes
　3　cloves minced garlic
　1　tablespoon olive oil
　2　cups cooked eggless elbow macaroni
　2　cups cooked navy beans
　½　cup minced fresh parsley
　1　teaspoon dried oregano
　½　teaspoon dried basil
　　　Herbal salt substitute (to taste)
　　　Ground black pepper (to taste)

In a large frying pan over medium-high heat, sauté the onions, tomatoes and garlic in the oil, stirring frequently to prevent browning. Add the pasta, beans, parsley, oregano and basil. Heat through. Season with the salt substitute and pepper.

*SERVES 4.*

PER SERVING: 285 CALORIES, 4.7 G. TOTAL FAT, 0.7 G. SATURATED FAT, 0 MG. CHOLESTEROL, 7.5 G. DIETARY FIBER, 12 MG. SODIUM.

## Red and Green Pasta with Walnut Sauce

*You might think of this as holiday pasta, with the bright colors of the beet and spinach noodles. It's topped with an unusual pesto made from walnuts and garlic.*

⅔  cup walnuts
⅓  cup hot water
3  tablespoons olive oil
½  teaspoon minced garlic
2  tablespoons chopped parsley
1  tablespoon herbal salt substitute
½  teaspoon ground black pepper
3  cups hot cooked Spinach Noodles (page 348)
3  cups hot cooked Beet Noodles (page 348)

In a blender or food processor, puree the walnuts, water, oil and garlic until a smooth paste forms. Spoon into a large bowl and stir in the parsley, salt substitute and pepper.

Add the pastas and toss well.

*Serves 6.*

---

Per serving: 602 calories, 21.4 g. total fat, 2.4 g. saturated fat, 0 mg. cholesterol, 16.3 g. dietary fiber, 28 mg. sodium.

## Baked Eggplant and Tomato Pasta Casserole

*Baking the eggplant allows it to dry out, so it absorbs more flavor from the sauce.*

1 large eggplant, thinly sliced
2 cups thinly sliced onions
4 tablespoons minced garlic
2 tablespoons olive oil
4 tomatoes, chopped
1 cup diced green peppers
1 cup diced sweet red peppers
½ cup nonalcoholic red wine or Vegetable Stock (page 316)
4 tablespoons tomato paste
2 tablespoons honey
1 tablespoon herbal salt substitute
3 cups cooked whole-wheat rotelle
½ cup toasted whole-wheat bread crumbs

Preheat the oven to 300°.

Place the eggplant slices directly on an oven rack and bake for 10 minutes. Turn the slices and bake for 10 minutes. Remove from the oven and set aside.

Increase the oven temperature to 350°. Lightly oil a 9″ × 13″ baking dish.

In a large frying pan over medium-low heat, sauté the onions and garlic in the oil for 10 minutes, stirring frequently to prevent browning. Add the tomatoes, green peppers, red peppers, wine or stock, tomato paste, honey and salt substitute. Cover and cook for 10 minutes.

Place half of the eggplant in the baking dish and top with the rotelle. Spoon half of the sauce over the rotelle. Add another layer of eggplant and the remaining sauce. Sprinkle with the bread crumbs. Bake for 25 minutes.

*SERVES 6.*

PER SERVING: 273 CALORIES, 5.9 G. TOTAL FAT, 0.8 G. SATURATED FAT, 0 MG. CHOLESTEROL, 5.6 G. DIETARY FIBER, 139 MG. SODIUM.

# Thai Noodle and Vegetable Salad

*The elegant cuisine of Thailand is the inspiration for this salad. Serve it with a glass of iced jasmine tea for an outdoor summer lunch.*

¼  cup water
3  tablespoons lemon juice
1½  tablespoons dark sesame oil
4  teaspoons low-sodium soy sauce or tamari
1  tablespoon reduced-fat peanut butter
1  tablespoon herbal salt substitute
1  teaspoon minced garlic
4  teaspoons rice-wine vinegar
2  teaspoons honey
1  cucumber
3  cups shredded romaine lettuce
3  cups cooked cellophane noodles
1  cup snow peas
½  cup julienned sweet red peppers
¼  cup diagonally sliced scallions

In a small bowl, whisk together the water, lemon juice, oil, soy sauce or tamari, peanut butter, salt substitute, garlic, vinegar and honey. Let stand for 10 minutes while you prepare the salad.

Peel the cucumber. Halve it lengthwise, scoop out the seeds and slice the flesh into half-moon shapes. Place in a large bowl. Add the lettuce, noodles, peas, peppers, peanuts and scallions.

Pour the dressing over the salad and toss well. Serve immediately.

*SERVES 4.*

PER SERVING: 256 CALORIES, 7.0 G. TOTAL FAT, 1.1 G. SATURATED FAT, 0 MG. CHOLESTEROL, 2.5 G. DIETARY FIBER, 194 MG. SODIUM.

**Noodle and White-Bean Salad with Low-Oil Vinaigrette**

*Make this salad in the morning, so the flavors have a chance to blend before dinner. Store, covered, in the refrigerator, then bring to room temperature to serve. You can find soba noodles in most health food stores and Asian markets.*

1 cup cooked soba
1 cup cooked white beans
1 cup julienned carrots
1 cup broccoli florets
½ cup sliced scallions
¼ cup minced fresh parsley
3 tablespoons apple cider vinegar
1 tablespoon olive oil
2 tablespoons low-sodium soy sauce or tamari
2 teaspoons dark sesame oil
1 tablespoon lemon juice
⅛ teaspoon ground red pepper

In a large bowl, combine the soba, beans, carrots, broccoli, scallions, parsley, vinegar, olive oil, soy sauce or tamari, sesame oil, lemon juice and pepper. Let marinate for at least 1 hour, or overnight. Serve at room temperature.

*Serves 4.*

Per serving: 168 calories, 6.0 g. total fat, 0.8 g. saturated fat, 0 mg. cholesterol, 4.6 g. dietary fiber, 302 mg. sodium.

## MAKE YOUR OWN NO-CHOLESTEROL PASTA

Perfect pasta is a delicate balance of three elements: flour, water and kneading. Too much of any one element, and the dough's silky elasticity vanishes.

Though traditional pasta dough recipes usually include eggs, they aren't essential. In fact, even oil isn't really necessary.

The following technique will guide you through the stages of making basic pasta dough. Once you practice and produce a passable pasta, try some of the variations.

### Basic Pasta Dough

1 cup whole-wheat pastry or unbleached flour
¼ cup water (approximate)
1 teaspoon olive oil (optional)
 Pinch of herbal salt substitute

*To make the dough with a food processor:* Place the flour, water, oil (if using) and salt substitute in a food processor. (The oil will make the pasta dough smoother but can be omitted to lower the calorie content.) Process with on/off turns to lightly combine. Continue to process until the dough forms a ball and cleans the sides of the bowl. (You may need to add 1 to 3 teaspoons more water to get to this point.) Proceed to the kneading step.

*To make the dough by hand:* In a large bowl, mix the flour and salt substitute. Make a well in the center of the flour and add the oil (if using). Use a fork to lightly incorporate the oil into the flour. When a loose lump of dough forms, begin adding water by tablespoonfuls. If needed, incorporate more flour and water in small amounts until a stiff dough forms. Proceed to the kneading step.

*To knead the dough:* Throughout kneading, be careful to add flour very gradually. In the beginning stages, the dough is apt to absorb flour and can get tough very quickly. Your goal is to knead the stickiness out of the dough rather than to cover it with flour.

Lightly sprinkle flour on your hands and all sides of the dough. Knead the dough on a lightly floured board or between your hands. After about 5 minutes, the dough should be smooth and elastic. You can test it by stretching a piece: It should stretch several inches without breaking. Flatten the dough into a pancake and flour it well. Now that it is fully kneaded, the flour will not be absorbed as much. Choose your rolling method.

*To roll the dough by machine:* Position the rollers at the widest setting. Roll the flattened dough through the machine. Fold the dough into thirds, turn it 90 degrees and roll it through again. This should give you an even rectangle of dough to cut into even strips.

Lightly flour both sides of the dough. Roll the rectangle of dough one time each through successively narrower settings until it is about 1/16" thick. Cut the strip in half for easier handling. Flour the dough well on both sides and feed through the cutting blades. Separate any sticky strands and hang on a rack or lay on a floured board to dry for 30 minutes. Proceed to cooking step.

*To roll the dough by hand:* With a lightly floured rolling pin, roll the dough to 1/16" thick. Lightly flour both sides of the dough. Starting at an edge, roll up the dough to form a jelly roll. Cut the roll into strips about 1/4" thick. Unroll each strip, separate sticky strands and let dry on a rack or floured board for 30 minutes. Proceed to cooking step.

*To cook:* In a large pot, bring 2 quarts of water to a rapid boil. Add the pasta and cook for 1 to 2 minutes. A teaspoon of olive oil in the water will help keep the noodles separate, but is not essential. Drain and serve.

*SERVES 2.*

PER SERVING: 223 CALORIES, 3.4 G. TOTAL FAT, 0.5 G. SATURATED FAT, 0 MG. CHOLESTEROL, 7.6 G. DIETARY FIBER, 3 MG. SODIUM.

*(continued)*

## MAKE YOUR OWN NO-CHOLESTEROL PASTA—CONTINUED

### Spinach Noodles

Basic Pasta Dough
2  tablespoons thawed and finely chopped frozen
spinach, squeezed dry

Follow the directions for the basic pasta. Add the
spinach during the kneading stage.

*SERVES 2.*

PER SERVING: 227 CALORIES, 3.4 G. TOTAL FAT, 0.5 G. SATURATED FAT,
0 MG. CHOLESTEROL, 7.8 G. DIETARY FIBER, 13 MG. SODIUM.

### Herb Noodles

Basic Pasta Dough
2  tablespoons minced fresh basil, oregano or thyme

Follow the directions for the basic pasta. Add the herbs
during the kneading stage.

*SERVES 2.*

PER SERVING: 224 CALORIES, 3.4 G. TOTAL FAT, 0.5 G. SATURATED FAT,
0 MG. CHOLESTEROL, 7.6 G. DIETARY FIBER, 3 MG. SODIUM.

### Beet Noodles

Basic Pasta Dough
2  tablespoons pureed cooked beets

Follow the directions for the basic pasta. Add the beets
during the kneading stage.

*SERVES 2.*

PER SERVING: 228 CALORIES, 3.4 G. TOTAL FAT, 0.5 G. SATURATED FAT,
0 MG. CHOLESTEROL, 7.9 G. DIETARY FIBER, 11 MG. SODIUM.

## Salt-Free Tomato Sauce with Mushrooms

*Thick and tasty, this sauce gets its flavor from a slow sauté of domestic and wild mushrooms in nonalcoholic red wine.*

1   cup minced onions
2   tablespoons minced garlic
½   cup nonalcoholic red wine
1   cup minced wild mushrooms, such as chanterelles
1   cup minced mushrooms
4   cups chopped tomatoes
2   tablespoons tomato paste
1   teaspoon herbal salt substitute
1   tablespoon honey
½   teaspoon dried basil
½   teaspoon dried oregano
    Ground black pepper (to taste)

In a 3- or 4-quart saucepan over medium-high heat, sauté the onions and garlic in the wine for 10 minutes, stirring frequently to prevent browning. Add both varieties of mushrooms. Cook for 15 minutes, or until the mushrooms exude moisture.

Add the tomatoes, tomato paste, salt substitute, honey, basil and oregano.

Reduce the heat to medium and cook, stirring occasionally, for 25 minutes. Season with the pepper.

*MAKES 4 CUPS.*

PER ¼ CUP: 30 CALORIES, 0.3 G. TOTAL FAT, <0.1 G. SATURATED FAT, 0 MG. CHOLESTEROL, 1.1 G. DIETARY FIBER, 23 MG. SODIUM.

## Tomato and Green-Olive Sauce

*Green olives give this rich sauce a tart bite, which complements the sweetness of garden-ripe tomatoes. Be sure to make extra sauce to freeze for a taste of summer during the winter months.*

    2   tablespoons minced garlic
    ¼   cup nonalcoholic red wine
    3   cups chopped fresh tomatoes
    2   tablespoons pitted chopped green olives
    1   tablespoon minced fresh parsley
    1   tablespoon dried oregano
    1   teaspoon olive oil

In a 2-quart saucepan over medium-high heat, sauté the garlic in the wine for 2 minutes. Add the tomatoes, olives, parsley, oregano and oil. Cook, stirring frequently, for 5 minutes.

Let cool, cover and refrigerate overnight to blend the flavors. Reheat before serving.

*MAKES ABOUT 3½ CUPS.*

PER ¼ CUP: 20 CALORIES, 0.7 G. TOTAL FAT, 0.1 G. SATURATED FAT, 0 MG. CHOLESTEROL, 0.7 G. DIETARY FIBER, 39 MG. SODIUM.

# Salt-Free Southern Italian Pasta Sauce

*This traditional recipe has been modified to fit today's healthy cooking standards: less oil and no salt.*

½ cup nonalcoholic red wine
1 teaspoon olive oil
1 tablespoon flour
1 cup minced onions
2 teaspoons minced garlic
5 cups chopped tomatoes
2 tablespoons tomato paste
2 tablespoons minced fresh parsley
½ teaspoon herbal salt substitute
½ teaspoon honey
¼–½ teaspoon dried basil
¼–½ teaspoon dried thyme
¼ teaspoon ground black pepper

In a 3-quart saucepan over medium-high heat, heat the wine and oil. Whisk in the flour and cook, whisking constantly, for 2 minutes. Add the onions and garlic. Cook, stirring frequently, for 5 minutes.

Add the tomatoes, tomato paste, parsley, salt substitute, honey, basil, thyme and pepper.

Cover, reduce the heat to low and simmer for 40 minutes, stirring occasionally. Let cool, then puree in a blender.

*Makes 3 cups.*

---

Per ¼ cup: 35 calories, 0.7 g. total fat, 0.1 g. saturated fat, 0 mg. cholesterol, 1.5 g. dietary fiber, 37 mg. sodium.

## Eggplant-Tomato Sauce

*Sautéed eggplant, nutmeg and nonalcoholic red wine give this sauce a thickness and rich flavor that are often missing from plain tomato sauces. It's excellent over pasta. It also freezes well and will keep for up to three months.*

¾  cup nonalcoholic red wine
1   teaspoon olive oil
1   small onion, finely chopped
1   cup cubed unpeeled eggplant
½   cup minced sweet red peppers
¼   cup chopped celery
2   cloves garlic, minced
3   cups Italian tomatoes, coarsely chopped
1   tablespoon chopped fresh basil
½   teaspoon ground nutmeg
    Herbal salt substitute (to taste)
    Ground black pepper (to taste)

In a 3-quart saucepan over medium-high heat, heat the wine and oil until bubbling. Add the onions and cook, stirring frequently, until soft but not browned, about 5 minutes. Add the eggplant, red peppers, celery and garlic. Cover and cook for 2 minutes.

Add the tomatoes, basil and nutmeg. Bring to a boil, then reduce the heat to medium. Simmer, uncovered, for 20 minutes. Season with the salt substitute and black pepper.

*MAKES ABOUT 5 CUPS.*

PER ¼ CUP: 15 CALORIES, 0.4 G. TOTAL FAT, 0.1 G. SATURATED FAT, 0 MG. CHOLESTEROL, 0.6 G. DIETARY FIBER, 10 MG. SODIUM.

## Green-Tomato Sauce

*You can make this unusual tomato sauce with tomatillos, the citrusy Mexican vegetable available year-round in supermarkets and gourmet stores. The sauce doubles as a delicious dipping salsa for chips.*

¼ cup chopped onions
1 teaspoon minced garlic
1 teaspoon olive oil
¼ cup nonalcoholic red wine
2 cups chopped green tomatoes or tomatillos
1 tablespoon minced fresh cilantro
1 teaspoon minced jalapeño peppers
1 teaspoon herbal salt substitute
½ teaspoon ground black pepper

In a 2-quart saucepan over medium-high heat, sauté the onions and garlic in the oil and wine for 10 minutes, stirring frequently to prevent browning.

Add the tomatoes or tomatillos, cilantro, jalapeño peppers, salt substitute and pepper. Cook, stirring, for 15 minutes. Let cool, then puree in a blender.

*MAKES ABOUT 2 CUPS.*

PER ¼ CUP: 20 CALORIES, 0.7 G. TOTAL FAT, 0.1 G. SATURATED FAT, 0 MG. CHOLESTEROL, 0.4 G. DIETARY FIBER, 17 MG. SODIUM.

## Pasta Sauce Provencale

*Olives, thyme and other seasonings of southern France create an aroma that's reminiscent of the herb-covered hillsides around Provence.*

  1  tablespoon olive oil
  6  large tomatoes, coarsely chopped (about 5 cups)
  1  teaspoon chopped black olives
  1  clove garlic, minced
  1  teaspoon herbal salt substitute
 ½  teaspoon honey
 ½  teaspoon chopped fresh parsley
 ½  teaspoon ground black pepper
 ¼  teaspoon dried thyme

In a 2- or 3-quart saucepan over medium-high heat, heat the oil until it almost smokes, about 4 to 5 minutes. Carefully add the tomatoes, olives and garlic. Cook, stirring frequently, until the tomatoes are soft, about 8 to 10 minutes. Add the salt substitute, honey, parsley, pepper and thyme. Reduce the heat to low and cook, uncovered, for 30 minutes.

*MAKES ABOUT 5 CUPS.*

PER ¼ CUP: 15 CALORIES, 0.9 G. TOTAL FAT, 0.1 G. SATURATED FAT, 0 MG. CHOLESTEROL, 0.5 G. DIETARY FIBER, 8 MG. SODIUM.

## Great Grains

While rice and other grains are diet staples in many countries, only recently have they begun to catch on in the United States. But word is spreading fast about their high-fiber goodness. These days, most supermarkets are well-stocked with an assortment of grains. Experiment with them to find out just how chameleon-like they can be, as they seem to take on different and exciting flavors from one recipe to the next.

  **Wild Rice with Mushrooms and Pecans**

*Wild rice is livened up with savory sautéed mushrooms and crunchy pecans.*

¼ cup diced onions
¼ cup diced celery
¼ cup diced carrots
¼ cup nonalcoholic white wine
1 tablespoon safflower oil
2 cups sliced mushrooms
1 cup wild rice
2½ cups Vegetable Stock (page 316)
2 tablespoons minced fresh parsley
2 tablespoons chopped toasted pecans

In a 3-quart saucepan over medium heat, sauté the onions, celery and carrots in the wine and oil for 5 minutes, stirring frequently to prevent browning.

Add the mushrooms and wild rice. Cook for 5 minutes, or until the mushrooms begin to exude moisture.

Add the stock and bring to a boil. Cover, reduce the heat to low and cook for 25 minutes, or until all the water has been absorbed. Stir in the parsley and pecans.

*Serves 4.*

Per serving: 215 calories, 6.3 g. total fat, 0.6 g. saturated fat, 0 mg. cholesterol, 1.8 g. dietary fiber, 16 mg. sodium.

# Jalapeño Pepper and Wild Mushroom Risotto

*Risotto—rice cooked to a cereal consistency—is made from Italian Arborio rice, the only rice that cooks to a creamy texture without dissolving.*

> 7 cups Garlic Broth (page 316)
> ½ cup minced onions
> ⅓ cup minced jalapeño peppers
> 2 cloves garlic, minced
> ½ cup nonalcoholic white wine
> 2 tablespoons olive oil
> 2 cups sliced wild mushrooms, such as shiitake or chanterelle
> 1½ cups Arborio rice

In a 2-quart saucepan over medium-high heat, bring the broth to a boil. Reduce the heat and keep the broth warm, just barely simmering.

In a 3-quart saucepan over medium-high heat, cook the onions, jalapeño peppers and garlic in the wine and 1 tablespoon of the oil for 2 minutes. Reduce the heat to medium and continue cooking the vegetables for 8 minutes, stirring frequently to prevent browning. Add the mushrooms and cook, stirring occasionally, until the mushrooms begin to exude moisture. Add the rice and stir to coat with the cooking liquid.

Add 1 cup of the hot broth and cook, stirring, until the liquid is absorbed. Add the broth ½ cup at a time, cooking after each addition until the liquid is absorbed. Continue until the rice is tender and all the broth has been absorbed, about 20 to 30 minutes. Serve hot, drizzled with the remaining olive oil.

*Serves 4.*

Per serving: 360 calories, 7.5 g. total fat, 1.1 g. saturated fat, 0 mg. cholesterol, 1.8 g. dietary fiber, 172 mg. sodium.

## Brown-Rice Salad with Mint in Lettuce Cups

*The delicate flavors of mint and lemon mingle in this salad, which is served in a curled lettuce leaf and garnished with sweet red pepper strips.*

| | |
|---|---|
| 3 | cups cooked short-grain brown rice |
| ½ | cup chopped red onions |
| ½ | cup chopped fresh mint |
| ½ | cup chopped fresh parsley |
| ¼ | cup peas |
| ¼ | cup minced sweet red peppers |
| 2 | tablespoons olive oil |
| ¼ | cup lemon juice |
| 1 | teaspoon minced garlic |
| 1 | teaspoon herbal salt substitute |
| ½ | teaspoon ground white pepper |
| 1 | head red-leaf lettuce |
| 12 | strips sweet red peppers |

In a large bowl, combine the rice, onions, mint, parsley, peas, red peppers, oil, lemon juice, garlic, salt substitute and ground pepper. Toss well and let marinate for 1 hour at room temperature.

Wash and separate the lettuce leaves; dry thoroughly. Place 2 or 3 leaves together, forming a cup. Repeat until you have 6 cups.

Divide the salad evenly among the cups. Garnish with the pepper strips.

*SERVES 6.*

PER SERVING: 183 CALORIES, 5.6 G. TOTAL FAT, 0.8 G. SATURATED FAT, 0 MG. CHOLESTEROL, 3.3 G. DIETARY FIBER, 20 MG. SODIUM.

# Three-Color Rice

*The three colors come from the vibrant vegetables in this recipe: peas, corn and carrots.*

¼　cup minced onions
2　teaspoons minced garlic
1　teaspoon olive oil
½　cup peas
½　cup corn
½　cup diced carrots
¼　cup apple juice
3　cups cooked short-grain brown rice
2　tablespoons minced fresh parsley

In a large frying pan over medium-high heat, sauté the onions and garlic in the oil for 5 minutes, stirring frequently to prevent browning. Add the peas, corn, carrots and apple juice. Let simmer for 5 minutes, then add the rice. Heat through, stirring frequently. Sprinkle with the parsley before serving.

*SERVES 4.*

PER SERVING: 228 CALORIES, 2.5 G. TOTAL FAT, 0.4 G. SATURATED FAT, 0 MG. CHOLESTEROL, 4.4 G. DIETARY FIBER, 27 MG. SODIUM.

# Indian Rice Pilaf

*Curried rice turns this pilaf into a spicy international dish. You can serve it as is or dress it up Indian-style with side dishes of chutney, peanuts and dried fruit.*

| | |
|---|---|
| 1 | cup chopped onions |
| 4 | cloves garlic, minced |
| 1 | tablespoon cumin seeds |
| 1 | tablespoon grated fresh ginger |
| 2 | teaspoons safflower oil |
| 2 | cups basmati rice, washed and drained |
| 4 | cups Vegetable Stock (page 316) |
| ⅔ | cup raisins |
| 2–3 | teaspoons curry powder |
| ⅓ | cup chopped scallions |
| ⅓ | cup raw peanuts or cashews |

In a large frying pan over medium-low heat, sauté the onions, garlic, cumin and ginger in the oil for 10 minutes, stirring frequently to prevent browning. Add the rice and sauté an additional 3 minutes, stirring constantly. Add the stock, raisins and curry.

Bring to a boil and let the mixture cook, uncovered, for 15 minutes. Cover the pan, reduce the heat and simmer for 10 to 15 minutes, or until all the liquid has been absorbed. Stir in the scallions and peanuts or cashews.

*SERVES 4.*

---

PER SERVING: 496 CALORIES, 11.0 G. TOTAL FAT, 1.1 G. SATURATED FAT, 0 MG. CHOLESTEROL, 3.2 G. DIETARY FIBER, 71 MG. SODIUM.

---

# Spinach Fried Rice

*This recipe cooks up in just 20 minutes. And it's a delicious way to satisfy a craving for fried rice without the high fat content.*

1½ cups chopped spinach
2 cloves garlic, minced
1 teaspoon dark sesame oil
⅓ cup nonalcoholic white wine
1 cup diagonally sliced celery or bok choy
1 cup thinly sliced mushrooms
3 cups cooked long-grain brown rice
¼ cup sliced scallions
2 tablespoons low-sodium soy sauce or tamari

In a wok or large frying pan over medium-high heat, sauté the spinach and garlic in the oil for 2 minutes, stirring constantly. Transfer to a platter.

In the same pan, heat the wine and sauté the celery or bok choy and mushrooms, stirring constantly, for 3 minutes. Add the rice, scallions and spinach. Heat through. Season with the soy sauce or tamari.

*Serves 4.*

PER SERVING: 195 CALORIES, 2.7 G. TOTAL FAT, 0.5 G. SATURATED FAT, 0 MG. CHOLESTEROL, 3.9 G. DIETARY FIBER, 316 MG. SODIUM.

## Asian-Style Quinoa

*Quinoa, a grain from the South American Andes, is rich in protein and other nutrients. Here it is combined with stir-fried vegetables.*

6 cups water
2 cups quinoa
1 tablespoon dark sesame oil
2 tablespoons low-sodium soy sauce or tamari
½ cup diagonally sliced scallions
½ cup diagonally sliced carrots
¼ cup nonalcoholic white wine
8 ounces firm tofu, cut into chunks

In a saucepan over medium-high heat, bring the water and quinoa to a boil. Cover the pan, reduce the heat to low and simmer for 20 minutes. Stir in the oil and 1 tablespoon of the soy sauce or tamari. Transfer to a large platter and keep warm.

In a wok or large frying pan over medium-high heat, sauté the scallions and carrots in the wine for 5 minutes, stirring constantly. Add the tofu and remaining soy sauce or tamari. Cook for 1 minute, stirring occasionally. Pour over the quinoa.

*Serves 6.*

PER SERVING: 296 CALORIES, 8.9 G. TOTAL FAT, 1.1 G. SATURATED FAT, 0 MG. CHOLESTEROL, 3.8 G. DIETARY FIBER, 197 MG. SODIUM.

## Creamy Polenta with Roasted Vegetables

*Polenta, a soft-cooked cornmeal, is perfect for a chilly winter evening. You can also bake the cooked polenta and serve it in slices for a more elegant presentation.*

| | |
|---|---|
| 1 | Japanese eggplant, halved lengthwise and sliced thickly |
| 8 | large mushrooms |
| 8 | scallions |
| 1 | cup cherry tomatoes |
| 2 | teaspoons olive oil |
| 1 | tablespoon low-sodium soy sauce or tamari |
| 1 | tablespoon dried thyme |
| 1 | cup coarse cornmeal |
| 1 | cup cold water |
| 2 | cups boiling Vegetable Stock (page 316) |

Preheat a broiler or stove-top grill.

In a large bowl, combine the eggplant, mushrooms, scallions and tomatoes. Drizzle with the oil and soy sauce or tamari and sprinkle with the thyme. Toss well and let marinate while you make the polenta.

In a heavy 2-quart saucepan, combine the cornmeal and water. Whisk in the hot stock. Bring to a boil over medium-high heat. Reduce the heat and cook, stirring with a whisk, until thick. Cover the pan and turn off the heat.

Remove the vegetables from their marinade (reserve the liquid). Broil or grill the vegetables until lightly browned, turning once halfway through the cooking time.

Divide the warm polenta among 3 or 4 plates and arrange the vegetables on top. Drizzle with the leftover marinade.

*SERVES 3.*

---

PER SERVING: 239 CALORIES, 5.0 G. TOTAL FAT, 0.7 G. SATURATED FAT, 0 MG. CHOLESTEROL, 8.7 G. DIETARY FIBER, 209 MG. SODIUM.

---

## Vegetarian Red Pepper and Artichoke Paella

*Paella means celebration—usually a feast saluting the catch of the day on the Spanish coast. Here's a vegetarian version with the same seasonings: saffron and garlic.*

¼ cup boiling water
¼ teaspoon saffron threads
2 large onions, thinly sliced
¼ cup olive oil
3 cups basmati rice, washed and drained
1 large sweet red pepper, thinly sliced
4 cloves garlic, minced
5½ cups Vegetable Stock (page 316)
1 tablespoon low-sodium soy sauce or tamari
½ teaspoon ground red pepper (or to taste)
1 teaspoon herbal salt substitute
½ teaspoon ground black pepper
8 ounces marinated artichokes, drained
¼ cup slivered almonds

In a small bowl, combine the water and saffron. Let steep for 20 minutes.

In a large frying pan over medium-low heat, sauté the onions in the oil for 10 minutes, stirring frequently.

Add the rice, red peppers and garlic. Sauté, stirring, for 5 minutes. Add the stock. Bring to a boil and let simmer, uncovered, for 15 minutes. Add the saffron and water.

Cover the pan, turn the heat to low and let steam for 10 to 15 minutes, or until all the water is absorbed. Add the soy sauce or tamari and ground red pepper. Season with the salt substitute and black pepper. Mix well.

Pour into a serving bowl. Serve topped with the artichokes and almonds.

*Serves 4.*

Per serving: 714 calories, 24.7 g. total fat, 2.2 g. saturated fat, 0 mg. cholesterol, 5.4 g. dietary fiber, 390 mg. sodium.

## Nuts about Beans

Beans have a surprisingly similar texture to meat that make them extra-hearty fare. They're often served as side dishes, but the recipes here dress them up as entrées. Add a tossed salad, some warm bread and a light dessert for a complete meal.

 **Mexican Corn Stew**

*This spicy stew gets its fire from minced fresh jalapeño peppers. Pass around a bowl of guacamole as a garnish.*

|   |   |
|---|---|
| 1 | cup dried small red beans, rinsed |
| 3 | tablespoons olive oil |
| 1 | cup chopped onions |
| 1 | tablespoon minced garlic |
| 2 | sweet red peppers, diced |
| ½ | cup thinly sliced carrots |
| ½ | cup thinly sliced celery |
| ¼ | cup diced jalapeño peppers |
| 6 | cups water or Vegetable Stock (page 316) |
| 3 | cups corn |
| 3 | tablespoons minced fresh cilantro |
| 2 | teaspoons ground cumin |
| 2 | teaspoons ground coriander |
| ½ | teaspoon ground red pepper (optional) |
| 2 | cups crushed tortilla chips |

Place the beans in a large bowl and cover with cold water. Let them soak overnight, then drain off the excess water. Place in a Crock-Pot.

In a large frying pan over medium-high heat, heat the oil. Add the onions and garlic. Sauté until the onions are soft, about 3 to 5 minutes. Add the red peppers, carrots, celery and jalapeño peppers. Cook for 3 minutes, stirring frequently. Add to the Crock-Pot.

Add the water or stock, corn, cilantro, cumin and coriander. Cover the pot and turn to low. Cook for 6 to 8 hours, or until the beans are tender and the stew is thick.

Add the ground pepper (if using) and serve in warmed bowls. Top each serving with the tortilla chips.

*Serves 6.*

PER SERVING: 367 CALORIES, 12.0 G. TOTAL FAT, 1.8 G. SATURATED FAT, 0 MG. CHOLESTEROL, 5.4 G. DIETARY FIBER, 194 MG. SODIUM.

## Sprouted Bean Burgers

*Top these burgers with mustard, lettuce, tomatoes and sprouts, and they could pass for the real thing.*

      1  cup sprouted chick-peas
      1  cup sprouted wheat berries
    ½  cup grated carrots
    ½  cup cooked cubed potatoes, mashed
    ¼  cup grated onions
    ½  teaspoon herbal salt substitute
    ¼  teaspoon dried basil
    ¼  teaspoon dried thyme
    ¼  teaspoon ground black pepper
    ⅛  teaspoon ground rosemary
        Low-sodium soy sauce or tamari (to taste)
  1–2  cups whole-wheat bread crumbs
      1  teaspoon canola oil

Place the chick-peas, wheat berries, carrots, potatoes, onions, salt substitute, basil, thyme, pepper and rosemary in a food processor. Puree. Add the soy sauce or tamari to taste.

Transfer to a large bowl. Stir in enough bread crumbs to make a mixture that holds together. Form into 6 patties.

Fry in the oil on a no-stick griddle over medium heat.

*Serves 6.*

PER SERVING: 100 CALORIES, 1.4 G. TOTAL FAT, 0.2 G. SATURATED FAT, 0 MG. CHOLESTEROL, 2.5 G. DIETARY FIBER, 48 MG. SODIUM.

# Cuban Black Beans and Rice

*Black beans are used in this recipe for their rich flavor, which combines well with cumin and garlic. You can make this dish spicier with a sprinkle of ground red pepper or hot pepper sauce.*

  1   cup washed black beans
  4   cups Vegetable Stock (page 316)
 ¾   cup chopped onions
  4   cloves garlic, minced
  1   tablespoon cumin seeds
  2   tablespoons olive oil
1½   cups long-grain brown rice
 ½   cup chopped green peppers
 ½   cup chopped sweet red peppers
  2   cups Garlic Broth (page 316)
      Low-sodium soy sauce or tamari, to taste

Place the beans in a large bowl and cover with cold water. Let soak overnight, then drain off the excess water. Transfer to a 3-quart saucepan. Add the stock. Bring to a boil over medium-high heat. Reduce the heat to medium and cook for 25 to 35 minutes, or until the beans are almost tender. Drain.

In a large frying pan over medium heat, sauté the onions, garlic and cumin in the oil for 10 minutes, stirring frequently to prevent browning. Add the rice, green peppers and red peppers. Cook, stirring, for 2 minutes. Add the beans and broth.

Bring to a boil, cover and cook for 40 minutes, or until the rice is tender. Season with the soy sauce or tamari.

*Serves 4.*

---

Per serving: 528 calories, 10.1 g. total fat, 1.5 g. saturated fat, 0 mg. cholesterol, 5.9 g. dietary fiber, 13 mg. sodium.

## Basic Bean Soup

*This thick soup has fiber-rich beans and vegetables in every spoonful. Make it ahead for a quick meal on a busy day.*

| | |
|---|---|
| 1 | cup dried beans, rinsed |
| 1 | cup chopped onions |
| 2 | teaspoons minced garlic |
| 1 | tablespoon olive oil |
| ½ | cup diced celery stalks and leaves |
| ½ | cup diced sweet potatoes or carrots |
| ½ | cup diced tomatoes |
| 5″ | piece kombu (kelp) |
| 6 | cups Vegetable Stock (page 316) |
| ¼ | cup white miso |
| 1 | tablespoon mirin (Japanese rice wine) |
| 1 | tablespoon minced fresh parsley |

Place the beans in a large bowl and cover with cold water. Let soak overnight, then drain off the excess water. Set aside.

In a 3- to 4-quart pot over medium-high heat, sauté the onions and garlic in the oil for 10 minutes, stirring frequently to prevent browning. Add the celery, sweet potatoes or carrots, tomatoes and kombu. Continue to sauté, stirring frequently, for 5 minutes. Add the stock and bring to a boil.

Reduce the heat to medium. Add the beans, cover and simmer for 1⅓ hours, or until the beans are tender. Remove and discard the kombu.

Pour ½ cup of the soup into a small bowl, add the miso and stir until the miso is blended. Pour back into the pot and add the mirin and parsley.

*SERVES 6.*

PER SERVING: 198 CALORIES, 3.5 G. TOTAL FAT, 0.6 G. SATURATED FAT, 0 MG. CHOLESTEROL, 14.5 G. DIETARY FIBER, 440 MG. SODIUM.

## **Vegetarian Sierra Stew**

*Heaping portions of beans and vegetables lend heartiness to this meatless stew, which is named for the High Sierras.*

    3   cups dried kidney beans, rinsed
    2   tablespoons olive oil
    1   large onion, thinly sliced
    4   cloves garlic, minced
    1   green pepper, coarsely chopped
   10   ounces canned tomatoes, with liquid
    1   cup coarsely chopped green cabbage
   ½   cup diced red potatoes
    1   tablespoon chili powder
   ½   teaspoon ground cumin
    4   cups water or Vegetable Stock (page 316)
   ½   cup brown rice
        Herbal salt substitute (to taste)
        Ground black pepper (to taste)

Place the beans in a large bowl and cover with cold water. Let soak overnight, then drain off the excess water. Place in a Crock-Pot.

In a large frying pan over medium-high heat, heat the oil. Add the onions and garlic. Sauté until the onions are soft, about 3 to 5 minutes. Add the peppers, tomatoes, cabbage, potatoes, chili powder and cumin. Continue cooking, stirring frequently, for 3 minutes, then transfer to the Crock-Pot.

Add the water or stock and rice. Cover the pot and turn to low. Let cook for 6 to 8 hours, or until the stew is thick and the beans and rice are tender. Season with the salt substitute and pepper.

*Serves 6.*

---

Per serving: 454 calories, 6.2 g. total fat, 0.8 g. saturated fat, 0 mg. cholesterol, 2.9 g. dietary fiber, 118 mg. sodium.

# Black Beans with Cumin and Garlic

*This dish is ultra-simple. You can freeze leftovers to wrap in sandwich burritos later.*

2  cups washed black beans
3  cups Vegetable Stock (page 316)
¼  cup minced onions
2  jalapeño peppers, minced
5  cloves garlic, minced
1  teaspoon ground cumin
2  tablespoons olive oil
¼  cup nonalcoholic red wine
¼  cup minced fresh parsley

Place the beans in a large bowl and cover with cold water. Let soak overnight, then drain off the excess water. Transfer to a 3-quart saucepan. Add the stock. Bring to a boil over medium-high heat. Reduce the heat to medium and cook for 45 to 60 minutes, or until the beans are almost tender. Drain.

In a large frying pan over medium-high heat, sauté the onions, jalapeño peppers, garlic and cumin in the oil for 5 minutes, stirring frequently to prevent browning. Add the wine and cook for 1 minute.

Add the beans and cook, stirring frequently, for 10 minutes. Serve sprinkled with the parsley.

*Serves 4.*

PER SERVING: 408 CALORIES, 8.3 G. TOTAL FAT, 1.3 G. SATURATED FAT, 0 MG. CHOLESTEROL, 0.5 G. DIETARY FIBER, 52 MG. SODIUM.

# Refried Mexican Beans

*You can make great refried beans without lard! This recipe gets its savory punch from Mexican spices.*

½   cup minced onions
2   tablespoons minced garlic
2   tablespoons olive oil
3   cups cooked pinto beans
1   tablespoon minced jalapeño peppers
½   teaspoon ground cumin
½   teaspoon salt (optional)

In a large frying pan over medium-high heat, sauté the onions and garlic in the oil for 10 minutes, stirring frequently to prevent browning. Add the beans and mash with a spoon. Add the jalapeño peppers, cumin and salt (if using). Heat through, stirring constantly.

*Serves 6.*

Per serving: 172 calories, 5.0 g. total fat, 0.7 g. saturated fat, 0 mg. cholesterol, 6.7 g. dietary fiber, 24 mg. sodium.

# SENSATIONAL SOY

## *Cooking with the Cholesterol-Crunching Superfood*

Here's some food for thought: The United States grows half of the world's supply of soy—and most of it ends up as chicken feed. That's too bad, really. Because as scientists are now discovering, soy foods have cholesterol-lowering properties that are indeed something to crow about.

Theories abound as to how soy works its heart-healthy magic. (For more information about what research has turned up so far, see Soy Foods on page 168.) But it's clear that folks who eat the most soy foods also have healthier cholesterol readings.

How can you get more of this superfood in your diet? Versatile products such as tofu, tempeh, miso and tamari make it easier than ever to enjoy soy. And these days, you can find them in most any supermarket—a testament to soy's growing popularity.

If you've never tried soy foods before—or if you've tried them but found them bland and boring—you're in for a real treat. The recipes in this chapter demonstrate just how well tofu, tempeh, soy and miso adapt to almost any dish. In fact, many of these selections are soy-based variations of traditional favorites, such as burgers, pot pie and chili. And if you've already made the switch to soy, these recipes will make wonderful additions to your repertoire.

Do keep in mind that while soy products have no cholesterol, they are moderately high in fat. About three ounces of firm tofu, for example, gets 54 percent of its calories from fat. Soy is still considered healthier than meats and dairy products because it has less saturated fat. Just be sure to use it wisely.

# Tofu Trickery

What does tofu taste like? Whatever you want it to. By itself, this soy product has a fairly indistinguishable flavor. But sauté it in chicken broth, and presto! It tastes just like chicken. Puree it with chives, and it becomes a sour cream–like topping for a baked potato. Or marinate it in a blend of vegetable stock and herbs, and it's an "imposter" cheese that works superbly in lasagna.

The recipes here make the most of tofu's conformist nature, combining it with an assortment of ingredients. Notice how its flavor changes from one dish to the next. Substituting light tofu for regular tofu will reduce the grams of fat in each serving without affecting the taste. Just be sure that the quantity and "firmness" of the tofu remain the same.

## Vegetarian Burritos

*These burritos make for a great Mexican meal. Make sure you plan ahead to allow the tofu to freeze solid and then thaw, which takes about five to six hours.*

1   pound tofu, frozen and thawed
2   cups Mexican salsa
8   flour tortillas, warmed
1   cup shredded nonfat soy mozzarella cheese
2   cups Refried Mexican Beans (page 370), warmed
1   cup shredded lettuce
½   cup chopped tomatoes

Squeeze the tofu to remove all excess moisture. Place in a small bowl and mash with a fork. Stir in 1 cup of the salsa. Let marinate at room temperature for 30 minutes.

To assemble the burritos, place a large spoonful of the tofu on each tortilla. Top with the cheese, beans, lettuce and tomatoes. Serve with the remaining salsa.

*Serves 8.*

---

Per serving: 359 calories, 11.3 g. total fat, 1.6 g. saturated fat, 0 mg. cholesterol, 7.4 g. dietary fiber, 743 mg. sodium.

---

## Better Than Sour Cream

*If you think no-cholesterol cooking means giving up the creamy taste and texture of dairy sour cream, here's a pleasant surprise. This sour cream substitute makes a healthy topping for baked potatoes and other side dishes as well as a perfect base for dips.*

    4  ounces soft tofu, crumbled
    1  teaspoon chopped chives
    1  teaspoon lemon juice

In a blender or food processor, combine the tofu, chives and lemon juice. Puree until smooth. Transfer to a jar, cover tightly and store in the refrigerator.

*MAKES ½ CUP.*

PER 2 TABLESPOONS: 19 CALORIES, 1.0 G. TOTAL FAT, 0.2 G. SATURATED FAT, 0 MG. CHOLESTEROL, 0.1 G. DIETARY FIBER, 8 MG. SODIUM.

## Charlie's Favorite Peanut Butter and Banana Sandwiches

*The pureed tofu in this recipe makes the peanut butter go farther with fewer calories.*

    1  pound soft tofu
    ⅔  cup reduced-fat chunky peanut butter
    2  tablespoons lemon juice
    1  tablespoon honey
    4  slices Oatmeal-Raisin Bread (page 404)
    ½  cup sliced bananas
    ¼  cup raisins

In a blender or food processor, puree the tofu, peanut butter, lemon juice and honey until smooth. Spread thickly on each slice of bread. Top with the bananas and raisins. Serve open-faced.

*SERVES 4.*

PER SERVING: 571 CALORIES, 22.5 G. TOTAL FAT, 4.3 G. SATURATED FAT, 0 MG. CHOLESTEROL, 6.9 G. DIETARY FIBER, 101 MG. SODIUM.

# Vegetarian Golden Potpie

*Though onions, carrots and peas are specified for this satisfying potpie, you can use whatever vegetables you have on hand.*

### Potpie

½   cup whole-wheat pastry flour
2   tablespoons nutritional yeast
2   teaspoons herbal salt substitute
½   teaspoon garlic powder
1   pound firm tofu, cut into 1″ cubes
1   teaspoon olive oil
½   cup water
1   onion, thinly sliced
1   carrot, thinly sliced
1   cup fresh peas
2   teaspoons minced garlic
2   tablespoons low-sodium soy sauce or tamari

### Gravy

⅓–½   cup nutritional yeast
¼   cup whole-wheat pastry flour
1   tablespoon safflower oil
1½   cups water
2   teaspoons low-sodium soy sauce or tamari
¾   teaspoon herbal salt substitute
¼   teaspoon ground pepper

*To make the potpie:* In a paper bag, combine the flour, yeast, salt substitute and garlic powder. Add the tofu and shake well to coat the pieces.

In a large frying pan over medium heat, heat the oil. Add the tofu and lightly brown on all sides, about 10 minutes. Transfer to a 1-quart casserole dish.

Add the water and onions to the pan. Sauté over medium heat until the onions are soft but not browned, about 5 minutes.

Add the carrots. Cover and cook for 5 minutes, or until tender. Add the peas and cook for 1 minute. Add the garlic and cook for 1 minute. Stir in the soy sauce or tamari.

Transfer the vegetables to the casserole and stir to combine with the tofu.

Preheat the oven to 350°.

*To make the gravy:* Wash and dry the frying pan. Add the yeast and flour. Stir over low heat for 3 minutes, or until fragrant. Add the oil and whisk until the mixture is smooth.

Stir in the water, soy sauce or tamari, salt substitute and pepper. Raise the heat to medium-high and whisk until the gravy thickens, about 2 to 3 minutes. Pour over the tofu and vegetables. Bake for 15 to 20 minutes or until bubbling.

*SERVES 6.*

PER SERVING: 265 CALORIES, 10.1 G. TOTAL FAT, 1.3 G. SATURATED FAT, 0 MG. CHOLESTEROL, 7.6 G. DIETARY FIBER, 266 MG. SODIUM.

## Meatless Tomato Sauce

*Use this versatile sauce over cooked pasta, lasagna and stuffed shells.*

|   |   |
|---|---|
| 2 | cloves garlic, minced |
| ⅓ | cup nonalcoholic red wine |
| 1 | teaspoon olive oil |
| 1 | cup minced onions |
| 1 | cup chopped mushrooms |
| 8 | ounces tofu, frozen and thawed |
| 2 | cups chopped Italian tomatoes |
| 2 | tablespoons tomato paste |
| 1 | tablespoon minced fresh basil |
| ½ | teaspoon dried oregano |

In a 2- or 3-quart saucepan over medium-high heat, sauté the garlic in the wine and oil for 2 minutes. Add the onions and mushrooms; sauté for 2 minutes.

Squeeze the tofu to remove excess moisture. Crumble and add to the pan. Cook for 5 to 8 minutes, stirring frequently. Add the tomatoes, tomato paste, basil and oregano. Reduce the heat and simmer for 20 minutes.

*SERVES 4.*

PER SERVING: 107 CALORIES, 4.5 G. TOTAL FAT, 0.6 G. SATURATED FAT, 0 MG. CHOLESTEROL, 2.6 G. DIETARY FIBER, 94 MG. SODIUM.

## Chinese Supper Stir-Fry

*Chunks of marinated firm tofu are stir-fried with bok choy, sweet potatoes and other vegetables to make this colorful supper dish.*

| | |
|---|---|
| 1 | tablespoon low-sodium soy sauce or tamari |
| 2 | teaspoons dark sesame oil |
| 1 | teaspoon grated fresh ginger |
| 6 | ounces firm tofu, cut into ½″ cubes |
| 1 | tablespoon safflower oil |
| ¼ | cup apple juice |
| 1 | cup thinly sliced scallions |
| ½ | cup cubed sweet potatoes |
| 3 | small beets, julienned |
| 1 | zucchini, thinly sliced |
| 4 | stalks bok choy, thinly sliced |
| 2 | cups mung bean sprouts |
| 2 | cups cooked brown rice |
| | Herbal salt substitute (to taste) |
| | Ground red pepper (to taste) |

In a small bowl, combine the soy sauce or tamari, sesame oil and ginger. Add the tofu and stir to combine. Let marinate, stirring occasionally, for 20 minutes.

In a wok or large frying pan over medium-high heat, heat the safflower oil and apple juice. Add the scallions and stir-fry for 1 minute. Add the sweet potatoes and beets; stir-fry for 3 minutes. Add the zucchini and bok choy; stir-fry for 5 minutes, or until the sweet potatoes are tender.

Add the tofu (with marinade), sprouts and rice. Stir-fry for 5 minutes. Season to taste with the salt substitute and pepper.

*Serves 4.*

---

Per serving: 340 calories, 10.8 g. total fat, 1.4 g. saturated fat, 0 mg. cholesterol, 7.8 g. dietary fiber, 219 mg. sodium.

---

# San Francisco Japantown Salad Spread

*Hijiki, a curly brown sea vegetable that looks like palm fronds underwater, is the secret seasoning in this salad. Look for it in health food stores.*

½ cup dried hijiki
16 ounces firm tofu
2 stalks celery, thinly sliced
2 carrots, shredded
6 scallions, thinly sliced
⅓ cup chopped fresh parsley
3 tablespoons nutritional yeast
2 tablespoons dark sesame oil
2 tablespoons low-sodium soy sauce or tamari
1 tablespoon lemon juice
2 cloves garlic, minced
¼ teaspoon dried dill
½ teaspoon paprika

Place the hijiki in a small bowl with water to cover. Let soak for 10 minutes. Drain well. Dry the hijiki between paper towels, then chop coarsely. Place in a large bowl.

Crumble the tofu into the bowl. Using a potato masher, mash together the hijiki and tofu. Add the celery, carrots, scallions, parsley and nutritional yeast.

In a small bowl, whisk together the oil, soy sauce or tamari, lemon juice, garlic, dill and paprika. Pour over the salad and toss well.

*SERVES 4.*

PER SERVING: 282 CALORIES, 16.9 G. TOTAL FAT, 2.4 G. SATURATED FAT, 0 MG. CHOLESTEROL, 6.2 G. DIETARY FIBER, 360 MG. SODIUM.

# Stuffed Mushrooms

*This recipe is a great alternative to veal- or beef-stuffed mushrooms. If you have leftover filling, you can freeze it for later use in casserole loaves, croquettes or stuffed bell peppers.*

  4  ounces tofu, frozen and thawed
12  large mushrooms
¼  cup minced onions
½  cup fine whole-wheat bread crumbs
  2  tablespoons apple juice
  1  tablespoon low-sodium soy sauce or tamari
     Pinch of dried marjoram

Squeeze the tofu to remove excess moisture. Crumble and set aside.

Preheat the broiler.

Twist or wiggle the mushroom stems to separate them from the caps. Mince the stems and set aside. Place the caps, open side down, on an ungreased baking sheet and broil for 1 minute. Remove from the oven and let cool.

Coat a large frying pan with no-stick spray. Add the onions and minced mushrooms and sauté over medium-high heat, stirring frequently, for 3 minutes. Add the bread crumbs and stir well. Cook for 2 minutes, or until lightly browned.

Add the tofu and apple juice to the pan. Cook for 1 minute, then remove from the heat.

Stir in the soy sauce or tamari and the marjoram. Mound the mixture in the mushroom caps. Broil for 1 to 2 minutes, or until lightly browned.

*SERVES 6.*

PER SERVING: 31 CALORIES, 0.8 G. TOTAL FAT, 0.1 G. SATURATED FAT, 0 MG. CHOLESTEROL, 0.2 G. DIETARY FIBER, 113 MG. SODIUM.

# Anaheim-Chili Casserole

*Another example of tofu's versatility, this delicious casserole can be made ahead and refrigerated for two days before reheating and serving.*

    1   cup finely chopped Anaheim chili peppers
    1½  cups tomato sauce
    14  ounces low-salt corn chips, broken into crumbs
    1   pound firm tofu, mashed
    1½  cups shredded low-fat soy cheese
    ½   cup sliced scallions
    ½   cup sliced black olives
    1   large bunch fresh cilantro, chopped

Preheat the oven to 350°.

In a 9″ × 13″ baking dish, spread half of the peppers. Top with half of the sauce, half of the chips and half of the tofu. Sprinkle with ¾ cup of the cheese. Top with half of the scallions, half of the olives and half of the cilantro.

Repeat to make a second set of layers. Sprinkle with the remaining cheese. Cover the casserole with foil. Bake for 30 minutes. Remove the foil and bake until the top is brown, about 15 minutes.

*SERVES 6.*

---

PER SERVING: 577 CALORIES, 31.2 G. TOTAL FAT, 1.9 G. SATURATED FAT, 0 MG. CHOLESTEROL, 3.5 G. DIETARY FIBER, 970 MG. SODIUM.

## Vegetable Breakfast Scramble

*In this recipe the crumbled tofu takes on a golden color—much like eggs—when it is mixed with the turmeric and other spices. Serve this scrambled-egg look-alike with a toasted slice of homemade Oatmeal-Raisin Bread (page 404).*

¼  cup hot water
1  tablespoon miso
1  tablespoon low-sodium soy sauce or tamari
¼  teaspoon turmeric powder
¼  teaspoon dried basil
¼  teaspoon dried dill
1  sweet red pepper, diced
6  large mushrooms, thinly sliced
1  small onion, minced
2  teaspoons safflower oil
¼  cup apple juice
8  ounces firm tofu

In a small bowl, combine the water, miso, soy sauce or tamari, turmeric, basil and dill. Set aside.

In a large frying pan over medium-high heat, sauté the peppers, mushrooms and onions in the oil and apple juice, stirring frequently, for 10 minutes, or until the onions soften.

Crumble the tofu into small chunks and add to the pan. Cook, stirring frequently, for 5 minutes.

Pour the liquid mixture over the tofu and sauté for 2 minutes.

*SERVES 2.*

---

PER SERVING: 300 CALORIES, 15.5 G. TOTAL FAT, 2.0 G. SATURATED FAT, 0 MG. CHOLESTEROL, 4.5 G. DIETARY FIBER, 596 MG. SODIUM.

# Baked Marinated Cutlets

*Here's a great no-cholesterol recipe for the meat-lovers in your family. Firm tofu is sliced into thin cutlets and marinated in a soy-ginger sauce before being baked to a veal-like consistency.*

  1 pound firm tofu
  3 tablespoons low-sodium soy sauce or tamari
  1 tablespoon dark sesame oil
  1 tablespoon grated fresh ginger
  1 cup thinly sliced onions
  2 cups thinly sliced mushrooms

Cut the tofu into cutlets about ⅓″ thick and 3″ square.

In a large shallow pan, combine the tofu, soy sauce or tamari, oil and ginger. Let marinate at room temperature for 2 hours, turning the slices occasionally.

Preheat the oven to 375°.

Lightly oil a large baking sheet. Place the tofu pieces on the sheet and bake for 15 minutes, flipping the pieces after 7 minutes. If desired, brush the pieces with leftover marinade once or twice as they bake.

While the tofu is baking, coat a large frying pan with no-stick spray. Add the onions and mushrooms and sauté over medium-high heat until the mushrooms exude moisture, about 15 minutes. Serve hot over the tofu.

*SERVES 4.*

---

PER SERVING: 227 CALORIES, 13.5 G. TOTAL FAT, 1.9 G. SATURATED FAT, 0 MG. CHOLESTEROL, 2.5 G. DIETARY FIBER, 415 MG. SODIUM.

# Vegetarian Sweet-and-Sour Tofu

*Chunks of firm tofu are paired with bell peppers, pineapple and onions in a sweet-and-sour sauce that tastes like it's right off the menu of your favorite Chinese restaurant.*

| | |
|---|---|
| 1 | cup diced green peppers |
| 1 | cup diced sweet red peppers |
| 2 | tablespoons safflower oil |
| 2 | tablespoons arrowroot powder |
| ¼ | cup low-sodium soy sauce or tamari |
| ½ | cup apple cider vinegar |
| ½ | cup pineapple juice |
| ½ | cup lemon juice |
| ¼–½ | cup honey |
| ½ | teaspoon herbal salt substitute |
| ½ | teaspoon grated fresh ginger |
| 8 | ounces firm tofu, cut into 1″ cubes |
| ½ | cup pineapple chunks |
| 4 | cups hot cooked basmati rice |

In a large frying pan over medium-high heat, sauté the green and red peppers in the oil for 10 minutes, stirring frequently to prevent browning.

In a large bowl, dissolve the arrowroot in the soy sauce or tamari. Add the vinegar, pineapple juice, lemon juice, honey, salt substitute and ginger.

Add the liquids to the pan and bring to a boil. Simmer until the sauce thickens, about 8 to 10 minutes. Add the tofu and pineapple. Heat through. Serve over the rice.

*Serves 4.*

---

Per serving: 501 calories, 13.5 g. total fat, 1.4 g. saturated fat, 0 mg. cholesterol, 3.3 g. dietary fiber, 580 mg. sodium.

# Mock Tuna Salad

*In this recipe tofu turns into tuna with the help of subtle seasonings that fool the palate with a mock fish flavor. Serve this salad on crackers or bread.*

14   ounces firm tofu
½   cup low-fat, cholesterol-free mayonnaise
½   cup chopped celery
⅓   cup nutritional yeast
1   scallion, chopped
1   tablespoon lemon juice
1   tablespoon low-sodium soy sauce or tamari
1   teaspoon herbal salt substitute
½   teaspoon minced garlic

Crumble the tofu into a colander placed over a bowl. Let drain for 15 minutes. Transfer the tofu to a large bowl.

Add the mayonnaise, celery, yeast, scallions, lemon juice, soy sauce or tamari, salt substitute and garlic. Mix well. Chill for 1 hour.

*Serves 4.*

Per serving: 265 calories, 16.7 g. total fat, 3.3 g. saturated fat, 0 mg. cholesterol, 4.9 g. dietary fiber, 393 mg. sodium.

# Dairyless Spinach Tarts

*Who says you have to give up quiche on a no-cholesterol diet? This savory version is made with creamy tofu, spinach and spices. Enjoy it warm or cold with a green salad.*

1    Light and Flaky No-Cholesterol Piecrust (page 426), unbaked
1    cup thinly sliced onions
3    cups chopped spinach
2    cups thinly sliced mushrooms
2    cloves garlic, minced
3    cups firm tofu, mashed or pureed
½    cup chopped fresh parsley
2    tablespoons dried dill
2    tablespoons low-sodium soy sauce or tamari

Preheat the oven to 350°.

Bake the crust for 10 minutes. Remove from the oven and let cool for 10 minutes. Keep the oven hot.

While the crust is baking, coat a large frying pan with no-stick spray. Add the onions and sauté over medium-high heat for 10 minutes, stirring frequently to prevent browning.

Lower the heat to medium, then add the spinach, mushrooms and garlic. Sauté for 10 minutes, stirring frequently, until the mushrooms exude moisture. Add the tofu, parsley, dill and soy sauce or tamari. Remove from the heat and pour into the baked pie shell.

Bake for 30 minutes, or until the top is browned.

*Serves 6.*

---

Per serving: 374 calories, 20.8 g. total fat, 2.6 g. saturated fat, 0 mg. cholesterol, 5.8 g. dietary fiber, 233 mg. sodium.

---

## Tasty Tempeh-tations

Tofu may be the best-known soy food in this country, but tempeh is quietly building its own legion of devotees. One reason is that it's an excellent source of vitamin $B_{12}$—great news for folks whose diets may run low in this nutrient, especially those who've given up meat and other $B_{12}$-rich animal products. Tempeh is perfect for delicious meatless meals, as these recipes demonstrate.

 **Barbecued Vegetarian Burgers**

*Tempeh is slowly baked in a zesty homemade barbecue sauce, piled on whole-wheat buns and topped with all the traditional hamburger trimmings.*

      16  ounces soy tempeh
       2  cups fat-free Russian dressing
       1  cup medium-hot Mexican salsa
       8  whole-wheat hamburger buns
          Lettuce
          Sprouts
          Red onion rings

Preheat the oven to 200°.

Cut the tempeh into 8 equal pieces. Cover a large baking sheet with aluminum foil and add the tempeh in a single layer.

In a small bowl, combine the dressing and salsa. Spread half of the sauce liberally over the tempeh.

Bake for 30 minutes. Flip the pieces, spread with the remaining sauce and bake for 30 minutes, or until the sauce thickens and sticks to the tempeh.

Warm the buns in the oven for 5 minutes. Fill each with a piece of the tempeh. Top with the lettuce, sprouts and onions.

*Serves 8.*

Per serving: 271 calories, 6.9 g. total fat, 1.2 g. saturated fat, 0 mg. cholesterol, 0.5 g. dietary fiber, 944 mg. sodium.

# French Mushroom Salad with Tempeh

*Steamed tempeh is thinly sliced and then marinated in a mustardy French vinaigrette dressing. This salad makes an elegant light meal or a high-protein side dish.*

8   ounces soy tempeh
1   teaspoon olive oil
2   cups chopped romaine lettuce
1   cup thinly sliced mushrooms
½   cup diagonally sliced green beans
½   cup thinly sliced cucumbers
2   tablespoons safflower oil
¼   cup + 2 tablespoons tomato juice
¼   cup lemon juice
1   teaspoon Dijon mustard
½   teaspoon herbal salt substitute

Steam the tempeh over boiling water for 20 minutes. Let cool, then slice into ½″ cubes.

Coat a large frying pan with no-stick spray. Add the tempeh and olive oil and sauté, turning once, for 5 minutes, or until lightly browned. Set aside.

Place the lettuce on a large platter or in a salad bowl. Top with the tempeh, mushrooms, beans and cucumbers.

In a small bowl, combine the safflower oil, tomato juice, lemon juice, mustard and salt substitute. Pour over the salad and let marinate at room temperature for 30 minutes. Toss well before serving.

*Serves 4.*

---

Per serving: 208 calories, 12.6 g. total fat, 1.5 g. saturated fat, 0 mg. cholesterol, 1.2 g. dietary fiber, 105 mg. sodium.

---

# Spicy Indonesian Cutlets with Peanut Sauce

*An authentic Indonesian recipe, perfect for friends and family members who love spicy food.*

### Cutlets

| | |
|---|---|
| 8 | ounces soy tempeh, cut into 3″ squares |
| ¾ | cup water |
| 2 | tablespoons low-sodium soy sauce or tamari |
| 2 | tablespoons grated fresh ginger |
| 1 | tablespoon minced fresh cilantro |
| 1 | teaspoon minced garlic |
| ¼ | teaspoon ground red pepper |
| ½ | cup coarse cornmeal |
| ½ | cup whole-wheat pastry flour |
| 1 | teaspoon dried basil |
| ½ | teaspoon dried oregano |
| ¼ | teaspoon curry powder |

### Peanut Sauce

| | |
|---|---|
| 2 | tablespoons reduced-fat peanut butter |
| 2 | tablespoons water |
| 3 | tablespoons low-sodium soy sauce or tamari |
| 1 | tablespoon rice-wine vinegar |
| 1 | tablespoon honey |
| 1 | teaspoon ground cumin |
| 1 | teaspoon ground coriander |

*To make the cutlets:* In a large shallow baking dish, combine the tempeh, water, soy sauce or tamari, ginger, cilantro, garlic and pepper. Let marinate at room temperature for 1 hour, turning frequently. Remove from the marinade with a slotted spoon.

In a small bowl or flat plate, combine the cornmeal, flour, basil, oregano and curry powder. Dredge the tempeh in the mixture, coating well.

Coat a large frying pan with no-stick spray. Add the tempeh and fry over medium-high heat for 5 to 10 minutes, turning once, until golden brown. Transfer to a platter and keep warm.

*To make the peanut sauce:* In a 1-quart saucepan, whisk together the peanut butter, water, soy sauce or tamari, vinegar, honey, cumin and coriander. Heat through. Pour over the tempeh and serve hot.

*Serves 4.*

PER SERVING: 305 CALORIES, 8.4 G. TOTAL FAT, 1.4 G. SATURATED FAT, 0 MG. CHOLESTEROL, 4.6 G. DIETARY FIBER, 677 MG. SODIUM.

## Dilled Party Spread

*This spread tastes just like a deli salad and is delicious as a sandwich filling. Or serve it on whole-grain crackers or with raw vegetable sticks.*

6–8  ounces soy tempeh, cut into ½″ cubes
1  teaspoon safflower oil
2  tablespoons low-sodium soy sauce or tamari
¼  cup minced celery
¼  cup chopped black olives (optional)
3  tablespoons nonfat, cholesterol-free mayonnaise
2  tablespoons minced fresh parsley
1  tablespoon minced scallions
½  teaspoon minced fresh dill
Pinch of ground red pepper

Steam the tempeh over boiling water for 15 minutes. Drain.

In a large frying pan, sauté the tempeh in the oil for 3 minutes, or until lightly browned. Remove the pan from the heat. Add the soy sauce or tamari, stir to coat the tempeh, then mash with a fork. Transfer to a large bowl.

Add the celery, olives (if using), mayonnaise, parsley, scallions, dill and pepper.

*Serves 4.*

PER SERVING: 111 CALORIES, 4.4 G. TOTAL FAT, 0.6 G. SATURATED FAT, 0 MG. CHOLESTEROL, 0.1 G. DIETARY FIBER, 417 MG. SODIUM.

**Onions Stuffed with Tempeh, Tomatoes and Peppers**

*These sweet onions are filled with a spicy mixture and then baked, creating a delicious blend of flavors.*

  4  large sweet onions, such as Vidalia
  2  teaspoons olive oil
  6  ounces crumbled soy tempeh
  2  cups coarsely chopped Italian tomatoes
  ½  cup diced canned mild chili peppers
  ⅓  cup diced sweet red peppers
  ¼  cup raisins
  2  tablespoons tomato paste
  2  cloves garlic, minced
  1  tablespoon apple cider vinegar
  1  teaspoon herbal salt substitute
  1  teaspoon ground black pepper
  ¼  teaspoon ground cinnamon
  ⅛  teaspoon ground cloves
  2  cups Garlic Broth (page 316)
  ¼  cup minced fresh parsley

With a melon baller, scoop the centers out of the onions, leaving a sturdy shell about ½" thick. Chop enough of the centers to equal 1 cup. Set aside.

Steam the shells over boiling water for 5 minutes. Drain and set aside.

Preheat the oven to 350°. Lightly oil a 9" × 13" baking dish. Place the shells in the dish, hollow sides up.

In a large frying pan over medium-high heat, sauté the chopped onions in the oil for 5 minutes, stirring frequently to prevent browning. Add the tempeh, tomatoes, chili peppers, red peppers, raisins, tomato paste and garlic. Lower the heat to medium and cook, stirring often, for 15 minutes.

Add the vinegar, salt substitute, black pepper, cinnamon and cloves. Cook for 5 to 10 minutes, or until most of the liquid has cooked away.

Spoon the filling into the reserved shells. Add the broth to the dish. Cover with foil and bake for 1 hour, or until the onions are very tender. Sprinkle with the parsley before serving.

*Serves 4.*

---

PER SERVING: 244 CALORIES, 6.4 G. TOTAL FAT, 0.9 G. SATURATED FAT, 0 MG. CHOLESTEROL, 5.7 G. DIETARY FIBER, 288 MG. SODIUM.

---

 ## Wheat Berry and Tempeh Salad with Curry Dressing

*Serve this exotic salad as a side dish to a Thai or Viet-namese entrée. You can buy wheat berries in health food stores; cook them like brown rice.*

- 6 ounces 5-grain tempeh, cut into thin strips
- 2 cups cooked wheat berries
- ½ cup halved cherry tomatoes
- ⅓ cup thinly sliced radishes
- ⅓ cup diagonally sliced green beans
- ½ cup thinly sliced cucumbers
- ⅓ cup low-fat, cholesterol-free mayonnaise
- 3 tablespoons minced fresh parsley
- 2 tablespoons minced onions or shallots
- 1 teaspoon curry powder
- 2 tablespoons lemon juice
- ¼ teaspoon salt
- ½ teaspoon ground black pepper

Steam the tempeh over boiling water for 15 minutes. Drain and place in a large bowl.

Add the wheat berries, tomatoes, radishes, beans, cucumbers, mayonnaise, parsley, onions or shallots, curry powder, lemon juice, salt and pepper. Toss well and let marinate at room temperature for 20 minutes before serving.

*Serves 4.*

---

PER SERVING: 228 CALORIES, 8.1 G. TOTAL FAT, 1.7 G. SATURATED FAT, 0 MG. CHOLESTEROL, 6.7 G. DIETARY FIBER, 293 MG. SODIUM.

---

# Rancho Bernadino Salad with Green Sauce

*A savory parsley sauce enhances slices of steamed tempeh and fresh vegetables in this salad.*

|   |   |
|---|---|
| 8 | ounces soy tempeh |
| 2 | scallions, thinly sliced |
| 3 | cups chopped spinach |
| 1 | cup thinly sliced cucumbers |
| 1 | cup alfalfa sprouts |
| 1 | cup chopped romaine lettuce |
| ½ | cup sliced celery |
| ¼ | cup minced fresh parsley |
| 2 | tablespoons olive oil |
| 1 | tablespoon rice-wine vinegar |
| 1 | tablespoon curry powder |
| 2–3 | teaspoons herbal salt substitute |
| 2 | teaspoons low-sodium soy sauce or tamari |

Steam the tempeh over boiling water for 20 minutes. Let cool, then slice into ½″ cubes.

Coat a large frying pan with no-stick spray. Add the tempeh and sauté for 10 minutes, turning the pieces once.

Add the scallions and cook for 2 minutes. Transfer to a large bowl. Add the spinach, cucumbers, sprouts, lettuce and celery.

In a blender or food processor, puree the parsley, olive oil, vinegar, curry powder, salt substitute and soy sauce or tamari. Pour over the salad and toss well. Let marinate for 1 hour at room temperature.

*Serves 6.*

PER SERVING: 135 CALORIES, 7.8 G. TOTAL FAT, 1.1 G. SATURATED FAT, 0 MG. CHOLESTEROL, 1.5 G. DIETARY FIBER, 97 MG. SODIUM.

# California Tempeh Spread

*With much less fat and none of the cholesterol of traditional pâté, this tasty spread is wonderful on crackers or vegetable spears or as a sandwich filling.*

4 ounces soy tempeh
¼ cup apple juice
2 tablespoons safflower oil
2 cups chopped mushrooms
1 cup minced onions
⅓ cup coarsely chopped almonds
½ cup bread crumbs
2 cloves garlic, minced
2 tablespoons herbal salt substitute
1 tablespoon low-sodium soy sauce or tamari
¼ teaspoon dried thyme
⅛ teaspoon dried sage

Steam the tempeh over boiling water for 20 minutes. Let cool, then slice into ½″ cubes.

In a large frying pan over medium-high heat, sauté the tempeh in the apple juice and oil for 10 minutes, stirring frequently.

Add the mushrooms, onions, almonds, bread crumbs and garlic. Sauté, stirring, for 15 minutes, or until the onions soften. Add the salt substitute, soy sauce or tamari, thyme and sage.

Transfer the mixture to a food processor. Blend with on/off turns to a thick pastelike consistency.

*SERVES 8.*

PER SERVING: 137 CALORIES, 7.8 G. TOTAL FAT, 0.8 G. SATURATED FAT, 0 MG. CHOLESTEROL, 1.1 G. DIETARY FIBER, 133 MG. SODIUM.

# Meatless Chili with Corn Chips

*Crumbled tempeh tastes just like ground beef in this mildly spicy chili. To turn up the heat, increase the quantities of jalapeño peppers and chili powder.*

1    cup dried kidney beans
8    ounces soy tempeh, crumbled
½    cup nonalcoholic red wine
½    cup low-sodium soy sauce or tamari
1    teaspoon ground cumin
1    teaspoon dried basil
1    teaspoon chili powder
1    cup coarsely chopped onions
¼    cup apple juice
2    tablespoons olive oil
2    cups sliced mushrooms
8    tomatoes, coarsely chopped
1    cup minced green peppers
1    cup minced carrots
1    cup minced celery
½    cup minced canned mild chili peppers
2    tablespoons minced jalapeño peppers
4    cloves garlic, minced
4    cups Vegetable Stock (page 316)
3    tablespoons tomato paste
     Herbal salt substitute (to taste)
2    cups crushed corn chips

Soak the beans in cold water to cover for 8 hours or overnight. Drain and set aside.

In a large bowl, combine the tempeh, wine, soy sauce or tamari, cumin, basil and chili powder. Let marinate at room temperature for 2 hours.

Meanwhile, in a 4- to 6-quart pot over medium-high heat, sauté the onions in the apple juice and oil for 10 minutes, stirring to prevent browning. Add the mushrooms and cook for 10 minutes, or until the mushrooms exude moisture.

Add the tomatoes, green peppers, carrots, celery, chili peppers, jalapeño peppers and garlic. Sauté, stirring frequently, for 5 minutes.

Add the beans, stock and tomato paste. Bring to a boil, cover and lower the heat. Simmer for 2 to 3 hours, or until the beans are tender and the chili is thick.

Add the tempeh and its marinade. Cook for 10 minutes. Season with the salt substitute. Serve garnished with the corn chips.

*SERVES 10.*

PER SERVING: 196 CALORIES, 5.3 G. TOTAL FAT, 0.7 G. SATURATED FAT, 0 MG. CHOLESTEROL, 3.2 G. DIETARY FIBER, 607 MG. SODIUM.

# FRESH FROM THE OVEN

## *Serve Up Good Health by the Slice*

Before the invention of bread machines, and before super-markets stocked entire aisles with loaves of all shapes and sizes, people often made their bread from scratch. It's practically a lost art nowadays. But not so long ago, Sunday dinner didn't seem complete unless there was a fresh homemade loaf to pass around the table.

Perhaps it's time to revive the tradition. To be sure, bread has a lot going for it, nutrition-wise. Whole-grain varieties in particular are superior sources of fiber, a proven cholesterol-buster. And new dietary guidelines from the U.S. Department of Agriculture recommend that we eat at least six servings of bread and other grain products every day for optimum health. (For more on the government's new nutrition standards, see The Main Event on page 337.)

But why bake your own? Well . . . there's just something about the taste, texture and aroma of a homemade loaf that makes it so much more satisfying than its store-bought counterpart. And because you prepare the dough yourself, you know that it has nothing but the freshest ingredients and is 100 percent preservative-free.

In this chapter you'll find recipes for more than 20 no-cholesterol breads and bread products, including English muffins, focaccia and sticky buns. For yeast breads, you'll need to allow at least 1½ hours to give the dough time to rise. There's also a selection of quick breads, yeastless loaves that require less time to prepare.

No matter which recipe you choose—and you're guaranteed to find several favorites—just remember not to slather slices of bread with fat-laden butter before you eat them. Opt for healthier spreads, such as jams, jellies and preserves. Or better yet, leave bread plain, so you can taste all of that homemade goodness.

## Bread and Breakfast

Folks who bypass breakfast may save a few minutes in the morning, but they also lose out on a lot of important nutrients. One study showed that people who eat breakfast get 40 percent more fiber, 38 percent more vitamin E and 50 percent more vitamin C—all proven cholesterol fighters—over the course of a day than people who skip breakfast.

These breads are perfect portable breakfasts: Just grab a slice and go. They taste great toasted, too.

### Walnut Poteca

*Take a slice of this bread with you to enjoy during your mid-morning coffee break or while you're running errands.*

      2   cups warm water (98°–110°)
      ½   cup honey
      1   tablespoon active dry yeast
    5–6   cups unbleached or whole-wheat pastry flour
      2   tablespoons safflower oil
     1½   cups date sugar
      1   cup ground walnuts
      ½   cup raisins
      ¼   cup maple syrup

In a large bowl, combine the water, honey and yeast. Let stand in a warm place until the mixture foams, about 10 minutes. Stir in 2 cups of the flour, mixing well with a wooden spoon. Let this batter rise in a warm place for 30 minutes. Stir in the oil and enough of the remaining flour to form a kneadable dough.

Turn onto a lightly floured surface and knead for 5 to 8 minutes, or until the dough becomes elastic and less sticky. Place in a clean, lightly oiled bowl. Cover and let rise in a warm, draft-free place for 1 hour. Punch down and let rise again for 30 minutes.

*(continued)*

While the dough is rising, in a medium bowl combine the date sugar, walnuts and raisins.

Lightly oil a large baking sheet.

Roll the dough into a large rectangle, about 8″ × 12″.

In a 1-quart saucepan, warm the maple syrup for 1 to 2 minutes. Brush it over the dough. Sprinkle with the walnut mixture, leaving a scant ½″ border all the way around. Roll up, starting with a short edge; the finished roll will measure about 8″ long × 3″ wide. Place, seam side down, on the baking sheet. With a sharp knife, cut 3 diagonal slits about ¼″ deep in the top of the roll for steam to escape. Let rise for 10 minutes.

Preheat the oven to 375°.

Bake the roll for 30 to 45 minutes, or until golden. Cut into slices and serve warm.

*Makes 1 roll; 16 slices.*

---

Per slice: 327 calories, 6.9 g. total fat, 0.6 g. saturated fat, 0 mg. cholesterol, 5.4 g. dietary fiber, 12 mg. sodium.

---

 ## Minnesota Christmas Stollen

*Of Scandinavian and German origin, this sweet torpedo-shaped loaf is studded with nuts and dried fruits. The cardamom-seed flavoring is the signature ingredient of traditional stollen.*

½   cup warm water (98°–110°)
¼   cup maple syrup
2   tablespoons active dry yeast
2   cups unbleached flour
1   cup chopped dried fruit (such as raisins, apricots, prunes or dates)
¼   cup finely chopped almonds
3   tablespoons safflower oil
1   tablespoon ground cardamom
1½  cups whole-wheat flour
2   tablespoons poppy seeds

In a large bowl, combine the water, maple syrup and yeast. Let stand in a warm place until the mixture foams, about 10 minutes. Stir in the unbleached flour, mixing well with a wooden spoon. Let this batter rise in a warm place for 30 minutes.

Stir in the fruit, almonds, oil and cardamom. Add enough of the whole-wheat flour to form a workable dough.

Turn the dough out onto a lightly floured surface and knead for 5 to 8 minutes, or until the dough becomes elastic and less sticky. Place in a clean, lightly oiled bowl. Cover and let rise in a warm, draft-free place for 1 hour. Punch down and let rise again for 30 minutes.

Preheat the oven to 350°.

Lightly oil a large baking sheet. Divide the dough in thirds. With your hands, roll each piece into a rope about 12" to 14" long. Place the ropes on the counter parallel to each other. Braid into a fat loaf. Pinch the ends together and tuck them under. Transfer the loaf to the baking sheet.

Lightly brush the top of the loaf with a little water. Sprinkle with the poppy seeds.

Bake for 45 minutes, or until the loaf is golden and sounds slightly hollow when tapped on the top. Let cool on a wire rack before slicing.

*MAKES 1 LARGE LOAF; ABOUT 10 SLICES.*

PER SLICE: 287 CALORIES, 7.3 G. TOTAL FAT, 0.8 G. SATURATED FAT, 0 MG. CHOLESTEROL, 4.3 G. DIETARY FIBER, 6 MG. SODIUM.

# English Muffins with Oat Bran

*Oat bran makes these muffins chewy and rich-tasting.*

| | |
|---|---|
| 1¼ | cups warm water (98°–110°) |
| 1 | tablespoon active dry yeast |
| 1 | tablespoon honey |
| 4–5 | cups unbleached or whole-wheat flour |
| 3 | tablespoons farina |
| 3 | tablespoons oat bran |
| 2 | tablespoons olive oil |
| 1 | tablespoons herbal salt substitute |
| ½ | cup coarse cornmeal |

In a large bowl, combine the water, yeast and honey. Let stand in a warm place until the mixture foams, about 10 minutes. Stir in 1 cup of the flour, mixing well with a wooden spoon. Let this batter rise in a warm place for 30 minutes. Stir in the farina, oat bran, oil, salt substitute and enough of the remaining flour to form a kneadable dough.

Turn onto a lightly floured surface and knead for 5 to 8 minutes, or until the dough becomes elastic and less sticky. Place in a clean, lightly oiled bowl. Cover and let rise in a warm, draft-free place for 1 hour. Punch down.

Halve the dough and roll out each half to ¼″ thickness on a lightly floured surface. Cut using a 3″ biscuit cutter. Lightly dredge each round in the cornmeal to coat both sides. Set the rounds on a piece of plastic and let rise for 30 minutes.

Heat a griddle or cast-iron skillet over medium-high heat until hot. Using a metal spatula, transfer several of the muffins to the pan and cook for 3 minutes on each side until lightly set and pale in color. Transfer to a wire rack. Repeat until all the muffins have received a preliminary cooking.

Again working in batches, return the muffins to the pan and cook for 5 minutes more on each side, or until they are golden brown on both sides and cooked through.

*Makes 14.*

---

PER MUFFIN: 182 CALORIES, 2.6 G. TOTAL FAT, 0.4 G. SATURATED FAT, 0 MG. CHOLESTEROL, 2.0 G. DIETARY FIBER, 4 MG. SODIUM.

# Almond-Chive Bread

*Almonds ground with water to a milky liquid take the place of milk in this recipe.*

1 tablespoon active dry yeast
1 tablespoon honey
1 cup warm water (98°–110°)
½ cup chopped almonds
1 cup whole-wheat pastry flour
2 cups unbleached flour
2 tablespoons minced fresh chives
1½ teaspoons herbal salt substitute

In a large bowl, combine the yeast, honey and ½ cup of the water. Let the bowl stand in a warm spot until the yeast mixture bubbles, about 10 minutes.

In a blender, combine the almonds and the remaining ½ cup water. Puree, then strain through a fine sieve. Add the liquid to the yeast mixture; reserve the solids.

Stir the pastry flour and ½ cup of the unbleached flour into the yeast mixture. Mix well with a wooden spoon. Let this batter rise in a warm place for 30 minutes.

Stir in the reserved almonds, chives, salt substitute and enough of the remaining flour to form a kneadable dough.

Turn onto a lightly floured surface and knead for 5 to 8 minutes, or until the dough becomes elastic and less sticky. Place in a clean, lightly oiled bowl. Cover and let rise in a warm, draft-free place for 1 hour. Punch down and let rise again for 30 minutes.

Preheat the oven to 350°.

Lightly oil a large baking sheet. Form a round loaf from the dough and place on the sheet. Bake for 45 to 60 minutes, or until the loaf and sounds slightly hollow when you tap it on the top. Transfer to a wire rack to cool.

*MAKES 1 LARGE LOAF; 15 SLICES.*

PER SLICE: 120 CALORIES, 2.6 G. TOTAL FAT, 0.3 G. SATURATED FAT, 0 MG. CHOLESTEROL, 2.0 G. DIETARY FIBER, 2 MG. SODIUM.

# Dark Rye with Molasses

*Topped with California Tempeh Spread (page 393), this bread makes especially good party fare.*

1½ cups warm water (98°–110°)
2 tablespoons molasses
2 tablespoons honey
1 tablespoon active dry yeast
3–4 cups whole-wheat flour
1½ cups dark rye flour
2 tablespoons minced garlic
2 tablespoons olive oil
1 tablespoon ground caraway
1 tablespoon dried sage

In a large bowl, combine the water, molasses, honey and yeast. Let stand in a warm place until the mixture foams, about 10 minutes.

Stir in 2 cups of the whole-wheat flour, mixing well with a wooden spoon. Let this batter rise in a warm place for 30 minutes. Stir in the rye flour, garlic, oil, caraway, sage and enough of the remaining whole-wheat flour to form a kneadable dough.

Turn onto a lightly floured surface and knead for 8 to 10 minutes, or until the dough becomes elastic and less sticky. Place in a clean, lightly oiled bowl. Cover and let rise in a warm, draft-free place for 1 hour.

Lightly oil a large baking sheet. Divide the dough into two equal balls and form each ball into a round. Let rise for 30 minutes.

Preheat the oven to 350°.

Bake the loaves for 45 to 60 minutes, or until they sound slightly hollow when you tap them on the top. Let cool before slicing.

*MAKES 2 LOAVES; ABOUT 20 VERY THIN SLICES.*

PER SLICE: 121 CALORIES, 2.0 G. TOTAL FAT, 0.3 G. SATURATED FAT, 0 MG. CHOLESTEROL, 2.7 G. DIETARY FIBER, 4 MG. SODIUM.

## Loaves That Liven Lunches

If comic-strip sandwich connoisseur Dagwood Bumstead could sample these delicious breads, he'd surely use them in his mile-high masterpieces. These breads go well with many different fixin's.

 ### Italian Tomato-Herb Bread

*Sun-dried tomatoes give these loaves a rosy color and, when paired with the olive oil, a distinct Mediterranean flavor.*

> 3   cups warm water (98°–110°)
> 2   tablespoons honey
> 1   tablespoon active dry yeast
> 6–7   cups whole-wheat flour
> ½   cup oil-packed sun-dried tomatoes, drained and diced
> ¼   cup olive oil
> 1   tablespoon tomato paste
> 2   teaspoons herbal salt substitute

In a large bowl, combine the water, honey and yeast. Let stand in a warm place until the mixture foams, about 10 minutes. Stir in 2 cups of the flour, mixing well with a wooden spoon. Let this batter rise in a warm place for 30 minutes.

Stir in the tomatoes, oil, tomato paste, salt substitute and enough flour to form a kneadable dough. On a lightly floured surface, knead for 5 to 8 minutes, until the dough is elastic and less sticky. Place in a lightly oiled bowl. Cover. Let rise in a warm place for 1 hour. Punch down and let rise again for 30 minutes.

Lightly oil 2 (9" × 5") loaf pans. Divide the dough in half, form each half into a loaf and place in the pans. Let rise for 20 minutes.

Preheat the oven to 375°.

Bake the loaves for 40 minutes, or until lightly browned. Turn out onto wire racks and let cool before slicing.

*Makes 2 loaves; about 20 slices.*

---

Per slice: 161 calories, 3.8 g. total fat, 0.5 g. saturated fat, 0 mg. cholesterol, 4.7 g. dietary fiber, 17 mg. sodium.

# Oatmeal-Raisin Bread

*The oatmeal in this recipe lends a wonderfully smooth texture to each bite of bread.*

|   |   |
|---|---|
| 1 | cup warm water (98°–110°) |
| ½ | cup molasses |
| 2 | tablespoons active dry yeast |
| 5–6 | cups whole-wheat flour |
| 2 | cups boiling water |
| 1 | cup rolled oats |
| 1 | cup raisins |
| ½ | teaspoon salt |
| ¼ | teaspoon grated fresh ginger |

In a large bowl, combine the warm water, molasses and yeast. Let stand in a warm place until the mixture foams, about 10 minutes. Stir in 2 cups of the flour, mixing well with a wooden spoon. Let this batter rise in a warm place for 30 minutes.

Meanwhile, in a small bowl, combine the boiling water and oats. Let stand until lukewarm, about 20 minutes.

Stir the oats into the yeast mixture. Add the raisins, salt and ginger. Stir in enough of the remaining flour to form a kneadable dough. Turn onto a lightly floured surface and knead for 5 to 8 minutes, or until the dough becomes elastic and less sticky. Place in a clean, lightly oiled bowl. Cover and let rise in a warm, draft-free place for 1 hour. Punch down and let rise again for 30 minutes.

Lightly oil 2 large baking sheets. Divide the dough in half. Form each half into a smooth ball. Place 1 ball in the center of each baking sheet. Let rise for 20 minutes.

Preheat the oven to 375°.

Bake the loaves for 40 to 45 minutes, or until the loaves sound hollow when tapped on the bottom.

*Makes 2 loaves; about 20 slices.*

Per slice: 160 calories, 0.9 g. total fat, 0.2 g. saturated fat, 0 mg. cholesterol, 4.7 g. dietary fiber, 64 mg. sodium.

# Alfalfa Sprout Bread

*Potatoes that are cooked and blended into a thick puree give this old-fashioned recipe a wonderfully light texture.*

|   |   |
|---|---|
| 2 | small baking potatoes, chopped |
| 4 | cups water |
| ¾ | cup honey |
| 2 | tablespoons active dry yeast |
| 8–10 | cups whole-wheat flour |
| 4 | cups alfalfa sprouts |
| ¼ | cup olive oil |
| ½ | teaspoon salt or 1½ tablespoons herbal salt substitute |

In a 2-quart saucepan over medium-high heat, cook the potatoes in the water until soft, about 10 to 15 minutes. Let cool for 5 minutes. Transfer the potatoes and water to a blender and puree.

Pour into a large bowl and let stand until lukewarm (98° to 110°). Add the honey and yeast. Let stand for 10 minutes.

Stir in 4 cups of the flour. Mix well, then let rise for 30 minutes. Stir in the sprouts, oil, salt or salt substitute, and enough of the remaining flour to form a kneadable dough. Turn onto a lightly floured surface and knead for 5 to 8 minutes, or until the dough becomes elastic and less sticky.

Place in a clean, lightly oiled bowl. Cover and let rise in a warm, draft-free place for 1 hour. Punch down and let rise again for 30 minutes.

Lightly oil 3 (9″ × 5″) loaf pans. Divide the dough into 3 equal balls and form into loaves. Place in the pans. Let rise for 15 to 20 minutes.

Preheat the oven to 350°.

Bake for 45 to 55 minutes, or until golden and the loaves sound slightly hollow when tapped on the top. Turn out onto wire racks and let cool before slicing.

*Makes 3 loaves; about 30 slices.*

Per slice: 168 calories, 2.5 g. total fat, 0.4 g. saturated fat, 0 mg. cholesterol, 4.6 g. dietary fiber, 39 mg. sodium.

## Focaccia

*Instead of being formed into a high, rounded loaf, focaccia is pancake-shaped, often baked on a baking sheet or pizza tile.*

½   cup warm water (98°–110°)
1   tablespoon active dry yeast
1   teaspoon honey
2–3   cups unbleached or whole-wheat pastry flour
½   teaspoon salt or 1 teaspoon herbal salt substitute
1   tablespoon olive oil
1   tablespoon red-wine vinegar
2   teaspoons dried marjoram
1   teaspoon dried dill
1   teaspoon dried oregano
¼   teaspoon ground black pepper

In a large bowl, combine the water, yeast and honey. Let stand in a warm place until the mixture foams, about 10 minutes. Stir in half of the flour, mixing well with a wooden spoon. Let this batter rise in a warm place for 30 minutes. Stir in the salt or salt substitute and enough of the remaining flour to form a kneadable dough.

Turn onto a lightly floured surface and knead for 5 to 8 minutes, or until the dough becomes elastic and less sticky. Place in a clean, lightly oiled bowl. Cover and let rise in a warm, draft-free place for 1 hour. Punch down.

Lightly oil a 15″ × 10″ baking sheet or jelly-roll pan. Roll the dough into a rectangle and fit it into the pan.

In a small bowl, whisk together the oil, vinegar, marjoram, dill, oregano and pepper. Brush over the surface of the dough. Let rise for 30 minutes.

Preheat the oven to 350°.

Bake the focaccia for 20 to 25 minutes, or until golden brown. Cut into pieces and serve warm.

*Makes about 8 pieces.*

Per piece: 125 calories, 2.3 g. total fat, 0.3 g. saturated fat, 0 mg. cholesterol, 4.1 g. dietary fiber, 136 mg. sodium.

## Dinnertime Delights

These hearty, rich-tasting loaves can hold their own as accompaniments to a variety of entrées. Served straight from the oven, they're sure to please everyone at your dinner table. You can also make them ahead of time; they freeze superbly and reheat quickly.

### Dilly Bread

*This recipe produces a green-flecked loaf with a pungent herb flavor. The combination of whole-wheat flour and honey is a nice complement to the dill.*

| | |
|---|---|
| 2 | cups warm water (98°–110°) |
| 2 | tablespoons active dry yeast |
| 2 | tablespoons honey |
| 5–6 | cups whole-wheat flour |
| 2 | tablespoons olive oil |
| 1½ | tablespoons dried dill |
| 2 | teaspoons herbal salt substitute |

In a large bowl, combine the water, yeast and honey. Let stand in a warm place until the mixture foams, about 10 minutes. Stir in 2 cups of the flour, mixing well with a wooden spoon.

Let this batter rise in a warm place for 30 minutes. Stir in the oil, dill, salt substitute and enough of the remaining flour to form a kneadable dough.

Turn onto a lightly floured surface and knead for 5 to 8 minutes, or until the dough becomes elastic and less sticky. Place in a clean, lightly oiled bowl. Cover and let rise in a warm, draft-free place for 1 hour. Punch down and let rise again for 30 minutes.

Lightly oil 2 (1- to 1½-quart) casserole dishes. Divide the dough in half, form into balls and place in the casseroles. Let rise for 10 minutes.

Preheat the oven to 350°.

*(continued)*

Bake the loaves for 45 minutes, or until the tops and sides sound hollow when tapped. Turn out onto wire racks and let cool before slicing.

*MAKES 2 LOAVES; ABOUT 15 SLICES.*

PER SLICE: 166 CALORIES, 2.6 G. TOTAL FAT, 0.4 G. SATURATED FAT, 0 MG. CHOLESTEROL, 5.4 G. DIETARY FIBER, 4 MG. SODIUM.

## California Sticky Buns

*This rich mixture of honey-sweetened dough and cinnamon-raisin filling will get rave reviews from family and friends.*

| | |
|---|---|
| 1½ | cups warm water (98°–110°) |
| ¼ | cup honey |
| 2 | tablespoons active dry yeast |
| 3½–4 | cups whole-wheat flour |
| ¼ | cup safflower oil |
| 1 | cup chopped walnuts |
| ¾ | cup raisins |
| ¾ | cup maple syrup |
| ⅓ | cup orange juice |
| 2 | tablespoons ground cinnamon |
| 1 | tablespoon grated orange rind |
| 1 | teaspoon ground cardamom |

In a large bowl, combine the water, honey and yeast. Let stand in a warm place until the mixture foams, about 10 minutes. Stir in 2 cups of the flour, mixing well with a wooden spoon. Let rise in a warm place for 30 minutes.

Stir in the oil and enough of the remaining flour to form a kneadable dough.

Turn onto a lightly floured surface and knead for 5 to 8 minutes, or until the dough becomes elastic and less sticky. Place in a clean, lightly oiled bowl. Cover and let rise in a warm, draft-free place for 1 hour. Punch down and let rise again for 30 minutes.

In a medium bowl, combine the walnuts, raisins, ½ cup of the maple syrup, orange juice, cinnamon, orange rind and cardamom. Set aside.

Lightly oil a 9″ × 13″ baking dish. Pour in the remaining ¼ cup maple syrup to coat the bottom of the pan.

Roll the dough into a large rectangle, about 24″ × 14″. Spread with the cinnamon mixture to within a scant ½″ of the borders. Roll up, starting at a short edge. Cut into segments about 2″ long.

Place the rolls, cut side up and sides touching, in the baking dish. Let rise for 10 minutes.

Preheat the oven to 350°.

Bake the buns for 25 minutes, or until browned.

*MAKES ABOUT 12.*

---

PER BUN: 332 CALORIES, 11.2 G. TOTAL FAT, 0.9 G. SATURATED FAT, 0 MG. CHOLESTEROL, 5.7 G. DIETARY FIBER, 7 MG. SODIUM.

## Onion Baguettes

*These miniature baguettes, perfect accessories for stream-lined family dinners, also transport well for picnics.*

| | |
|---|---|
| 1 | cup finely chopped onions |
| 2 | tablespoons olive oil |
| 2¼ | cups warm water (98°–110°) |
| ¼ | cup honey |
| 2 | tablespoons active dry yeast |
| 5–6 | cups whole-wheat flour |
| 1 | tablespoon chopped fresh rosemary or 1 teaspoon dried |
| 1 | teaspoon dried thyme |
| 1 | teaspoon dried basil |

In a small frying pan over medium-low heat, sauté the onions in the oil until limp, about 10 minutes, stirring frequently to prevent browning. Remove from the heat and set aside.

In a large bowl, combine the water, honey and yeast. Let stand in a warm place until the mixture foams, about 10 minutes. Stir in 2 cups of the flour, mixing well with a wooden spoon. Let this batter rise in a warm place for 30 minutes.

Stir in the onions, rosemary, thyme, basil and enough of the remaining flour to form a kneadable dough. Turn onto a lightly floured surface and knead for 5 to 8 minutes, or until the dough becomes elastic. Place in a clean, lightly oiled bowl. Cover and let rise in a warm, draft-free place for 1 hour. Punch down and let rise again for 30 minutes.

Lightly oil 2 large baking sheets. Divide the dough into 16 equal balls and roll each into a cylinder no more than 5″ long. Place on baking sheets. Cut 3 diagonal slits about ¼″ deep in the top of each cylinder. Let rise for 10 minutes.

Preheat the oven to 375°.

Bake the baguettes for 25 to 30 minutes, or until golden.

*MAKES 16.*

PER BAGUETTE: 167 CALORIES, 2.4 G. TOTAL FAT, 0.4 G. SATURATED FAT, 0 MG. CHOLESTEROL, 5.2 G. DIETARY FIBER, 3 MG. SODIUM.

# Wednesday Bread

*Great any day of the week, this bread derives its sweet flavor from the combination of honey and cinnamon.*

- 2 cups warm water (98°–110°)
- 1 cup honey
- 2 tablespoons active dry yeast
- 4 cups stone-ground whole-wheat flour
- 3 cups unbleached flour
- ¼ cup safflower oil
- 1 tablespoon ground cinnamon
- ½ teaspoon salt

In a large bowl, combine the water, honey and yeast. Let stand in a warm place until the mixture foams, about 10 minutes. Stir in 2 cups of the whole-wheat flour, mixing well with a wooden spoon. Let this batter rise in a warm place for 30 minutes.

Stir in the unbleached flour, oil, cinnamon and salt. Stir in enough of the remaining flour to form a kneadable dough.

Turn onto a lightly floured surface and knead for 5 to 8 minutes, or until the dough becomes elastic and less sticky. Place in a clean, lightly oiled bowl. Cover and let rise in a warm, draft-free place for 1 hour. Punch down and let rise again for 30 minutes.

Lightly oil 2 (9″ × 5″) loaf pans. Divide the dough in half. Form each piece into a loaf and place in a pan, seam side down. Let rise for 10 minutes.

Preheat the oven to 350°.

Bake the loaves for 45 minutes, or until the top and sides sound hollow when tapped. Turn out onto wire racks and let cool before slicing.

*Makes 2 loaves; about 20 slices.*

---

Per slice: 230 calories, 3.4 g. total fat, 0.4 g. saturated fat, 0 mg. cholesterol, 3.8 g. dietary fiber, 56 mg. sodium.

# Thyme, Sage and Olive Loaf

*The secret of this recipe is the thyme and sage, two richly flavored herbs that blend well with the wheat flour and honey.*

| | |
|---|---|
| 1 | cup warm water (98°–110°) |
| ⅓ | cup honey |
| 2 | tablespoons active dry yeast |
| 3 | cups whole-wheat flour |
| ¾ | cup buckwheat flour |
| ½ | cup chopped Kalamata or other black olives |
| 2 | tablespoons olive oil |
| 1 | teaspoon dried thyme |
| 1 | teaspoon ground black pepper |
| ½ | teaspoon dried sage |

In a large bowl, combine the water, honey and yeast. Let stand in a warm place until the mixture foams, about 10 minutes. Stir in 1 cup of the whole-wheat flour, mixing well with a wooden spoon. Let this batter rise in a warm place for 30 minutes.

Stir in the buckwheat flour, olives, oil, thyme, pepper and sage. Add enough of the remaining flour to form a kneadable dough.

Turn onto a lightly floured surface and knead for 5 to 8 minutes, or until the dough becomes elastic and less sticky. Place in a clean, lightly oiled bowl. Cover and let rise in a warm, draft-free place for 1 hour. Punch down and let rise again for 30 minutes.

Lightly oil a 1½-quart casserole. Form the dough into a ball and press into the casserole. Let rise for 10 minutes.

Preheat the oven to 350°.

Bake the bread for 35 to 45 minutes, or until the top and sides sound hollow when tapped. Let cool on a wire rack before slicing.

*Makes 1 loaf; 10 slices.*

Per slice: 241 calories, 6.1 g. total fat, 0.8 g. saturated fat, 0 mg. cholesterol, 6.4 g. dietary fiber, 227 mg. sodium.

## Celery Biscuits

*The flavor of these biscuits is reminiscent of turkey stuffing—celery leaves, plus familiar herbs such as sage, thyme and basil. Because they're made from a yeasted dough, they have less than one-third of the fat of regular biscuits.*

1½  cups warm water (98°–110°)
½  cup honey
1½  tablespoons active dry yeast
6  cups whole-wheat flour
1  cup minced onions
½  cup olive oil
⅓  cup minced celery leaves
1½  teaspoons dried sage
1  teaspoon celery seed
1  teaspoon dried thyme
1  teaspoon dried basil
½  teaspoon salt or 2 teaspoons herbal salt substitute
½  teaspoon ground black pepper

In a large bowl, combine the water, honey and yeast. Let stand in a warm place until the mixture foams, about 10 minutes. Stir in 2 cups of the flour, mixing well with a wooden spoon. Let this batter rise in a warm place for 30 minutes.

Stir in the onions, oil, celery leaves, sage, celery seed, thyme, basil, salt or salt substitute, and pepper.

Add enough of the remaining flour to form a kneadable dough.

Turn onto a lightly floured surface and knead for 5 to 8 minutes, or until the dough becomes elastic and less sticky.

Place the dough in a clean, lightly oiled bowl. Cover and let rise in a warm, draft-free place for 1 hour. Punch down and let rise again for 30 minutes.

Lightly oil 2 baking sheets.

*(continued)*

Turn the dough onto a floured work surface and roll to a thickness of about 1″. Using a floured 2″ biscuit cutter, cut circles of the dough.

Place the circles on the sheets, either ½″ or 2″ apart (depending on whether you want the finished biscuits to be touching). Cover and let rise for 20 minutes, or until doubled in bulk.

Preheat the oven to 350°.

Bake the biscuits for about 25 minutes, or until they're browned and the bottoms sound hollow when tapped.

*Makes 40.*

Per biscuit: 101 calories, 3.1 g. total fat, 0.4 g. saturated fat, 0 mg. cholesterol, 2.5 g. dietary fiber, 29 mg. sodium.

## Make It Quick

As their name implies, quick breads take less time to make than traditional breads. The recipes don't use yeast, so there's no kneading or waiting for the dough to rise. They're perfect for occasions when you want a freshly baked loaf fast.

### Irish Raisin Bread

*This recipe uses lots of raisins and other dried fruit. The bread is crumbly and sweet, like its Irish soda bread cousin.*

| | |
|---|---|
| ⅓ | cup raisins |
| ¼ | cup chopped dried apricots |
| 2 | tablespoons apricot nectar |
| 1 | cup warm water (98°–110°) |
| 2 | tablespoons honey |
| 2 | tablespoons safflower oil |
| 3½–4 | cups unbleached or whole-wheat pastry flour |
| 1½ | teaspoons baking soda |
| 1½ | teaspoons baking powder |

In a medium bowl, combine the raisins, apricots and apricot nectar. Let stand for 1 hour, then drain. Add the water, honey and oil.

Preheat the oven to 375°. Lightly oil a large baking sheet.

Into a large bowl, sift 3 cups of the flour with the baking soda and baking powder.

Pour the liquid ingredients over the flour mixture. Mix well and knead lightly to combine, adding enough of the remaining flour to keep the dough from sticking.

Pat the dough into a 7″ round and place on the baking sheet. Cut a shallow X in the top with a sharp knife.

Bake for 45 to 50 minutes, or until lightly browned. Transfer to a wire rack and let cool before slicing thinly.

*MAKES 1 LOAF; ABOUT 15 SLICES.*

PER SLICE: 147 CALORIES, 2.1 G. TOTAL FAT, 0.2 G. SATURATED FAT, 0 MG. CHOLESTEROL, 1.1 G. DIETARY FIBER, 160 MG. SODIUM.

## Blue Cornbread with Fresh Sweet and Hot Peppers

*Blue cornmeal originated in Hopi Indian territory in northeastern Arizona. The kernels are actually blue, and they lend a sweeter taste to the dough than their yellow cousins.*

|       |                                      |
|-------|--------------------------------------|
| 2     | sweet red peppers, finely diced      |
| 3     | jalapeño peppers, finely diced       |
| 2     | tablespoons apple juice              |
| 3     | cloves garlic, minced                |
| 1     | cup water                            |
| ½     | cup egg substitute                   |
| 2     | tablespoons olive oil                |
| 2     | tablespoons unsweetened applesauce   |
| 2     | tablespoons honey                    |
| 1¼    | cups blue cornmeal                   |
| 1     | cup unbleached flour                 |
| 1     | tablespoon baking powder             |
| 1     | teaspoon herbal salt substitute      |
| ¼     | teaspoon baking soda                 |

In a 1-quart saucepan over medium-high heat, simmer the red peppers, jalapeño peppers, apple juice and garlic, stirring constantly, for 10 minutes. Transfer to a medium bowl and let cool.

Preheat the oven to 400°.

Lightly oil a 9" × 13" baking dish. Place the dish in the oven to heat for 5 minutes.

Add the water, egg substitute, oil, applesauce and honey to the bowl with the peppers.

Into a large bowl, sift the cornmeal, flour, baking powder, salt substitute and baking soda.

Pour the liquid ingredients over the cornmeal mixture. Mix well. Pour the batter into the hot dish. Bake for 25 to 30 minutes, or until browned. Let cool before cutting.

*MAKES 12 PIECES.*

PER PIECE: 137 CALORIES, 2.9 G. TOTAL FAT, 0.4 G. SATURATED FAT, 0 MG. CHOLESTEROL, 3.1 G. DIETARY FIBER, 148 MG. SODIUM.

# Orange, Cranberry and Date Bread

*Cranberries and orange rind give this sweet bread a tart taste and jewel-like colors when sliced. You may use fresh or frozen cranberries.*

| | |
|---|---|
| 1 | cup orange juice |
| ½ | cup chopped dates |
| ½ | cup raisins |
| ½ | cup cranberries |
| ½ | cup honey |
| 1–2 | tablespoons grated orange rind |
| ¼ | cup safflower oil |
| 2½ | cups whole-wheat pastry or unbleached flour |
| 1 | tablespoon baking powder |
| 1 | teaspoon baking soda |

In a 2-quart saucepan over medium heat, cook the orange juice, dates, raisins, cranberries, honey and orange rind for 10 minutes, or until the cranberries pop. Remove from the heat and let cool. Stir in the oil.

Preheat the oven to 375°. Lightly oil a 9″ × 5″ loaf pan.

In a large bowl, combine the flour, baking powder and baking soda. Add the cranberry mixture and stir well to combine.

Pour the batter into the pan and bake for 40 to 45 minutes, or until a knife inserted in the center of the loaf comes out clean. Let cool before slicing thinly.

*MAKES 1 LOAF; ABOUT 15 SLICES.*

---

PER SLICE: 176 CALORIES, 4.1 G. TOTAL FAT, 0.4 G. SATURATED FAT, 0 MG. CHOLESTEROL, 3.6 G. DIETARY FIBER, 152 MG. SODIUM.

# For the Sweet Tooth

## *Delectable Guilt-Free Desserts*

Okay, you'll go along with eating a little less red meat. And you promise to lay off the eggs and to lighten up on those fatty snacks. But there's just no way that you're going to desert your dessert!

Fortunately, there's good news for all patrons of pastries and proponents of puddings. When it comes to cholesterol control, you can have your cake—or pie or parfait—and eat it, too.

Dessert has a well-earned reputation as a diet saboteur. Underneath that whipped-cream camouflage is a nutritional land mine of calories, fat and cholesterol. But you can defuse the heart-hostile effects of your favorite food finales with clever ingredient substitutions. By replacing whole eggs with egg whites and oil with applesauce, for example, you can slash the fat content of homemade cakes. (For more ways to slim down your baked goods, see Desserts on page 71.)

Of course, fresh fruit is a naturally nutritious ending to any meal. But when your sweet tooth clamors for something rich and creamy and gooey, go ahead and treat it to one of the no-cholesterol creations below. You'll find healthy renditions of some old standbys, as well as tempting new creations that will quickly become household favorites.

The fact that all of these recipes are low-fat and cholesterol-free can be your little secret. They're so downright delicious that no one would believe they're heart-smart, too!

### Pastries with Pizzazz

When it comes to dessert, the pies have it. Whether it's Boston cream or blueberry, pecan or pumpkin, this pièce de résistance has a way of rounding out a meal that few other foods can match. Here you'll find healthful remakes of a couple of classics—and some other fresh-baked goodies, too.

# French Apple Pie

*The ingredients in this pie combine to produce an aroma that is reminiscent of a Parisian bakery.*

| | |
|---|---|
| 1 | Light and Flaky No-Cholesterol Piecrust (page 426) |
| 1½ | cups thick unsweetened applesauce |
| ½ | cup honey |
| 3 | tablespoons apple brandy (optional) |
| 1 | tablespoon vanilla |
| | Grated rind of 1 lemon |
| 3 | green apples, thinly sliced |
| ½ | cup all-fruit apricot jam |

Prepare and bake the crust; set aside.

Preheat the oven to 375°.

In a 2-quart saucepan over medium-high heat, simmer the applesauce, honey, brandy (if using), vanilla and lemon rind until quite thick, about 10 to 15 minutes.

Pour the mixture into the prepared crust. Arrange the apples in concentric circles on top of the sauce.

In a 1-quart saucepan over medium-high heat, melt the apricot jam, then press it through a sieve. Use a pastry brush to glaze the apples with the jam.

Bake the pie for 30 minutes. Let cool before slicing.

*SERVES 8.*

PER SERVING: 295 CALORIES, 7.4 G. TOTAL FAT, 0.7 G. SATURATED FAT, 0 MG. CHOLESTEROL, 4.2 G. DIETARY FIBER, 12 MG. SODIUM.

# Heavenly Rhubarb Pie

*Rhubarb, a tasty member of the buckwheat family, glows like a ruby when it's cooked as a pie filling. Maple syrup provides a sweet counterpoint to the rhubarb's tartness.*

    Pastry for 2 Light and Flaky No-Cholesterol Piecrusts (page 426)
- 6 cups chopped fresh or frozen rhubarb
- 1½ cups maple syrup
- ⅓ cup arrowroot powder
- 7 tablespoons whole-wheat pastry flour

Prepare the piecrust dough according to the recipe directions. Roll half of the dough into an 11″ circle and fit it into a 9″ pie plate. Roll the remainder into an 11″ circle and set aside.

Preheat the oven to 350°.

In a large bowl, combine the rhubarb, maple syrup, arrowroot and flour. Pour into the bottom piecrust. Top with the remaining dough. Trim, seal and crimp the edges. Cut 3 steam slits in the top crust.

Bake for 60 to 70 minutes, or until the filling bubbles out of the steam slits and the top is lightly browned. Let cool before serving.

*SERVES 8.*

PER SERVING: 445 CALORIES, 14.6 G. TOTAL FAT, 1.4 G. SATURATED FAT, 0 MG. CHOLESTEROL, 6.9 G. DIETARY FIBER, 25 MG. SODIUM.

# Oat-Almond Piecrust

*Safflower oil works exceptionally well in this recipe, but feel free to try canola or any other mild vegetable oil. The oats and almonds add crunch to the crust.*

¾ cup rolled oats
1 tablespoon blanched almonds
¾ cup whole-wheat pastry flour
2–3 tablespoons oil
1–2 tablespoons ice water

In a blender or food processor, combine the oats and almonds and grind to a coarse powder. Transfer to a large bowl. Add the flour and mix well.

Drizzle on the oil and incorporate it with a pastry blender or your fingertips until the mixture resembles coarse cornmeal. Sprinkle in enough of the water (mixing it lightly with a fork) to moisten all of the flour and make a dough that you can form into a ball.

Flatten the dough into a circle about ½″ thick. On a lightly floured board or a sheet of waxed paper, roll the dough into a thin (about ⅛″) circle about 11″ in diameter. Line a 9″ pie pan with the dough and trim the edges to leave a ½″ overhang all around. Use the overhang to form a fluted edge.

Place the crust in the freezer for at least 20 minutes.

Fill the shell and bake it according to the directions of your specific recipe.

*To bake the crust without a filling:* Preheat the oven to 425°.

Line the prepared piecrust with aluminum foil and place it on a baking sheet. Bake for 8 minutes. Remove it from the oven and discard the foil. Bake for 7 minutes. Let the crust cool before filling.

*MAKES 1 (9″) CRUST; SERVES 8.*

PER SERVING: 100 CALORIES, 4.3 G. TOTAL FAT, 0.5 G. SATURATED FAT, 0 MG. CHOLESTEROL, 2.2 G. DIETARY FIBER, 1 MG. SODIUM.

## Blueberry Turnovers

*The blueberries, lemon juice and lemon rind combine to give these turnovers a sweet-tart flavor.*

### Dough

    1   cup warm water (98°–110°)
    ¼   cup honey
    1   tablespoon active dry yeast
    3   cups whole-wheat or unbleached flour
    3   tablespoons safflower oil

### Filling

    2   cups thinly sliced tart apples, such as Granny Smith
    1½  cups fresh or frozen blueberries
    ½   cup apple juice
    ¼   cup currants
    1   cup plus 2 tablespoons maple syrup
    3   tablespoons arrowroot powder
    1   tablespoon lemon juice
    1   tablespoon grated lemon rind
    ½   teaspoon ground cinnamon

*To make the dough:* In a large bowl, combine the water, honey and yeast. Stir well, then let rise for 10 minutes, or until the mixture foams. Stir in 1½ cups of the flour, mixing well to form a batter. Let rise in a warm place for 40 minutes. Add the oil and enough of the remaining flour to form a sticky dough.

Lightly flour a clean countertop or breadboard and knead the dough for 10 minutes, or until the dough becomes elastic and less sticky (if necessary, incorporate extra flour into the dough as you go). Place in a clean, lightly oiled bowl. Cover and let rise in a warm, draft-free place for 45 minutes.

*To make the filling:* While the dough is rising, combine the apples, blueberries, apple juice and currants in a

2-quart saucepan. Simmer over medium-high heat for 10 minutes, or until the apples soften.

In a small bowl, combine 1 cup of the maple syrup with the arrowroot and lemon juice. Add to the apple mixture and cook, stirring constantly, until the mixture thickens, about 8 to 10 minutes. Remove from the heat and stir in the lemon rind and cinnamon. Let cool for 10 minutes while you roll out the dough.

Preheat the oven to 350°.

Lightly oil a large baking sheet. Divide the dough into 8 portions and roll each into a very thin circle about 5″ in diameter. Place ⅓ cup filling in the center of each circle. Brush a thin line of water around the edge of each circle and fold each piece in half to form a half-moon shape. Press the edges together to seal. Reserve any remaining filling.

Transfer the turnovers to the baking sheet. Brush the tops with the remaining 2 tablespoons maple syrup. Bake for 20 minutes, or until browned.

If desired, puree any reserved filling and serve as a sauce over the turnovers.

*Serves 8.*

Per serving: 396 calories, 6.2 g. total fat, 0.7 g. saturated fat, 0 mg. cholesterol, 7.6 g. dietary fiber, 10 mg. sodium.

# Apple Dumplings

*These dumplings taste fabulous "as is," but you can also top
each one with the tofu whipped cream on page 450.*

2⅓  cups whole-wheat pastry or unbleached flour
 ½  teaspoon finely ground date sugar
 ⅓  cup safflower oil, chilled
 ⅓  cup cold water
 ¼  cup honey
 1  teaspoon ground cinnamon
 4  tart apples, thinly sliced
1½  cups apple juice
 ⅔  cup maple syrup
 1  tablespoon lemon juice
 ¼  teaspoon ground nutmeg

Preheat the oven to 425°.

In a large bowl, combine the flour and date sugar. Add the
oil and incorporate it with a pastry blender or your fingertips
until the dough resembles coarse cornmeal. Sprinkle lightly
with the water and blend it in with a fork to make a dough
that you can form into a ball. Divide into 4 equal portions.

Lightly flour a clean countertop or breadboard. Roll
each portion of the dough into a 7″ square. In the center of
each, place 1 tablespoon of the honey and sprinkle with ¼
teaspoon of the cinnamon. Top with ¼ of the apple slices.

Fold up the corners of each square to meet in the center
and seal the edges with water. Place each dumpling in a
small baking or gratin dish large enough to hold the
dumpling and about ½ cup of syrup.

In a 1-quart saucepan over medium-high heat, simmer
the apple juice, maple syrup, lemon juice and nutmeg for
10 minutes, stirring frequently. Pour the syrup over the
dumplings. Bake for 40 minutes (if the syrup starts to
scorch, add a little water to each dish).

*Serves 4.*

Per serving: 721 calories, 20.1 g. total fat, 2.1 g. saturated fat,
0 mg. cholesterol, 12.1 g. dietary fiber, 14 mg. sodium.

# Apple, Kiwifruit and Berry Tart

*This stunningly beautiful dessert is worthy of your most elegant dinner party. The Oat-Almond Piecrust is an excellent complement to the filling of jelled fruit juice, fresh kiwifruit and berries.*

1 Oat-Almond Piecrust (page 421)
2 cups apple juice
1 tablespoon agar-agar flakes
3 kiwifruit, peeled and sliced
1 cup fresh raspberries
2 tablespoons all-fruit apricot jam

Prepare and bake the crust; set aside.

In a 1-quart saucepan, combine 1 cup of the apple juice with the agar. Cook over medium heat, stirring constantly, until the flakes dissolve, about 15 minutes. Remove from the heat and stir in the remaining 1 cup apple juice. Place the pan in the refrigerator and let stand until the mixture cools and begins to thicken to the consistency of unbeaten egg whites, about 25 to 30 minutes.

Pour the juice mixture into the prepared crust. Top with the kiwis and berries in a decorative pattern. Place the tart in the refrigerator and chill for 45 minutes, or until the filling is set.

In a 1-quart saucepan over low heat, melt the apricot jam, stirring constantly. Press the jam through a fine sieve to remove any bits of peel. Brush over the fruit. Refrigerate for 15 minutes to set the glaze.

*SERVES 8.*

PER SERVING: 178 CALORIES, 6.1 G. TOTAL FAT, 0.7 G. SATURATED FAT, 0 MG. CHOLESTEROL, 4.1 G. DIETARY FIBER, 5 MG. SODIUM.

## PIECRUST MADE PERFECT

Egg white and vinegar help increase this crust's flakiness. Vinegar also helps keep the gluten from developing, which would toughen the dough. Be sure to use flours that are naturally lower in gluten, such as whole-wheat pastry or unbleached flour.

Just double this recipe if you need a top and a bottom crust.

### Light and Flaky No-Cholesterol Piecrust

  1  cup plus 2 tablespoons whole-wheat pastry or
     unbleached flour
     Pinch of salt (optional)
  2  tablespoons safflower oil, chilled
  1  egg white, lightly beaten
  1  teaspoon apple cider vinegar
     Ice water (as needed)

*To mix the dough by hand:* In a medium bowl, mix together the flour and the salt (if using). Make a well in the center of the flour and add the oil. Lightly mix it in with your fingertips until you have a cornmeal-like texture. Do not let the dough become warm from overmixing, especially if your hands are warm, because the crust will turn out tough.

Add the egg white and vinegar to the bowl. Mix lightly with your fingertips until incorporated. Try to form the dough into a ball. If it is still dry and crumbly, add the water, 1 tablespoon at a time, until you get a slightly sticky dough that holds together. Proceed to the dough-rolling step.

*To mix the dough in a food processor:* Place the steel blade into the workbowl, pushing it down until it fits snugly in the bowl. Add the flour and salt (if using); mix for 1 second.

Add the oil, egg white and vinegar. Use on/off turns to mix lightly. With the machine running, dribble in as much water as needed for the dough to form a ball. (This may take only a tiny bit of water. Don't overwork the dough by mixing too long.)

*To roll the dough:* Using your hands, form the dough into a flattened circle about ½" thick. If the dough is still cold, you can roll it out immediately or press it into an ungreased pie pan. Otherwise, wrap it in plastic wrap or waxed paper and refrigerate for at least 20 minutes.

Working on a very lightly floured surface, roll the dough into an 11″ circle. Carefully ease the dough into a 9″ pie plate, being careful not to stretch it. Trim the excess dough, leaving a ½″ overhang. Form the overhang into a fluted edge.

Cover the dough with plastic wrap and place in the freezer while you prepare the filling. When the filling is ready, discard the plastic and add the filling to the crust. Either freeze the unbaked pie (tightly wrapped) at this point or bake it according to your recipe directions.

*To bake the crust without a filling:* Roll out the dough and fit it into a pie plate as directed above. Line the shell with aluminum foil and place in the freezer for at least 20 minutes. Set the pie plate on a baking sheet and bake the crust at 400° for 8 to 12 minutes. Remove it from the oven, discard the foil and let the crust cool.

*Makes 1 crust; serves 6.*

---

PER SERVING: 119 CALORIES, 5.0 G. TOTAL FAT, 0.5 G. SATURATED FAT, 0 MG. CHOLESTEROL, 2.8 G. DIETARY FIBER, 10 MG. SODIUM.

---

*To make a double-crust pie:* Double the basic dough recipe. Divide the ball of dough in half and roll each half into an 11″ circle. Fit 1 circle into your pie plate and cover with plastic wrap. Sandwich the second circle of dough between 2 layers of plastic wrap. Place both pieces in the freezer while you prepare the filling.

When the filling is ready, remove the dough from the freezer, discard the plastic wrap from both pieces and immediately place the filling in the bottom crust. Lay the second piece of dough over the filling. Trim the edges and pinch them together to seal the gaps and form a fluted edge. Cut 3 slits in the top crust to allow steam to escape during baking. (This helps lessen the chances of the filling bubbling over onto the floor of your oven as the pie bakes.) You can either freeze your unbaked pie (tightly wrapped) at this stage or bake it according to your recipe directions.

# Creative No-Cholesterol Crisps

Filled with fruit and sporting a light, crumbly topping, a crisp could pass for a naturally healthy dessert. Problem is, those innocent-looking crumbs actually contain lots of butter. But you can make your own " guiltless" topping that has zero cholesterol but tastes just as delicious. The only difference is in appearance: Crumbs made with butter rise like biscuits, while the cholesterol-free variety bake into a crunchy crust.

Be sure to select fresh or frozen fruit that has a rich color and that will produce plenty of juice while baking. If you choose unsweetened frozen raspberries or strawberries, pair them with apples or another high-pectin fruit to give body and texture to the filling. Or add arrowroot powder to the uncooked fruit to help thicken the juices as the crisp bakes.

 **Raspberry-Apple Crisp**

*The raspberries and apples in this crisp are perfectly matched for sweetness and color. Choose tart apples that will hold together well as they cook, such as Pippin or Granny Smith.*

|   |   |
|---|---|
| 6 | cups thinly sliced tart apples |
| 2 | cups fresh or frozen raspberries |
| ½ | cup honey |
| 1 | tablespoon lemon juice |
| 1 | tablespoon arrowroot powder |
| ¾ | cup apple juice |
| ¾ | cup whole-wheat pastry or unbleached flour |
| ½ | cup rolled oats |
| 3 | tablespoons yellow cornmeal |
| ½ | teaspoon ground nutmeg |
| 1 | teaspoon vanilla |

Preheat the oven to 350°.

In a 3-quart saucepan, combine the apples, raspberries, honey, lemon juice and arrowroot. Stir in ½ cup of the apple juice. Bring to a boil over medium-high heat. Reduce the heat and simmer, stirring frequently, until the apples begin to soften, about 5 to 10 minutes.

Lightly oil a 9″ × 13″ baking dish. Add the apple mixture.

In a medium bowl, combine the flour, oats, cornmeal and nutmeg. Sprinkle with the remaining ¼ cup apple juice and the vanilla. Mix well. Sprinkle this mixture over the apples. Bake for 20 minutes, or until lightly browned. Serve hot.

*SERVES 6.*

PER SERVING: 286 CALORIES, 1.6 G. TOTAL FAT, 0.3 G. SATURATED FAT, 0 MG. CHOLESTEROL, 7.6 G. DIETARY FIBER, 5 MG. SODIUM.

## Vermont Maple Crisp

*Enjoy the cholesterol-lowering benefits of apple pectin in a dessert flavored with maple syrup and raisin puree.*

    10  small tart apples
     1  teaspoon ground cinnamon
    ¾  cup apple juice
    ⅓  cup maple syrup
    ¼  cup raisins
    ¼  cup boiling water
     1  cup rolled oats
     1  cup whole-wheat pastry flour
    ½  teaspoon salt (optional)
    ¼  cup safflower oil

Lightly oil a 9″ × 13″ baking dish.

Core the apples, but don't peel them. Slice into thin rings, place in the baking dish and sprinkle with the cinnamon. Add ½ cup of the apple juice and the maple syrup. In a blender, puree the raisins and water. Pour over the apples.

In a medium bowl, combine the oats, flour and salt (if using). Add the oil and remaining ¼ cup apple juice and mix into a crumbly dough. Spread over the apples. Let stand for 30 minutes.

Preheat the oven to 400°. Bake for 45 minutes, or until the filling bubbles and the top crust is evenly browned.

*SERVES 6.*

PER SERVING: 412 CALORIES, 11.2 G. TOTAL FAT, 1.2 G. SATURATED FAT, 0 MG. CHOLESTEROL, 9.1 G. DIETARY FIBER, 7 MG. SODIUM.

# Pear Crisp with Oat Bran Crust

*Serve this crisp at your next dinner party. The oat bran adds a chewy texture, while the date sugar—which is simply ground dried dates—enhances even off-season pears.*

|       |                                              |
|-------|----------------------------------------------|
| 7     | cups thinly sliced pears, such as Bosc       |
| ½     | cup plus 2 tablespoons date sugar            |
| ¼     | cup pear juice                               |
| 1     | tablespoon lemon juice                       |
| 1     | tablespoon arrowroot powder                  |
| 1     | cup whole-wheat pastry or unbleached flour   |
| ⅔     | cup oat bran                                 |
| 1½    | teaspoons baking powder                      |
| ⅓     | cup apple juice                              |
| 2     | tablespoons safflower oil                    |
| 1     | teaspoon vanilla                             |

Preheat the oven to 375°.

In a large bowl, combine the pears, ½ cup of the date sugar, the pear juice, lemon juice and arrowroot.

Lightly oil a 9″ × 13″ baking dish. Add the pear mixture.

In a medium bowl, combine the flour, oat bran, baking powder and remaining 2 tablespoons date sugar. Add the apple juice, oil and vanilla. Stir just until a dough forms. Drop by spoonfuls on top of the pears. Bake for 20 to 30 minutes, or until the top is browned.

*Serves 6.*

PER SERVING: 374 CALORIES, 6.8 G. TOTAL FAT, 0.7 G. SATURATED FAT, 0 MG. CHOLESTEROL, 12.3 G. DIETARY FIBER, 91 MG. SODIUM.

# Cape Cod Cranberry-Blueberry Crisp

*Cranberry fans who do not get enough of the tart fruit during the holidays will love this crisp from Cape Cod, where the best cranberries grow.*

| | |
|---|---|
| 2 | cups fresh or frozen blueberries |
| 1¾ | cups fresh or frozen cranberries |
| 1 | cup maple syrup |
| ¼ | cup currants |
| 3 | tablespoons arrowroot powder |
| 2 | tablespoons lemon juice |
| ¾ | cup whole-wheat pastry or unbleached flour |
| ½ | cup rolled oats |
| ¼ | cup blanched almonds, ground |
| 1 | teaspoon toasted sesame seeds |
| ¼ | teaspoon ground cinnamon |
| ¼ | cup apple juice |

Preheat the oven to 350°.

In a large bowl, combine the blueberries, cranberries, maple syrup, currants, arrowroot and lemon juice.

Lightly oil a 9″ × 13″ baking dish. Add the fruit mixture.

In a medium bowl, combine the flour, oats, almonds, sesame seeds and cinnamon. Sprinkle with the apple juice and mix well. Spoon over the fruit. Bake for 40 minutes, or until lightly browned.

*Serves 6.*

PER SERVING: 303 CALORIES, 3.7 G. TOTAL FAT, 0.4 G. SATURATED FAT, 0 MG. CHOLESTEROL, 6.1 G. DIETARY FIBER, 10 MG. SODIUM.

# Cooling Confections

Fresh and frosty, these no-cholesterol treats will become year-round favorites in your household. Pureeing the frozen desserts twice—once when they've frozen to the slush point and again before serving—will make them as smooth as silk.

## Watermelon Sherbet

*Choose the ripest melon—it should sound dense and heavy when you thump it—for this rose-colored sherbet. Freeze an extra batch for an out-of-season treat.*

  8   cups seeded, chopped watermelon
  1   cup honey (or to taste)
1½  tablespoons lemon juice
1½  teaspoons agar-agar flakes

Place the watermelon in a fine sieve set over a large bowl. Using a large spoon, press the chunks against the sieve to extract as much liquid as possible. Reserve the juice and remaining pulp separately.

In a 3-quart saucepan, combine the watermelon juice, honey, lemon juice and agar. Bring to a simmer over medium heat and cook, stirring frequently, for 5 minutes. Remove from the heat and let cool in the pan for 10 minutes.

Transfer the reserved watermelon pulp to a blender or food processor. Process until smooth. Add to the agar mixture and mix well. Pour into a large shallow pan and freeze for 2 hours.

Cut into cubes and place in a blender or food processor, then puree to a slushy consistency. Pour back into the pan and freeze for 2 hours. Cut into cubes and puree until smooth. Serve in chilled bowls.

*SERVES 8.*

PER SERVING: 183 CALORIES, 0.7 G. TOTAL FAT, 0 G. SATURATED FAT, 0 MG. CHOLESTEROL, 0.8 G. DIETARY FIBER, 5 MG. SODIUM.

# Cranberry Sherbet Parfait

*Layered with slices of bright green kiwifruit, this parfait can double as a palate cleanser between courses.*

3 cups fresh or frozen cranberries
2 cups apple juice
½ cup honey (or to taste)
¼ cup orange juice concentrate
¼ cup maple syrup
2 cups sliced kiwifruit

In a 3-quart saucepan, combine the cranberries, apple juice, honey, orange juice concentrate and maple syrup. Cover and cook over medium-high heat until the berries pop, about 5 minutes. Let the mixture cool slightly, then puree in a blender or food processor. Taste for sweetness and add more honey if needed.

Press the mixture through a sieve into a large bowl, using the back of a wooden spoon to extract as much liquid as possible. Pour into a large shallow pan and freeze for 2 hours.

Cut into cubes and place in a blender or food processor, then puree to a slushy consistency. Pour back into the pan and freeze for 2 hours. Cut into cubes and puree until smooth. Pour into parfait glasses, alternating with layers of kiwi.

*Serves 6.*

---

Per serving: 234 calories, 0.5 g. total fat, 0.1 g. saturated fat, 0 mg. cholesterol, 4.4 g. dietary fiber, 8 mg. sodium.

## Summer Fruit Parfaits

*Be sure to use soft tofu in this recipe. The firm kind gives the parfaits a gritty texture.*

    8   ounces soft tofu
    1   teaspoon almonds
    ½   teaspoon vanilla
    1   cup fresh or frozen blueberries
    1   cup sliced fresh peaches
    1   cup sliced fresh strawberries

In a blender, puree the tofu, almonds and vanilla until smooth. Divide among 4 parfait glasses.

In the blender, puree the blueberries and peaches. Pour over the tofu layer in the parfait glasses.

Rinse the blender jar, then puree the strawberries. Pour over the blueberry layer in the parfait glasses. Chill for 20 minutes.

*Serves 4.*

PER SERVING: 94 CALORIES, 2.6 G. TOTAL FAT, 0.3 G. SATURATED FAT, 0 MG. CHOLESTEROL, 2.4 G. DIETARY FIBER, 19 MG. SODIUM.

## Carob-Date Pops

*These taste just like old-fashioned fudge pops, but with no chocolate or dairy products.*

1 cup chopped dates
1 ripe banana, sliced
½ cup almonds
½ cup apple juice
4 ounces soft tofu
¼ cup raisins
¼ cup roasted carob powder
1 teaspoon vanilla
½ teaspoon ground cinnamon
¼ teaspoon ground nutmeg

In a food processor or blender, combine the dates, bananas, almonds, apple juice, tofu, raisins, carob, vanilla, cinnamon and nutmeg. Puree until very smooth.

Pour into 5 (6-ounce) paper cups and place a wooden or plastic ice-pop stick in the center of each. Freeze solid. To serve, tear off the paper cup.

*Serves 5.*

PER SERVING: 256 CALORIES, 8.0 G. TOTAL FAT, 0.9 G. SATURATED FAT, 0 MG. CHOLESTEROL, 5.3 G. DIETARY FIBER, 12 MG. SODIUM.

## Smooth Sensations

Mousses and puddings are standard dessert fare. And it's easy to understand why they've remained so popular over the years: Spoonful after spoonful, they gently glide over your taste buds, filling your mouth with their ambrosial flavor. In these recipes, ingredients such as agar-agar flakes and pureed fruit mimic the creamy texture usually imbued by whole milk and eggs.

 **Mocha Mousse**

*Flavored with roasted-grain coffee substitute and roasted carob powder, this mousse will satisfy a craving for something rich.*

    4  cups apple juice
    3  tablespoons agar-agar flakes
    3  tablespoons maple syrup
    2  tablespoons almond butter
    1  tablespoon roasted carob powder
    1  tablespoon roasted-grain coffee substitute

In a blender, combine the apple juice, agar, maple syrup, almond butter and carob. Puree until smooth.

Transfer to a 2-quart saucepan and cook over medium heat for 10 minutes, stirring constantly. Remove from the heat and let cool for 10 minutes. Add the coffee substitute and stir to dissolve it. Pour into 6 dessert goblets. Refrigerate until firm, about 30 minutes.

*Serves 6.*

PER SERVING: 146 CALORIES, 3.4 G. TOTAL FAT, 0.3 G. SATURATED FAT, 0 MG. CHOLESTEROL, 1.1 G. DIETARY FIBER, 9 MG. SODIUM.

# Berry and Banana Kanten

*Kanten is the Japanese name for agar-agar, an all-purpose vegetable gelatin that thickens to a creamy consistency reminiscent of dairy-rich puddings. You can find kanten in health food stores.*

4   cups apple juice
1   ripe banana, sliced
2   cups sliced fresh or frozen strawberries
1   cup fresh or frozen raspberries
1   (½ ounce) bar kanten, broken into small pieces
¼   cup maple syrup
1   teaspoon lime juice
1   teaspoon vanilla

In a blender or food processor, process the apple juice and bananas until smooth. Transfer to a 3-quart saucepan.

Add the strawberries, raspberries, kanten, maple syrup, lime juice and vanilla. Cook over medium-high heat, stirring constantly, until the kanten dissolves, about 12 to 15 minutes. Let cool slightly.

Pour into 8 individual bowls. Chill until set, about 2 hours.

*Serves 8.*

---

PER SERVING: 121 CALORIES, 0.4 G. TOTAL FAT, 0.1 G. SATURATED FAT, 0 MG. CHOLESTEROL, 1.9 G. DIETARY FIBER, 7 MG. SODIUM.

---

## English Summer Pudding

*Leftover bread or pastry is covered with berries and apple juice, then left to soak until it becomes a thick pudding.*

  6  cups mixed berries
  ¼  cup honey
  ¼  cup apple juice
  3  cups cubed Minnesota Christmas Stollen (page 398)
     or Oatmeal-Raisin Bread (page 404)
     Tofu whipped cream (page 450)

In a 3-quart saucepan, combine the berries, honey and apple juice. Bring to a boil and simmer for 5 minutes.

Place the bread cubes in a large heatproof bowl. Add the berry mixture. Cover with plastic wrap and refrigerate overnight. Serve with the whipped cream.

*SERVES 8.*

---

PER SERVING: 223 CALORIES, 4.0 G. TOTAL FAT, 0.4 G. SATURATED FAT, 0 MG. CHOLESTEROL, 6.1 G. DIETARY FIBER, 8 MG. SODIUM.

---

## Maple-Cashew Mousse

*You can serve this dessert in goblets or pour it into a pre-baked piecrust for an elegant ending to a meal.*

  2  cups cashew Nut Milk (page 439)
  ¼  cup maple syrup
  3  tablespoons agar-agar flakes
  1  tablespoon vanilla
  1  tablespoon tahini
  1  tablespoon cashews

In a 2-quart saucepan, combine the nut milk, maple syrup, agar and vanilla. Cook over medium heat, stirring constantly, until the agar dissolves, about 5 minutes. Stir in the tahini.

Pour into a medium bowl and refrigerate until firm,

about 50 minutes. Transfer to a blender or food processor and process until creamy. Spoon into 6 dessert goblets.

In a small frying pan over medium heat, toast the cashews until a nutty aroma emerges, about 3 to 5 minutes. Chop coarsely and sprinkle over the mousse. Chill and serve.

*SERVES 6.*

PER SERVING: 162 CALORIES, 8.0 G. TOTAL FAT, 1.2 G. SATURATED FAT, 0 MG. CHOLESTEROL, 0.8 G. DIETARY FIBER, 6 MG. SODIUM.

## BUT HOW DO YOU MILK A NUT?

Nut "milk" makes an excellent substitute for regular dairy milk. It is delicious on cereals, in baked goods and as the base for creamy sauces. Depending on the use, you can either sweeten the milk or leave it plain.

This recipe makes 2 cups, but you can easily double it. Store your nut milk in a sealed container in the refrigerator, where it will keep for about three or four days. If you'd like, you can save the resulting nut pulp to add to breads, pastries or even casseroles.

### Nut Milk

2 cups water
½ cup raw almonds or cashews
½ cup oats
1 tablespoon molasses or honey (optional)

In a blender, puree the water, almonds or cashews, and oats on high speed for about 3 minutes, or until the nuts are very finely chopped. Pour into a fine sieve and strain into a bowl. Press on the nut pulp with the back of a spoon to extract as much liquid as possible.

If desired, stir in the molasses or honey. If not using immediately, transfer to a container with a tight lid and store in the refrigerator.

*MAKES 2 CUPS.*

PER CUP: 269 CALORIES, 18.1 G. TOTAL FAT, 0.2 G. SATURATED FAT, 0 MG. CHOLESTEROL, 3.0 G. DIETARY FIBER, 5 MG. SODIUM.

## Fresh Peach Pudding

*In this recipe, the tartness of the lemon juice and orange rind provides a wonderful counterpoint to the sweetness of the perfectly ripe peaches.*

    8   large ripe peaches, sliced
    2   teaspoons lemon juice
    2   tablespoons agar-agar flakes
    1   tablespoon honey
        Grated rind of ½ orange
    ½   teaspoon ground cinnamon
        Sweet Cherry Sauce (page 448)

In a blender or food processor, combine the peaches, lemon juice, agar, honey, orange rind and cinnamon. Puree until smooth. Transfer to a 2-quart saucepan.

Simmer over medium heat, stirring constantly, for 5 minutes, or until the agar dissolves. Pour into 6 to 8 custard cups or ramekins and refrigerate until firm. Serve with the cherry sauce.

*SERVES 6.*

PER SERVING: 191 CALORIES, 0.8 G. TOTAL FAT, 0.2 G. SATURATED FAT, 0 MG. CHOLESTEROL, 3.2 G. DIETARY FIBER, 5 MG. SODIUM.

## Fresh Berry Tapioca

*Make this pudding when strawberries are in season, at their freshest and most flavorful.*

    4   cups sliced fresh or frozen strawberries
    1   cup apple juice
    3   tablespoons quick-cooking tapioca
    3   tablespoons honey
    1   cup raspberries

Puree the strawberries in a blender or food processor. In a 2-quart saucepan over medium-high heat, bring the strawberries, apple juice, tapioca and honey to a boil, stirring constantly.

Remove the pan from the heat. Stir in the raspberries. Pour into 6 dessert goblets and chill in the refrigerator until set, about 1 hour.

*Serves 6.*

---

PER SERVING: 108 CALORIES, 0.5 G. TOTAL FAT, 0.1 G. SATURATED FAT, 0 MG. CHOLESTEROL, 2.8 G. DIETARY FIBER, 3 MG. SODIUM.

---

# Carob Pudding

*Carob lends its rich flavor, color and texture to this pudding, which makes a great alternative to the high-fat chocolate variety.*

16 ounces soft tofu, cut into cubes
3 medium bananas
¼ cup carob powder
1 teaspoon vanilla
1 tablespoon honey or maple syrup

In a blender, puree the tofu, bananas, carob, vanilla, and honey or maple syrup until smooth and creamy. Pour into dessert glasses and chill for 30 minutes.

*Serves 4.*

---

PER SERVING: 189 CALORIES, 4.4 G. TOTAL FAT, 0.8 G. SATURATED FAT, 0 MG. CHOLESTEROL, 2.1 G. DIETARY FIBER, 36 MG. SODIUM.

---

# Almond Rice Pudding

*Rice pudding with a twist: This variation is sweetened with vanilla and honey and thickened with almond milk.*

3–4½ cups cooked short-grain brown rice
  ½ cup currants
  2 cups apple juice
  ½ cup almonds
  ⅓ cup honey
  1 teaspoon vanilla
  ½ teaspoon ground cinnamon
  ¼ teaspoon ground nutmeg

Preheat the oven to 350°.

Lightly oil a 9″ × 5″ loaf pan. Combine the rice and currants in the pan and set aside.

In a blender, puree the apple juice, almonds, honey, vanilla, cinnamon and nutmeg. Pour over the rice.

Bake for 45 minutes, or until all the liquid has been absorbed. Serve warm or cold.

*Serves 4.*

PER SERVING: 288 CALORIES, 5.7 G. TOTAL FAT, 0.7 G. SATURATED FAT, 0 MG. CHOLESTEROL, 4.1 G. DIETARY FIBER, 6 MG. SODIUM.

# Fresh and Fast

Served plain, fruit makes a naturally no-cholesterol dessert. But these recipes dress up peaches, pineapples and other favorites to create special treats that are light but satisfying. Best of all, they can be prepared in less than 20 minutes. Keep a selection of fresh fruit on hand, so you can whip up something on a moment's notice.

     **Peaches with Melba Sauce**

*This version of melba sauce combines pureed berries, vanilla and honey. Served over sliced fresh peaches, it makes a simple yet delicious dessert for busy evenings.*

    4  large ripe peaches, peeled and sliced
    1  cup fresh or frozen raspberries
    ¼  cup honey
    1  tablespoon vanilla

Divide the peaches among 4 dessert dishes.

In a blender or food processor, puree ½ cup of the raspberries with the honey and vanilla. Pour into a small bowl and stir in the remaining ½ cup berries. Spoon over the peaches. Serve at room temperature or chilled.

*Serves 4.*

---

PER SERVING: 128 CALORIES, 0.2 G. TOTAL FAT, 0.1 G. SATURATED FAT, 0 MG. CHOLESTEROL, 2.8 G. DIETARY FIBER, 1 MG. SODIUM.

---

# Pineapple-Fig Bake

*The sugary figs make the plain apples in this dessert taste sinfully sweet.*

    3   cups pineapple juice
    2   cups chopped tart apples
 1½   cups chopped dried figs
    ¾   cup chopped dried pineapple
    ⅓   cup chopped dates
    ¾   teaspoon ground cinnamon
    ½   teaspoon ground nutmeg

Preheat the oven to 300°.

In a 3-quart saucepan, combine the pineapple juice, apples, figs, pineapple, dates, cinnamon and nutmeg. Bring to a boil over medium-high heat. Reduce the heat and simmer for 5 minutes, stirring frequently.

Transfer the fruit to a 9″ × 13″ baking dish. Bake for 1 hour, or until the fruit is very soft. Serve hot or cold.

*Serves 4.*

PER SERVING: 471 CALORIES, 2.3 G. TOTAL FAT, 0.3 G. SATURATED FAT, 0 MG. CHOLESTEROL, 10.7 G. DIETARY FIBER, 13 MG. SODIUM.

# Maple-Apple Bake

*These baked apples are stuffed with bananas, which add a fruity sweetness that's unusual and very tasty.*

    2   large tart apples, such as Granny Smith
    ¼   cup maple syrup
    1   teaspoon ground cinnamon
    1   teaspoon ground nutmeg
    ½   ripe banana, thinly sliced
    ½   cup apple juice concentrate

Preheat the oven to 350°.

With an apple corer, core each apple to within ⅛″ from the bottom, leaving a small amount of skin intact. Place the apples in a 9″ × 9″ baking dish. Place 1 tablespoon of the maple syrup in each cavity. Sprinkle with the cinnamon and nutmeg. Pack the cavities with the bananas.

In a cup, mix the apple juice concentrate and the remaining 2 tablespoons maple syrup. Pour around the apples in the dish. Bake for 20 minutes. Serve hot.

*Serves 2.*

PER SERVING: 330 CALORIES, 1.3 G. TOTAL FAT, 0.5 G. SATURATED FAT, 0 MG. CHOLESTEROL, 3.5 G. DIETARY FIBER, 23 MG. SODIUM.

## Chinese Melon Dessert

*Canned litchi nuts and mandarin orange slices add a touch of the Orient to this simple fruit dessert. The date sugar evokes the delicate flavors of the melon and oranges.*

4 cups cantaloupe balls
1 cup pineapple chunks
1 cup canned litchi nuts, rinsed and drained
1 cup canned mandarin orange slices, rinsed and drained
1 cup orange juice
¼ cup maple syrup
¼ cup date sugar
1 teaspoon chopped fresh mint leaves

In a large bowl, combine the cantaloupe, pineapple, litchi nuts and oranges.

In a small bowl, combine the orange juice, maple syrup, date sugar and mint. Pour over the fruit and toss well. Let marinate at room temperature for 1 hour before serving.

*Serves 6.*

PER SERVING: 151 CALORIES, 0.5 G. TOTAL FAT, 0.1 G. SATURATED FAT, 0 MG. CHOLESTEROL, 2.1 G. DIETARY FIBER, 18 MG. SODIUM.

# Ruby Apples

*You can make these apples ahead and keep them in the refrigerator for up to six days. They make great hostess and holiday gifts.*

6   medium tart apples
2   cups nonalcoholic red wine
1   cinnamon stick
1   tablespoon honey
2   tablespoons grated orange rind

Peel the apples, leaving them whole and keeping the stems intact, if possible. Using a sharp knife or melon baller, core the apples from the bottom. Place the apples, right side up, in a large pot. Add the wine, cinnamon and honey.

Bring to a boil over medium-high heat. Then reduce the heat to medium and simmer, uncovered, for 25 to 30 minutes, or until the apples are soft but not ready to collapse.

Transfer the apples to small dessert dishes and spoon some of the poaching liquid over them. Sprinkle with the orange rind.

*Serves 6.*

PER SERVING: 99 CALORIES, 0.5 G. TOTAL FAT, 0.1 G. SATURATED FAT, 0 MG. CHOLESTEROL, 3.1 G. DIETARY FIBER, 7 MG. SODIUM.

## Sweet Golden Pears

*Just-underripe, brown-skinned pears, such as Bosc, work best for this dessert; they hold together in the hot poaching liquid.*

6 Bosc or other firm pears
1 cup nonalcoholic white wine
1 cup apple juice
  Juice of 1 large lemon
5 whole cloves

Peel the pears, leaving them whole. Using a sharp knife or melon baller, core the pears from the bottom.

Place them upright in a large pot. Add the wine, apple juice, lemon juice and cloves. Bring to a boil over medium-high heat. Reduce the heat to medium and simmer, uncovered, for 25 to 30 minutes, or until the pears are soft but not ready to collapse.

Transfer to small dessert dishes. Discard the cloves and spoon some of the poaching liquid over the pears. Serve hot.

*SERVES 6.*

PER SERVING: 105 CALORIES, 0.6 G. TOTAL FAT, <0.1 G. SATURATED FAT, 0 MG. CHOLESTEROL, 3.8 G. DIETARY FIBER, 4 MG. SODIUM.

# Over-the-Top Fruit Sauces

Giving up full-fat whipped cream is easier said than done. But these fruit sauces will quickly make you forget about the white stuff. They can be made up to ten days ahead and stored in the refrigerator.

## Peach Sauce

*The tang of orange, lemon and peach makes this a tasty topping for sherbet, pudding or a slice of pie.*

- 4 large peaches, sliced
- ½ cup honey
- 2 tablespoons lemon juice
- 1 tablespoon orange juice or orange-juice concentrate

In a 3-quart saucepan over medium-high heat, simmer the peaches, honey and lemon juice, stirring often, for 20 minutes, or until the peaches soften. Add the orange juice or orange-juice concentrate.

Transfer the sauce to a blender or food processor and puree until smooth. Serve warm.

*Makes about 3 cups.*

---

Per 2 tablespoons: 29 calories, <0.1 g. total fat, <0.1 g. saturated fat, 0 mg. cholesterol, 0.3 g. dietary fiber, 0 mg. sodium.

---

## Sweet Cherry Sauce

*Give rice pudding a tantalizingly different taste with this fruity sauce.*

- 2½ cups pitted sweet cherries
- 1 cup apple juice
- ⅓ cup rice bran syrup or maple syrup
- 3 tablespoons arrowroot powder

In a blender, combine 1 cup of the cherries, apple juice, rice bran syrup or maple syrup, and arrowroot. Process for 1 minute.

Pour into a 2-quart saucepan. Add the remaining cherries. Bring to a boil over medium-high heat, stirring constantly, and cook until thick. Let cool slightly before using.

*Makes about 3½ cups.*

Per 2 tablespoons: 26 calories, 0.1 g. total fat, 0.1 g. saturated fat, 0 mg. cholesterol, 0.3 g. dietary fiber, 1 mg. sodium.

## Blueberry Sauce with Nutmeg

*The sweet flavor of grated nutmeg enhances the blueberries in this easy sauce. Serve it over slices of angel food cake or poached fruit.*

    2   cups fresh or frozen blueberries
  ⅓–½   cup honey
    1   tablespoon arrowroot or kuzu powder
    1   teaspoon ground nutmeg
    1   teaspoon grated lemon rind

In a blender, combine the blueberries, ⅓ cup of the honey, arrowroot or kuzu, nutmeg and lemon rind. Transfer to a 1-quart saucepan. Cook over medium-high heat, whisking frequently, until the sauce thickens, about 10 to 12 minutes. Taste and adjust the sweetener, if necessary. Let cool slightly before serving.

*Makes 1½ cups.*

Per 2 tablespoons: 19 calories, 0.2 g. total fat, 0.1 g. saturated fat, 0 mg. cholesterol, 0.7 g. dietary fiber, 2 mg. sodium.

## Fresh Raspberry Sauce

*An elegant sauce, this works well over Blueberry Turnovers (page 422) or Almond Rice Pudding (page 442).*

¼  cup all-fruit raspberry or currant jelly
3  tablespoons cold water
1  tablespoon arrowroot powder
2  cups fresh raspberries

In a 1-quart saucepan over medium-low heat, melt the jelly.

In a small bowl, combine the water and arrowroot, stirring until smooth. Add to the jelly and cook, stirring constantly, until clear and thick. Add the berries. Cook over low heat until the sauce is slightly thickened, about 5 minutes. Serve warm or cold.

*MAKES ABOUT 2½ CUPS.*

PER 2 TABLESPOONS: 18 CALORIES, 0.1 G. TOTAL FAT, 0.1 G. SATURATED FAT, 0 MG. CHOLESTEROL, 0.6 G. DIETARY FIBER, 1 MG. SODIUM.

## Whip Up an Imitation

This tofu-based topping tastes just like high-fat, cholesterol-rich dairy whipped cream. Be sure to use soft tofu.

4  ounces soft tofu
2  tablespoons maple syrup
½  teaspoon vanilla

In a food processor or blender, puree the tofu, maple syrup and vanilla until very smooth.

*MAKES ½ CUP.*

PER 2 TABLESPOONS: 45 CALORIES, 1.0 G. TOTAL FAT, 0.2 G. SATURATED FAT, 0 MG. CHOLESTEROL, 0 G. DIETARY FIBER, 9 MG. SODIUM.

# PART V

# The Fat and Cholesterol Finder

# HEART-SMART EATING
# BY THE NUMBERS
## *How Does Your Diet Add Up?*

**P**ut away your calculator: The chart beginning on page 454 can make it simpler to stick to a low-fat, low-cholesterol diet than you might think. The best part? No number crunching necessary (unless you want to, of course).

Like most other fat and cholesterol counters, this chart divvies up food into categories, from beans to vegetables. In between you'll find breakfast foods, desserts, snack foods, fish and shellfish, meats and so forth. But this chart is designed a bit differently than those you may have used in the past. The difference? It ranks foods by the amount of saturated fat per serving—"low," "acceptable" or "high"—rather than by the amount of dietary cholesterol. Most experts agree that saturated fat is the healthy heart's worst enemy. The more you stick to foods in the "low" category—and there's a delicious array to choose from—the less saturated fat you'll eat and the healthier your diet will be.

As long as your overall calorie and cholesterol intake is reasonable, that is. As odd as it may seem, some foods contain a low percentage of saturated fat but pack lots of calories and cholesterol. For example, a couple of slices of frozen French toast drizzled with low-calorie syrup will "cost" you less than two grams of saturated fat. But they contain a significant amount of calories and cholesterol. Another example: Both three ounces of tofu and a fast-food ham-and-cheese breakfast croissant get 54 percent of their calories from fat. But compare the calories, cholesterol and saturated fat content, and it's easy to see why breakfast croissants should be an occasional indulgence.

Here's some other information you'll need to use this chart.

- We've rounded calorie and cholesterol counts to the nearest whole number.

| Food | Portion | Calories |
|---|---|---|
| **BEANS, BEAN PRODUCTS AND OTHER LEGUMES** | | |
| **Low** | | |
| Adzuki beans, boiled | ½ cup | 147 |
| Baked beans with pork, canned | ½ cup | 134 |
| Black beans, boiled | ½ cup | 114 |
| Broad beans (fava beans), boiled | ½ cup | 94 |
| Chick-peas, canned | ½ cup | 143 |
| Green peas, boiled | ½ cup | 67 |
| Lentils, boiled | ½ cup | 114 |
| Lima beans, boiled | ½ cup | 108 |
| Refried beans, canned | ½ cup | 135 |
| Snap beans (green beans), boiled | ½ cup | 22 |
| Soybeans, boiled | ½ cup | 149 |
| Soybean sprouts, raw | ½ cup | 45 |
| Split peas, boiled | ½ cup | 116 |
| Three-bean salad, canned | ⅓ cup | 100 |
| Tempeh | ½ cup | 165 |
| **ACCEPTABLE** | | |
| Tofu, firm, raw | ¼ block (about 3 oz.) | 118 |

- Foods that get less than 1 percent of their calories from fat or saturated fat per serving are designated by the symbol "<1".
- Unless otherwise specified, the foods are commercially prepared.
- While brand names are used in some cases, the nutrient information for many commercially prepared foods (such as frozen entrées) should be viewed as sample values. So expect variations among different brands and read labels carefully.
- Since beans, fruits and vegetables typically contain little or no saturated fat and cholesterol, we've devoted the most space to other food categories.

| Fat (g.) | Saturated Fat (g.) | % Calories from Fat | % Calories from Saturated Fat | Cholesterol (mg.) |
|---|---|---|---|---|
| 0.1 | 0.04 | <1 | <1 | 0 |
| 2 | 0.8 | 13.4 | 5.4 | 9 |
| 0.5 | 0.1 | 3.9 | <1 | 0 |
| 0.3 | 0.1 | 2.9 | 1 | 0 |
| 1.4 | 0.1 | 8.8 | <1 | 0 |
| 0.2 | 0.05 | 2.7 | <1 | 0 |
| 0.4 | 0.1 | 3.2 | <1 | 0 |
| 0.4 | 0.1 | 3.3 | <1 | 0 |
| 1.4 | 0.5 | 9.3 | 3.3 | 0 |
| 0.2 | 0.04 | 8.2 | 1.6 | 0 |
| 7.7 | 1.1 | 46.5 | 6.6 | 0 |
| 2.4 | 0.3 | 48 | 6 | 0 |
| 0.4 | 0.1 | 3.1 | <1 | 0 |
| 0.5 | 0 | 4.5 | 0 | 0 |
| 6.4 | 0.9 | 34.9 | 4.9 | 0 |
| 7.1 | 1 | 54.1 | 7.6 | 0 |

*(continued)*

| Food | Portion | Calories |
|------|---------|----------|

## Beans, Bean Products and Other Legumes — Continued

### High

| | | |
|------|---------|----------|
| Chili, vegetarian, canned | 1 cup | 286 |
| Chili with beans and meat, canned | 1 cup | 250 |

## Breads and Bread Products

### Low

| | | |
|------|---------|----------|
| Bagel, plain or onion | 1 (about 2½ oz.) | 195 |
| Blueberry muffin | | |
|     homemade with 2% low-fat milk | 1 (about 2 oz.) | 163 |
|     low-fat, frozen | 1 (about 2½ oz.) | 190 |
| Breadstick, plain | 1 (about ¼ oz.) | 25 |
| Cornbread, homemade with 2% low-fat milk | 1 piece (about 2¼ oz.) | 173 |
| Corn muffin, homemade with 2% low-fat milk | 1 (about 2 oz.) | 180 |
| Cracked wheat bread | 1 slice (about 1 oz.) | 65 |
| English muffin, plain, toasted | 1 (about 2 oz.) | 133 |
| French, Vienna or sourdough bread | 1 slice (about 1 oz.) | 69 |
| Italian bread | 1 slice (about 1 oz.) | 81 |
| Pita bread, white | 1 (about 2 oz.) | 165 |
| Pumpernickel bread | 1 slice (about 1 oz.) | 80 |
| Raisin bread | 1 slice (about 1 oz.) | 71 |
| Roll or bun, homemade with whole milk | 1 (about 1 oz.) | 112 |
| Rye bread | 1 slice (about 1 oz.) | 83 |
| Wheat bread, reduced-calorie | 1 slice (about 1 oz.) | 46 |
| White bread, soft crumb | 1 slice (about 1 oz.) | 67 |

| Fat (g.) | Saturated Fat (g.) | % Calories from Fat | % Calories from Saturated Fat | Cholesterol (mg.) |
|---|---|---|---|---|
| 14 | 6 | 44.1 | 18.9 | 43 |
| 11 | 5 | 39.6 | 18 | 50 |
| 1.1 | 0.2 | 5.1 | <1 | 0 |
| 6.2 | 1.2 | 34.2 | 6.6 | 21 |
| 5 | 1 | 23.7 | 4.7 | 5 |
| 0.6 | 0.1 | 21.6 | 3.6 | 0 |
| 4.6 | 1 | 23.9 | 5.2 | 26 |
| 7 | 1.3 | 35 | 6.5 | 24 |
| 1 | 0.2 | 13.8 | 2.8 | 0 |
| 1 | 0.2 | 6.8 | 1.4 | 0 |
| 0.8 | 0.2 | 10.4 | 2.6 | 0 |
| 1.1 | 0.3 | 12.2 | 3.3 | 0 |
| 0.7 | 0.1 | 3.8 | <1 | 0 |
| 1 | 0.1 | 11.3 | 1.1 | 0 |
| 1.1 | 0.3 | 13.9 | 3.8 | 0 |
| 2.7 | 0.7 | 21.7 | 5.6 | 13 |
| 1.1 | 0.2 | 11.9 | 2.2 | 0 |
| 0.5 | 0.1 | 9.8 | 2 | 0 |
| 0.9 | 0.2 | 12.1 | 2.7 | <1 |

*(continued)*

| Food | Portion | Calories |
|------|---------|----------|

## BREADS AND BREAD PRODUCTS — CONTINUED

### ACCEPTABLE

| Food | Portion | Calories |
|------|---------|----------|
| Biscuit, buttermilk, refrigerator | 2 (about 2 oz. total) | 170 |
| Bran muffin, homemade with wheat bran and 2% low-fat milk | 1 (about 2 oz.) | 161 |
| Cinnamon roll, refrigerator, baked, with frosting | 1 (about 1 oz.) | 109 |
| Zwieback rusks | 5 pieces (about 1 oz.) | 149 |

### HIGH

| Food | Portion | Calories |
|------|---------|----------|
| Biscuit, baking powder, homemade | 1 (about 1 oz.) | 103 |
| Croissant | 1 (about 2 oz.) | 235 |
| Popover, homemade | 1 (about 1½ oz.) | 90 |
| Spoon bread, homemade with vegetable shortening | 1 cup | 468 |

## BREAKFAST FOODS

### LOW

| Food | Portion | Calories |
|------|---------|----------|
| Danish, cinnamon nut (Arby's) | 1 (3½ oz.) | 360 |
| French toast, frozen, with low-calorie syrup | 2 slices (about 4 oz. total) with 4 Tbsp. syrup | 340 |
| Hash brown, frozen, oven-heated | 1 patty (about 2½ oz.) | 110 |
| Pancakes with 2 pats butter and syrup (McDonald's) | 3 (about 9 oz.) | 560 |
| Toaster pastry with fruit | 1 | 204 |
| Waffle, frozen, with low-calorie syrup | 1 (about 1¼ oz.) with 2 Tbsp. syrup | 136 |

### ACCEPTABLE

| Food | Portion | Calories |
|------|---------|----------|
| Coffee cake, carmel nut | 1 slice (about 2 oz.) | 240 |
| Doughnut, plain, made without yeast | 1 (about 2 oz.) | 198 |

### HIGH

| Food | Portion | Calories |
|------|---------|----------|
| Biscuit with egg, cheese and sausage, frozen | 1 (about 5½ oz.) | 490 |
| Biscuit with egg and sausage (McDonald's) | 1 (about 6½ oz.) | 520 |

| Fat (g.) | Saturated Fat (g.) | % Calories from Fat | % Calories from Saturated Fat | Cholesterol (mg.) |
|---|---|---|---|---|
| 7 | 1.5 | 37.1 | 7.9 | 0 |
| 7 | 1.3 | 39.1 | 7.3 | 19 |
| 4 | 1 | 33 | 8.3 | 0 |
| 3.4 | 1.4 | 20.5 | 8.3 | 7 |
| 4.8 | 1.2 | 41.9 | 10.5 | <1 |
| 12 | 3.5 | 46 | 13.4 | 13 |
| 3.7 | 1.3 | 37 | 13 | 59 |
| 27.4 | 8.7 | 52.7 | 16.7 | 293 |
| 11 | 1 | 27.5 | 2.5 | 0 |
| 6 | 1.5 | 15.9 | 4 | 80 |
| 6 | 0 | 49.1 | 0 | 0 |
| 14 | 2.5 | 22.5 | 4 | 10 |
| 5.3 | 0.8 | 23.4 | 3.5 | 0 |
| 2.1 | 0.5 | 13.9 | 3.3 | 0 |
| 12 | 2.5 | 45 | 9.4 | 20 |
| 10.8 | 1.8 | 49.1 | 8.2 | 17 |
| 30 | 12 | 55.1 | 22 | 145 |
| 35 | 10 | 60.6 | 17.3 | 245 |

*(continued)*

| FOOD | PORTION | CALORIES |
|------|---------|----------|

## BREAKFAST FOODS — CONTINUED

### HIGH — CONTINUED

| | | |
|------|---------|----------|
| Croissant with egg, cheese and sausage (Burger King) | 1 (about 6 oz.) | 530 |
| Croissant with ham and cheese (Arby's) | 1 (about 4¼ oz.) | 345 |
| Danish, cheese (McDonald's) | 1 (about 4 oz.) | 410 |
| Doughnut, cream-filled, yeast or raised | 1 (about 3 oz.) | 307 |
| English muffin with egg, cheese and Canadian bacon (McDonald's) | 1 (about 5 oz.) | 290 |
| French toast sticks without butter and syrup (Burger King) | 5 (about 5½ oz. total) | 500 |
| Hash brown (McDonald's) | 1 patty (about 2 oz.) | 130 |

### COLD CEREALS

#### LOW

| | | |
|------|---------|----------|
| Cheerios with skim milk | 1 cup with ½ cup milk | 150 |
| Granola without raisins, low-fat, with skim milk | ½ cup with ½ cup milk | 250 |
| Kellogg's Frosted Flakes with skim milk | ¾ cup with ½ cup milk | 160 |
| Raisin Bran with skim milk | 1 cup with ½ cup milk | 210 |
| Shredded Wheat without milk | 2 biscuits | 160 |
| Trix with skim milk | 1 cup with ½ cup milk | 160 |

#### ACCEPTABLE

| | | |
|------|---------|----------|
| Cinnamon Toast Crunch with 2% low-fat milk | ¾ cup with ½ cup milk | 190 |

#### HIGH

| | | |
|------|---------|----------|
| Cracklin' Oat Bran with skim milk | ¾ cup with ½ cup milk | 270 |
| 100% Natural with fruit and nuts, with 2% low-fat milk | ⅔ cup with ½ cup milk | 310 |

| Fat (g.) | Saturated Fat (g.) | % Calories from Fat | % Calories from Saturated Fat | Cholesterol (mg.) |
|---|---|---|---|---|
| 41 | 14 | 69.6 | 23.8 | 255 |
| 20.7 | 12.1 | 54 | 31.6 | 90 |
| 22 | 8 | 48.3 | 17.6 | 70 |
| 20.8 | 5.7 | 61 | 16.7 | 20 |
| 13 | 4.5 | 40.3 | 14 | 235 |
| 27 | 7 | 48.6 | 12.6 | 0 |
| 8 | 1.5 | 55.4 | 10.4 | 0 |
| 2 | 0.5 | 12 | 3 | <5 |
| 3 | 0 | 10.8 | 0 | 0 |
| 0 | 0 | 0 | 0 | 0 |
| 1 | 0 | 4.3 | 0 | 0 |
| 0.5 | 0 | 2.8 | 0 | 0 |
| 1.5 | 0.5 | 8.4 | 2.8 | <5 |
| 6 | 2 | 28.4 | 9.5 | 0 |
| 8 | 3 | 26.7 | 10 | 0 |
| 13.5 | 3.5 | 39.2 | 10.2 | 0 |

(continued)

| FOOD | PORTION | CALORIES |
|------|---------|----------|

## BREAKFAST FOODS—CONTINUED

### HOT CEREALS

**LOW**

| Food | Portion | Calories |
|------|---------|----------|
| Cream of Rice, cooked | ¾ cup | 95 |
| Cream of Wheat, quick-cooking, cooked | ¾ cup | 97 |
| Farina, enriched, cooked | ¾ cup | 88 |
| Oatmeal, cooked | ¾ cup | 109 |
| Ralston, cooked | ¾ cup | 101 |
| Wheatena, cooked | ¾ cup | 102 |

## CANDY AND SWEETS

**LOW**

| Food | Portion | Calories |
|------|---------|----------|
| Butterscotch | 4 pieces (about 1 oz. total) | 112 |
| Hard candy | 3 pieces (about ½ oz. total) | 60 |
| Marshmallow chicks | 5 small (about 2 oz. total) | 160 |
| Peanut brittle | 1 piece (about 1⅓ oz.) | 180 |

**ACCEPTABLE**

| Food | Portion | Calories |
|------|---------|----------|
| Fudge, vanilla, homemade | 1 piece (about 1 oz.) | 105 |

**HIGH**

| Food | Portion | Calories |
|------|---------|----------|
| Almonds, chocolate-coated | 7 (about 1 oz. total) | 159 |
| Caramels | 3 (about 1 oz. total) | 108 |
| Chocolate bar, semisweet | 1 (about 1½ oz.) | 230 |
| Coconut bar, chocolate-coated | 1 (about 2 oz.) | 195 |
| Fudge, chocolate with nuts, homemade | 1 piece (about 1 oz.) | 121 |
| Mints, chocolate-coated | 2 (about ⅓ oz. total) | 29 |
| Peanuts, chocolate-coated | 10 (about 1½ oz. total) | 208 |
| Raisins, chocolate-coated | 10 (about ⅓ oz. total) | 39 |
| Vanilla creams, chocolate-coated | 1 oz. | 122 |

| Fat (g.) | Saturated Fat (g.) | % Calories from Fat | % Calories from Saturated Fat | Cholesterol (mg.) |
|---|---|---|---|---|
| 0.2 | 0 | 1.9 | 0 | 0 |
| 0.4 | 0 | 3.7 | 0 | 0 |
| 0.2 | 0.02 | 2 | <1 | 0 |
| 1.8 | 0.3 | 14.9 | 2.5 | 0 |
| 0.6 | 0 | 5.3 | 0 | 0 |
| 0.9 | 0 | 7.9 | 0 | 0 |
| | | | | |
| 1 | 0.3 | 8 | 2.4 | 3 |
| 0 | 0 | 0 | 0 | 0 |
| 0 | 0 | 0 | 0 | 0 |
| 5 | 1 | 25 | 5 | 0 |
| 1.5 | 1 | 12.9 | 8.6 | 5 |
| 12.2 | 2.1 | 69.1 | 11.9 | 0 |
| 2.3 | 1.9 | 19.2 | 15.8 | 2 |
| 13 | 9 | 50.9 | 35.2 | 10 |
| 11.7 | 6.2 | 54 | 28.6 | 0 |
| 4.6 | 1.6 | 34.2 | 11.9 | 4 |
| 1.1 | 0.7 | 34.1 | 21.7 | 0 |
| 13.4 | 5.8 | 58 | 25.1 | 4 |
| 1.5 | 0.9 | 34.6 | 20.8 | <1 |
| 4.8 | 1.4 | 35.4 | 10.3 | 1 |

*(continued)*

| Food | Portion | Calories |
|------|---------|----------|

## Cheese and Cheese Products

### Low

| Food | Portion | Calories |
|------|---------|----------|
| American, nonfat | 1 slice (about ¾ oz.) | 30 |
| Cheddar, nonfat | 1 oz. | 45 |
| Cream cheese, nonfat | 2 Tbsp. | 30 |
| Swiss, nonfat | 1 slice (about ¾ oz.) | 30 |
| Yogurt cheese, low-fat | 1 oz. | 30 |

### Acceptable

| Food | Portion | Calories |
|------|---------|----------|
| Cottage cheese, 1% low-fat | ½ cup | 82 |

### High

| Food | Portion | Calories |
|------|---------|----------|
| American | 1 oz. | 106 |
| Blue cheese | 1 oz. | 99 |
| Brie | 1 oz. | 93 |
| Camembert | 1 oz. | 84 |
| Caraway | 1 oz. | 105 |
| Cheddar | | |
| reduced-fat | 1 oz. | 80 |
| regular | 1 oz. | 110 |
| Colby | 1 oz. | 110 |
| Cottage cheese | | |
| creamed, small or large curd | ½ cup | 109 |
| 2% low-fat | ½ cup | 101 |
| Cream cheese | | |
| reduced-fat | 2 Tbsp. | 70 |
| regular | 1 oz. | 100 |
| Feta | 1 oz. | 74 |
| Fondue | ¼ cup | 151 |
| Gouda | 1 oz. | 100 |
| Gruyère | 1 oz. | 116 |
| Limburger | 1 oz. | 92 |
| Monterey Jack | 1 oz. | 105 |
| Mozzarella | | |
| part–skim milk | 1 oz. | 71 |
| whole milk | 1 oz. | 79 |

| Fat (G.) | Saturated Fat (G.) | % Calories from Fat | % Calories from Saturated Fat | Cholesterol (MG.) |
|---|---|---|---|---|
| 0 | 0 | 0 | 0 | 0 |
| 0 | 0 | 0 | 0 | 25 |
| 0 | 0 | 0 | 0 | <5 |
| 0 | 0 | 0 | 0 | 0 |
| 0.6 | Trace | 18 | Trace | 0 |
| 1.2 | 0.7 | 13.2 | 7.7 | 5 |
| 8.9 | 5.6 | 75.6 | 47.5 | 27 |
| 8.1 | 5.2 | 73.6 | 47.3 | 21 |
| 7.6 | 4.9 | 73.5 | 47.4 | 28 |
| 6.8 | 4.3 | 72.9 | 46.1 | 20 |
| 8.2 | 5.2 | 70.3 | 44.6 | 26 |
| 5 | 3 | 56.3 | 33.8 | 20 |
| 9 | 6 | 73.6 | 49 | 30 |
| 9 | 5.7 | 73.6 | 46.6 | 27 |
| 4.7 | 3 | 38.8 | 24.8 | 16 |
| 2.2 | 1.4 | 19.6 | 12.5 | 10 |
| 5 | 3.5 | 64.3 | 45 | 15 |
| 10 | 6 | 90 | 54 | 30 |
| 6 | 4.2 | 72.9 | 51.1 | 25 |
| 10.4 | 5.1 | 62 | 30.4 | 128 |
| 7.7 | 4.9 | 69.3 | 44.1 | 32 |
| 9.1 | 5.3 | 70.6 | 41.1 | 31 |
| 7.6 | 4.7 | 74.3 | 46 | 25 |
| 8.5 | 5.3 | 72.9 | 45.4 | 25 |
| 4.5 | 2.8 | 57 | 35.5 | 16 |
| 6.1 | 3.7 | 69.5 | 42.2 | 22 |

*(continued)*

| FOOD | PORTION | CALORIES |
|------|---------|----------|

## CHEESE AND CHEESE PRODUCTS — CONTINUED

### HIGH — CONTINUED

| FOOD | PORTION | CALORIES |
|------|---------|----------|
| Muenster | | |
|     reduced-fat | 1 oz. | 80 |
|     regular | 1 oz. | 103 |
| Neufchâtel | 1 oz. | 73 |
| Parmesan, grated | 1 Tbsp. | 23 |
| Provolone | 1 oz. | 98 |
| Ricotta | | |
|     part–skim milk | ½ cup | 171 |
|     whole milk | ½ cup | 216 |
| Romano, grated | 1 Tbsp. | 19 |
| Soufflé, homemade | 1 cup | 207 |
| Swiss | 1 oz. | 105 |
| Welsh rarebit, frozen | ¼ cup (about 2 oz.) | 120 |

## DESSERTS

### CAKES

#### LOW

| FOOD | PORTION | CALORIES |
|------|---------|----------|
| Angel food | 1 slice (¹⁄₁₂ of cake) | 73 |
| Fruitcake | 1 slice (about 2 oz.) | 139 |
| Sponge | 1 slice (¹⁄₁₂ of cake) | 110 |

#### ACCEPTABLE

| FOOD | PORTION | CALORIES |
|------|---------|----------|
| Boston cream | 1 slice (⅙ of cake) | 232 |
| Devil's food, made from mix with eggs and oil, with 2 Tbsp. chocolate icing | 1 slice (¹⁄₁₂ of cake) | 440 |
| Pound, made with margarine | 1 slice (¹⁄₁₆ of loaf cake) | 206 |
| White, made from mix with egg whites and oil, with 2 Tbsp. reduced-calorie chocolate icing | 1 slice (¹⁄₁₂ of cake) | 370 |

| Fat (g.) | **Saturated Fat (g.)** | % Calories from Fat | **% Calories from Saturated Fat** | Cholesterol (mg.) |
|---|---|---|---|---|
| 5 | **3** | 56.3 | **33.8** | 20 |
| 8.4 | **5.4** | 73.4 | **47.2** | 27 |
| 6.6 | **4.1** | 81.4 | **50.5** | 21 |
| 1.5 | **1** | 58.7 | **39.1** | 4 |
| 7.5 | **4.8** | 68.9 | **44.1** | 19 |
| | | | | |
| 9.8 | **6.1** | 51.6 | **32.1** | 38 |
| 16.1 | **10.3** | 67.1 | **42.9** | 63 |
| 1.4 | **0.9** | 66.3 | **42.6** | 5 |
| 16.2 | **8.2** | 70.4 | **35.7** | 176 |
| 7.7 | **5** | 66 | **42.9** | 26 |
| 9 | **4** | 67.5 | **30** | 20 |
| | | | | |
| 0.2 | **0.03** | 2.5 | **<1** | 0 |
| 3.9 | **0.5** | 25.3 | **3.2** | 2 |
| 1 | **0.3** | 8.2 | **2.5** | 39 |
| | | | | |
| 7.8 | **2.3** | 30.3 | **8.9** | 35 |
| 21 | **4.5** | 43 | **9.2** | 45 |
| 9 | **1.9** | 39.3 | **8.3** | 41 |
| 11 | **3** | 26.8 | **7.3** | 0 |

*(continued)*

| FOOD | PORTION | CALORIES |
|------|---------|----------|

## DESSERTS — CONTINUED

### CAKES — CONTINUED

#### HIGH

| | | |
|------|---------|----------|
| Carrot cake, homemade with cream cheese icing | 1 slice (¹⁄₁₂ of cake) | 484 |
| Cheesecake, frozen | ¼ cake (about 4¼ oz.) | 350 |
| Pound, made with butter | 1 slice (¹⁄₁₂ of cake) | 110 |
| Yellow with pudding, made from mix with eggs and margarine, with 2 Tbsp. chocolate icing | 1 slice (¹⁄₁₂ of cake) | 410 |

### COOKIES

#### LOW

| | | |
|------|---------|----------|
| Brownie with nuts, made from mix | 1 (about ¾ oz.) | 81 |
| Fig bars, nonfat | 2 (about 1 oz.) | 100 |
| Gingersnaps | 5 (about 1¼ oz. total) | 147 |
| Ladyfingers | 4 (about 1½ oz. total) | 158 |
| Molasses | 2 (about 2 oz. total) | 274 |
| Oatmeal with raisins | | |
| homemade | 1 (about ½ oz.) | 65 |
| reduced-fat | 2 (about 1 oz.) | 110 |

#### ACCEPTABLE

| | | |
|------|---------|----------|
| Fig bars | 2 (about 1 oz. total) | 110 |
| Peanut butter, homemade | 1 (about ¾ oz.) | 95 |
| Sugar, homemade with margarine | 1 (about ½ oz.) | 66 |

#### HIGH

| | | |
|------|---------|----------|
| Chocolate chip, homemade with margarine | 1 (about ½ oz.) | 78 |
| Macaroon, homemade | 1 (about 1 oz.) | 97 |
| Sandwich, vanilla with cream filling | 4 (about 2 oz. total) | 297 |
| Sugar wafer with cream filling | 1 small | 18 |
| Vanilla wafers | 8 (about 1 oz. total) | 150 |

| Fat (g.) | Saturated Fat (g.) | % Calories from Fat | % Calories from Saturated Fat | Cholesterol (mg.) |
|---|---|---|---|---|
| 29.3 | **5.4** | 54.5 | **10** | 60 |
| 18 | **9** | 46.3 | **23.1** | 50 |
| 5.6 | **3.2** | 45.8 | **26.2** | 63 |
| | | | | |
| 17 | **7.5** | 37.3 | **16.5** | 75 |
| | | | | |
| 3.7 | **0.6** | 41.1 | **6.6** | 13 |
| 0 | **0** | 0 | **0** | 0 |
| 3.1 | **0.8** | 19 | **4.9** | 14 |
| 3.4 | **1.1** | 19.4 | **6.7** | 157 |
| 6.9 | **1.7** | 22.7 | **5.6** | 25 |
| | | | | |
| 2.4 | **0.5** | 33.2 | **6.9** | 5 |
| 2.5 | **0** | 20.5 | **0** | 0 |
| | | | | |
| 2.5 | **1** | 20.5 | **8.2** | 0 |
| 4.8 | **0.9** | 45.5 | **8.5** | 6 |
| 3.3 | **0.7** | 45 | **9.5** | 4 |
| | | | | |
| 4.5 | **1.3** | 51.9 | **15** | 5 |
| 3.1 | **2.7** | 28.8 | **25.1** | 0 |
| 13.5 | **3.7** | 41 | **11.2** | 23 |
| 0.9 | **0.2** | 45 | **10** | 0 |
| 7 | **2** | 42 | **12** | 0 |

*(continued)*

| FOOD | PORTION | CALORIES |
|---|---|---|
| **DESSERTS — CONTINUED** | | |
| **PIES** | | |
| **LOW** | | |
| Apple, low-fat, frozen | 1 slice (⅕ of pie) | 220 |
| Pecan, fresh | 1 slice (⅛ of pie) | 431 |
| **ACCEPTABLE** | | |
| Rhubarb, fresh | 1 slice (⅛ of pie) | 299 |
| **HIGH** | | |
| Apple, fresh | 1 slice (⅛ of pie) | 302 |
| Banana custard, fresh | 1 slice (⅛ of pie) | 252 |
| Blueberry, fresh | 1 slice (⅛ of pie) | 286 |
| Cherry, fresh | 1 slice (⅛ of pie) | 308 |
| Chocolate meringue, fresh | 1 slice (⅛ of pie) | 287 |
| Custard, fresh | 1 slice (⅛ of pie) | 249 |
| Lemon meringue, fresh | 1 slice (⅛ of pie) | 268 |
| Mince, fresh | 1 slice (⅛ of pie) | 320 |
| Pumpkin, fresh | 1 slice (⅛ of pie) | 241 |
| **PUDDING** | | |
| **ACCEPTABLE** | | |
| Vanilla, made from mix with 2% low-fat milk | ½ cup | 148 |
| **HIGH** | | |
| Chocolate, made from mix with whole milk | ½ cup | 163 |
| Custard, homemade, baked | ½ cup | 148 |
| Rice with raisins, homemade | ½ cup | 194 |
| Tapioca, made from mix with whole milk | ½ cup | 161 |
| **OTHER** | | |
| **LOW** | | |
| Fruit cocktail, canned in light syrup | ½ cup | 72 |
| Gelatin, made from powder, with fruit | ½ cup | 80 |

| Fat (g.) | Saturated Fat (g.) | % Calories from Fat | % Calories from Saturated Fat | Cholesterol (mg.) |
|---|---|---|---|---|
| 5 | 1 | 20.5 | 4.1 | 0 |
| 23.6 | 3.3 | 49.3 | 6.9 | 65 |
| 12.6 | 3.1 | 37.9 | 9.3 | 0 |
| 13.1 | 3.4 | 39 | 10.1 | 0 |
| 10.6 | 3.4 | 37.9 | 12.1 | 66 |
| 12.7 | 3.2 | 40 | 10.1 | 0 |
| 13.3 | 3.5 | 38.9 | 10.2 | 0 |
| 13.7 | 5.1 | 43 | 16 | 64 |
| 12.7 | 4.3 | 45.9 | 15.5 | 120 |
| 10.7 | 3.2 | 35.9 | 10.7 | 98 |
| 13.6 | 3.6 | 38.3 | 10.1 | 1 |
| 12.8 | 4.5 | 47.8 | 16.8 | 70 |
| 2.4 | 1.4 | 14.6 | 8.5 | 9 |
| 4.6 | 2.7 | 25.4 | 14.9 | 16 |
| 6.6 | 3.3 | 40.1 | 20.1 | 123 |
| 4.1 | 2.2 | 19 | 10.2 | 15 |
| 4.1 | 2.5 | 22.9 | 14 | 17 |
| 0.1 | 0.01 | 1.3 | <1 | 0 |
| 0.1 | 0 | 1.1 | 0 | 0 |

*(continued)*

| FOOD | PORTION | CALORIES |
|---|---|---|
| **DESSERTS—CONTINUED** | | |
| **OTHER—CONTINUED** | | |
| **HIGH** | | |
| Coconut cream, canned | ¼ cup | 142 |
| Eclair | 1 (about 3½ oz.) | 239 |
| **DIPS AND SNACKS** | | |
| **DIPS** | | |
| **LOW** | | |
| Hummus | ⅓ cup | 140 |
| Onion, low-fat | 2 Tbsp. | 30 |
| Salsa | 2 Tbsp. | 10 |
| **HIGH** | | |
| Bacon and horseradish | 2 Tbsp. | 60 |
| Cheese | | |
| low-fat | 2 Tbsp. | 80 |
| regular | 2 Tbsp. | 90 |
| Clam | 2 Tbsp. | 50 |
| Onion | 2 Tbsp. | 60 |
| Ranch | 2 Tbsp. | 140 |
| **SNACKS** | | |
| **LOW** | | |
| Caramel corn | ½ cup | 140 |
| Cereal mix | ¾ cup | 130 |
| Cracker Jacks | 1 box | 150 |
| Crackers | | |
| graham | 1 (½ oz.) | 55 |
| saltine | 5 (½ oz. total) | 61 |
| Crispbread, rye | 1 slice | 35 |
| Fruit rolls | 2 | 110 |

| Fat (G.) | Saturated Fat (G.) | % Calories from Fat | % Calories from Saturated Fat | Cholesterol (MG.) |
|---|---|---|---|---|
| 13.1 | 11.6 | 83 | 73.5 | 0 |
| 13.6 | 4.4 | 51.2 | 16.6 | 136 |
| 6.9 | 1 | 44.4 | 6.4 | 0 |
| 0 | 0 | 0 | 0 | <5 |
| 0 | 0 | 0 | 0 | 0 |
| 5 | 3 | 75 | 45 | 20 |
| 3 | 2 | 33.6 | 22.5 | 15 |
| 7 | 5 | 70 | 50 | 20 |
| 4.5 | 3 | 81 | 54 | 20 |
| 5 | 3 | 75 | 45 | 20 |
| 14 | 2.5 | 90 | 16.1 | 10 |
| 4 | 1 | 25.7 | 6.4 | <5 |
| 5 | 1 | 34.6 | 6.9 | 0 |
| 3 | 0.5 | 18 | 3 | 0 |
| 1.3 | 0.3 | 21.3 | 4.9 | 0 |
| 1.7 | 0.4 | 25.1 | 5.9 | 0 |
| 0 | 0 | 0 | 0 | 0 |
| 1 | Trace | 8.2 | Trace | 0 |

*(continued)*

| FOOD | PORTION | CALORIES |
|---|---|---|

### DIPS AND SNACKS — CONTINUED

#### SNACKS — CONTINUED

##### LOW — CONTINUED

| FOOD | PORTION | CALORIES |
|---|---|---|
| Granola bar, chocolate chip, low-fat | 1 (about 1 oz.) | 110 |
| Melba toast | 3 pieces (about ½ oz. total) | 55 |
| Pretzels | | |
| baked | 16 (about 1 oz. total) | 120 |
| cheese-flavored | 1 oz. | 160 |
| Dutch-type | 2 large (about 1 oz. total) | 125 |
| Popcorn | | |
| air-popped, plain | 1 cup | 31 |
| microwave, butter-flavored, light | 1 bag (about 13 cups) | 110 |
| Potato chips, nonfat | 30 (about 1 oz. total) | 110 |
| Rice cakes, flavored | 1 (about ½ oz.) | 50 |
| Toffee corn (popcorn and peanuts) | ⅔ cup (about 1 oz.) | 140 |
| Tortilla chips, plain | 13 (about 1 oz. total) | 140 |

##### ACCEPTABLE

| FOOD | PORTION | CALORIES |
|---|---|---|
| Corn chips | 30 small (about 1 oz. total) | 155 |
| Popcorn, microwave | | |
| butter-flavored | 1 bag (about 13 cups) | 150 |
| plain | 1 bag (about 13 cups) | 140 |

##### HIGH

| FOOD | PORTION | CALORIES |
|---|---|---|
| Cheez Doodles | 17 (about 1 oz. total) | 150 |
| Crackers | | |
| butter-flavored | 4 (about ½ oz. total) | 64 |
| cheese | 4 round (½ oz. total) | 67 |
| cheese and peanut butter | 2 (½ oz. total) | 69 |
| wheat | 7 (½ oz. total) | 61 |
| Granola bar, chocolate chip | 1 (about 1 oz.) | 120 |

| Fat (g.) | Saturated Fat (g.) | % Calories from Fat | % Calories from Saturated Fat | Cholesterol (mg.) |
|---|---|---|---|---|
| 2 | 0.5 | 16.4 | 4.1 | 0 |
| 0.5 | 0.1 | 8.2 | 1.6 | 0 |
| 2.5 | 0 | 18.8 | 0 | 0 |
| 7 | 1 | 39.4 | 5.6 | 0 |
| 1.4 | 0.3 | 10.1 | 2.2 | 0 |
| 0.3 | 0.1 | 8.7 | 2.9 | 0 |
| 4 | 0.5 | 32.7 | 4.1 | 0 |
| 0 | 0 | 0 | 0 | 0 |
| 0 | 0 | 0 | 0 | 0 |
| 4 | 1 | 25.7 | 6.4 | <5 |
| 6 | 1 | 38.6 | 6.4 | 0 |
| 9.1 | 1.5 | 52.8 | 8.7 | 0 |
| 10 | 1.5 | 60 | 9 | 0 |
| 10 | 1.5 | 64.3 | 9.6 | 0 |
| 8 | 2.5 | 48 | 15 | 0 |
| 2.5 | 0.8 | 35.2 | 11.3 | 0 |
| 3 | 1.2 | 40.2 | 16.1 | 4 |
| 3.4 | 0.9 | 44.3 | 11.7 | 2 |
| 1.8 | 0.9 | 26.6 | 13.3 | 0 |
| 3.5 | 1.5 | 26.3 | 11.3 | 0 |

*(continued)*

| FOOD | PORTION | CALORIES |
|---|---|---|
| **DIPS AND SNACKS — CONTINUED** | | |
| **SNACKS — CONTINUED** | | |
| **HIGH — CONTINUED** | | |
| Popcorn, buttered | 1 cup | 41 |
| Potato chips | 10 (about ¾ oz. total) | 105 |
| Potato sticks | 1 oz. | 148 |
| Sesame sticks | 30 pieces (about 1 oz.) | 170 |
| Wheat Nuts (wheat germ nuggets) | 1 oz. | 200 |
| **DRESSINGS** | | |
| **LOW** | | |
| Blue cheese, nonfat | 2 Tbsp. | 35 |
| Caesar, low-fat | 2 Tbsp. | 70 |
| French, nonfat | 2 Tbsp. | 50 |
| Garlic, creamy, nonfat | 2 Tbsp. | 40 |
| Honey dijon, nonfat | 2 Tbsp. | 50 |
| Italian | | |
| low-fat | 2 Tbsp. | 15 |
| nonfat | 2 Tbsp. | 15 |
| Oil and vinegar, imitation, nonfat | 2 Tbsp. | 15 |
| Ranch | | |
| low-fat | 2 Tbsp. | 80 |
| nonfat | 2 Tbsp. | 45 |
| Thousand Island | | |
| low-fat | 2 Tbsp. | 45 |
| nonfat | 2 Tbsp. | 35 |
| **ACCEPTABLE** | | |
| French, low-fat | 2 Tbsp. | 50 |
| Ranch | 2 Tbsp. | 140 |
| Russian | 2 Tbsp. | 110 |

| Fat (g.) | Saturated Fat (g.) | % Calories from Fat | % Calories from Saturated Fat | Cholesterol (mg.) |
|---|---|---|---|---|
| 2 | 0.9 | 43.9 | 19.8 | 4 |
| 7.1 | 1.8 | 60.9 | 15.4 | 0 |
| 9.8 | 2.5 | 59.6 | 15.2 | 0 |
| 12 | 2 | 63.5 | 10.6 | 0 |
| 19 | 3 | 85.5 | 13.5 | 0 |
| 0 | 0 | 0 | 0 | 0 |
| 6 | 0.5 | 77.1 | 6.4 | 5 |
| 0 | 0 | 0 | 0 | 0 |
| 0 | 0 | 0 | 0 | 0 |
| 0 | 0 | 0 | 0 | 0 |
| 0.5 | 0 | 30 | 0 | 0 |
| 0 | 0 | 0 | 0 | 0 |
| 0 | 0 | 0 | 0 | 0 |
| 7 | 0.5 | 78.8 | 5.6 | 0 |
| 0 | 0 | 0 | 0 | 0 |
| 1 | 0 | 20 | 0 | <5 |
| 0 | 0 | 0 | 0 | 0 |
| 3 | 0.5 | 54 | 9 | 0 |
| 14 | 1.5 | 90 | 9.6 | 10 |
| 6 | 1 | 49.1 | 8.2 | 0 |

*(continued)*

| FOOD | PORTION | CALORIES |
|------|---------|----------|

### DRESSINGS — CONTINUED

**HIGH**

| Food | Portion | Calories |
|------|---------|----------|
| Blue cheese | | |
| low-fat | 2 Tbsp. | 80 |
| regular | 2 Tbsp. | 170 |
| Caesar | 2 Tbsp. | 170 |
| French | 2 Tbsp. | 120 |
| Garlic, creamy | 2 Tbsp. | 140 |
| Honey dijon | 2 Tbsp. | 130 |
| Italian | 2 Tbsp. | 100 |
| Italian, creamy | | |
| low-fat | 2 Tbsp. | 50 |
| regular | 2 Tbsp. | 110 |
| Oil and vinegar | | |
| low-fat | 2 Tbsp. | 60 |
| regular | 2 Tbsp. | 110 |
| Sweet-and-sour | 2 Tbsp. | 150 |
| Thousand Island | 2 Tbsp. | 110 |

### EGGS AND EGG SUBSTITUTE

**LOW**

| Food | Portion | Calories |
|------|---------|----------|
| Egg white | 1 large | 16 |

**ACCEPTABLE**

| Food | Portion | Calories |
|------|---------|----------|
| Egg substitute, liquid | ¼ cup | 53 |

**HIGH**

| Food | Portion | Calories |
|------|---------|----------|
| Egg | | |
| fried with margarine | 1 large | 92 |
| hard-boiled | 1 large | 78 |
| scrambled with butter and whole milk | 1 large | 95 |
| Egg substitute, frozen | ¼ cup | 96 |
| Egg yolk | 1 large | 59 |

| Fat (g.) | Saturated Fat (g.) | % Calories from Fat | % Calories from Saturated Fat | Cholesterol (mg.) |
|---|---|---|---|---|
| 8 | 2 | 90 | 22.5 | 0 |
| 17 | 3 | 90 | 15.9 | 10 |
| 18 | 2.5 | 95.3 | 13.2 | 0 |
| 12 | 2 | 90 | 15 | 0 |
| 13 | 2 | 83.6 | 12.9 | 0 |
| 10 | 1.5 | 69.2 | 10.4 | 0 |
| 10 | 1.5 | 90 | 13.5 | 0 |
| 5 | 1 | 90 | 18 | 0 |
| 11 | 4 | 90 | 32.7 | 0 |
| 5 | 1 | 75 | 15 | 0 |
| 11 | 2 | 90 | 16.4 | 0 |
| 13 | 2 | 78 | 12 | 0 |
| 10 | 1.5 | 81.8 | 12.3 | 10 |
| Trace | 0 | Trace | 0 | 0 |
| 2.1 | 0.4 | 35.7 | 7 | 1 |
| 6.9 | 1.9 | 67.5 | 18.6 | 211 |
| 5.3 | 1.6 | 61.2 | 18.5 | 212 |
| 7.1 | 2.8 | 67.3 | 26.5 | 248 |
| 6.7 | 1.2 | 62.8 | 11.3 | 1 |
| 5.1 | 1.6 | 77.8 | 24.4 | 213 |

*(continued)*

| FOOD | PORTION | CALORIES |
|---|---|---|

### EGGS AND EGG SUBSTITUTE—CONTINUED

**HIGH—CONTINUED**

Quiche

| | | |
|---|---|---|
| Lorraine | 1 slice (about 6¼ oz.) | 600 |
| spinach, frozen | 1 (about 6 oz.) | 480 |

### FAST FOODS

**LOW**

| | | |
|---|---|---|
| Baked potato with cheese and bacon (Wendy's) | 1 (about 10 oz.) | 530 |
| BBQ Beef Sandwich on bun (Dairy Queen/Brazier) | 1 (about 4 oz.) | 225 |
| Fish, breaded, baked, without bun (Long John Silver's) | 3 pieces (about 5 oz. total) | 150 |
| Onion rings, breaded (Burger King) | 1 order (about 5 oz.) | 310 |

**ACCEPTABLE**

| | | |
|---|---|---|
| Baked potato with sour cream and chives (Wendy's) | 1 (about 10 oz.) | 380 |
| Burrito, bean (Taco Bell) | 1 | 391 |
| Chicken, breaded, with mayonnaise, lettuce and tomato on bun (Wendy's) | 1 (about 9 oz.) | 450 |
| Chicken breast and wing quarter, roasted, without skin (KFC) | (about 4 oz. total) | 199 |
| Fish, breaded, with tartar sauce on bun (McDonald's) | 1 (about 6 oz.) | 360 |
| French fries (McDonald's) | 1 large (about 6 oz.) | 450 |
| Garden salad with 2 Tbsp. reduced-fat, reduced-calorie Italian dressing (Wendy's) | 1 (about 10 oz.) | 150 |
| Pie, apple (Burger King) | 1 (about 4 oz.) | 310 |
| Shake, chocolate (McDonald's) | 1 small (about 16 oz.) | 350 |

**HIGH**

| | | |
|---|---|---|
| Baked potato with chili and cheese (Wendy's) | 1 (about 10 oz.) | 610 |

| Fat (G.) | Saturated Fat (G.) | % Calories from Fat | % Calories from Saturated Fat | Cholesterol (MG.) |
|---|---|---|---|---|
| 48 | 23.2 | 72 | 34.8 | 285 |
| 32 | 16 | 60 | 30 | 205 |
| 18 | 4 | 30.6 | 6.8 | 20 |
| 4 | 1 | 16 | 4 | 20 |
| 1 | 0.6 | 6 | 3.6 | 110 |
| 14 | 2 | 40.6 | 5.8 | 0 |
| 6 | 4 | 14.2 | 9.5 | 15 |
| 12 | 4 | 27.6 | 9.2 | 5 |
| 20 | 4 | 40 | 8 | 60 |
| 5.9 | 1.7 | 26.7 | 7.7 | 97 |
| 16 | 3.5 | 40 | 8.8 | 35 |
| 22 | 4 | 44 | 8 | 0 |
| 9 | 1.5 | 54 | 9 | 0 |
| 15 | 3 | 43.5 | 8.7 | 0 |
| 6 | 3.5 | 15.4 | 9 | 25 |
| 24 | 9 | 35.4 | 13.3 | 45 |

*(continued)*

| FOOD | PORTION | CALORIES |
|------|---------|----------|

## FAST FOODS—CONTINUED

### HIGH—CONTINUED

| FOOD | PORTION | CALORIES |
|------|---------|----------|
| Baked potato with broccoli and cheese (Arby's) | 1 (about 10 oz.) | 417 |
| Burrito | | |
|    chicken (Taco Bell) | 1 | 345 |
| Cheeseburger with condiments on bun (Burger King) | 1 (about 5 oz.) | 320 |
| Cheese steak with onions and peppers on bun (Arby's) | 1 (about 7 oz.) | 467 |
| Chef's salad with turkey, ham, cheese and Thousand Island dressing (Arby's) | 1 (about 14 oz.) | 503 |
| Chicken breast, fried (KFC) | 1 (about 5 oz.) | 360 |
| Chicken nuggets without sauce (KFC) | 6 (about 3 oz. total) | 284 |
| Double cheeseburger with condiments on bun (Burger King) | 1 (about 8 oz.) | 600 |
| Hamburger with condiments on bun (McDonald's) | 1 (about 4 oz.) | 270 |
| Hot dog, plain, on bun (Dairy Queen/ Brazier) | 1 (about 3 oz.) | 280 |
| Nachos Supreme (Taco Bell) | 1 order | 364 |
| Roast beef on bun (Arby's) | 1 (about 6 oz.) | 383 |
| Shake, vanilla (McDonald's) | 1 small (about 16 oz.) | 310 |
| Submarine | | |
|    Italian (cold cuts) (Arby's) | 1 (about 10 oz.) | 671 |
|    Tuna (Arby's) | 1 (about 10 oz.) | 663 |
| Taco, beef (Taco Bell) | 1 | 180 |
| Taco salad with small chili and 1 packet sour cream (Wendy's) | 1 (about 30 oz.) | 830 |
| Tostada (Taco Bell) | 1 | 242 |

| Fat (G.) | Saturated Fat (G.) | % Calories from Fat | % Calories from Saturated Fat | Cholesterol (MG.) |
|---|---|---|---|---|
| 17.9 | 6.9 | 38.6 | 14.9 | 22 |
| 13 | 5 | 33.9 | 13 | 57 |
| 13 | 6 | 36.6 | 16.9 | 40 |
| 25.3 | 9.7 | 48.8 | 18.7 | 53 |
| 38.7 | 8.2 | 69.2 | 14.7 | 150 |
| 20 | 5 | 50 | 12.5 | 115 |
| 18 | 4 | 57 | 12.7 | 68 |
| 36 | 17 | 54 | 25.5 | 135 |
| 9 | 3 | 30 | 10 | 30 |
| 16 | 6 | 51.4 | 19.3 | 25 |
| 18 | 5 | 44.5 | 12.4 | 17 |
| 18.2 | 7 | 42.8 | 16.4 | 43 |
| 5 | 3.5 | 14.5 | 10.2 | 25 |
| 38.8 | 12.8 | 52 | 17.2 | 69 |
| 37 | 8.2 | 50.2 | 11.1 | 43 |
| 11 | 5 | 55 | 25 | 32 |
| 42 | 17.5 | 45.5 | 19 | 125 |
| 11 | 4 | 40.9 | 14.9 | 14 |

*(continued)*

| FOOD | PORTION | CALORIES |
|------|---------|----------|
| **FATS, OILS AND SPREADS** | | |
| **FATS** | | |
| **HIGH** | | |
| Chicken | 1 Tbsp. | 115 |
| Lard | 1 Tbsp. | 115 |
| Shortening | 1 Tbsp. | 113 |
| **OILS** | | |
| **ACCEPTABLE** | | |
| Almond | 1 Tbsp. | 120 |
| Canola | 1 Tbsp. | 124 |
| Grapeseed | 1 Tbsp. | 120 |
| Safflower | 1 Tbsp. | 120 |
| Walnut | 1 Tbsp. | 120 |
| **HIGH** | | |
| Avocado | 1 Tbsp. | 124 |
| Coconut | 1 Tbsp. | 120 |
| Corn | 1 Tbsp. | 120 |
| Cottonseed | 1 Tbsp. | 120 |
| Olive | 1 Tbsp. | 119 |
| Palm | 1 Tbsp. | 120 |
| Peanut | 1 Tbsp. | 119 |
| Sesame | 1 Tbsp. | 120 |
| Soybean | 1 Tbsp. | 120 |
| Sunflower | 1 Tbsp. | 120 |
| **SPREADS** | | |
| **LOW** | | |
| Apple butter | 1 Tbsp. | 33 |
| Mayonnaise, low-fat | 1 Tbsp. | 25 |

| Fat (g.) | Saturated Fat (g.) | % Calories from Fat | % Calories from Saturated Fat | Cholesterol (mg.) |
|---|---|---|---|---|
| 12.8 | 3.8 | 100 | 29.7 | 11 |
| 12.8 | 5 | 100 | 39.1 | 4 |
| 12.8 | 3.2 | 100 | 25.5 | 0 |
| | | | | |
| 13.6 | 1.1 | 100 | 8.3 | 0 |
| 14 | 1 | 100 | 7.3 | 0 |
| 13.6 | 1.3 | 100 | 9.8 | 0 |
| 13.6 | 1.2 | 100 | 9 | 0 |
| 13.6 | 1.2 | 100 | 9 | 0 |
| | | | | |
| 14 | 1.6 | 100 | 11.6 | 0 |
| 13.6 | 11.8 | 100 | 88.5 | 0 |
| 13.6 | 1.7 | 100 | 12.8 | 0 |
| 13.6 | 3.5 | 100 | 26.3 | 0 |
| 13.5 | 1.8 | 100 | 13.6 | 0 |
| 13.6 | 6.7 | 100 | 50.3 | 0 |
| 13.5 | 2.3 | 100 | 17.4 | 0 |
| 13.6 | 1.9 | 100 | 14.3 | 0 |
| 13.6 | 2 | 100 | 15 | 0 |
| 13.6 | 1.4 | 100 | 10.5 | 0 |
| | | | | |
| 0.1 | 0 | 2.7 | 0 | 0 |
| 1 | 0 | 36 | 0 | 0 |

*(continued)*

| FOOD | PORTION | CALORIES |
|------|---------|----------|

## FATS, OILS AND SPREADS—CONTINUED

### SPREADS—CONTINUED

**ACCEPTABLE**

| | | |
|------|---------|----------|
| Almond butter, unsalted | 1 Tbsp. | 101 |
| Peanut butter without added oils | 2 Tbsp. | 200 |

**HIGH**

| | | |
|------|---------|----------|
| Butter, salted, unsalted stick or whipped | 1 Tbsp. | 102 |
| Butter blend, made with butter and vegetable oil | 1 Tbsp. | 50 |
| Margarine | | |
|     squeeze | 1 Tbsp. | 80 |
|     stick | | |
|         reduced-fat | 1 Tbsp. | 60 |
|         regular | 1 Tbsp. | 100 |
|     tub | | |
|         reduced-fat | 1 Tbsp. | 45 |
|         regular | 1 Tbsp. | 100 |
| Mayonnaise | | |
|     reduced-fat | 1 Tbsp. | 50 |
|     regular | 1 Tbsp. | 100 |
| Peanut butter with added oils, smooth | 2 Tbsp. | 188 |

## FISH AND SHELLFISH

### FISH

**LOW**

| | | |
|------|---------|----------|
| Bass, striped, uncooked | 3 oz. | 82 |
| Bluefish, uncooked | 3 oz. | 105 |
| Cod, Atlantic, broiled, baked or microwaved | 3 oz. | 89 |
| Flounder, broiled, baked or microwaved | 3 oz. | 99 |
| Grouper, broiled, baked or microwaved | 3 oz. | 100 |
| Haddock, broiled, baked or microwaved | 3 oz. | 95 |
| Halibut, broiled, baked or microwaved | 3 oz. | 119 |

| FAT (G.) | SATURATED FAT (G.) | % CALORIES FROM FAT | % CALORIES FROM SATURATED FAT | CHOLESTEROL (MG.) |
|---|---|---|---|---|
| 9.5 | 0.9 | 84.7 | 8 | 0 |
| 16 | 2 | 72 | 9 | 0 |
| 11.5 | 7.2 | 100 | 63.5 | 31 |
| 6 | 3 | 100 | 54 | 10 |
| 9 | 1.5 | 100 | 16.9 | 0 |
| 6 | 1 | 90 | 15 | 0 |
| 11 | 2 | 99 | 18 | 0 |
| 4.5 | 1 | 90 | 20 | 0 |
| 11 | 2 | 99 | 18 | 0 |
| 5 | 1 | 90 | 18 | 5 |
| 11 | 1.5 | 99 | 13.5 | 5 |
| 16 | 3.1 | 76.6 | 14.8 | 0 |
| 2 | 0.4 | 22 | 4.4 | 68 |
| 3.6 | 0.8 | 30.9 | 6.9 | 50 |
| 0.7 | 0.1 | 7.1 | 1 | 47 |
| 1.3 | 0.3 | 11.8 | 2.7 | 58 |
| 1.1 | 0.3 | 9.9 | 2.7 | 40 |
| 0.8 | 0.1 | 7.6 | <1 | 63 |
| 2.5 | 0.4 | 18.9 | 3 | 35 |

*(continued)*

| Food | Portion | Calories |
|---|---|---|

## FISH AND SHELLFISH—CONTINUED

### FISH—CONTINUED

**LOW—CONTINUED**

| Food | Portion | Calories |
|---|---|---|
| Mahimahi, uncooked | 3 oz. | 72 |
| Monkfish, uncooked | 3 oz. | 65 |
| Ocean perch, Atlantic, broiled, baked or microwaved | 3 oz. | 103 |
| Orange roughy, broiled, baked or microwaved | 3 oz. | 75 |
| Pollack, broiled, baked or microwaved | 3 oz. | 96 |
| Shark, mixed species, uncooked | 3 oz. | 111 |
| Smelt, rainbow, broiled, baked or microwaved | 3 oz. | 105 |
| Snapper, mixed species, broiled, baked or microwaved | 3 oz. | 109 |
| Sole, broiled, baked or microwaved | 3 oz. | 99 |
| Surimi, uncooked | 3 oz. | 84 |
| Trout, rainbow, broiled, baked or microwaved | 3 oz. | 128 |
| Tuna, light meat, canned in water | 3 oz. | 99 |
| Turbot, European, uncooked | 3 oz. | 81 |
| Whitefish, mixed species, smoked | 3 oz. | 92 |

**ACCEPTABLE**

| Food | Portion | Calories |
|---|---|---|
| Anchovies, canned in olive oil | 5 (about ¾ oz. total) | 42 |
| Carp, broiled, baked or microwaved | 3 oz. | 138 |
| Salmon | | |
|     pink, canned, with bones and liquid | 3 oz. | 118 |
|     sockeye, fresh, broiled, baked or microwaved | 3 oz. | 184 |
| Sardines, Atlantic, canned in oil, drained, with bones | 2 (about 1 oz. total) | 50 |
| Swordfish, broiled, baked or microwaved | 3 oz. | 132 |
| Tuna, fresh, broiled, baked or microwaved | 3 oz. | 156 |
| Tuna salad, prepared with mayonnaise | 3 oz. | 159 |

| Fat (G.) | Saturated Fat (G.) | % Calories from Fat | % Calories from Saturated Fat | Cholesterol (MG.) |
|---|---|---|---|---|
| 0.6 | 0.2 | 7.5 | 2.5 | 62 |
| 1.3 | 0.3 | 18 | 4.2 | 21 |
| 1.8 | 0.3 | 15.7 | 2.6 | 46 |
| 0.8 | 0.02 | 9.6 | <1 | 22 |
| 1 | 0.2 | 9.4 | 1.9 | 82 |
| 3.8 | 0.8 | 30.8 | 6.5 | 43 |
| 2.6 | 0.5 | 22.3 | 4.3 | 77 |
| 1.5 | 0.3 | 12.4 | 2.5 | 40 |
| 1.3 | 0.3 | 11.8 | 2.7 | 58 |
| 0.7 | 0.2 | 7.5 | 2.1 | 26 |
| 3.7 | 0.7 | 26 | 4.9 | 62 |
| 0.7 | 0.2 | 6.4 | 1.8 | 26 |
| 2.5 | 0.6 | 27.8 | 6.7 | 41 |
| 0.8 | 0.2 | 7.8 | 2 | 28 |
| 1.9 | 0.4 | 40.7 | 8.6 | 17 |
| 6.1 | 1.2 | 39.8 | 7.8 | 71 |
| 5.1 | 1.3 | 38.9 | 9.9 | 47 |
| 9.3 | 1.6 | 45.5 | 7.8 | 74 |
| 2.8 | 0.4 | 50.4 | 7.2 | 34 |
| 4.4 | 1.2 | 30 | 8.2 | 43 |
| 5.3 | 1.4 | 30.6 | 8.1 | 42 |
| 7.9 | 1.3 | 44.7 | 7.4 | 11 |

*(continued)*

| Food | Portion | Calories |
|------|---------|----------|

### FISH AND SHELLFISH — CONTINUED

#### FISH — CONTINUED

**HIGH**

| Food | Portion | Calories |
|------|---------|----------|
| Catfish, channel, breaded and fried | 3 oz. | 195 |
| Caviar, black or red | 1 Tbsp. | 40 |
| Eel, broiled, baked or microwaved | 3 oz. | 201 |
| Herring, kippered | 1 fillet (about 1½ oz.) | 87 |
| Mackerel, Atlantic, broiled, baked or microwaved | 3 oz. | 223 |
| Pompano, Florida, broiled, baked or microwaved | 3 oz. | 179 |

#### SHELLFISH

**LOW**

| Food | Portion | Calories |
|------|---------|----------|
| Clams, steamed | 20 small (about 3 oz.) | 133 |
| Crab, Alaskan king, steamed | 3 oz. | 82 |
| Crayfish (crawfish), steamed | 3 oz. | 97 |
| Lobster, boiled, poached or steamed | 3 oz. | 83 |
| Mussels, blue, boiled, poached or steamed | 3 oz. | 146 |
| Scallops, uncooked | 3 oz. | 75 |
| Shrimp, mixed species, steamed | 3 oz. | 84 |

**ACCEPTABLE**

| Food | Portion | Calories |
|------|---------|----------|
| Lobster salad, prepared with mayonnaise | ½ cup | 286 |
| Oysters, eastern, steamed | 6 medium (about 1½ oz. total) | 57 |
| Shrimp, mixed species, breaded and fried | 3 oz. | 206 |

**HIGH**

| Food | Portion | Calories |
|------|---------|----------|
| Clams, mixed species, breaded and fried | 20 small (about 6¾ oz. total) | 380 |
| Crab, soft-shell, fried | 1 (about 4½ oz.) | 334 |
| Oysters, eastern, breaded and fried | 6 medium (about 3 oz. total) | 173 |
| Scallops, mixed species, breaded and fried | 2 large (about 1 oz. total) | 67 |

| Fat (G.) | Saturated Fat (G.) | % Calories from Fat | % Calories from Saturated Fat | Cholesterol (MG.) |
|---|---|---|---|---|
| 11.3 | 2.8 | 52.2 | 12.9 | 69 |
| 2.9 | 0.7 | 65.3 | 15.6 | 94 |
| 12.7 | 2.6 | 56.9 | 11.6 | 137 |
| 5 | 1.1 | 51.7 | 11.4 | 33 |
| 15.1 | 3.6 | 60.9 | 14.5 | 64 |
| 10.3 | 3.8 | 51.8 | 19.1 | 54 |
| 1.8 | 0.2 | 12.2 | 1.4 | 60 |
| 1.3 | 0.1 | 14.3 | 1.1 | 45 |
| 1.2 | 0.2 | 11.1 | 1.9 | 151 |
| 0.5 | 0.1 | 5.4 | 1.1 | 61 |
| 3.8 | 0.7 | 23.4 | 4.3 | 48 |
| 0.7 | 0.1 | 8.4 | 1.2 | 28 |
| 0.9 | 0.3 | 9.8 | 3.2 | 166 |
| 16.6 | 2.6 | 52.2 | 8.2 | 120 |
| 2.1 | 0.6 | 33.2 | 9.5 | 44 |
| 10.4 | 1.8 | 45.4 | 7.9 | 151 |
| 21 | 5 | 49.7 | 11.8 | 115 |
| 17.9 | 4.4 | 48.2 | 11.9 | 45 |
| 11.1 | 2.8 | 57.7 | 14.6 | 71 |
| 3.4 | 0.8 | 45.7 | 10.7 | 19 |

*(continued)*

| Food | Portion | Calories |
|------|---------|----------|

### Fruits and Fruit Juices

**Low**

| | | |
|------|---------|----------|
| Apple, raw, with skin | 1 (about 5 oz.) | 81 |
| Apple juice, unsweetened, canned or bottled | 1 cup | 117 |
| Cherries, sweet, without pits | 1 cup | 104 |
| Figs, dried | 3 (about 2 oz. total) | 145 |
| Grapefruit, pink | ½ (about 4 oz.) | 37 |
| Grapes, green or red | 1 cup | 114 |
| Orange juice, frozen, from concentrate | 1 cup | 112 |
| Peach, raw | 1 (about 3 oz.) | 37 |
| Pears, canned in light syrup | ½ cup | 72 |
| Raisins, seedless | ½ cup | 218 |
| Strawberries | 1 cup | 45 |

**High**

| | | |
|------|---------|----------|
| Avocado | ½ (about 3 oz.) | 162 |

### Grains

**Low**

| | | |
|------|---------|----------|
| Barley, pearled, cooked | ½ cup | 97 |
| Bran | | |
| oat, raw | 2 Tbsp. | 29 |
| wheat, raw | 2 Tbsp. | 15 |
| Buckwheat groats, cooked | ½ cup | 91 |
| Bulgur wheat, cooked | ½ cup | 76 |
| Corn grits, white or yellow, cooked | ½ cup | 73 |
| Cornmeal, whole-grain, white or yellow, raw | ¼ cup | 109 |
| Couscous, cooked | ½ cup | 101 |
| Hominy, white or yellow, canned, raw | ½ cup | 58 |
| Millet, cooked | ½ cup | 143 |
| Quinoa, raw | ¼ cup | 159 |
| Rye, raw | ¼ cup | 141 |
| Wheat germ, toasted | ¼ cup | 108 |

| Fat (G.) | Saturated Fat (G.) | % Calories from Fat | % Calories from Saturated Fat | Cholesterol (MG.) |
|---|---|---|---|---|
| 0.5 | 0.1 | 5.5 | 1.1 | 0 |
| 0.3 | 0.1 | 2.3 | <1 | 0 |
| 1.4 | 0.3 | 12.1 | 2.6 | 0 |
| 0.7 | 0.1 | 4.3 | <1 | 0 |
| 0.1 | 0.02 | 2.4 | <1 | 0 |
| 0.9 | 0.3 | 7.1 | 2.4 | 0 |
| 0.2 | 0.02 | 1.6 | <1 | 0 |
| 0.1 | 0.01 | 2.4 | <1 | 0 |
| 0.04 | 0 | <1 | 0 | 0 |
| 0.3 | 0.1 | 1.2 | <1 | 0 |
| 0.6 | 0.03 | 12 | <1 | 0 |
| 15.4 | 2.5 | 85.6 | 13.9 | 0 |
| 0.4 | 0.1 | 3.7 | <1 | 0 |
| 0.8 | 0.2 | 24.8 | 6.2 | 0 |
| 0.3 | 0.04 | 18 | 2.4 | 0 |
| 0.6 | 0.1 | 6 | <1 | 0 |
| 0.2 | 0.04 | 2.4 | <1 | 0 |
| 0.2 | 0.04 | 2.5 | <1 | 0 |
| 1.1 | 0.2 | 9.1 | 1.7 | 0 |
| 0.1 | 0.03 | <1 | <1 | 0 |
| 0.7 | 0.1 | 10.9 | 1.6 | 0 |
| 1.2 | 0.2 | 7.5 | 1.3 | 0 |
| 2.5 | 0.3 | 14.2 | 1.7 | 0 |
| 1.1 | 0.1 | 7 | <1 | 0 |
| 3 | 0.5 | 25 | 4.2 | 0 |

*(continued)*

| FOOD | PORTION | CALORIES |
|------|---------|----------|
| **GRAINS — CONTINUED** | | |
| **HIGH** | | |
| Bran, rice, raw | 2 Tbsp. | 33 |
| **RICE** | | |
| **LOW** | | |
| Brown, cooked | ½ cup | 109 |
| Chicken-flavored, made from mix with 2 Tbsp. margarine (Rice-A-Roni) | 1 cup | 320 |
| Fried, made from mix with 2 Tbsp. margarine (Rice-A-Roni) | 1 cup | 320 |
| Spanish, homemade | ½ cup | 107 |
| White | | |
|     enriched, cooked | ½ cup | 133 |
|     instant, cooked | ½ cup | 80 |
| Wild, cooked | ½ cup | 83 |
| **GRAVIES AND SAUCES** | | |
| **GRAVIES** | | |
| **LOW** | | |
| Mushroom, canned | ¼ cup | 30 |
| Onion, dry mix, prepared | ¼ cup | 20 |
| **ACCEPTABLE** | | |
| Au jus, canned | ¼ cup | 10 |
| Brown, dry mix, prepared | ¼ cup | 19 |
| **HIGH** | | |
| Beef, canned | ¼ cup | 31 |
| Chicken, canned | ¼ cup | 47 |
| Turkey, canned | ¼ cup | 30 |

| FAT (G.) | SATURATED FAT (G.) | % CALORIES FROM FAT | % CALORIES FROM SATURATED FAT | CHOLESTEROL (MG.) |
|---|---|---|---|---|
| 2.2 | 0.4 | 60 | 10.9 | 0 |
| | | | | |
| 0.9 | 0.2 | 7.4 | 1.7 | 0 |
| 9.5 | 1 | 26.7 | 2.8 | 0 |
| 11 | 2 | 30.9 | 5.6 | 0 |
| 2.1 | 0 | 17.7 | 0 | 0 |
| 0.3 | 0.1 | 2 | <1 | 0 |
| 0.1 | 0.04 | 1.1 | <1 | 0 |
| 0.3 | 0.04 | 3.3 | <1 | 0 |
| | | | | |
| 1.6 | 0.2 | 48 | 6 | 0 |
| 0.2 | 0.1 | 9 | 4.5 | 0 |
| 0.1 | 0.1 | 9 | 9 | 0 |
| 0.4 | 0.2 | 18.9 | 9.5 | 1 |
| 1.4 | 0.7 | 40.6 | 20.3 | 2 |
| 3.4 | 0.8 | 65.1 | 15.3 | 1 |
| 1.3 | 0.4 | 39 | 12 | 1 |

*(continued)*

| FOOD | PORTION | CALORIES |
|------|---------|----------|

## GRAVIES AND SAUCES — CONTINUED

### SAUCES

**LOW**

| | | |
|------|---------|----------|
| Barbecue, bottled | ¼ cup | 47 |
| Marinara, canned | ½ cup | 85 |
| Soy, tamari, bottled | 1 Tbsp. | 11 |
| Spaghetti, canned | ½ cup | 136 |
| Sweet-and-sour, dry mix, made with water and vinegar | ¼ cup | 74 |
| Teriyaki, bottled | ¼ cup | 60 |
| Tomato, canned | 1 cup | 74 |
| Worcestershire, bottled | 1 tsp. | 0 |

**HIGH**

| | | |
|------|---------|----------|
| Alfredo, canned | ½ cup | 310 |
| Bernaise, dry mix, made with milk and butter | ¼ cup | 175 |
| Curry, dry mix, made with milk | ¼ cup | 67 |
| Hollandaise, dry mix, made with milk and butter | ¼ cup | 176 |
| Tartar | 1 Tbsp. | 74 |
| White | | |
| dry mix, made with milk | ¼ cup | 60 |
| medium, homemade | ¼ cup | 101 |

## ICE CREAM AND FROZEN TREATS

**LOW**

| | | |
|------|---------|----------|
| Frozen yogurt, vanilla, nonfat | ½ cup | 110 |
| Fruit ice | 1 cup | 247 |
| Fruit juice bar | 1 (about 1¾ oz.) | 42 |

**ACCEPTABLE**

| | | |
|------|---------|----------|
| Frozen yogurt, vanilla | ½ cup | 110 |
| Ice cream, vanilla, low-fat | ½ cup | 100 |
| Sherbet, orange | ½ cup | 135 |
| Tofutti, all flavors | ½ cup | 217 |

| Fat (G.) | Saturated Fat (G.) | % Calories from Fat | % Calories from Saturated Fat | Cholesterol (MG.) |
|---|---|---|---|---|
| 1.1 | 0.2 | 21.1 | 3.8 | 0 |
| 4.2 | 0.6 | 44.5 | 6.4 | 0 |
| 0.1 | 0.01 | 8.2 | <1 | 0 |
| 5.9 | 0.9 | 39.4 | 6 | 0 |
| | | | | |
| 0.02 | 0 | <1 | 0 | 0 |
| 0 | 0 | 0 | 0 | 0 |
| 0.4 | 0.1 | 4.9 | 1.2 | 0 |
| 0 | 0 | 0 | 0 | 0 |
| | | | | |
| 27 | 15 | 78.4 | 43.5 | 75 |
| 17.1 | 10.5 | 87.9 | 54 | 47 |
| 3.7 | 1.5 | 49.7 | 20.1 | 9 |
| 17.1 | 10.5 | 87.4 | 53.7 | 47 |
| 8.1 | 1.5 | 98.5 | 18.4 | 7 |
| | | | | |
| 3.4 | 1.6 | 51 | 24 | 9 |
| 7.8 | 4.3 | 69.5 | 38.3 | 26 |
| | | | | |
| 0 | 0 | 0 | 0 | 0 |
| 0 | 0 | 0 | 0 | 0 |
| 0 | 0 | 0 | 0 | 0 |
| | | | | |
| 1.5 | 1 | 12.3 | 8.2 | 5 |
| 2 | 1 | 18 | 9 | 5 |
| 1.9 | 1.2 | 12.7 | 8 | 7 |
| 12 | 2 | 49.8 | 8.3 | 0 |

*(continued)*

| FOOD | PORTION | CALORIES |
|------|---------|----------|

## ICE CREAM AND FROZEN TREATS — CONTINUED

### HIGH

| Food | Portion | Calories |
|------|---------|----------|
| Frozen yogurt, cherry, premium | ½ cup | 110 |
| Ice cream, soft-serve, chocolate or vanilla, on cone | 1 (about 5 oz.) | 230 |
| Ice cream, vanilla | | |
| reduced-fat | ½ cup | 130 |
| regular | ½ cup | 170 |
| Ice cream sundae, chocolate | 1 (about 6 oz.) | 300 |
| Ice milk, soft-serve, vanilla | ½ cup | 112 |

## MEATS

### BEEF

#### ACCEPTABLE

| Food | Portion | Calories |
|------|---------|----------|
| Steak, top round, lean, broiled | 3 oz. | 153 |

#### HIGH

| Food | Portion | Calories |
|------|---------|----------|
| Brisket, lean, braised | 3 oz. | 206 |
| Corned beef hash, canned | 1 cup | 398 |
| Ground, broiled | | |
| extra-lean | 3 oz. | 225 |
| lean | 3 oz. | 238 |
| regular | 3 oz. | 248 |
| Liver, braised | 3 oz. | 137 |
| Meat loaf | 3 oz. | 170 |
| Roast | | |
| bottom round, lean, braised | 3 oz. | 178 |
| pot, arm, lean, braised | 3 oz. | 184 |
| Shank cross cut, lean, simmered | 3 oz. | 171 |
| Short rib, lean, braised | 3 oz. | 251 |

| Fat (g.) | Saturated Fat (g.) | % Calories from Fat | % Calories from Saturated Fat | Cholesterol (mg.) |
|---|---|---|---|---|
| 2.5 | 1.5 | 20.5 | 12.3 | 10 |
| 7 | 5 | 27.4 | 19.6 | 20 |
| 4.5 | 3 | 31.2 | 20.8 | 35 |
| 10 | 6 | 52.9 | 31.8 | 105 |
| 7 | 5 | 21 | 15 | 20 |
| 2.3 | 1.4 | 18.5 | 11.3 | 7 |
| 4.2 | 1.4 | 24.7 | 8.2 | 71 |
| 10.9 | 3.9 | 47.6 | 17 | 79 |
| 24.9 | 11.9 | 56.3 | 26.9 | 73 |
| 13.4 | 5.3 | 53.6 | 21.2 | 84 |
| 15 | 5.9 | 56.7 | 22.3 | 86 |
| 16.5 | 6.5 | 59.9 | 23.6 | 86 |
| 4.2 | 1.6 | 27.6 | 10.5 | 331 |
| 11.2 | 5.1 | 59.3 | 27 | 55 |
| 7 | 2.4 | 35.4 | 12.1 | 82 |
| 7.1 | 2.6 | 34.7 | 12.7 | 86 |
| 5.4 | 2 | 28.4 | 10.5 | 66 |
| 15.4 | 6.6 | 55.2 | 23.7 | 79 |

*(continued)*

| FOOD | PORTION | CALORIES |
|---|---|---|
| **MEATS — CONTINUED** | | |
| **BEEF — CONTINUED** | | |
| **HIGH — CONTINUED** | | |
| Steak | | |
|     filet mignon, lean, broiled | 3 oz. | 179 |
|     flank, lean, broiled | 3 oz. | 176 |
|     porterhouse, lean, broiled | 3 oz. | 185 |
|     rib eye, lean, broiled | 3 oz. | 191 |
|     sirloin, wedge bone, lean, broiled | 3 oz. | 166 |
|     T-bone, lean, broiled | 3 oz. | 182 |
| **LAMB** | | |
| **HIGH** | | |
| Ground, broiled | 3 oz. | 241 |
| Kabob cubes, lean, broiled | 3 oz. | 156 |
| Leg, lean, roasted | 3 oz. | 162 |
| Rib roast, crown, lean, roasted | 3 oz. | 197 |
| **LUNCHMEATS/PROCESSED MEATS** | | |
| **LOW** | | |
| Turkey breast | 2 slices (about 1½ oz. total) | 47 |
| **HIGH** | | |
| Bologna | | |
|     beef | 2 slices (about 2 oz. total) | 177 |
|     turkey | 2 slices (about 2 oz. total) | 113 |
| Chicken roll, light meat | 2 slices (about 2 oz. total) | 90 |
| Corned beef | 2 slices (about 2 oz. total) | 142 |

| Fat (G.) | Saturated Fat (G.) | % Calories from Fat | % Calories from Saturated Fat | Cholesterol (MG.) |
|---|---|---|---|---|
| 8.5 | 3.2 | 42.7 | 16.1 | 71 |
| 8.6 | 3.7 | 44 | 18.9 | 57 |
| 9.2 | 3.7 | 44.8 | 18 | 68 |
| 10 | 4 | 47.1 | 18.8 | 68 |
| 6.1 | 2.4 | 33.1 | 13 | 76 |
| 8.8 | 3.5 | 43.5 | 17.3 | 68 |
| | | | | |
| 16.7 | 6.9 | 62.4 | 25.8 | 82 |
| 6.2 | 2.2 | 35.8 | 12.7 | 77 |
| 6.6 | 2.4 | 36.7 | 13.3 | 76 |
| 11.3 | 4.1 | 51.6 | 18.7 | 75 |
| | | | | |
| 0.7 | 0.2 | 13.4 | 3.8 | 17 |
| | | | | |
| 16.2 | 6.9 | 82.4 | 35.1 | 33 |
| 8.6 | 2.9 | 68.5 | 23.1 | 56 |
| 4.2 | 1.2 | 42 | 12 | 28 |
| 8.5 | 3.5 | 53.9 | 22.2 | 49 |

*(continued)*

| Food | Portion | Calories |
|------|---------|----------|

### Meats — Continued

### Lunchmeats/Processed Meats — Continued

**High — Continued**

| Food | Portion | Calories |
|------|---------|----------|
| Frankfurter | | |
| beef | 1 | 180 |
| chicken | 1 | 116 |
| Ham, boiled, extra-lean | 2 slices (about 2 oz. total) | 74 |
| Liverwurst, fresh | 3 slices (about 2 oz. total) | 185 |
| Olive loaf | 2 slices (about 2 oz. total) | 133 |
| Pastrami | | |
| beef | 2 slices (about 2 oz. total) | 198 |
| turkey | 2 slices (about 2 oz. total) | 80 |
| Pepperoni | 10 slices (about 2 oz. total) | 273 |
| Salami, pork | 3 slices (about 2 oz. total) | 230 |
| Sausage | | |
| bratwurst, fresh | 1 link (about 3 oz.) | 256 |
| kielbasa, smoked | 2 slices (about 2 oz. total) | 176 |
| knockwurst, smoked | 1 link (about 2½ oz.) | 209 |
| pork, fresh | 4 links (about 2 oz. total) | 192 |
| scrapple | 2 oz. | 120 |
| Turkey ham | 2 slices (about 2 oz. total) | 73 |

| Fat (G.) | Saturated Fat (G.) | % Calories from Fat | % Calories from Saturated Fat | Cholesterol (MG.) |
|---|---|---|---|---|
| 16.3 | 6.9 | 81.5 | 34.5 | 35 |
| 8.8 | 2.5 | 68.3 | 19.4 | 45 |
| 2.8 | 0.9 | 34.1 | 10.9 | 27 |
| 16.2 | 6 | 78.8 | 29.2 | 90 |
| 9.4 | 3.3 | 63.6 | 22.3 | 22 |
| 16.6 | 5.9 | 75.5 | 26.8 | 53 |
| 3.5 | 1 | 39.4 | 11.3 | 31 |
| 24.2 | 8.9 | 79.8 | 29.3 | 44 |
| 19.1 | 6.7 | 74.7 | 26.2 | 45 |
| 22 | 7.9 | 77.3 | 27.8 | 51 |
| 15.4 | 5.6 | 78.8 | 28.6 | 38 |
| 18.9 | 6.9 | 81.4 | 29.7 | 39 |
| 16.2 | 5.6 | 75.9 | 26.3 | 43 |
| 7.6 | 2.8 | 57 | 21 | 25 |
| 2.8 | 1 | 34.5 | 12.3 | 32 |

*(continued)*

| FOOD | PORTION | CALORIES |
|---|---|---|
| **MEATS — CONTINUED** | | |
| **PORK** | | |
| **HIGH** | | |
| Bacon | | |
|     Canadian | 2 medium slices (about 1½ oz. total) | 86 |
|     smoked | 3 medium slices (about ¾ oz. total) | 109 |
|       smoked, thickly sliced | 1 slice (about ⅓ oz.) | 50 |
| Chop, center rib, lean, roasted | 3 oz. | 208 |
| Ham, cured, roasted | 3 oz. | 140 |
| Roast, center loin, lean, roasted | 3 oz. | 204 |
| Sparerib, lean, braised | 3 oz. | 337 |
| **VEAL** | | |
| **HIGH** | | |
| Ground, broiled | 3 oz. | 146 |
| Loin, lean, roasted | 3 oz. | 149 |
| **MILK AND MILK PRODUCTS** | | |
| **CREAM** | | |
| **LOW** | | |
| Sour cream, nonfat | 2 Tbsp. | 30 |
| **HIGH** | | |
| Half-and-half | 2 Tbsp. | 39 |
| Heavy | 2 Tbsp. | 103 |
| Light | 2 Tbsp. | 59 |
| Nondairy, powdered | 1 tsp. | 10 |
|     flavored | 1 tsp. | 60 |
| Sour cream | | |
|     reduced-fat | 2 Tbsp. | 35 |
|     regular | 2 Tbsp. | 62 |

| Fat (G.) | Saturated Fat (G.) | % Calories from Fat | % Calories from Saturated Fat | Cholesterol (MG.) |
|---|---|---|---|---|
| 3.9 | 1.3 | 40.8 | 13.6 | 27 |
| 9.4 | 3.3 | 77.6 | 27.2 | 16 |
| 4.5 | 2 | 81 | 36 | 10 |
| 11.7 | 4.1 | 50.6 | 17.7 | 67 |
| 6.5 | 2.2 | 41.8 | 14.1 | 48 |
| 11.1 | 3.8 | 49 | 16.8 | 77 |
| 25.8 | 10 | 68.9 | 26.7 | 103 |
| 6.4 | 2.6 | 39.5 | 16 | 88 |
| 5.9 | 2.2 | 35.6 | 13.3 | 90 |
| 0 | 0 | 0 | 0 | 2 |
| 3.5 | 2.2 | 80.8 | 50.8 | 11 |
| 11 | 6.9 | 96.1 | 60.3 | 41 |
| 5.8 | 3.6 | 88.5 | 54.9 | 20 |
| 0.5 | 0.5 | 45 | 45 | 0 |
| 3 | 2.5 | 45 | 37.5 | 0 |
| 2 | 1.5 | 51.4 | 38.6 | 10 |
| 6 | 3.8 | 87.1 | 55.2 | 13 |

*(continued)*

| FOOD | PORTION | CALORIES |
|------|---------|----------|

## MILK AND MILK PRODUCTS — CONTINUED

### CREAM — CONTINUED

#### HIGH — CONTINUED

| FOOD | PORTION | CALORIES |
|------|---------|----------|
| Whipped cream | 2 Tbsp. | 19 |
| Whipped topping, nondairy | 2 Tbsp. | 30 |

### MILK

#### LOW

| FOOD | PORTION | CALORIES |
|------|---------|----------|
| Dairy shake mix, chocolate, prepared with water | About 6 oz. | 80 |
| Evaporated skim | 2 Tbsp. | 25 |
| Powdered skim, prepared | 1 cup | 82 |
| Skim | 1 cup | 86 |

#### ACCEPTABLE

| FOOD | PORTION | CALORIES |
|------|---------|----------|
| 1% low-fat, chocolate | 1 cup | 158 |

#### HIGH

| FOOD | PORTION | CALORIES |
|------|---------|----------|
| Buttermilk | 1 cup | 99 |
| Eggnog | ½ cup | 171 |
| Evaporated | 2 Tbsp. | 40 |
| 1% low-fat | 1 cup | 102 |
| 2% low-fat | 1 cup | 121 |
| Whole | 1 cup | 157 |
| Whole, chocolate | 1 cup | 208 |

### YOGURT

#### LOW

| FOOD | PORTION | CALORIES |
|------|---------|----------|
| Fruit | | |
| light (low-calorie) | 1 cup | 100 |
| regular | 1 cup | 240 |
| Fruit with crunch-type topping | | |
| light (low-calorie) | ¾ cup | 130 |
| regular | ¾ cup | 220 |

| Fat (g.) | Saturated Fat (g.) | % Calories from Fat | % Calories from Saturated Fat | Cholesterol (mg.) |
|---|---|---|---|---|
| 1.7 | 1 | 80.5 | 47.4 | 6 |
| 2.4 | 2 | 72 | 60 | 0 |
| | | | | |
| 1 | 0 | 11.3 | 0 | 0 |
| 0 | 0 | 0 | 0 | 0 |
| 0.2 | 0.1 | 2.2 | 1.1 | 4 |
| 0.4 | 0.3 | 4.2 | 3.1 | 4 |
| | | | | |
| 2.5 | 1.5 | 14.2 | 8.5 | 7 |
| | | | | |
| 2.2 | 1.3 | 20 | 11.8 | 9 |
| 9.5 | 5.7 | 50 | 30 | 75 |
| 2 | 1 | 45 | 22.5 | 5 |
| 2.6 | 1.6 | 22.9 | 14.1 | 10 |
| 4.7 | 2.9 | 35 | 21.6 | 18 |
| 8.9 | 5.6 | 51 | 32.1 | 35 |
| 8.5 | 5.3 | 36.8 | 22.9 | 31 |
| | | | | |
| 0 | 0 | 0 | 0 | 0 |
| 3 | 1.5 | 11.3 | 5.6 | 15 |
| | | | | |
| 1 | 0 | 6.9 | 0 | 0 |
| 2 | 0.5 | 8.2 | 2 | <5 |

*(continued)*

| FOOD | PORTION | CALORIES |
|---|---|---|
| **MILK AND MILK PRODUCTS — CONTINUED** | | |
| **YOGURT — CONTINUED** | | |
| **LOW — CONTINUED** | | |
| Plain, nonfat | 1 cup | 120 |
| **HIGH** | | |
| Plain | | |
|     low-fat (1½% milk-fat) | 1 cup | 150 |
|     whole milk | 1 cup | 139 |
| **NUTS AND SEEDS** | | |
| **NUTS** | | |
| **LOW** | | |
| Chestnuts, European, roasted | 1 oz. | 70 |
| Filberts (hazelnuts), unblanched, dried | 1 oz. | 179 |
| **ACCEPTABLE** | | |
| Almonds, unblanched, dried | 1 oz. | 167 |
| Pecans, dried | 1 oz. | 189 |
| Pistachios, dried | 1 oz. | 164 |
| Walnuts, English, dried | 1 oz. | 182 |
| **HIGH** | | |
| Brazil, unblanched, dried | 1 oz. | 186 |
| Cashews, dry-roasted | 1 oz. | 163 |
| Coconut, sweetened, flaked | 1 oz. | 126 |
| Macadamia, dried | 1 oz. | 199 |
| Mixed, dry-roasted | 1 oz. | 169 |
| Peanuts, dry-roasted | 1 oz. | 164 |
| Pine, pignolia, dried | 1 oz. | 146 |

| Fat (G.) | Saturated Fat (G.) | % Calories from Fat | % Calories from Saturated Fat | Cholesterol (MG.) |
|---|---|---|---|---|
| 0 | 0 | 0 | 0 | 0 |
| | | | | - |
| 4 | 2.5 | 24 | 15 | 20 |
| 7.4 | 4.8 | 47.9 | 31.1 | 29 |
| | | | | |
| 0.6 | 0.1 | 7.7 | 1.3 | 0 |
| 17.8 | 1.3 | 89.5 | 6.5 | 0 |
| | | | | |
| 14.8 | 1.4 | 79.8 | 7.5 | 0 |
| 19.2 | 1.5 | 91.4 | 7.1 | 0 |
| 13.7 | 1.7 | 75.2 | 9.3 | 0 |
| 17.6 | 1.6 | 87 | 7.9 | 0 |
| | | | | |
| 18.8 | 4.6 | 91 | 22.3 | 0 |
| 13.2 | 2.6 | 72.9 | 14.4 | 0 |
| 9 | 8 | 64.3 | 57.1 | 0 |
| 20.9 | 3.1 | 94.5 | 14 | 0 |
| 14.6 | 2 | 77.8 | 10.7 | 0 |
| 13.9 | 1.9 | 76.3 | 10.4 | 0 |
| 14.4 | 2.2 | 88.8 | 13.6 | 0 |

*(continued)*

| Food | Portion | Calories |
|------|---------|----------|
| **NUTS AND SEEDS—CONTINUED** | | |
| **SEEDS** | | |
| **ACCEPTABLE** | | |
| Sunflower, dried | 1 oz. | 162 |
| **HIGH** | | |
| Pumpkin, dried, hulled | 1 oz. | 154 |
| Sesame, dried, hulled | 1 Tbsp. | 47 |
| **PASTAS** | | |
| **LOW** | | |
| Fresh, cooked | 1 cup | 183 |
| Macaroni, enriched, cooked | 1 cup | 197 |
| Noodles | | |
|     egg, enriched, cooked | 1 cup | 213 |
|     soba, cooked | 1 cup | 113 |
|     spinach, enriched, cooked | 1 cup | 211 |
| Spaghetti | | |
|     enriched, cooked | 1 cup | 197 |
|     whole-wheat, cooked | 1 cup | 174 |
| Spinach, fresh, cooked | 1 cup | 182 |
| Vegetable, cooked | ¾ cup | 210 |
| **HIGH** | | |
| Tortellini, cheese | ½ cup | 220 |
| **DISHES** | | |
| **LOW** | | |
| Pasta salad with seafood, without dressing | 3½ oz. | 90 |
| **ACCEPTABLE** | | |
| Lasagna with meat sauce, frozen | About 10 oz. | 270 |
| Pasta primavera, frozen | About 10 oz. | 260 |
| Spaghetti and meatballs, homemade | 1 cup | 332 |

| Fat (G.) | Saturated Fat (G.) | % Calories from Fat | % Calories from Saturated Fat | Cholesterol (MG.) |
|---|---|---|---|---|
| 14.1 | 1.5 | 78.3 | 8.3 | 0 |
| 13 | 2.5 | 76 | 14.6 | 0 |
| 4.4 | 0.6 | 84.3 | 11.5 | 0 |
| 1.5 | 0.2 | 7.4 | 1 | 46 |
| 0.9 | 0.1 | 4.1 | <1 | 0 |
| 2.4 | 0.5 | 10.1 | 2.1 | 53 |
| 0.1 | 0.02 | <1 | <1 | 0 |
| 2.5 | 0.6 | 10.7 | 2.6 | 53 |
| 0.9 | 0.1 | 4.1 | <1 | 0 |
| 0.8 | 0.1 | 4.1 | <1 | 0 |
| 1.3 | 0.3 | 6.4 | 1.5 | 46 |
| 1 | 0 | 4.3 | 0 | 0 |
| 5 | 3 | 20.5 | 12.3 | 40 |
| 5 | 0.6 | 50 | 6 | 12 |
| 6 | 2.5 | 20 | 8.3 | 25 |
| 8 | 2.5 | 27.7 | 8.7 | 35 |
| 11.7 | 3.3 | 31.7 | 8.9 | 74 |

*(continued)*

| FOOD | PORTION | CALORIES |
|------|---------|----------|

## PASTAS — CONTINUED

### DISHES — CONTINUED

**HIGH**

| | | |
|------|---------|----------|
| Fettuccine Alfredo, frozen | About 9 oz. | 270 |
| Lasagna with meat sauce, frozen | About 10 oz. | 360 |
| Macaroni and cheese, homemade, baked | 1 cup | 430 |
| Manicotti, cheese, frozen | About 3 oz. | 290 |
| Ravioli, cheese, with tomato sauce, frozen | About 9½ oz. | 360 |
| Tortellini, cheese, with tomato sauce, frozen | About 9 oz. | 290 |

## PIZZA

**LOW**

Cheese

| | | |
|------|---------|----------|
| Healthy Choice French bread pizza | 1 (about 5½ oz.) | 310 |

Italian sausage

| | | |
|------|---------|----------|
| Healthy Choice sausage French bread pizza | 1 (about 6 oz.) | 330 |
| Supreme Lean Cuisine deluxe French bread pizza | 1 (about 6 oz.) | 330 |

**ACCEPTABLE**

Cheese

| | | |
|------|---------|----------|
| Chef Boyardee, dry mix, prepared | 1 slice (about 5 oz.) | 320 |
| Weight Watchers extra cheese | 1 (about 5¾ oz.) | 390 |

Pepperoni

| | | |
|------|---------|----------|
| Weight Watchers | 1 (about 5½ oz.) | 390 |

Supreme

| | | |
|------|---------|----------|
| Weight Watchers deluxe combo | 1 (about 6½ oz.) | 380 |

**HIGH**

Cheese

| | | |
|------|---------|----------|
| Domino's thin crust | ⅓ of 12″ pie (about 5½ oz.) | 364 |
| Pizza Hut thin crust | 1 slice of medium pie (about 3½ oz.) | 205 |

| FAT (G.) | SATURATED FAT (G.) | % CALORIES FROM FAT | % CALORIES FROM SATURATED FAT | CHOLESTEROL (MG.) |
|---|---|---|---|---|
| 7 | 3 | 23.3 | 10 | 15 |
| 13 | 5 | 32.5 | 12.5 | 50 |
| 22.2 | 8.9 | 46.5 | 18.6 | 42 |
| 9 | 3.5 | 27.9 | 10.9 | 20 |
| 14 | 5 | 35 | 12.5 | 85 |
| 6 | 5 | 18.6 | 15.5 | 105 |
| 4 | 2 | 11.6 | 5.8 | 10 |
| 4 | 1.5 | 10.9 | 4.1 | 20 |
| 6 | 2.5 | 16.4 | 6.8 | 30 |
| 8 | 2.5 | 22.5 | 7 | 15 |
| 12 | 4 | 27.7 | 9.2 | 35 |
| 12 | 4 | 27.7 | 9.2 | 45 |
| 11 | 3.5 | 26.1 | 8.3 | 40 |
| 15.5 | 6.3 | 38.3 | 15.6 | 26 |
| 8 | 4 | 35.1 | 17.6 | 25 |

*(continued)*

| FOOD | PORTION | CALORIES |
|------|---------|----------|

## PIZZA—CONTINUED

### HIGH—CONTINUED

Italian sausage

| | | |
|------|---------|----------|
| Domino's hand-tossed, with mushrooms | 2 slices of 12″ pie (about 6 oz. total) | 402 |
| Pizza Hut hand-tossed | 1 slice of medium pie (about 4 oz.) | 267 |

Pepperoni

| | | |
|------|---------|----------|
| Domino's hand-tossed | 2 slices of 12″ pie (about 6 oz.) | 406 |
| Healthy Choice pepperoni French bread pizza | 1 (about 6 oz.) | 350 |
| Pizza Hut hand-tossed | 1 slice of medium pie (about 4 oz.) | 238 |

Supreme

| | | |
|------|---------|----------|
| Pizza Hut hand-tossed | 1 slice of medium pie (about 5 oz.) | 284 |

Veggie

| | | |
|------|---------|----------|
| Domino's hand-tossed | 2 slices of 12″ pie (about 6¾ oz. total) | 360 |
| Pizza Hut hand-tossed | 1 slice of medium pie (about 5 oz.) | 216 |

## POULTRY, FOWL AND GAME

### LOW

Chicken breast, without skin

| | | |
|------|---------|----------|
| fried in batter | ½ (about 3 oz.) | 161 |
| roasted | ½ (about 3 oz.) | 142 |
| Frogs' legs, uncooked | 3 oz. | 62 |

Turkey

| | | |
|------|---------|----------|
| breast, prebasted, roasted, without skin | 3 oz. | 107 |
| light meat, roasted, without skin | 3 oz. | 34 |

| Fat (g.) | Saturated Fat (g.) | % Calories from Fat | % Calories from Saturated Fat | Cholesterol (mg.) |
|---|---|---|---|---|
| 13.9 | 6.1 | 31.1 | 13.7 | 31 |
| 11 | 5 | 37 | 16 | 31 |
| 15.1 | 6.6 | 33.8 | 14.6 | 32 |
| 9 | 4 | 23.1 | 10.3 | 25 |
| 8 | 4 | 30.3 | 15.1 | 24 |
| 12 | 5 | 38 | 15.8 | 30 |
| 10.4 | 4.5 | 26 | 11.3 | 19 |
| 6 | 3 | 25 | 12.5 | 17 |
| 4.1 | 1.1 | 22.9 | 6.1 | 78 |
| 3.1 | 0.9 | 19.6 | 5.7 | 73 |
| 0.3 | 0 | 4.4 | 0 | 43 |
| 2.9 | 0.8 | 24.4 | 6.7 | 36 |
| 0.7 | 0.2 | 18.5 | 5.3 | 15 |

*(continued)*

| Food | Portion | Calories |
|------|---------|----------|

### POULTRY, FOWL AND GAME—CONTINUED

**ACCEPTABLE**

| Food | Portion | Calories |
|------|---------|----------|
| Pheasant, meat only, uncooked | 3 oz. | 113 |
| Venison, roasted | 3 oz. | 134 |

**HIGH**

| Food | Portion | Calories |
|------|---------|----------|
| Capon, roasted, without skin | 3 oz. | 195 |
| Chicken | | |
|     breast, with skin | | |
|         fried in batter | ½ (about 5 oz.) | 364 |
|         roasted | ½ (about 4 oz.) | 193 |
|         roasted, ready-to-serve | ½ (about 5 oz.) | 250 |
|     drumstick, with skin | | |
|         fried in batter | 1 (about 3 oz.) | 193 |
|         roasted | 1 (about 2 oz.) | 112 |
|     liver, simmered | 3 oz. | 133 |
|     thigh, without skin | | |
|         fried in batter | 1 (about 2 oz.) | 113 |
|         roasted | 1 (about 2 oz.) | 109 |
| Duck, roasted, without skin | 3 oz. | 171 |
| Pâté | | |
|     chicken, canned | 1 oz. | 57 |
|     goose, smoked, canned | 1 oz. | 131 |
| Potpie, turkey, homemade | 1 piece (about 8 oz.) | 550 |
| Rabbit, roasted | 3 oz. | 131 |
| Squab (pigeon), uncooked | 1 (about 6 oz.) | 239 |
| Turkey | | |
|     dark meat, roasted, without skin | 3 oz. | 32 |
|     dark meat, roasted, with skin | 3 oz. | 188 |
|     light meat, roasted, with skin | 3 oz. | 168 |
|     liver, simmered | 3 oz. | 144 |

| Fat (G.) | **Saturated Fat (G.)** | % Calories from Fat | **% Calories from Saturated Fat** | Cholesterol (MG.) |
|---|---|---|---|---|
| 3.1 | **1.1** | 24.7 | **8.8** | 56 |
| 2.7 | **1.1** | 18.1 | **7.4** | 95 |
| 9.9 | **2.8** | 45.7 | **12.9** | 73 |
| 18.5 | **4.9** | 45.7 | **12.1** | 119 |
| 7.6 | **2.2** | 35.4 | **10.3** | 82 |
| 13 | **4** | 46.8 | **14.4** | 110 |
| 11.3 | **3** | 52.7 | **14** | 62 |
| 5.8 | **1.6** | 46.6 | **12.9** | 47 |
| 4.6 | **1.6** | 31.1 | **10.8** | 536 |
| 5.4 | **1.5** | 43 | **11.9** | 53 |
| 5.7 | **1.6** | 47.1 | **13.2** | 49 |
| 9.5 | **3.6** | 50 | **18.9** | 76 |
| 3.7 | **1.1** | 58.4 | **17.4** | 111 |
| 12.4 | **4.1** | 85.2 | **28.2** | 43 |
| 31.3 | **10.5** | 51.2 | **17.2** | 72 |
| 5.4 | **1.6** | 37.1 | **11** | 54 |
| 12.6 | **3.3** | 47.4 | **12.4** | 151 |
| 1.2 | **0.4** | 33.8 | **11.3** | 15 |
| 9.8 | **3** | 46.9 | **14.4** | 76 |
| 7.1 | **2** | 38 | **10.7** | 65 |
| 5.1 | **1.6** | 31.9 | **10** | 532 |

*(continued)*

| FOOD | PORTION | CALORIES |
|------|---------|----------|

## SOUPS AND STEWS

### SOUPS

**LOW**

| | | |
|------|---------|----------|
| Black bean, condensed, made with water | 1 cup | 116 |
| Clam chowder | | |
|     Manhattan, condensed, made with water | 1 cup | 78 |
|     New England, low-fat | 1 cup | 120 |
| Crab | 1 cup | 76 |
| Gazpacho | 1 cup | 56 |
| Minestrone, low-fat | 1 cup | 120 |
| Onion, condensed, made with water | 1 cup | 58 |
| Split pea with ham, low-fat | 1 cup | 170 |
| Tomato | | |
|     condensed, made with water | ½ cup | 100 |
|     low-fat | ½ cup | 90 |
| Vegetarian vegetable, condensed, made with water | 1 cup | 72 |

**ACCEPTABLE**

| | | |
|------|---------|----------|
| Bouillon cube, chicken, made with water | 1 cup | 12 |
| Chicken noodle, condensed, made with water | 1 cup | 75 |
| Chicken rice, condensed, made with water | 1 cup | 60 |
| Green pea, condensed, made with water | 1 cup | 165 |
| Lentil with ham | 1 cup | 139 |

**HIGH**

| | | |
|------|---------|----------|
| Beef noodle, condensed, made with water | 1 cup | 83 |
| Beef vegetable, condensed, made with water | 1 cup | 78 |
| Bouillon cube, beef, made with water | 1 cup | 7 |
| Cheese, condensed, made with water | 1 cup | 156 |
| Cream of celery, condensed, made with water | 1 cup | 90 |
| Cream of chicken, condensed, made with water | 1 cup | 117 |
| Cream of mushroom, condensed, made with water | 1 cup | 129 |

| Fat (g.) | Saturated Fat (g.) | % Calories from Fat | % Calories from Saturated Fat | Cholesterol (mg.) |
|---|---|---|---|---|
| 1.5 | 0.4 | 11.6 | 3.1 | 0 |
| 2.2 | 0.4 | 25.4 | 4.6 | 2 |
| 2 | 0.5 | 15 | 3.8 | 5 |
| 1.5 | 0.4 | 17.8 | 4.7 | 10 |
| 2.2 | 0.3 | 35.4 | 4.8 | 0 |
| 2 | 0.5 | 15 | 3.8 | <1 |
| 1.7 | 0.3 | 26.4 | 4.7 | 0 |
| 2.5 | 1 | 13.2 | 5.3 | 10 |
| 2 | 0 | 18 | 0 | 0 |
| 2 | 0.5 | 20 | 5 | 0 |
| 1.9 | 0.3 | 23.8 | 3.8 | 0 |
| 0.3 | 0.1 | 22.5 | 7.5 | 0 |
| 2.5 | 0.7 | 30 | 8.4 | 7 |
| 1.9 | 0.5 | 28.5 | 7.5 | 7 |
| 2.9 | 1.4 | 15.8 | 7.6 | 0 |
| 2.8 | 1.1 | 18.1 | 7.1 | 7 |
| 3.1 | 1.2 | 33.6 | 13 | 5 |
| 1.9 | 0.9 | 21.9 | 10.4 | 5 |
| 0.2 | 0.1 | 25.7 | 12.9 | 0 |
| 10.5 | 6.7 | 60.6 | 38.7 | 30 |
| 5.6 | 1.4 | 56 | 14 | 15 |
| 7.4 | 2.1 | 56.9 | 16.2 | 10 |
| 9 | 2.4 | 62.8 | 16.7 | 2 |

*(continued)*

| FOOD | PORTION | CALORIES |
|------|---------|----------|

## SOUPS AND STEWS — CONTINUED

### SOUPS — CONTINUED

#### HIGH — CONTINUED

| | | |
|------|---------|----------|
| Cream of potato, condensed, made with water | 1 cup | 73 |
| Scotch broth, condensed, made with water | 1 cup | 80 |
| Turkey vegetable, condensed, made with water | 1 cup | 72 |

### STEWS

#### HIGH

| | | |
|------|---------|----------|
| Beef, ready-to-serve | 1 cup | 194 |
| Oyster, condensed, made with water | 1 cup | 58 |

## VEGETABLES

### LOW

| | | |
|------|---------|----------|
| Broccoli, boiled | ½ cup | 22 |
| Cabbage, boiled, shredded | ½ cup | 17 |
| Carrot, raw | 1 (about 7½", 2½ oz.) | 31 |
| Chili peppers, raw, chopped | ½ cup | 30 |
| Corn, sweet yellow, boiled | Kernels from 1 ear | 83 |
| Eggplant, boiled, cubed | ½ cup | 13 |
| Garlic, raw | 1 clove | 4 |
| Okra, boiled | ½ cup | 26 |
| Onions, raw, chopped | ½ cup | 30 |
| Pumpkin, canned | ½ cup | 41 |
| Tomatoes, raw, chopped | 1 cup | 38 |
| Zucchini, raw, sliced | ½ cup | 9 |

### POTATOES

#### LOW

| | | |
|------|---------|----------|
| Baked | | |
|     plain, flesh only | 1 (about 6 oz.) | 145 |
|     plain, microwaved, flesh and skin | 1 (about 8 oz.) | 212 |

| Fat (G.) | Saturated Fat (G.) | % Calories from Fat | % Calories from Saturated Fat | Cholesterol (MG.) |
|---|---|---|---|---|
| 2.4 | 1.2 | 29.6 | 14.8 | 5 |
| 2.6 | 1.1 | 29.3 | 12.4 | 5 |
| 3 | 0.9 | 37.5 | 11.3 | 2 |
| 7.6 | 2.5 | 35.3 | 11.6 | 34 |
| 3.8 | 2.5 | 59 | 38.8 | 14 |
| 0.3 | 0.04 | 12.3 | 1.6 | 0 |
| 0.3 | 0.04 | 15.9 | 2.1 | 0 |
| 0.1 | 0.02 | 2.9 | <1 | 0 |
| 0.2 | 0.02 | 6 | <1 | 0 |
| 1 | 0.2 | 10.8 | 2.2 | 0 |
| 0.1 | 0.02 | 6.9 | 1.4 | 0 |
| 0.02 | 0 | 4.5 | 0 | 0 |
| 0.1 | 0.04 | 3.5 | 1.4 | 0 |
| 0.1 | 0.02 | 3 | <1 | 0 |
| 0.3 | 0.2 | 6.6 | 4.4 | 0 |
| 0.6 | 0.1 | 14.2 | 2.4 | 0 |
| 0.1 | 0.02 | 10 | 2 | 0 |
| 0.2 | 0.04 | 1.2 | <1 | 0 |
| 0.2 | 0.1 | <1 | <1 | 0 |

*(continued)*

| FOOD | PORTION | CALORIES |
|---|---|---|
| **VEGETABLES — CONTINUED** | | |
| **POTATOES — CONTINUED** | | |
| **LOW — CONTINUED** | | |
| Boiled, flesh only | 1 | 67 |
| Sweet potato, baked | 1 (about 4 oz.) | 117 |
| **ACCEPTABLE** | | |
| Mashed, made with whole milk and margarine | ½ cup | 111 |
| O'Brien | ½ cup | 79 |
| Potato salad | ½ cup | 179 |
| **HIGH** | | |
| Au gratin | ½ cup | 161 |
| Baked, with sour cream and chives | 1 (about 6 oz.) | 221 |
| French fries | | |
|     deep-fried | 20–25 1″–2″ strips | 235 |
|     frozen, oven-heated | 20 (about 4 oz.) | 222 |
|     microwave | 1 box (about 3 oz.) | 230 |
| Potato pancake | 1 (about 3 oz.) | 234 |
| Scalloped | ½ cup | 105 |

| Fat (G.) | Saturated Fat (G.) | % Calories from Fat | % Calories from Saturated Fat | Cholesterol (MG.) |
|---|---|---|---|---|
| 0.1 | 0.02 | 1.3 | <1 | 0 |
| 0.1 | 0.03 | <1 | <1 | 0 |
| 4.4 | 1.1 | 35.7 | 8.9 | 2 |
| 1.2 | 0.8 | 13.7 | 9.1 | 4 |
| 10.3 | 1.8 | 51.8 | 9.1 | 85 |
| 9.2 | 5.8 | 51.4 | 32.4 | 28 |
| 12.6 | 5.6 | 51.3 | 22.8 | 14 |
| 12.2 | 3.8 | 46.7 | 14.6 | 0 |
| 8.8 | 4.5 | 35.7 | 18.2 | 0 |
| 12 | 3 | 47 | 11.7 | 0 |
| 12.6 | 3.4 | 48.5 | 13.1 | 93 |
| 4.5 | 2.8 | 38.6 | 24 | 15 |

# ABOUT THE AUTHORS

RICHARD TRUBO is a medical writer and co-author of *The H.A.R.T. Program: Controlling Your High Blood Pressure without Drugs.* His articles have appeared in *American Health, Reader's Digest* and other national magazines.

MARY CARROLL has been in the food business for more than 20 years. The former owner and operator of Cuisine Naturelle Cooking School in Mill Valley, California, she writes a weekly column for the *Los Angeles Times* Syndicate on gourmet natural foods and vegetarian cooking and is a frequent contributor to *Food & Wine, American Health* and *Cooking Light* magazines.

WILLIAM P. CASTELLI, M.D., is the medical director of the Framingham Cardiovascular Insitute (formerly the Framingham Heart Study), a wellness program at Metro West Medical Center in Framingham, Massachusetts. He received his B.S. degree from Yale University in 1953 and his M.D. in 1959 from the Catholic University of Louvain in Belgium. In 1979 Dr. Castelli became the third director of the Framingham Heart Study, which now encompasses four generations of Framingham townspeople. Dr. Castelli has also taught at Harvard Medical School, the Boston University School of Medicine and the University of Massachusetts Medical School.

# SUBJECT INDEX

*Underscored page references indicate boxed text.*

## A

Alcohol, 13-16. *See also* Wine
  triglycerides and, 186
Allicin, in garlic, 100
Almonds, 16-19
Angel food cake, as low-fat dessert, 72
Anticlotting activity
  flavonoids and, 109
  garlic and, 100
  wine and, <u>207</u>
Antioxidants, 19-24
  Daily Values, 20-21
  food sources of, <u>23</u>
    tea, 177
    wine, 208-9
  scientific studies on, 19-24, 38
  supplements, 22-24
Apolipoprotein B, wheat germ and, 204
Apples, 24-26
Arginine, in nuts, 17
Artificial sweeteners, pregnancy and, 214
Aspirin, beta-carotene and, for reducing
    risk of heart attack, 37-38
Atherosclerosis, 4-5. *See also* Plaque
  smoking and, 165
Avocados, 27-29, 99

## B

Baked goods
  apples in, 26
  barley in, 32
  egg reduction in, <u>76</u>
  fat, calories and cholesterol in, 456-59
  flaxseed in, 94-95, <u>95</u>
  low-fat, 26, 72-73
  oat bran in, 146
  wheat germ in, 205
  yogurt in, 213-14
Bananas
  in health shake, 164
  as low-fat dessert, 71
Barley, 29-32, <u>31</u>
Beano, 36
Beans, 33-36
  fat, calories and cholesterol in, 454-57
  fiber in, <u>34</u>
  gas prevention and, 35-36
  in Mediterranean diet, 138
  scientific studies on, 33-34
  serving suggestions, 34-35
Beef
  fat, calories and cholesterol in, 498-501
  lean, 113-17, <u>115</u>

# M

# N

# O

# RECIPE INDEX

*Underscored page references indicate boxed text.*

# N

# O